TRANSYLVANIA:
Tutor To The West

Transylvania University

Lexington, Kentucky

1975

TRANSYLVANIA:
Tutor To The West

by John D. Wright, Jr.

THE UNIVERSITY PRESS OF KENTUCKY

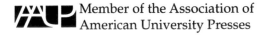

To Fran

Contents

1 Learning in the Wilderness   1

2 Division and Reunion   16

3 James Moore and the New University   33

4 Problems and Slow Growth of the University   47

5 Horace Holley and the Making of a University   65

6 The Making of a Martyr   99

7 The Phoenix Rises   118

8 The Failure of Innovative Education   132

9 The Crisis in the Medical Department   145

10 The Methodists Take Their Turn   158

11 The Period of Decline, 1850–1865   172

12 The Great Experiment: Kentucky University   190

13 The Embattled Sectarians, 1865–1877   212

14 Apes, Girls, and "Daddy" Loos   234

15 The Creative Administration of Burris Jenkins   258

16 Student Life From the Civil War to World War I   281

17 The Struggle for Survival and Identity   312

18 World War I and the Heresy Trial   331

19 Transylvania Survives the Twenties   344

20 Depression and War   364

21 Innovation and Expansion   390

22 Expansion and Consolidation   407

    Epilogue   431

    Bibliography   435

    Index   441

Introduction

It is most appropriate that as this nation celebrates the bicentennial of its independence that Transylvania University, which was born during that crucial era, should also commemorate its bicentennial with a new history of its long and colorful existence. Chartered in 1780, Transylvania played a significant role as an educational pioneer in the developing trans-Allegheny West. Strategically located in the growing cultural and mercantile center of Lexington, Kentucky, this University was to draw upon the young elite of the South and Southwest for its clientele as it gradually overcame the obstacles of its frontier existence to achieve a national reputation for its excellent medical, legal, and liberal arts education.

It was remarkable that as early as 1799, this young University had established and staffed medical and law departments when few such centers for instruction existed anywhere in the nation. By 1820 the quality of the medical training here, based upon outstanding faculty and rich and varied library and apparatus resources, closely matched that of any of the other medical schools in the country. Enrollments soared during the decades of 1820–1850, and it is not too much to say that probably the majority of trained physicians practicing in the South and Southwest in the ante-bellum period received their education at Transylvania.

Even in its early years, Transylvania was fortunate to have among its trustees some of the noted leaders in Kentucky's political, military, and judicial life. These included Isaac Shelby, the first governor of Kentucky, George Rogers Clark, the Revolutionary War hero who won the Northwest from the British, Caleb Wallace, one of the first appointees to the Kentucky Supreme Court, and Henry Clay. National leaders such as George Washington and John Adams contributed funds to this pioneer educational venture in Kentucky. During the 1818–1827 period under the leadership of Horace Holley, a transplanted New Englander, the University progressed so rapidly as to rank among the leading institutions of higher learning in the country. Its alumni provided a significant part of the professional, political, and business leadership not only in the South and West, but on a national level as well. Men like Stephen Austin, who opened up Texas for settlement, Albert Sidney Johnston, who lost his life as a Confederate general at Shiloh, Cassius M. Clay, the fighting abolitionist, Jefferson Davis, president of the Confederacy, and Richard M. Johnson and

John C. Breckinridge, both vice-presidents of the United States, formed a part of this distinguished roster.

Thomas Jefferson, who was governor of Virginia when that state chartered Transylvania in 1780, was a longtime friend and supporter of the institution and corresponded with Horace Holley about their mutual interests in university education. In January 1820, Jefferson, who was having difficulty persuading the Virginia legislature to establish a state university, wrote a friend that "we must send our children for education to Kentucky (Transylvania) or Cambridge (Harvard). The latter will return them to us fanatics and tories, and the former will keep them to add to their population. If however we are to go a begging anywhere for education, I would rather it should be to Kentucky than any other state, because she has more flavor of the old cask than any other."

As one who has spent much of his life researching, collecting and writing books about Kentucky, I have never ceased to be impressed by the important contributions Transylvania University has made, and continues to make, to higher education. Despite a history of adversities that might well have spelled demise for most institutions, this University has battled courageously and successfully to overcome them. It approaches its bicentennial with a justified pride in its historical achievements and with confidence in its future.

It is fitting that a member of the faculty whose teaching career has long been associated with the school should write this history of Transylvania. Since coming to Transylvania in 1950 with degrees from Dartmouth and Columbia, Dr. John Wright has earned a reputation as a scholar and historian whose first interest is teaching. In this history of the University, Dr. Wright has based his account on a wide range of sources, and has attempted to place the ongoing life of the institution in a meaningful relation to the educational history of the nation and to the political, economic, social, and cultural forces that influenced that history. Alumni, students of higher education, and Kentuckians should find this an engrossing narrative of this nation's first western University.

J. Winston Coleman, Jr.

August 10, 1975
Lexington, Kentucky

Acknowledgments

It comes as no surprise to any historian that a work of history is a joint enterprise. Yet, until I became engaged in producing this volume on the history of Transylvania University the reality of that experience had not been brought home. It is truly amazing the many diverse ways in which historians are dependent on others for the accumulation of data, the editing and rewriting of the numerous drafts, and the host of details in converting a manuscript into a book. All-in-all it is a most rewarding experience and while this brief acknowledgment falls far short of adequately compensating these individuals for their assistance, I am pleased to express my gratitude now.

To President Irvin E. Lunger must go the credit for the project in the first place. He persuaded me to undertake a task which I had been avoiding because I regarded the writing of institutional history as difficult and tedious. While it has on occasion proven to be both, the satisfaction and excitement of the task have far outweighed those aspects. Dr. Lunger gave me his full support in making all records available to me, in carefully reading the entire manuscript, and in providing valuable insights into the recent years of Transylvania's history.

There is no way to assess the invaluable assistance I received from Roemel Henry, Transylvania's librarian, archivist, and repository of more local and school information than a historical society. As a historian herself, she knows the needs of the researcher, and she supplied the resources of the Transylvania University archives and files with effectiveness, grace, and good humor.

To J. Winston Coleman, Jr., Kentucky's historian par excellence, I am indebted more than I can say to his willingness to wade through the early draft and to bring to bear upon it his rich store of Kentucky historical lore. I am proud to be a member of that large fraternity of writers who are fortunate recipients of the kind assistance of this fine gentleman.

To my cherished colleagues, Joseph Binford and Paul Fuller, I wish to express my gratitude for the hours they wrestled with the manuscript and in assisting me in the tortuous task of revising and rewriting the several drafts. I wish also to thank John R. Bryden for reading the manuscript and using his keen proofreading talent and his intimate knowledge of a good deal of Transylvania history to improve the final product. My heartfelt thanks, too, to Ann Williamson who brought a wealth of good judgment and valuable expertise to the editing of the work and turned a tedious task into an exciting introduction to the art of publication. I wish also to acknowledge my debt to the extensive collection of data on Transylvania accumulated carefully by Dr. L. R. Dingus, a devoted member of the University faculty for many years. Certainly no author has had a more genial and competent guide to handling the hundred and one details involved in preparing a book for press than Edward Houlihan with his irrepressible good humor, common sense, and experience.

I wish to extend my thanks to the staffs of the Massachusetts Historical Society, the Presbyterian Historical Society, the Lexington Public Library, and the Transylvania University library for their thoughtfulness and assistance. I am grateful to the Transylvania alumni, young and old, who shared with me recollections of their days at this institution. I hope that this history may in some small way enrich their sense of pride and tradition in their cherished association with this university.

To my wife Fran, whose loving encouragement and bright perceptive comments on the various drafts and galley proof she conscientiously read immeasurably assisted this writer, I owe more than these words can ever express.

John D. Wright, Jr.

September, 1975

In Memoriam

Transylvania University has been greatly assisted in the publication of this volume by a gift in memory of Dr. Edward McShane Waits, by his cousin Mrs. Tilton J. Cassidy.

A native of Cynthiana, Kentucky, Edward McShane Waits enrolled at Transylvania University in 1892. Following his graduation he was ordained a minister in the Christian Church (Disciples of Christ). He had served churches in Kentucky and Texas when he was named to the presidency of Texas Christian University in Fort Worth in 1916.

Often referred to as the father of modern Texas Christian University, Dr. Waits served as president of the college for 25 years and was directing the continuing development program as president emeritus when he died in 1949. During this tenure he guided the growth of T.C.U. from 301 students to over 6,000, from a debt-ridden church school to one of the nation's showplaces of private higher education.

During his lifetime he served in several national leadership positions both in education and his church, authored two books, and was recognized by his alma mater with an honorary Doctor of Laws.

Preface to Second Edition

It has been most gratifying to see the warm reception given the first edition of *Transylvania: Tutor to the West*. The exhaustion of the first printing has necessitated another. However, this is more than a reprinting of the first edition. It is, in many respects, a new edition, incorporating not only numerous corrections of errata discovered in the first edition, but substantial rewriting of the last two chapters. The passage of time, the impact of a new administration, changing conditions, all give a new perspective on the recent decades of Transylvania's history as well as providing new information.

I do wish to thank the readers who have called my attention to errors of commission and omission, and although—human frailty being what it is—all corrections may not have been made, I hope that most of them have been included in this new edition.

As the printing of this new edition comes in the bicentennial year of Transylvania's existence, it may justifiably be considered the bicentennial edition. It is my hope that the reading of the past two hundred years of Transylvania's rich history will not only provide perspective on this university today but be a useful resource for the generations of Transylvanians yet to come as this institution moves into its third century.

TRANSYLVANIA:
Tutor To The West

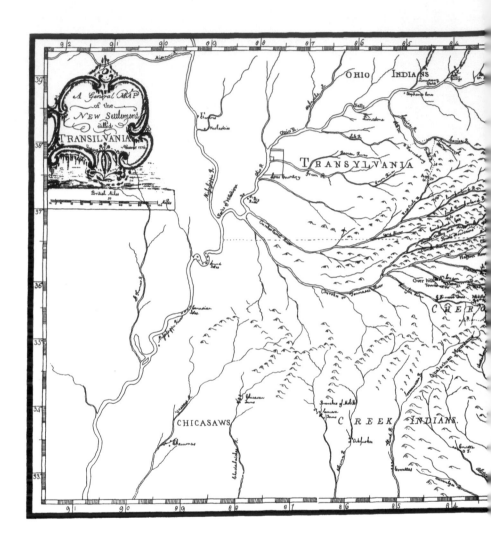

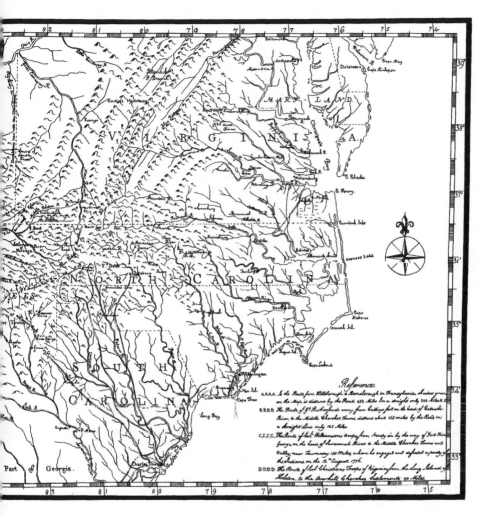

A 1776 map of Kentucky referring to the area as the new settlement called Transylvania.

1

Learning in the Wilderness

It was the year 1780. It was a time of revolution in America, and the end of the War for Independence was nowhere in sight. British forces, frustrated in their attempts in the northern and middle colonies to corner General Washington and the Continental army and force a surrender, had turned to the southern colonies. In May 1780, Charleston, South Carolina, fell to the British, and General Cornwallis assumed command of the army and began moving northward through North Carolina towards Virginia. The threat of invasion alarmed the Virginia assembly which had convened in the very month Charleston had fallen. The record of that assembly's activities reveals the priority given to military matters. Thomas Jefferson had just been elected governor of Virginia, and it was his misfortune to be chief executive during a period of military crises for which his great talents were unsuited. Yet it was remarkable that in the turbulence of this crisis matters unrelated to military preparedness were introduced, discussed and acted upon. Among them was a charter to establish a seminary of learning in the trans-Allegheny region of that Virginia-owned region called Kentucky. Nothing, certainly, could have pleased Governor Jefferson more than this evidence of concern for the educational future of this country. The seminary would be a spearhead of learning in the wilderness.

KENTUCKY IN 1780 was a battlefield, not a schoolground. This region, historically the domain of the Indian and the buffalo and for many years a rich source of legend and attraction for the westward-bound, was only gradually yielding its wildness to the impact of organized settlement. Both French explorers, hunters and traders using the Ohio River, and English hunters and traders using the Ohio but also pushing across the mountains from Virginia, had penetrated the region perhaps as early as the mid-seventeenth century. Real competition came in the eighteenth century as land speculators entered the field. In 1748 the Ohio Company was organized (two of George Washington's half-brothers were among the leaders) and lay claim to 200,000 acres in the Ohio Valley. To make a reality of this claim, systematic exploration, mapping and surveying had to be undertaken. In 1750 Dr. Thomas Walker was employed to head a party across the mountains. This physician, a graduate of William and Mary, led his followers into the uncharted Appalachian mountain chain. These mountain ranges, stretching from northeast to southwest blocked the way west until the men spied a break in the mountain wall which they named for the Duke of Cumberland. It was to become one of the most famous mountain passes in the history of the American westward migration.[1]

The Ohio Company sent Christopher Gist on another Kentucky exploration shortly after Walker's trip, but the competition between France and Great Britain for the control of the North American continent once more exploded into warfare, this time known as the French and Indian War, which blocked any serious movement into Kentucky. The end of the war and the Treaty of Paris in 1763 ended French control in Canada and in the region east of the Mississippi River, and Britain temporarily prohibited settlers from moving into the trans-Appalachian West by the Proclamation Act of 1763. This did not stop hunters, however, who passed through the Cumberland Gap to exploit Kentucky's rich resources of furs and deerskins. Among these hunters was Daniel Boone, who with John Find-

---

[1] A good recent account of this phase of Kentucky history may be found in Thomas D. Clark, *Kentucky: Land of Contrast* (New York, 1968). See Chapters 1 and 2.

ley traveled through Kentucky in 1768. After two years of wandering about the region, dodging Indians, autographing trees and familiarizing himself with the land, Boone returned to his patient wife in North Carolina.

Despite the fact that Kentucky was a favorite hunting-ground for the Cherokees from the south and the Shawnees and Wyandottes from the north, Boone persuaded six families to join his own in a move to Kentucky in the fall of 1773. In a surprise attack on the party Cherokees killed two boys, one of whom was Boone's son, and the frantic survivors pulled back to North Carolina. Boone's ambition to found the first Kentucky settlement was frustrated by James Harrod and a small but enterprising band of Pennsylvania traders who, in June 1774, had begun to clear land on a site eight miles south of the Kentucky River.

Meanwhile, a grandiose scheme to carve a private frontier colony out of Kentucky south of the Kentucky River and reaching into northern Tennessee was being hatched by Judge Richard Henderson of North Carolina and some influential friends. In March 1774, they had formed a land company, and a year later, bringing with them a generous supply of attractive merchandise, they met with a council of the Cherokees at Sycamore Shoals on the Watauga River in Tennessee. Here the Cherokees signed a treaty surrendering their vaguely-defined claims to the region.

To this new colony the name Transylvania was given, thus introducing into this region the name that ultimately would be associated with the infant seminary some years later. The deed from the Cherokees had used the name Chenoa to designate the land, but the pioneer company was composed of men educated in a classical and European tradition. These men perhaps recalled that the Romans had once named a region in eastern Europe Transylvania because it lay beyond a great forest. Now these New World empire builders were creating their own colony beyond the forests and mountains, their own Transylvania.[2]

[2] We have no first hand evidence on this matter of the name of Transylvania. Robert Peter, *Transylvania University: Its Origins, Rise, Decline, and Fall* (Louisville, 1896), p. 14, surmises that it may have been the classical tradition that suggested the name.

Judge Henderson employed Daniel Boone to head a group of trail-blazers to mark off a permanent trail into central Kentucky and establish an outpost for the company on the Kentucky River. This Boone did in March 1775, and the famed settlement of Boonesboro came into existence. Shortly thereafter, the Revolutionary War began. Indian allies of the British waged a campaign of terror in Kentucky for the next seven years, climaxed by their fearful ambush of settlers at lower Blue Licks in August 1782.

Despite the constant threat of Indian attacks, however, settlers continued to move into Kentucky. From Pennsylvania, Virginia and the Carolinas they came. It is estimated that as many as 150,000 men, women and children passed over the Wilderness Road through the Cumberland Gap between 1775 and 1800. While most settlers were looking for better farm land, or for other ways to improve their economic condition, some were religiously-motivated. There was, for example, a sizeable group of Baptists from Spotsylvania, Virginia, who were tired of the religious conflicts in the Old Dominion, and who, in September 1781, moved across the mountains into the Dick's River valley, south of the Kentucky River. Other Baptist groups followed, and Baptist churches began to spring up along the frontier. Presbyterians, who along with the Baptists had been active in fighting the domination of the established Anglican Church in Virginia years before Jefferson entered upon his campaign for religious liberty, also came into this region of Kentucky.[3]

One of the most challenging problems confronting colonists from the earliest settlements at Jamestown and Plymouth was that of preserving and transmitting the British cultural heritage in the wilderness. This problem followed the moving frontier as it edged its way westward for the next two centuries. This transfer of culture, which Bernard Bailyn views as the basic educational process in American society, had in Europe largely been taken care of by the traditional inter-relationship between family, the apprenticeship system and the community. Under the constant impact of the wilderness, this traditional pattern disintegrated, and colonial leaders, fearful that people would

[3] Clark, *Kentucky: Land of Contrast*, Chapter 5.

The fort at Lexington in 1782,
From Ranck's History of Lexington

relapse into barbarism, placed on schools the new and heavy
responsibility of cultural transference.[4]

Louis Wright has also pointed out that

on every frontier, as the American continent was settled, a group
who sometimes described themselves as the "better element"
waged a persistent warfare against the disintegrating forces
which the liberty of a wild country unloosed. This group were
the conservatives of traditional conduct, traditional way of doing
things, traditional manners and morals, and they sought to preserve and perpetuate the ancient inheritance of things of the
mind and spirit.[5]

THE MEN WHO SPONSORED the new seminary chartered
by the Virginia assembly in the spring of 1780 were Presbyterians whose dedication to education and a literate ministry
was part of their proud tradition. The Presbyterians had already
established several schools in Virginia including Liberty Hall

[4]Bernard Bailyn, *Education in the Forming of American Society* (Chapel
Hill, 1960), *passim*.

[5]Louis Wright, *Culture on the Moving Frontier* (Bloomington, Indiana,
1955).

(later Washington and Lee) and Hampden-Sydney. Now they were taking the lead in establishing a school, or seminary as it was then so frequently called, in the trans-Allegheny West. Most active in securing the charter were the Reverend John Todd of Hanover Presbytery in Virginia, and his nephew, Colonel John Todd. Colonel Todd, with his brothers Levi and Robert, were Pennsylvania-born, but had gone to Virginia to attend a school conducted by their uncle. Forsaking law study for the frontier, they moved to Kentucky where John immediately became prominent in political and military affairs. He was chosen to represent Kentucky in the Virginia legislature.[6]

Conditions were hardly favorable to the establishment of a school in a barely-settled wilderness where at least six of the early school trustees lost their lives in Indian warfare. Motivation for chartering the school is found in the original charter which was entitled "An Act to vest certain Escheated Lands in the County of Kentucke in Trustees for a Public School."

> Whereas it is represented to this General Assembly that there are certain lands within the country of Kentucky, formerly belonging to British subjects, not yet sold under the Law of Escheats and Forfeitures, which might at a future day be a valuable fund for the maintenance and education of youth, and it being the interest of this Commonwealth always to promote and encourage every design which may tend to the improvement of the mind and the diffusion of knowledge even amongst the remote citizens, whose situation a barbarous neighborhood and a savage intercourse might otherwise render unfriendly to science. . . .[7]

[6] William H. Whitsitt, *Life and Times of Judge Caleb Wallace* (Louisville, 1888), p. 99. Whitsitt claims that Col. Todd deserves the greatest credit for the passage of the act establishing the seminary. Other accounts of the founding and early days of Transylvania may be found in William Foote, *Sketches of Virginia, Historical and Biographical* (2nd ser., 2nd ed., Philadelphia, 1856); Walter Wilson Jennings, *Transylvania: Pioneer University of the West* (New York, 1955); Robert Peter, *Transylvania University: Its Origins, Rise, Decline, and Fall*; Alvin F. Lewis, *History of Higher Education in Kentucky* (Washington, D.C., 1899); James F. Hopkins, *The University of Kentucky: Origins and Early Years* (Lexington, Ky., 1951).

[7] This act is printed in William W. Hening, *The Statutes at Large: Being a Collection of All the Laws of Virginia, From the First Session of the Legislature in the Year 1619* (13 vols., Richmond, 1809–1823), X, 287–288.

It was specified that eight thousand acres formerly belonging to British subjects should be vested in thirteen trustees "as a free donation from the Commonwealth for the purpose of a public school or Seminary of Learning, to be erected in said country as soon as the circumstances of the country and the state of the funds will admit. . . ."[8]

What is noteworthy about the charter for the Kentucky school is the emphasis on the new institution's being a "public school." From the founding of Harvard College and throughout the colonial period, establishment of colleges was due to denominational sponsorship. As in the case of Puritan institutions, this support of education arose from a concern for a trained ministry and a literate congregation. During the eighteenth century, however, the growing emphasis on rationalism, secularism and science among intellectuals aroused their interest in an educational system not linked with denominational sponsorship. Thomas Jefferson's educational plans for Virginia certainly reflected this trend. Virginia legislators were also tending to think of education more in public terms than in private and restrictive ones. Thus, when the bill to charter a new school in recently-settled regions in the West came before them, its language reflected this changing attitude. Not only did the charter reveal this concern for education as a public responsibility, but it also reflected the fear of educated leaders that frontier conditions were indifferent if not hostile to learning. Certainly many frontiersmen would have put education low on the list of priorities for survival.

Unsettled conditions in Kentucky discouraged immediate activity on the part of the trustees who were more concerned with survival than education. When the trustees were finally able to meet for the first time in 1783, they found the original charter did not adequately define either their powers or specify the procedures by which new trustees would be chosen and general business conducted. They petitioned the Virginia assembly to amend the charter to correct these deficiencies. The man introducing the bill to amend the charter was Caleb Wallace, a

[8]*Ibid.*

Princeton graduate, Presbyterian clergyman and representative from Lincoln County, Kentucky. He had been a longtime associate of the Reverend Todd and shared his concern for encouragement of education on the frontier. In late June 1783, the bill was passed by the assembly. It passed in the form of an amendment to the original 1780 charter and specifically attached the name Transylvania Seminary to the school.

Under the new bill the number of trustees was increased to twenty-five, constituting a self-perpetuating board given all the "powers and privileges that are enjoyed by visitors and governors of any college or university within this state not herein limited or otherwise directed." To the original grant of 8,000 acres was now added 12,000 more acres of escheated land, this total of 20,000 acres to be permanently tax-free. The faculty and students under the new charter were to be exempt from militia duty, a significant consideration in the days when able-bodied men were on call for such duty to combat Indians. The seminary was empowered to grant degrees of Bachelor and Master of Arts as well as honorary degrees. The trustees were made responsible for overseeing examinations of the students twice a year to evaluate the quality of instruction. In keeping with the original intent to establish a public institution, it was clearly stated that no religious test should be required of trustees, officers or instructors. Students were to be examined for their knowledge, "virtue and erudition," and not for religious dogma. Finally, the trustees were made accountable to the legislature for their administration of the seminary.[9]

The twenty-five new trustees included among their number some of the most outstanding leaders of the day. The Reverend Caleb Wallace was one. This devout Presbyterian gave up his duties as clergyman for the law. He was one of three appointees to the Kentucky Supreme Court (later to become the Kentucky Court of Appeals in 1792) on which he served until his resignation in 1813. Another of the trustees was Isaac Shelby, the very able and energetic military leader in the American Revolution who had supplied George Rogers Clark's campaign in Illinois and who distinguished himself at the battles of King's

[9]Hening, *Statutes*, XI, 282–287.

Mountain and Cowpens. Shelby later became Kentucky's first governor. Christopher Greenup, a Virginia lawyer who moved to Lexington in 1783, and later to Frankfort, was a trustee of the new seminary. He was one of Kentucky's first two Representatives to the U.S. Congress in 1792, and was elected governor of the state in 1804.

Fresh from his exploits at Kaskaskia and Vincennes and a Kentucky hero to stand beside Boone and Kenton, George Rogers Clark was appointed a trustee of Transylvania. No one ever accused Clark of being overly concerned with educational matters, however, and his seat on the board became vacated after a few years for non-attendance. Samuel McDowell, father of the famed surgeon Ephraim McDowell, was also a trustee until he was appointed a judge of the Kentucky Supreme Court and fearing a conflict of professional interests resigned his seat in 1788. Two years later James Garrard, the second governor of Kentucky, became a trustee. And, finally, the infamous General James Wilkinson appeared for two years on the roster of trustees, as he briefly shared his winning personality and varied talents with Kentuckians while secretly scheming with Spanish authorities in New Orleans to exploit the troubled relations between Congress and the trans-Appalachian West. While it is true that some of these men did not make the best, or even the most conscientious, of Transylvania's trustees, the fact remains they were appointed because the legislature believed the institution and the cause of education deserved the service of such men. If the enterprise was worthy, then worthy men should support and lead it.

None of these new trustees was more devoted to making a success of this educational venture than the Reverend David Rice. He was among the earliest Presbyterian ministers to settle near the cluster of new settlements along the Kentucky and Dick's Rivers, and was known affectionately then and thereafter as "Father" Rice. Born in Hanover, Virginia in 1733 of Welsh farmer folk, Rice had experienced a deep conversion in his youth while listening to the preaching of a local Presbyterian minister, and decided to dedicate himself to the ministry. After graduating from Princeton, he returned to Hanover Pres-

bytery to study under the Reverend John Todd and was ordained in 1763. He was preaching in Bedford County, Virginia,
when the American Revolution started, and he immediately
gave his whole-hearted support to the cause, actively participating in the committee of public safety for his county.

In 1783 at fifty years of age, Rice responded to a call from
three hundred Kentucky Presbyterians to come and establish a
church. Taking his wife and eleven children with him, he
moved into the frontier area and laid the foundation for Presbyterianism in Kentucky. This tall, slender, active man impressed
people with his solemn, dignified manner. His vigorous campaign against slavery and his attempts to prevent its introduction into Kentucky marked him as a man of courage and fore-
sight.[10]

ON NOVEMBER 10, 1783, the necessary quorum of thirteen
trustees met "in pursuance of an act of the General Assembly
of Virginia" in the rough surroundings of Crow's station near
Danville. Isaac Shelby was there, as were Benjamin Logan,
David Rice, Caleb Wallace and Christopher Greenup. The
trustees elected Rice chairman and considered what could be
done to start the school. They had no cash. Their gift from the
legislature was in land — unsurveyed and some of it almost inaccessible and difficult to sell or lease. A committee was appointed to draw up subscriptions for the procurement of funds
from real or personal property of interested persons in the area.
There being no quorum for the December meeting, the Board
did not convene again until March 4, 1784, when they received
the welcome news that the Reverend John Todd, early sponsor
of the school and now a resident of Louisa, Virginia, had presented the school with a gift of a library and philosophical apparatus as an "encouragement to science to this Institution."
Such a gift was invaluable to the school at this time, but trans-

10 Ernest Trice Thompson, *Presbyterians in the South* (Richmond, Va.,
1963), I, 93–116; Robert Davidson, *The History of the Presbyterian Church in
the State of Kentucky* (New York, 1847), 65–71; Asa Earl Martin, *The
Anti-Slavery Movement in Kentucky Prior to 1850* (Louisville, 1918), pp. 12–
13.

portation of the books and apparatus over the mountains was costly. It took the trustees five years and personal solicitation among themselves to bring Todd's gift to Kentucky.[11]

In November 1784, the trustees, though discouraged about the failure to secure funds by subscription, decided that a start must be made. They resolved "that one or more Grammar schools, as the funds of the Seminary and other circumstances will permit," be erected at or near the dwelling of Rice. So Rice re-arranged his living quarters to permit the first classes to be held in his log cabin. Tuition was placed at four pistoles a year, there being no national currency worthy of the name at this time. In the West where men with goods to sell looked down the river to New Orleans, the Spanish appeared a more significant factor, and Spanish gold was the best currency available.[12]

David Rice's cabin

[11]Minutes of the Board of Trustees, November 10, 1783.
[12]*Ibid.*, November 4, 1784.

In February 1785, the first students of Transylvania Seminary trudged through the snow and wintry air to Father Rice's commodious cabin close by Harrod's Run between Danville and Fort Harrod.[13] The unsettled conditions of the country, the distances between houses, the lack of interest and money of many settlers kept the attendance small. Yet it was a beginning. Certainly at this time it could have been little more than an elementary school in most respects. Even the basic supplies of books, paper and writing utensils were lacking.

The first teacher was, not surprisingly, another Presbyterian minister. Although the Board did not confirm the arrangement until they mustered a quorum for the May 26, 1785 meeting, they approved retroactively the employment of the Reverend James Mitchell at a yearly salary of thirty pounds. A Pennsylvanian by birth Mitchell had moved to Virginia as a youth where he became associated with David Rice and Caleb Wallace. Licensed a Presbyterian minister in October 1781, and sent on a tour of Kentucky by his presbytery, he was much impressed by the new land. Returning to Virginia, he married one of Rice's daughters and shortly moved to Kentucky. He may have been influential in founding the early Presbyterian congregations at Danville, Cane Run and the Forks of Dick's River which presented the petition of three hundred signatures to Rice that brought him to Kentucky. Though Mitchell returned to Virginia for his ordination in August 1784, he was apparently prevailed upon by his father-in-law to settle in Kentucky. When a teacher was needed for the classes in Rice's cabin, Mitchell was willing and available to fill the position. This arrangement lasted a little over a year. In March 1786, Mitchell returned to Bedford, Virginia, where he remained as pastor until his death in 1841.[14]

With the departure of Mitchell, classes were apparently discontinued since no further mention is made of teachers, stu-

---

[13]Though there has been some debate over the issue of the location of Rice's home, Annie Stuart Anderson made a careful investigation of the matter, and in her article in the *Register* of the Kentucky Historical Society made a convincing case as to the correct site. An historical marker now identifies it.

[14]Whitsitt, *Caleb Wallace*, p. 103.

dents, classes or tuition until the school was moved to Lexington in 1789. In the meantime Rice resigned as chairman of the Board in July 1787. He was replaced by Harry Innes, who later was to be appointed as the first Chief Justice of the Kentucky Court of Appeals.

The chief concern of the trustees was the acquisition of funds. Various committees were appointed to survey and lease the escheated lands which composed the school's endowment. A petition was sent to the Virginia legislature to assign to Transylvania Seminary one-sixth of the surveyors' fees collected within the district which, at the time, were payable to William and Mary. This request was granted by an act of the legislature in 1787, but though various acts were passed later to strengthen the bill, the fees did not provide a great deal of money and the procedure was abolished in 1802.[15]

DESPITE THE FACT that Transylvania had scarcely begun its existence and its very survival was precarious, it had aroused sufficient interest among residents of the area to lead to a controversy concerning religion in the school. This controversy was manifested in the columns of the district's first newspaper, the *Kentucky Gazette*, published in Lexington. The controversy signalled the ominous development of a storm center that was to grow rapidly in size and intensity. The period of the American Revolution and the concurrent influence of eighteenth century Enlightenment had left a legacy of spreading indifference to traditional religious thought and denominational loyalties. Though vigorously condemned by ministers of most sects, the trend towards secularism and deism was not substantially checked until the religious revival at the opening of the nineteenth century. The collision between eighteenth-century enlightened ideals and religiously-orthodox views was a powerful one and led to the increasing influence of the latter and its gradual predominance in the second and third decades of the

[15] See James R. Robertson, *Petitions of the Early Inhabitants of Kentucky to the General Assembly of Virginia, 1769 to 1792* (Filson Club Publications, No. 27, Louisville, 1914).

nineteenth century. From its earliest days Transylvania, as was the case with many other colleges, was to be the agency which polarized these conflicting viewpoints. Reading the vehement attacks proponents of these differing opinions made on each other, one cannot but conclude that these men regarded control of the schools, and by implication control over the minds of the young, as of the highest priority.[16]

Obvious Presbyterian control of Transylvania Seminary at this time had apparently aroused sufficient critical comment to motivate Caleb Wallace to respond to it in the columns of the *Kentucky Gazette*. He wrote under the pseudonym of "Catholicus." Wallace may have felt a more than usual pressure to assume a pseudonym since he was a judge on the highest bench in the district, a situation which eventually compelled him to resign from the Board of the seminary in 1788. His relationship to the conflicting issues was a complex one. He was a Jeffersonian in his political affiliations, strongly supporting representative democracy, and in 1798 was a leading supporter of the Kentucky Resolution against the Federalist Alien and Sedition Acts. In Virginia before the American Revolution, he was a leader of a dissenting sect struggling against the monopoly of the established Anglican Church, and had stood firmly behind Jefferson's campaign for religious liberty in the Old Dominion. But as a staunch Presbyterian of orthodox views, he denounced the secularizing trend of Jeffersonian thought which he believed encouraged religious infidelity. In his letter printed in the *Kentucky Gazette* in September 1787, Wallace made it clear that he did not believe morals could be taught without theology. He avoided the mistake of proposing that only Presbyterian tenets be taught, suggesting that ministers of various sects be invited to preach in the school. Prayers and singing of hymns and psalms would be, of course, an essential part of the student's daily routine. The Christian religion and the education of young men could not, and should not, be separated. Students, he concluded, could make up their own minds regarding religious beliefs after they left school.[17]

[16]Niels Sonne, *Liberal Kentucky, 1780–1828* (New York, 1939). This is the best single account of the clash of eighteenth century rationalism with orthodox religious revivalism in Kentucky.
[17]*Ibid.*, pp. 48–50.

Col. Robert Patterson's cabin

Several other writers entered the lists, bearing such names as "Paddy Money-Man," "A Transylvanian" and "A Sectarian." One urged that religion be entirely removed from the curriculum, another that the newly established American principle of the separation of church and state be applied to the seminary, while another countered these views by advocating outright sectarian control.

This was the situation when the Board of Trustees made the momentous decision in the fall of 1788 to move from the rural surroundings of Dick's River Valley to the growing urban center of nearby Lexington.

2

Division and Reunion

Harry Toulmin

Lexington, along with Pittsburgh, Cincinnati, Louisville and St. Louis, was representative of what Richard Wade has called the "urban frontier." In his authoritative study, *The Urban Frontier: The Rise of the Western Cities, 1790–1830*, Wade has convincingly shown that as Americans pushed westward two frontiers were established. One was the more familiar and traditional rural frontier with its particular way of life and values, and the other was the urban frontier. Contrary to the usual view the urban frontier was not merely a gradual evolution of a rural community into a more concentrated and diversified town community; it was a distinct area in its own right with the wholesale transfer of eastern economic and social institutions and values to a frontier site. Of the cities in the Ohio River Valley, Lexington was among the earliest and grew the fastest.[1]

When hunters from Harrodsburg camping on the future site of the town in 1775 heard the news of the famous battle far to the north in the small Massachusetts town of Lexington, they commemorated the event by naming the site Lexington. Not until four years later did Robert Patterson and about twenty-five others hack out a clearing in the heavy canebrake beside a small branch of the Elkhorn River near a good spring and build a crude fort. Patterson was a vigorous leader in this new community and became a trustee of the young Transylvania in

---

[1] Richard C. Wade, *The Urban Frontier: The Rise of the Western Cities, 1790–1830* (Cambridge, 1959).

1795. His small log cabin, one of the first in Lexington, is still preserved on the Transylvania campus.

By 1790 Lexington had a population of 835. Ten years later the town had grown to 1795, exceeding Pittsburgh and twice as large as Louisville. Despite the fact it was the only one of the major towns studied by Wade that was not located on a major river (the Kentucky River was ten miles away), it was the axis of main trade and migration routes. New settlers purchased their goods here and later brought in their produce to sell. Goods were bought and sold in the Cheapside Market, and traders quenched their thirst and exchanged news and views at the taverns Sheaf of Wheat, the Indian Queen, or the Sign of the Buffalo.

Town leaders were ambitious to make Lexington a social and cultural leader in the West, as well as a busy mercantile center. Many of them had come from Philadelphia and other Pennsylvania towns, others from Virginia and Carolina towns. They wished to create a western Philadelphia as soon as possible, laying out streets on a grid plan and getting rid of the vestiges of frontier living. As early as 1785 the town fathers ordered "all persons having cabbins [sic], cow pens, hog pens, or other in-closures [sic] whatever within the main street of Lexington" to remove them in sixty days. Visitors who had seen the town in 1790 and came back ten years later were amazed at the transformation and the rapidity with which old log structures had been replaced with permanent and handsome brick structures. Many of these fine new homes were built on the two hills dominating the town, one sharply rising from the Town Branch of the Elkhorn to what is now High Street, the other more gradually sloping up toward the present Transylvania campus.[2]

Economically Lexington developed into a major trade mart, exchanging rich agricultural production of the fertile farm-lands — hemp, corn, wheat and tobacco — for goods brought down the Ohio and overland from Limestone (now Maysville). In the first decades of the nineteenth century Lexington turned to manufacturing as well. With a plentiful crop of hemp, it was not surprising that rope manufacturing became a major in-

[2]*Ibid.*, pp. 18, 21. Also *Kentucky Gazette*, January 23, February 13, 1790.

dustry. By 1810 one visitor claimed that Lexington had nearly every type of American industry. The War of 1812 intensified this development and *Niles Register* was predicting that Lexington would be "the greatest inland city in the western world." The successful trip of the steamboat *Enterprise* from New Orleans to Louisville that same year, however, presaged Lexington's economic decline, for the rapidly growing river towns of Louisville and Cincinnati soon surpassed her.[3]

The economic base of the town was essential to its social, cultural, and educational development. Because of the confluence from north and south of two streams of immigration, the town's population could not but reflect some sectional differences. Yet slavery was generally accepted by most. In fact, the labor shortage in such a rapidly-growing area led to the large-scale use and importation of slaves. There had been some attempt by the Reverend David Rice and other ministers, delegates to the Kentucky Constitutional Convention of 1792, to prohibit the importation of slaves, but under the forceful leadership of Virginians such as George Nicholas the move was defeated. In 1800 there were 461 slaves listed in Lexington, but the number rapidly rose by 1810 to 1,594 — over thirty-five percent of the town's population — giving Lexington a distinctly southern character. However, the presence of many residents from non-slave-holding states modified this character.[4]

In this frontier area there was probably a greater emphasis on egalitarianism than in many eastern communities, yet distinct social classes emerged rather quickly as wealth tended to be concentrated in relatively few hands. In 1808 sixteen men owned over a third of the total town assessment of a million dollars. According to Wade's classification, "the merchants headed this rapidly stratifying social structure," followed by the professional classes, then the numerically large number of skilled and unskilled laborers, clerks and shopkeepers. Beneath them were the transients, such as the wagoners and rivermen, and at the bottom Negroes, slave and free.[5]

[3]Lewis Collins, *History of Kentucky* (Covington, Ky., 1874), pp. 262–263; Bernard Mayo, "Lexington: Frontier Metropolis," *Historiography and Urbanization* (Baltimore, 1941), p. 29.

[4]Wade, *The Urban Frontier*, pp. 49–52.

[5]*Ibid.*, p. 109.

It was the obvious intent of Lexington's economic elite to become the social and cultural elite as well. The merchant aristocracy not only became predominant in the town's political councils and thus influential in raising the physical standards of Lexington; they were also leaders in establishing and supporting libraries, schools, churches and public buildings. They encouraged Transylvania to move to — and remain in — Lexington by purchasing and giving the school a choice lot in town. They became trustees of the school and sent their sons there.

Despite the growing class stratification there were many urban and recreational activities shared by all. In addition to meeting together at churches, schools and various civic organizations, Lexingtonians shared the same amusements of horseracing, billiards, drinking, gambling and the theater. Visitors frequently commented that amusements predominated in the city's life. Yet there were five churches in Lexington by 1815, with stable and traditional congregations.

Finally, Lexington supported the arts and literature. Amateur theatricals appeared early in the form of plays presented by Transylvania students on a stage in the court house in 1799. Later the appearance of professional road companies overshadowed local talent. Musical and artistic talent was less apparent, although amateur musical organizations were presenting concerts by 1808. It was remarkable, therefore, that on November 12, 1817 a performance of the first symphony of Beethoven was given by a local musical organization under the conductorship of Anthony Heinrich, probably the first performance of a Beethoven symphony in America. Not until Matthew Jouett began his amazing career of portrait painting late in the second decade of the nineteenth century could Lexington claim a painter of note.

As was true of cultural developments in most American communities, writing and publishing appeared first. Lexington's pioneer publishing event was the arrival of John Bradford and his press in 1787 and his editing and publishing of the West's early newspaper, the *Kentucky Gazette*. A half-dozen other publishers had joined Bradford by the first decades of the nineteenth century. Books, pamphlets and literary magazines were printed, though many of the latter publications were of short duration. Two of the most interesting books to appear were John Robert Shaw's *The Life and Travels of John Robert Shaw* (1807) and Joseph Buchanan's *The Philosophy of Human Nature* (1812). The first is the picaresque tale of an English-born well-digger who spent some years of his life in Lexington, which gives a vivid picture of the life of a western workingman. The book by Buchanan, who attended Transylvania and studied medicine under Dr. Samuel Brown, is based on a series of lectures Buchanan had prepared for his courses. It is a tour de force as a pioneer study in American materialism and psychology, and has recently been the study of a number of psychologists and philosophers interested in the development of American philosophical and psychological thought. One historian of American philosophy called Buchanan "The earliest native physiological psychologist."[6]

IN LIGHT OF LEXINGTON'S development, it was hardly surprising that trustees of Transylvania chose this community as the permanent seat of the school. As its first action in Lexington, the Board elected a professor and a grammar-school master, but only the latter materialized in the person of Isaac Wilson who "produced satisfactory testimonials of his good demeanor, also a Diploma from the College and Academy of Philadelphia as Batchelor [sic] of Arts." Convinced that he was qualified to teach rudiments of the Greek and Latin languages, the trustees hired Wilson for six months beginning June 1, 1789 "at the public school-house near Lexington." The school was adjacent to the Presbyterian Meeting House then located on the east side of South Limestone Street on the present site of the Agricultural Experiment Station of the University of Kentucky. A committee of the Board inspected the schoolhouse and made arrangements to employ someone to "repair, clean and roughly lay a floor, fill up the hearths, and make a door. . . ." Tuition was set at three pounds a year. Hard cash being scarce, payment was accepted in property, corn, pork or tobacco. Though the library and apparatus donated by the Reverend John Todd had now arrived, it was not used by the grammar-school but

[6] Sonne, *Liberal Kentucky*, Ch. 3; Wade, *The Urban Frontier*, pp. 153–155.

deposited at the home of Levi Todd, a trustee of Transylvania and the future grandfather of Mary Todd.[7]

In January 1790, the trustees renewed Wilson's contract, and paid him fifty pounds for his past six months' services. Many trustees, we assume, were present at the exercises of the small school on April 10, 1790. According to the account in the *Kentucky Gazette*, it was an all-day affair.

> In the presence of a very respectable audience, several very elegant speeches were delivered by the boys, and in the evening a tragedy acted, and the whole concluded with a farce. The several masterly strokes of Elocution throughout the performance obtained a general applause, and were acknowledged by a universal clap from all present. The good order and decorum observed throughout the whole together with the rapid progress of the school in literature reflects great honor on the President.[8]

Some writers have referred to this occasion as the first college commencement in the West, but this is an exaggeration of a modest class-day exercise of a small grammar-school of thirteen students. Yet a start had been made, although it was discouraging that enrollment dropped to five students within a year. There seems to be no simple explanation for this, although it may have been due in part to the continuing threat of Indian attacks. It was reported to Secretary of War Knox in 1790 that during the previous seven years 1500 persons had been killed or captured by Indians in Kentucky. The *Kentucky Gazette* reported on January 23, 1790, that Indians had kidnapped and killed three settlers near Lexington, and this was followed by similar reports during the next few months.

Nevertheless Lexington continued to grow, and the trustees believed they might tap some of the growing wealth in the community by the timeworn device of a lottery, permission for which they secured from the legislature in 1790. Though the lottery proved to be a failure, the grammar-school continued with the appointment of a new schoolmaster, James Moore, in September 1791. A native of Virginia, Moore had moved to Kentucky where he hoped to become a Presbyterian minister. He was received as a candidate by the Transylvania (the name was popular) Presbytery in April 1792, but his trial sermon was

[7]Minutes of the Board, May 22, 1789; *Kentucky Gazette*, August 29, 1789.
[8]*Kentucky Gazette*, April 29, 1790.

not satisfactory and he was asked to deliver another. Apparently there were doubts as to his "experimental piety," and Moore, refusing to undergo another test, was dismissed by the Presbytery. He entered the Episcopalian ministry instead and became the first rector of Christ Church in Lexington.[9]

ON TO-MORROW AFTERNOON
By 3 O'clock,

IT is expected that the sales of Tickets in the Medical College Lottery will be suficient to **JUSTIFY THE DRAWING**, which is already announced to take place at that time.

THE AGENT

MUST, however, be permitted to observe, that he is apprehensive if he does not receive that encouragement from **THE CITIZENS OF TOWN PARTICULARLY**, which he had reason to expect, when he engaged in the undertaking, he will be compelled to disappoint those who *have* purchased, by postponement; as the object would be completely defeated, should the drawing of the Lottery commence before a sufficient number of the tickets are sold.

Let him therefore hope, that he will not be obliged to attribute a postponement to the inattention of the *CITIZENS* towards the advancement and prosperity of Transylvania University.   *JULY 25, 1823*

☞Tickets can be found at *all* the Book Stores, at the Post Office, at Washington Hotel, at Wallingsford's Tavern, at D. A. Sayre's, at T. Anderson's, at J. Graves's, at W. Connell's, and at J. Norton's.

An early lottery announcement

During 1791–1792 classes met in Moore's house. He was paid twenty-five pounds the first year and fifty pounds the next, half of his salary being paid in land and the rest from tuition money. He could accommodate the entire seminary in his house because there were not more than nineteen students in attendance during the year. Yet Moore managed to subdivide this small

[9]Davidson, *The History of the Presbyterian Church in Kentucky*, p. 295.

number into six classes ranging from those advanced in Greek classics and studying natural and mathematical science to those just beginning to construe Latin. Use of the John Todd library and apparatus was now made. However, the low pay and poor prospects led him to warn the trustees he would probably have to resign his position in the spring of 1793 as his "present finances will not admit" his continuing. He was even gloomier in his report to the chairman of the Board in April 1793:

> I am sorry to have to confess that our success has not answered the most moderate expectations. Circumstances to which our failure may be attributed will occur to every person on reflection. Our unaccomodated [sic] situation, want of teachers, neglect on the part of those who ought to be our patrons, no prospect of honorary degrees to stimulate the ambition and dilligence [sic] of students, and nothing to draw the attention of the public from which we have a right to expect additional funds as well as students.

In addition, Moore accused the trustees of being indifferent and failing to provide adequate rules for academic discipline.

The trustees in 1792 might be forgiven for having other things on their minds than fostering a seminary, legally responsible though they might be for its welfare. This was a fateful year for Kentucky. After nine conventions called during the past seven years in which Kentucky's future independence from Virginia and statehood were discussed, Virginia passed an enabling act authorizing Kentucky's admittance into the United States and Congress confirmed the action in February 1791. After fulfilling the necessary requirements for admission, Kentucky was admitted as the fifteenth state in 1792.

Lexington was the center of great excitement in the summer of 1792 when newly-elected governor Isaac Shelby and the legislature met in Lexington to organize the state government. It had certainly been Lexington's hope, and realistic expectation, that the state capital would be located there, but the decision was made to move the state government to Frankfort, a small community situated in a bowl of hills on the banks of the Kentucky River. Such a location, it was argued, was more nearly the center of the population, and it was more accessible to important river communications. Thus, while Lexington was to become the cultural and educational leader in the new state, it would not be the political center.

Other issues also agitated Lexington. One was the French Revolution which had aroused intense sentiment, either for or against, among many Americans. The revolution was supported by anti-Federalists as a means of crystallizing local political opinion to promote republicanism and Jefferson. Another source of excitement was a fantastic project, headed by the now-broken hero George Rogers Clark, to lead a large force of men from Kentucky and Tennessee to New Orleans against the Spanish who had recently closed the mouth of the Mississippi and New Orleans to western trade. Swift action from President Washington, who urged Governor Shelby to quash such an expedition, successfully prevented this folly.

Amid all this excitement, a meeting of the trustees to consider Transylvania's progress must have seemed tame, yet the trustees were seriously concerned to make the school succeed as their constant efforts to procure funds and recruit able leadership testified. Nor were the trustees the only men vitally interested in Transylvania's future. A group of Lexington men, fearful the seminary might move elsewhere if it failed to succeed, formed the Transylvania Land Company (no relation to Colonel Henderson's famous company of an earlier day), purchased an excellent town lot north of Main Street, and began the erection of a brick house. This lot and building they offered to the trustees if they would agree to locate the school permanently in Lexington. At their meeting of April 8, 1793, the trustees accepted the offer and resolved "that the permanent seat of the Seminary be established on the lot of ground in the Town of Lexington adjoining Messr. January's. . . ." This was the college lot, later named Gratz Park.

IN THE FALL OF 1793 it was increasingly apparent that a number of the recently-appointed trustees to the Transylvania Board, including John Bradford, editor of the *Kentucky Gazette*, were discontent with the strongly-orthodox Presbyterian influence on the Board. Though the Board at its stated meeting in October elected James Moore as the school's first president, a title empty of prestige at that time, a new majority acted a few months later during the February 1794 meeting to secure a more promising president for the fall of that year. The conservative Presbyterians denounced this action as illegal on technical grounds, but their main grievance was the intended choice as the new administrator — Harry Toulmin, a man whom they considered as having the most dubious religious and political credentials. However the decision to appoint Toulmin was reaffirmed at the April meeting by a narrow margin, and Moore resigned, along with most of the Presbyterian trustees.[10]

Transylvania's first permanent building, located in Gratz Park

Harry Toulmin, reason for the Presbyterian discontent, was newly-arrived from England where he had been born in 1767. He was strongly influenced by his father, a man of liberal convictions who leaned towards Unitarianism, and the views of close friend Joseph Priestley. Not only famous as a chemist for his discovery of oxygen but also well-known as an ardent proponent of the French Revolution, Priestley was a dedicated and eloquent churchman whose Unitarian beliefs made him the ob-

[10]*Senate Journal*, 1795–1796, p. 111.

ject of considerable criticism by leaders and followers of the Anglican Church.

Toulmin was attracted by the prospects in the new republic and read many of the published travels about America, especially Kentucky. In fact, he himself had written a series of short tracts giving reasons for migrating to America, plus a sketch of Kentucky including a reference to a new college established there by the Virginia legislature. He sailed for Virginia in 1793 and became acquainted, through Priestley's introduction, with Jefferson who was delighted with this young Englishman. Jefferson may well have encouraged Toulmin to accept the presidency of the new school in Lexington and exert his leadership in the western land where it was needed.

Toulmin received John Bradford's letter of February 6, 1794, informing him of his appointment as president of Transylvania Seminary at a salary which consisted of half the tuition money, "a small plantation now in the occupancy of the present President" and 100 pounds. Toulmin accepted immediately "with sentiments of the warmest gratitude," expressing the hope that his talents would equal his enthusiasm and requesting that the trustees not expect too much of him. He also stated that if greater unanimity could be achieved among the trustees by rescinding his appointment, he hoped they would feel free to do so.[11]

The views of the Presbyterian trustees who resigned over Toulmin's appointment were probably accurately reflected by the Reverend Robert Davidson, a Presbyterian clergyman, who recounted the incident in his very partial *History of the Presbyterian Church in Kentucky.*

> Mr. Toulmin was by birth an Englishman, and by profession a Baptist preacher, but in sentiment he was a Unitarian, and a follower of Doctor Priestly. . . . Toulmin was, moreover, a hot politician and a sycophantic satellite of Thomas Jefferson, to whom he dedicated several adulatory stanzas in a small volume of very indifferent poems, which he published in Lexington, in 1805. His democratical partisanship and Socinian doctrine made him popular with the Deistical clubs, and through their influence he was invited to preside over Transylvania Seminary.

[11] John Bradford to Harry Toulmin, February 6, 1794; Harry Toulmin to John Bradford, February 12, 1794. Shane Collection, Presbyterian Historical Society, Philadelphia.

It was only a "mad and misguided majority" of the trustees, said Davidson, who elected Toulmin, and they thus dealt a fatal blow to the prosperity of the school.[12]

Toulmin arrived in Lexington in June 1794, and took the oath of office on the 30th of that month. He found a great diversity among the thirty students as far as their ages and attainments were concerned. On Saturday mornings those who lived nearby came to recite "some moral or political piece they had previously committed to memory." On Sundays he met with the older students to discuss the subject of moral philosophy. He asked younger students to memorize some scriptural selections to impress on them a sense of duty and moral obligation. He once exclaimed:

> Would to heaven, that the principles of piety were ever with them to restrain them from evil and to incite them to the practice of what is good! But whilst the name of the judgments of God are slighted and profaned! how can the principles of piety be expected to influence the heart?[13]

Although these hardly seem the sentiments of a dissolute man, it must be remembered that Toulmin was a clergyman and that his differences with the Presbyterians centered around theological premises. It was Toulmin's Unitarian views, combined with his Jeffersonian political principles that outraged his opponents. The political affiliation becomes even more significant when we find the trustees recommending to Toulmin that French be introduced into the curriculum for its value "as connecting us more closely with the only free Nation upon earth but ourselves . . . and unfolding to our youth the writings and learning of a nation, now holding pre-eminently the first rank in the world for virtue, for patriotism, and for science. . . ."[14] This was October 1794. Pro-French sentiment still remained strong in many parts of the country despite the excesses of the Reign of Terror. For the westerner in particular, it was the British with their reluctance to surrender the forts in the Old

---

[12]Davidson, *The History of the Presbyterian Church in Kentucky*, p. 290.

[13]Harry Toulmin, "Report to the Board of Trustees," October, n.d., 1794. Shane Collection.

[14]Trustees' Committee, "Recommendations on Curriculum," October, n.d., 1794. Shane Collection.

Northwest and their rumored encouragement of Indian attacks on western settlements that were the enemy.

Though enrollment dropped to twenty-one by April 1795, Toulmin was not discouraged, buoyed as he was by compliments of the parents of his students. The boarding-out problem remained a bothersome one, both from the point of supervision and expense, and Toulmin suggested that a third floor be added to the present brick building now housing the seminary. This structure, located on the north end of the college lot facing toward Second Street with its back to Third Street, had been under construction when Transylvania received both house and lot from the Transylvania Land Company in 1793, and the trustees had completed the building a year later. The Board at first decided to follow Toulmin's suggestion to add a third story, but thought better of it later and authorized a committee to erect "a brick building to adjoin the Colege [sic] on ye West, and have the same completed for the reception of students." Not more than $1,073 was to be expended, and a kitchen was supposed to be constructed out of this same money.[15]

ADDED TO OTHER PROBLEMS was the challenge to Transylvania presented by the Presbyterians in the form of a competing school. Within a few weeks after the controversial Board meeting of April 1794, from which there had been the mass exodus of Presbyterians, the Transylvania Presbytery authorized plans to establish a new school — one in which, as Davidson later said, "their sons might enjoy the advantages of a liberal education without the contamination of their religious principles, and which might furnish the churches with able and faithful ministers."[16]

The Presbyterians proposed to establish two schools, a grammar school and an academy. The grammar school they started almost immediately by hiring Andrew Steele and convening classes near the Pisgah Presbyterian Church, about eight miles

[15]Minutes of the Board, June 10, 1975.
[16]Davidson, *The History of the Presbyterian Church in the State of Kentucky*, p. 291.

from Lexington. A charter for Kentucky Academy was secured from the legislature in December 1794, which provided that one-half of the trustees must always be Presbyterian ministers from the Transylvania Presbytery. A well-devised fund-raising campaign was set in motion. Kentucky congregations were systematically solicited, as well as interested donors. An effective team consisting of David Rice and James Blythe was sent to raise money along the Atlantic seaboard from Washington to Boston. These two gentlemen started with President George

Kentucky Academy

Washington, who contributed $100, then to John Adams who pledged $100, Aaron Burr $40, and to James Wilson who, demonstrating his strong Scotch Presbyterian background, pledged $300. All told, $10,000 in pledges was collected on this tour, of which Blythe brought back 1,023 pounds in cash. An additional 882 pounds, 16 shillings, was collected in Kentucky. The academy would also benefit from a grant of 6,000 acres by action of the legislature in 1798. From as far away as London, it received a gift from a Reverend Gordon of books and apparatus valued at more than 80 pounds, and the telescope, microscope, air-pump and prisms may be those in the present collection of early scientific equipment long-preserved by Transylvania.[17]

Despite this remarkable success in raising funds (which must have irked the Transylvania Board), the Presbyterian trustees moved slowly to establish the academy. They spent months discussing the future site, for which they claimed they had no money, but they finally settled on Pisgah. Andrew Steele, who had been serving as teacher in the grammar school, was replaced by the peripatetic James Moore, while Steele assumed a new role as head of the academy.

THE WHOLE AFFAIR, in retrospect, has all the appearances of an academic charade. Kentucky Academy as a potential competitor to Transylvania was being used as a lever to regain Presbyterian control of the latter institution. Not only had the Presbyterians successfully chartered a new school, they persuaded the Kentucky legislature to take punitive action against the Transylvania trustees on the grounds that they had violated the charter.[18]

Toulmin was quite aware that he was one of the chief causes of this controversy. At the April 1796 Board meeting he gave notice he would resign effective in September. Though he complained that his low salary was one reason for his leaving, his main worry was the legislature which had taken action placing the president on a yearly-contractual basis. This made the position "too precarious for a man to direct his views towards it as a permanent object." Nor was he unconscious of the continuing attacks on him based, he was sorry to say, on "National

[17]*Ibid.*, 291–294. Various MS dealing with the founding of Kentucky Academy, lists of subscribers, etc., may be found in the Shane Collection and in the archives of Transylvania University.

[18]The Act was copied into the Minutes Book of the trustees. See the action of the Board recorded in the Minutes for November 23, 1795.

and religious prejudices." He wished the Board luck in achieving unanimity in the future.[19]

While it was most certainly a disappointment for Toulmin to relinquish his brief but to some extent satisfying experience as an educator, it was by no means the end of his career. In the fall of 1796 he was named by Governor Garrard to the post of Secretary of State of Kentucky. Close to the seat of political action, he immersed himself in law and later published a *Digest of the Laws of Kentucky*. In 1804 his old friend, now President Jefferson, named him to a federal judgeship of the Tombigbee district of the Mississippi Territory.

The resignation of Toulmin had removed a major obstacle to the reunion of the Presbyterians and the Transylvania trustees. At the June 3, 1796, meeting the Transylvania Board acknowledged receipt of overtures from the Kentucky Academy Society that "they are desirous to communicate on the subject of a Union of the two seminaries," and the Board appointed a committee to meet with representatives from the Presbyterian institution. Both schools saw very practical benefits resulting from union in addition to the official declaration expressing their concern for the public good. Transylvania trustees, short of cash, could well use the accumulated funds of the academy which, unfortunately for their expectations, proved to be considerably less than they had been led to believe. The academy would benefit from union with Transylvania with its landed endowment, two school buildings, a home for the president, one sixth of the surveyors' fees and an excellent location near downtown Lexington. The superior advantages offered by Transylvania motivated the Kentucky Academy representatives to be quite accommodating in the proposed terms of union drawn up by a joint committee at McGowan's Tavern in Lexington, September 14, 1796.[20]

Among various proposals were those making the laws of Transylvania Seminary the laws of the united institutions, and the name, seat and seal of Transylvania would be those of the combined schools. It was also proposed that the two boards be

[19]Harry Toulmin to the Board of Trustees, April 4, 1796. Shane Collection.
[20]Minutes of the Board, June 3, 1796, September 23, 1796, October 10, 1796.

merged, and that no vacancies be filled until the total number was reduced to twenty-one. This proposal was not immediately accepted by Transylvania trustees, and they engaged in delaying tactics until the financial condition of the school appeared critical. In the fall of 1798 the prospect of acquiring the funds of Kentucky Academy, expected to total 600 pounds at the time, was irresistible. A lengthy petition spelling out a suggested plan for the union of the two institutions was submitted to the Kentucky legislature in the fall of 1798, and on December 22, the act creating Transylvania University was approved. The new institution became legally alive on January 1, 1799.[21]

[21]*Ibid.*, November 2, 3, 1798.

3

James Moore and the New University

James Moore

With more expectations and hopes than money, the newly-appointed trustees sat down to draw the blueprint for their university. The very title of university opened visions for the institution that the former status of seminary never had. At the first meeting the trustees resolved to appoint a professor of medicine and a professor of law and politics. To fill these posts they appointed Frederick Ridgely and Samuel Brown as professors of medicine and George Nicholas as professor of law and politics. Medical training associated with educational institutions was relatively recent, beginning in 1765 at Benjamin Franklin's College of Philadelphia. Harvard, King's College (Columbia), Dartmouth, and William and Mary had later established medical departments, but they did not always function consistently or effectively. Nor, indeed, did the Transylvania Medical Department really begin its truly successful period until 1818. The same was true of the Law Department, for which there were even fewer precedents at eastern institutions.[1]

Although an announcement in the *Kentucky Gazette* indicated the first session in the University would begin on April 29, 1799, there is little evidence that such a session materialized, and it may be assumed that the regular session began later in the fall of that year. Meanwhile the trustees busied themselves with outlining the curriculum and drawing up class schedules and rules of conduct. In fact, most matters which today would

[1]Minutes of the Board, January 8, 1799.

be handled by faculty and various deans were administered by trustees, with some advice from the president. This reveals clearly the unique character of the early American college as compared with its European counterpart.

The American college was patterned on the English system, as might be expected, though with significant modifications. As Richard Hofstadter and Walter Metzger have pointed out in their work on *The Development of Academic Freedom in the United States*, the American college differed from European universities first in being a mixture of private denominational sponsorship with some state supervision; secondly, in lacking professional faculties; thirdly, in having lay, non-resident governing boards. Teachers were employed primarily as tutors with no independent status, either individually or collectively. Academic freedom, as we have come to know it, was practically unknown on the campus. Nor did the college president have much freedom. Despite the fact his status was higher than the teacher in the colonial and ante-bellum periods, he too suffered from the lack of a tradition to protect his independence of thought and action. Trustees reigned supreme, and they suffered from no sense of inferiority in dealing with all matters pertaining to the campus. Thus, the curriculum, classes, student discipline, student chapel, and the hiring and firing of presidents and teachers occupied their time, as well as that of raising money and supervising maintenance of the physical plant.[2]

Given unchallenged supremacy in these matters, the trustees followed traditional patterns in devising a curriculum and organizing student life. Institutionally they separated the non-professional or academic from the law and medical areas, and divided the academic structure into an academy and a college. The academy was to be a preparatory department for students who had not been adequately trained in the basic studies required for entrance into college. In the absence of an adequate public school system in Kentucky and in most other states at this time, a preparatory department was essential. Some stu-

[2]Richard Hofstadter and Walter Metzger, *The Development of Academic Freedom in the United States* (New York, 1955), pp. 61–63, 115.

dents may have had the opportunity of attending private schools or being privately tutored, but many did not. The trustees stipulated that the academy should teach Greek, Latin, arithmetic and the fundamentals of reading and writing English. In the fields of Greek and Latin, the academy student had to be able to read selections from Erasmus, Caesar's *Commentaries*, Ovid's *Metamorphisis*, Vergil's *The Aeneid*, Horace, Cicero's *Select Orations*, and four books of Homer's *Iliad*. A French teacher was also to be available for instruction in that language.[3]

After mastering these subjects, the student might be admitted to the college — if he were of good moral character — where he would start off his first year with algebra, geometry, trigonometry, navigation, conic sections and English composition. The next year he would struggle with natural philosophy (which presumably touched on the basics of physics and chemistry), astronomy, moral philosophy (Paley was the standard), logic, chronology and general history, rhetoric, and belles lettres. Only two years were required to complete the college course at this time, which perhaps accounts for the weight placed on the academy training in classical languages, later to be incorporated into the college's four-year course. The curriculum as thus devised was a rubber-stamp imitation of the curriculum of eastern colleges, which in turn had followed the lead of Harvard and William and Mary in transferring the traditional forms from England. This curriculum, centuries old, had been based on the assumption that man's education should free him from ignorance, and that through the use of his natural faculties he would discover the nature and meaning of the universe and man's place in it. The source of this quest was the golden age of Greek thinkers and the later contributions of Roman writers. To know these sources a man must first master the languages in which their thoughts were expressed. Thus, while Latin and Greek studies might well have been valued for their so-called "intellectual discipline" and bases for origins of many English

[3] Minutes of the Board, October 18, 1799.

words, they assumed importance as avenues to the great ideas in Western civilization, a knowledge of which was essential to any gentleman's education.[4]

The ultimate product of an American college education in this era was the Christian gentleman. Harvard College had stated this early in its charter of 1650, when it said its purpose was "the advancement of all good literature, artes [sic] and Sciences," while emphasizing the fact that "the maine [sic] end of life and studies is, to know God and Jesus Christ which is eternall [sic] life." Two hundred years later a president of Columbia echoed this purpose: "Here in college is to be fashioned, in the highest attainable perfection, the scholar, the citizen, the good man, and the Christian gentleman."[5]

American experience began to challenge this absolute and traditional dedication to learning classical languages, but in 1799 the old ideal remained supreme. The frequent use of Latin and Greek quotations — in current literature, delivery of Latin orations at commencements, interjection of classical phrases into formal orations and political debates, and learned treatises of lawyers, doctors and ministers — was acceptable and indeed required among educated men of the day.

In addition to establishing the curriculum, the trustees also paid close attention to daily schedules, examinations and rules for student behavior. There were no doubts in their minds that the college must act *in loco parentis* for the students. Discipline was the constant worry of the college president who in the pre-Civil War period was the chief judge and disciplinarian on campus, whether at Harvard or anywhere else. Edward Everett's diary, written while he was president of Harvard for a brief period in the late 1840's, is filled with poignant complaints about the never-ending round of disciplinary cases appearing before him. For a scholar such as Everett, who had envisioned the presidency of Harvard as a pleasant and peaceful interlude of encouraging and guiding the intellectual pursuits of his young charges, the experience was a traumatic one. And so it must

---

[4]*Ibid.*

[5]George P. Schmidt, *The Liberal Arts College* (New Brunswick, N.J., 1957), p. 44.

have been for many other college presidents.

The trustees established the hours of study during the summer session from sunrise to 8 a.m., from 9 to 12 noon, and from 2 to 5:30 p.m. Hours were the same in the winter except for the afternoon when the hours were 1:30 to 4 p.m. and 5 to 8 p.m., the school closing at noon on Saturdays. Prayers were to begin the morning's routine and conclude the evening's, with "decency and reverence." Every student was required to attend public worship on Sunday "at such place as he himself shall choose." In addition, "no student shall frequent Taverns, nor places of licentious or unprofitable amusement, nor use any immoral or indecent language, or behavior, nor play at cards, dice, or any unlawful game." Nor was any student to have liquor in his room except with express permission. "The punishments of the institution, being wholly of the moral kind, and addressed to the sense of duty, and the principles of honour and shame . . ." ranged from private admonition to public admonition, public confession, expression of penitence, suspension, and expulsion.[6]

Finally, the trustees stipulated that at the end of each session all students were to be publicly examined in the presence of the trustees. A great deal of emphasis was placed on public speaking, and seniors were required to present public orations. College men frequently went into professions such as ministry or law, or into public or political careers where, in those days of public declamation and oratory the capacity to speak effectively was a necessity.

With the curriculum outlined and class routine and student discipline defined, there remained the matter of appointing personnel, starting with the president. It came as no surprise that James Moore was elected to the top position. He had been persuaded to leave Kentucky Academy in the fall of 1798 to head Transylvania Seminary. He was a man of traditional views and moderate manners, relatively uncontroversial and generally acceptable to both sides of the previously-opposing camps.

There is not a great deal of personal information available

---

[6] Minutes of the Board, November 4, 1799.

about this early president. We do know he attended Washington Academy (now Washington and Lee) and that he had been regarded by his fellow students there as being so serious as to provoke ridicule, "and his timidity and reserve perhaps accounted for his few friends." He played the flute, a fact which inspired a Transylvania graduate of a later day, James Lane Allen, to write a charming short story about Moore called *The Flute and the Violin*. Moore has been described as "tall, gaunt, somewhat neglectful of dress." His portrait by Matthew Jouett, painted before Jouett refined his technique under the tutelage of Gilbert Stuart, shows Moore in profile, revealing a narrow, thin face with high forehead, soft brown hair, rather light brown or blue eyes, and a long, thin nose. He had a fair complexion and a rather full, gentle mouth. Though one senses a certain lack of vigor and strength in the man — his impact on Transylvania's development was modest — he played a significant role in building the first Episcopalian congregation and church in Lexington. On the wall of Christ Church today is a plaque commemorating that fact and describing Moore as learned, liberal, amiable and pious.[7]

Two addresses which Moore delivered while president in 1800–1801 give some insight into his educational philosophy. He believed the essentials of a successful educational experience were an eager curiosity for knowledge and a strong conviction of the dignity and usefulness of learning apart from any utilitarian advantage. Abhor vice and everything low and mean, he advised, and be patient and develop discipline of labor and its application to assigned duties. He urged students to care for their manners and general deportment, to realize that as college students more was expected of them than of other boys the same age. Place confidence in your teachers, he said. Waste no time on non-essentials, use the library and read history. Finally, there is a note of affection and reconciliation that he may well have been directing to a wider audience than the students:

> Be kind, affectionate and forgiving towards one another. Let us never hear of quarreling or falling out among ourselves. It is disgraceful in all ranks of men, but particularly in students, who

[7]*Ibid.*, October 25, 1799; Jennings, *Transylvania*, pp. 36–37.

should live together as brethren of the same family. . . . To forgive an injury is magnanimous; but to resent imaginary offenses is meanness itself, and betrays littleness of soul.[8]

In addition to the election of Moore as president were the appointments of Samuel Brown and Frederick Ridgely to the Medical Department and George Nicholas to the Law Department. Nicholas died a few months after his appointment, however, and James Brown was selected to replace him. Another Virginian and a graduate of William and Mary, Brown had studied law, been admitted to the bar, moved to Lexington in 1789 and commanded the Lexington riflemen in the war against the Indians in 1791. He became Secretary of State under Governor Shelby and was a trustee of Transylvania from 1793–1797. He now became the school's first active law professor until his departure in 1804 to New Orleans as Secretary of the Territory.

Other appointments included that of the Reverend James Blythe as professor of mathematics and natural philosophy. This ardent Presbyterian had been active in promoting the cause of Kentucky Academy. Reverend James Welsh was appointed as professor of languages. President Moore's salary was set at $500 a year, that of Blythe at $450, and Welsh at $400. The professors of law and medicine received their remuneration from the sale of tickets to their students. Tuition for students in the Academic Department was four pounds, payable quarterly, and twenty dollars a year for law and medical students with extra fees for use of the books in the library.[9]

At the time Transylvania became a university it was located on a lot one block long and a half-block wide, on a gentle slope north of Main Street. The lot was bounded on the south by Second Street and on the north by Third Street. Market and Mill Streets were to be its eastern and western boundaries, but these streets were not actually extended through the campus until the fall of 1807.

William Leavy, who attended the University shortly after it began operation, recalled that

the lot, when I first went to the college, had post and rail fences

[8]*Kentucky Gazette*, May 25, 1800; November 13, 1801.
[9]Minutes of the Board, October 25, 1799.

on Second Street and on Third Street, but the northwest side
was Thos. January's inclosure. His hemp building was on Second Street, corner of Mill, and the rope-walk was adjoining the
college lot. The southeast side also had a ropewalk adjoining the
college lot. The lot was commonly used at the noon intermission
as a playground by the boys, — wrestling and jumping, foot ball,
bandy, etc. The eastern side of the college building was a "five"
alley, there being no break in the wall. [The President, at that
time lived in the college building on the west side.] The library
and apparatus were all kept in a small room over the entry front.
The academical department was alone in operation at that time,
and three or four rooms served for all the classes. The whole
school was assembled in the large room below, on the right as
you enter; the roll of the school was called and prayers by one of
the professors at the hour, I think, commencing at eight
o'clock.[10]

Gratz Kitchen, the oldest University building

Some physical improvements were made with the limited
funds available. The college lot was sowed with bluegrass, locust trees were planted and fencing erected. A brick kitchen

[10] Quoted in Peter, *Transylvania University*, p. 47.

was built, large enough to accommodate a caretaker family and student boarders. It must have created a bucolic scene when the college lot was leased for use as a pasture to James Moore and Col. Morrison. In January 1798, the trustees contracted with Mrs. Catherine Richardson

> that she is to have the house rent free: — to have an oven built and a well dug as soon as the work can be done. . . . To have use of the whole Lot, with the privilege of making a garden and Clover Lot. . . . And that she will diet [sic], wash and mend for the Scholars, etc., at fifteen pounds per year . . . the Trustees to furnish the diningroom with a table & seats. The Boarders to furnish themselves with firewood and candles for their own rooms, and also their own beds; and the Trustees to build a milk house eight or ten feet square adjacent to the well.[11]

More vigorous advertising of the University was initiated in early 1800, with public announcements appearing in the local press. A familiar theme ran through these announcements — the desirability of training western students in western institutions. Until the establishment of Transylvania University there had been no college worthy of the name in the area. Now this was changed. Notices emphasized the various factors of convenience, economy and local pride. Later, in the 1830's and up to the Civil War, the theme also incorporated the argument that northern ideas were alien, hostile and subversive to southern ideals and institutions. The religious concern of the trustees, undoubtedly reinforced by strong Presbyterian influence on the Board, was reflected in the announcement that

> it has been, and still shall be, the care of the Trustees and Professors, to guard against the baneful influence of sceptical principles; and while they carefully prevent the inculcation of the peculiar opinions of any Christian sect, they feel themselves bound to see, that the great leading doctrines of Christianity be warmly inculcated by precept and example.[12]

Evidence that there was still a division among members of the Board was dramatized in an extraordinary affair which occurred in the summer of 1801. A student petition to the trustees containing charges against one of the professors, James Welsh,

[11] Minutes of the Board, August 12, October 10, 1797; January 1, 1798.
[12] Sonne, *Liberal Kentucky*, p. 76.

resulted in a "trial" or series of hearings examining the charges. This incident was unusual in several respects. For one thing, it was an unprecedented and bold action on the part of students to petition trustees directly for redress of a grievance, thus by-passing the president who would have been the proper administrative official to approach. For another, it was a remarkable display of student bravado to charge a duly-appointed professor with such a variety of complaints and to be exposed to the full weight of the trustees' displeasure.

The subject of this difficulty was the Reverend James Welsh, one of the pioneer Presbyterian clergymen in Kentucky and pastor of a number of Lexington and Georgetown churches from 1796 to 1804. He was associated at one time with James Blythe in the Lexington church, but this relationship was so inharmonious that action was required by the Presbytery to prevent a violent rupture. From all available evidence it seems Welsh was temperamentally unsuited both as a teacher and resident supervisor of the boarding students. An erratic and overbearing disciplinarian, he intruded into meetings of the students' debating club — laughing, coughing, making faces and grimaces at students who expressed views he disliked, and reprimanding them for supporting Jeffersonian principles because he feared the Federalist parents of some of the students would hear of it and remove their children from school. One faction of the Board had at first voted to forbid student petitioners from presenting evidence against Welsh, but this action was later revoked. When depositions of the witnesses were taken, some twenty students — certainly close to a majority of them — had given testimony against Welsh. In addition to charges previously levied, he was accused of neglecting his teaching, ridiculing Baptist ministers, and denouncing students whom he believed held deistical and Republican opinions.[13]

Despite the fact the Presbyterian trustees were not especially fond of Welsh, they supported him against the students. They may have been impelled to do so for several reasons: their dis-

[13] The whole manuscript record of the trial is in the archives of Transylvania University. See also the accounts of this incident in Sonne, *Liberal Kentucky*, pp. 68–73 and Jennings, *Transylvania*, pp. 45–49.

like of student impertinence in bringing charges against a professor; their disapproval of the religious, if not political, views of the students who were against Welsh; the fear that any success of students might weaken Presbyterian control of the institution, and their desire to unite behind one of their clergymen in a crisis. A series of resolutions, passed by very close margins, generally criticized the students, acquitted Welsh, and ordered that both students and Welsh return to their previous status and routine. No punishment was imposed on the students, however, on the grounds that no procedure for redress of student grievances had been provided, a deficiency which the Board immediately set out to remedy.[14]

This action allowing Welsh his former position was unacceptable to many students, fifteen of whom withdrew from school the following day. This serious threat to the prosperity of the University was so great that even the more conservative trustees were convinced they should reconsider their action, which they did. A resolution was passed stating that in the opinion of the Board "Mr. James Welsh can no longer be serviceable to this University as a professor." A week later he submitted his resignation and was replaced by Alexander McKeehan as the new professor of languages. At the same time, the trustees established a procedure by which a student who "shall conceive himself improperly treated by a professor" could turn first to the president, who, if he believed the complaint well-founded, might then consult with the standing committee of the trustees. If the president did not believe the complaint well-founded, then a faculty committee was to examine the case. If they concurred with the president and the student still wished to press the matter, then he, too, was allowed an appeal to the standing committee.[15]

In April 1802, the trustees conferred the first A.B. degree in the school's history on Robert Barr. Though we have no record of the number of medical and law students in these early days, it was doubtless small, but as early as the fall of 1799 some students wishing to study law had expressed their concern on

[14]*Ibid.* Minutes of the Board, June 17, 23, 25, 27, 29, July 1, 1801.
[15]Minutes of the Board, July 16, 1801.

hearing of the death of George Nicholas. The Board, as mentioned earlier, remedied the situation with the appointment of James Brown, of whom it was said that he taught not only law but the Republican philosophy "with such fidelity that Thomas Jefferson advised young Virginians to study at Transylvania." In the spring of 1799 the Board authorized $600 for the purchase of a law library.[16]

Dr. Frederick Ridgely's house at Second & Market, now the headquarters of the Christian Church in Kentucky

Medical students probably met in the homes and offices of Samuel Brown and Ridgely. Instruction could hardly have been systematic. Anatomical laboratories were practically non-existent, and it is doubtful whether these physicians provided any cadavers for dissection. It has been recorded by Robert Peter in his *History of the Medical Department of Transylvania University* that Ridgely in 1799–1800 "delivered to the small class of medical students then in attendance a course of public instruction which did him credit." Ridgely and Brown may well

[16]*Ibid.*, April 7, 1802; Sonne, *Liberal Kentucky*, p. 68.

have been the first to teach by lecture in a formalized department in western America. In the fall of 1799, the Board authorized the appropriation of $500 for the purchase of a medical library.[17]

The Academic Department had originally been dependent for its library and apparatus on the gift of the Reverend John Todd. Although as early as 1785 the Board had expended fifty pounds for books "judged to be immediately necessary," it appears they were to be sold to students as they needed them and thus could not be considered a true basis for a library. When Moore began teaching, the college library was almost exclusively Todd's. Moore was instructed to catalogue it and to "charge the scholars what he shall judge reasonable for the use of the Roman and Greek Classicks. . . ." In October 1794, a committee was appointed to open up subscriptions for the library — 200 shares at $5 each. There is no record of just how much if anything was collected by this method. Some public financial support of the library seems evident, however, because public demand to be allowed to use these library books caused the Board's regulation that the college library should be for student use only. This situation was shortly relieved by the establishment in January 1795, of the "Transylvania Library" (a confusion of these names compounds the historian's difficulties) which was to be a public library funded by public subscriptions. A year later the first consignment of 400 books arrived, available for public use. As a matter of convenience the books were stored in the building housing the Transylvania Seminary where they remained until directors acted to remove them to a separate building in 1799.[18]

In 1802 a remarkable effort by some of Lexington's leaders to forward the cause and progress of Transylvania University was revealed in a petition to the trustees signed by thirty-nine men urging the Board to secure the services of the president of William and Mary. Indeed, some of these men pledged what

[17]Robert Peter, *The History of the Medical Department of Transylvania University* (Filson Club Publications No. 20, Louisville, 1905), p. 11. Minutes of the Board, October 18, 1799.

[18]See articles on "The Lexington Library" in *The Transylvanian*, XIV, No. 1.

funds would be necessary to make a total of $1,000 to offer as an annual salary. James Moore had indicated his willingness to step aside and James Madison (not the more famous Madison then serving as Jefferson's Secretary of State) apparently was willing to leave William and Mary to accept the challenge of heading the western university. We have no record of why the agreement was never consummated. In the fall of 1804 Moore relinquished his post as president, and though he stayed as a trustee for a few years thereafter, he resigned even this post in 1808.

The trustees voted to elect the Reverend James Blythe Acting-President, to serve also as professor of natural philosophy, geography and mathematics. That he was designated acting-president would seem to indicate that the Board wished to continue searching for a man to fill the post permanently. It is unlikely that either Blythe or the trustees could have predicted that he was to occupy that position for the next fourteen years.

4

Problems and Slow Growth of the New University

James Blythe

James Blythe had been born in North Carolina in 1765 and educated at Hampden-Sydney College. He was a dedicated Christian and staunch Presbyterian, and the ministry was his calling. Licensed in 1791, he moved to Kentucky shortly thereafter and was ordained pastor of the historic Pisgah Church and also the Clear Creek Church in July 1793. He remained associated with the Pisgah Presbyterian Church for nearly forty years. Robert Peter writes in his history of the school that "as a preacher Doctor Blythe was energetic and animated, and was a staunch advocate of orthodoxy. . . ."

William Leavy, who attended Transylvania during Blythe's administration recalled later that Blythe was a

> powerful and strenuous advocate for the Bible and Missionary Societies connected with the Presbyterian Church. His labours in the pulpit and in writing were incessant. . . . He was constant and spirited in the family and prayer meetings as well as in the church. He was ever active, and no one could think of formality in relation to any of his services. Prompt, ardent, and impetuous, he was apt to be impatient and dogmatic. He was at times severe and dictatorial, if not arrogant, in his manner to students. These peculiarities of temper and manner rendered him exceedingly unpopular with the young men.

Leavy ranked Blythe highly as a teacher of science. Another student recalled that "Blythe was a large, square-made man, five feet eleven, with a remarkably stern and heavy brow and a deep toned harsh voice with positive manners, and too exclusive and taciturn to be popular, and yet a firm and good teacher.''[1]

He was joined on the faculty by Robert Hamilton Bishop, professor of moral philosophy, and a recent immigrant from Scotland. Bishop was a devout Presbyterian who had recently published a work entitled *An Apology for Calvinism*, a defense of orthodoxy against the heresies of that apostate Barton W. Stone, one of the leaders at the Cane Ridge revival a few years before. Bishop's narrow Presbyterian family training was broadened by his education at the University of Edinburgh. Trained at a Presbyterian seminary, he responded to a call for missionary commitment and left for America shortly after he married in 1802. He was assigned to work in Kentucky by the New York Synod, travelling widely through the area before accepting a position on the Transylvania faculty in 1804. While at Transylvania, Bishop assisted the Reverend James McChord in establishing the Market Street Presbyterian Church, a stone's throw from the university campus. Thus Bishop filled the roles of minister and professor for the next twenty years. Not surprisingly, Bishop had a strong brogue, and American students had some difficulty in understanding him at first.[2] Of Ebenezer Sharpe, who taught Latin and Greek during this period, we know little.

With the election of Blythe to the position of acting-president, the Presbyterians came into unquestioned control of Transylvania. The institution at this time was hardly in a flourishing condition. Rarely were as many as fifty students in attendance. Plans for a medical and legal education were only fitfully executed by what amounted to casual, tutorial arrangements. Yet compared with other institutions of its time and considering the brief period of its existence, Transylvania was doing moderately well. But the ambitious community leaders were not satisfied, as was indicated by their campaign to bring

[1]Robert Davidson, *The History of the Presbyterian Church in Kentucky*, pp. 123–125; William Leavy, "A Memoir of Lexington and Its Vicinity," *Register of the Kentucky Historical Society*, XL, No. 134 (January, 1943), p. 46; C. E. Graham to Robert Peter, February 2, 1876 in archives of Transylvania University.

[2]James H. Rodabaugh, *Robert Hamilton Bishop* (Columbus, Ohio, 1935), *passim*.

James Madison of William and Mary to Lexington. Views of a critical visitor, printed in the local press, may well have been shared by these men. This correspondent, hearing there was a university in Lexington, paid a visit. After finding only a few modest structures clustered at the upper end of a small park and examining students and faculty, he concluded that Transylvania hardly compared with even the most insignificant English academies. "There were professors, but few students," he wrote, "and the latter appeared to be composed generally of youth in the pursuit of the inferior and less dignified departments of literature, to the almost total rejection of scientific and classical learning." The students spoke contemptuously of classical learning, which the writer thought may have been due in part to poor teaching. He saw no proper education here for the future scholar, statesman or minister. Added to the other problems, he concluded, was a board of trustees marked by division and bigotry, and a faculty whose low fixed salaries offered them no incentive for the more capable to work harder for the improvement of the institution.[3]

From the fall of 1802 Dr. Blythe and his family had occupied the west half of the college building, promising the trustees to keep the house in good order and give general maintenance supervision over the house, stable, garden, smoke house and lot. The acting-president lived there until he moved to a house of his own three years later, located on a lot immediately to the north of the college. The trustees busied themselves with such details of maintenance as securing a pump, making repairs to the well, and erecting "a necessary" on the University lot. Adding an unusual feature to this mundane fact is the record that states Blythe himself dug the pit for the necessary and was paid $5 by the Board for his effort. Blythe had always complained that his salary was too low.[4]

To bolster the academic quality of the school, the trustees authorized Blythe to spend $800 in the summer of 1805 for apparatus for teaching natural science, then referred to as natural philosophy. Part of this equipment had to be purchased from

[3]*Kentucky Gazette*, January 24, February 21, 1804.
[4]Minutes of the Board, October 30, 1802, March 4, 1808.

Europe and included chemical apparatus and a galvanic battery. The Board, in a public announcement in the fall, proudly proclaimed the arrival of this apparatus, as well as additions to the college library which now totaled some 1300 volumes. The trustees optimistically reported to the public "the prosperous condition of the Seminary [sic] committed to their direction" and expressed the opinion "that a Liberal Education can be obtained in our own state with as much facility and certainty as anywhere else in America and certainly with much less expense." In addition to the standard curriculum, they promised the French language would continue to be taught, providing a suitable teacher could be obtained. Curriculum generally remained the same. The trustees urged parents to send their sons for a full course of two terms, the first beginning in November, the second in May. With six pounds' tuition being charged to scientific students and four pounds to students of languages, a student's estimated annual expense including living costs was $100 or less. The trustees warned parents against giving too much money to their sons, having found by long experience that "nothing is so pernicious to the Morals of Students as unlimited credit, or a large remittance of Money." Finally, the trustees promised that the University would do everything possible for the protection of students against the dangers of immorality and irreligion.[5]

To undergird Blythe's administration financially, the trustees voted to sell as much of the landed endowment as would bring in $10,000. According to the best estimates, Transylvania University at the time of its establishment in 1799 had a total landed endowment of 20,000 acres, 8,000 of which had come with the original charter. The 12,000 acres added in the 1783 amended charter had been negated by action of the Kentucky legislature in 1792 when it prohibited the escheating of this land. Kentucky Academy brought 12,000 acres of its own as a gift from the state into the union with Transylvania, thus, in a sense, restoring the lost land; but the school officials continued to complain that the state had deprived it of a sizeable portion of its endowment. By 1804 the annual income amounted to 477

[5]*Ibid.*, April 3, 1805; Jennings, *Transylvania*, pp. 60–62.

pounds, of which 326 pounds came from rents, the rest being derived from tuition. Expenditures were listed at 419. The sale of the land was imperative to give the trustees some financial elbow room, and in the next six or seven years, the trustees disposed of a sizeable portion of its landed endowment. A sale of 8,000 acres in 1806 brought $30,000 which was invested in shares of the Bank of Kentucky and insurance company stock. By 1812 the conversion of land into cash and investments may have brought the endowment of the school to about $67,000, the interest and dividends from which provided the basic income for the school. Rents proved to be a variable and hard-to-collect source of revenue and frequently came in the form of corn, wheat and pork.[6]

Henry Clay by Jouett

[6]Resumé of Transylvania's financial history was outlined in the "Report to the Joint Committee Appointed to Examine into the Condition of Transylvania University, January, 1842," *Kentucky Documents*, 1841–1842. See also Charles Caldwell's summary of the financial history in his *A Discourse on the Genius and Character of the Reverend Horace Holley* (Boston, 1828), pp. 193–195. Also, Minutes of the Board, April 8, 1809.

The most interesting faculty appointment in 1805 was that of Henry Clay as law professor, replacing James Brown. Clay had arrived in Lexington in 1797, a twenty-year-old, Virginia-trained lawyer. Immediately he used his talents, legal and ora-torical, to become one of the town's leading defense attorneys with a legendary capacity for swaying juries. He taught law for two years at Transylvania and then resigned his post, immedi-ately being elected one of the trustees. Though serving only an occasional term as trustee because his national political career kept him in Washington, he remained from this time forward a loyal friend and counsellor to the institution until his death in 1852.

At the same time Clay was appointed professor of law, the trustees appointed James Fishback professor of medicine. Dr. Fishback had a varied career as a physician, newspaper editor and, finally, Baptist minister. He resigned his seat as trustee of Transylvania to assume his teaching post which he kept for two years. During the War of 1812 he was active as editor of *The Western Monitor*, a vigorous mouthpiece for the anti-war, Fed-eralist viewpoint.

On October 8, 1806, three A.B. degrees were conferred. Whatever may have been the fluctuating educational standards of that day, the faculty and trustees were maintaining rigorous requirements for the degree, if the small number granted is any indication. It was not until three years later that two more de-grees were awarded, one of them to Joseph Buchanan.

The trustees forbade undesirable student organizations, and faculty permission was required for participation in any theatri-cal performance. Student organizations, however, were inevita-ble. As early as 1802 the Transylvania Philosophical Society was organized by students, and prior to that there apparently were some informal debating clubs.[7]

About this time, the trustees adopted the first official seal of the University. The device was a globe and a telescope mount-ed on their stands, and an open book inscribed "Euclid." The motto underneath was "Pietate et doctrina tuta libertas" which was encircled by the inscription "Sigillum Transylvaniae Universitates."

[7]Minutes of the Board, March 2, 1808.

The University's first seal

DURING THE YEARS of the Blythe administration, Lexington continued to grow. From a population of 1,795 at the turn of the century, it had increased to 4,426 by 1810, and by the end of the War of 1812 — a very prosperous period for the town — the population was estimated at over 6,000. Hemp production and rope manufacturing were central to the town's economy as the increase of ropewalks — some of them adjacent to the Transylvania campus — would indicate. Land values soared, and visitors reported that town lots sold for prices nearly as high as those found in Boston, New York or Philadelphia. Lexington was the first western town to provide street lighting, starting with twenty oil lamps, five of them on Main Street. The town also offered free oil to any citizen providing his own lamp. Lexington was among the earliest of western towns to provide an adequate police force, establishing a modest watch as early as 1796. This was due, in part, to the sizeable Negro population in town. Citizens had complained that "large assemblages of Negroes had become troublesome to the Citizens," particularly on the week-ends.[8]

To prevent fires a town charter forbade wooden chimneys on buildings within the town limits, and three fire engines were in operation in 1815. Because of the great limestone shelf underlying the Lexington area close to the surface, adequate drainage

[8]Wade, *The Urban Frontier*, pp. 50–52, 90.

remained a problem from that day to this. Town fathers warned citizens that cesspools, improperly located or dug to an undesirable depth, threatened to spread contagion to wells, and thus would "jeopardize the health of our citizens."[9]

Proud country estates were built by wealthy citizens on the outskirts of town, such as Henry Clay's "Ashland." Fashionable hotels and taverns were built, such as Postlethwait's and its chief competitor, Bradley's.

A major event concerning all citizens of Lexington, and Kentucky as well, was the War of 1812. Considering the fact that Henry Clay was an ardent War Hawk in Congress with Kentucky generally giving him its support, it comes as a surprise to see Blythe, acting-president of Transylvania, vigorously opposing the war; however, losing a son in the brutal massacre at the River Raisin only intensified his hostility. Some, though not all, of the Presbyterians backed Blythe. For example James Fishback, then editor of *The Western Monitor*, gave editorial support to the position of John Pope, the maverick U.S. Senator from Kentucky who had voted against the declaration of war. Pope, it might be noted, was appointed professor of law in the University in 1814. Fishback's views apparently represented the Presbyterian, pro-Federalist, anti-war party. A number of Presbyterians tried to disengage themselves from the position of being anti-war and pro-Federalist, but this was not easy since leaders of the pro-war faction were, in many cases, proponents of religious liberalism and strongly advocated separation of church and state.[10]

Blythe was not only outspoken in his condemnation of the war, but also in his public denunciation of what he regarded as widespread and dangerous religious infidelity among Kentucky's leaders, and among those of the nation as well. In a sermon suggestively titled *Our Sins Acknowledged* delivered on January 12, 1815 (a date declared by President James Madison to be a national fast day), he said "America is confessedly a christian nation." Yet, where are the facts to back up such a claim? He saw woefully few. If the national leaders have any

[9]*Ibid.*
[10]Sonne, *Liberal Kentucky*, Chapter on Dr. Joseph Buchanan, *passim*.

religion at all, it "resembles infinitely more the religion of the heathens than of Christians. . . ." Kentucky was even worse. He said, "We form one, among a very few of the American States, who in our legislative capacity acknowledge no God, no Providence, no Savior." Blythe stated that the belief religion and politics should be separated was a product of French atheism and had infected the American mind on a large scale. President Timothy Dwight of Yale was likewise conducting an unceasing campaign against French atheism and Jeffersonian sentiments.[11]

These issues were not the only matters contributing to Blythe's discontent. Five years after he took the position of acting-president he complained his salary of $450 was most inadequate, even with the additional compensation of $25 a year as librarian, a chore he refused to perform any longer. Out of this miserable pittance, he remonstrated, he was supposed to entertain "visiting literary gentlemen." He said he persevered under these hardships only "because the Seminary was an old and continues to be a favorite subject of mine, and because I knew the funds were embarrassed." He no longer believed this to be the case. The Board's only reaction to his complaints was to raise his salary to $500 and leave it there. Blythe, of course, must have received additional compensation for his pastoral services at the Pisgah church, and occasionally other churches, though there is no record of the amount.[12]

Meanwhile, the search for a new president had been going on since Blythe had always held the post on a temporary basis. In July 1812, the trustees appointed a committee which included Henry Clay to look for a new president, but the war forced postponement of any action. Later, at a stormy meeting of the Board in June 1815, a resolution was offered stating that the appointment of Blythe "will be permanently injurious to the interest and prosperity of the University" and that he should not be reappointed. By an eleven to seven vote this resolution was tabled, but the trustees were unanimous in their election of the Reverend John B. Romeyne, a prominent New York Pres-

[11] Sonne, *Liberal Kentucky*, pp. 118–130.
[12] James Blythe to Colonel James Trotter, April 29, 1809. Shane Collection.

byterian, as president. In those days appointments were made without consulting the appointee beforehand, so it was not surprising that Romeyne refused the appointment.

The anti-Blythe sentiment extended beyond a few trustees as was dramatically shown by a student meeting a week after the Board' meeting in which the resolution expressing no confidence in Blythe had been tabled. The students passed resolutions, later published, in which they expressed their disapproval of Blythe and of the trustees for continuing to appoint him. The Board found this action censuring trustees intolerable. They found such student meetings "impudent" and such student resolutions "highly censurable." This dampened the students' enthusiasm markedly, and they expressed their regrets in an address to the Board, stating they had not intended "any reflection on any member of the board." This calmed the crisis, but the students were instructed to forbear from public expression of their opinion of the Board, officers and faculty of Transylvania University without the consent of the faculty.[13]

The trustees, however, could not repress continued newspaper attacks on them and on the stagnant condition of the University. These attacks had taken an ominous turn, at least from the viewpoint of Presbyterians. With a renewed emphasis on the public character of the institution, the responsibility of the legislature to examine the condition of the school and the record of the trustees was becoming evident. Despite the obvious discontent with Blythe, however, the Board persisted in re-appointing him as head of the University. The haphazard search for a permanent president went on, but the procedure must by now have convinced critics that it was a perpetual dodge employed by the Presbyterians. In the spring of 1816 the trustees amazingly voted to appoint Horace Holley as president, and a committee was selected to inform the outstanding Boston clergyman of this action. In the same session they elected Dr. Thomas Cooper as the first professor of a new chair of chemistry. Considering that Holley was a Unitarian and Cooper an ardent exponent of everything the more conservative Presbyterians hated, these acts seem to have been sheer lunacy.

[13] Minutes of the Board, July 5, 22, 1815.

But there was a strategy — which turned somewhat devious: the trustees had been misinformed concerning Holley's religious orthodoxy and therefore quickly rescinded their action; and in the case of Cooper they offered such a small salary ($400) that they knew he would refuse — which he did.[14]

Given this situation at Transylvania it was not surprising that the Kentucky legislature, for the first time since the University was chartered, made a serious move to examine and evaluate conditions at the only institution approximating a state university in Kentucky. In December 1815, the House appointed a committee to investigate, and this committee requested the trustees to prepare a report on the condition of the school. Reflecting the prevailing sectarian control of the Board, this report was largely an ingenious exercise in self-justification, ignoring some facts and distorting others. It did admit, though reluctantly, that public estimation of the institution was "very low." But it asserted that the factors creating difficulties for the school — such as the character of the western country, the desire for a brief education, the war, competing academies and similar difficulties — were all external. Further the trustees defended themselves against the accusation of sectarian control, indicating that of three professors only one was a real Presbyterian, and of the total number of trustees only seven were Presbyterian.[15]

The legislative committee was not particularly impressed by this report, nor by what they saw of the University. Though agreeing the financial condition of the school was reasonably sound, all other aspects of the operation seemed to evidence weakness and decline, and the committee was convinced that the causes were rooted in the divided Board, split by political and religious issues. Nor was the committee impressed by recent Board actions in electing a capable man such as Horace Holley and then rescinding the appointment on sectarian grounds. In addition to the Presbyterian domination of the school, the committee discovered unpatriotic political activities in the classroom as well. "The politics taught in the institution

[14]Minutes of the Board, November 11, 1815; March 23, 1816.
[15]Sonne, *Liberal Kentucky*, pp. 145–148.

have not been pure," the committee asserted. Criticism of the
American government and praise for the British constitution
had been voiced in students' presence, much to the young
men's irritation. Apparently Bishop was the source of this difficulty.[16]

All-in-all, the House committee was convinced that the legislature should sweep out the old trustees and replace them with
new ones. If the Board needed any incitement to bestir themselves and renovate the University, they had it now. They filled
vacancies in the medical department and appropriated $1,000
for the purchase of chemical equipment. They accepted, indeed
they may have encouraged, the resignation of James Blythe
from all his positions at Transylvania as of March 12, 1816.
Plans were made for enlargement of the physical plant — even
to the consideration of selling the college lot and buildings for
$20,000 and erecting buildings at a new location. This proposal
was set aside, but plans for a new building on the present
campus were finalized. By borrowing funds, selling stock and
soliciting cash gifts, the trustees accumulated $25,648 for erect-
ing the main college building, and $18,681 for other buildings
such as the adjoining kitchen and housing for the maintenance
men. This main college building, completed in September 1818,
was constructed on the upper part of the college lot in front of
the old college buildings and faced south toward town. It was
an impressive structure. Robert Peter described it as "a handsome edifice of three stories, surmounted by a tall and orna-
mental cupola, affording not only capacious lecture and recitation rooms, etc., but numerous apartments for students." The
Kentucky Gazette reported that "in addition to the old buildings a new one has just been opened, containing a chapel, lecture rooms. A refectory will be opened at the beginning of the
next session, 100 students can now be provided with board and
lodging, plus what is available in town." In addition to the
chapel, the building contained at least thirty rooms. The refectory was built to the east of the main building.[17]

[16]*Ibid.*, pp. 149–151.
[17]Minutes of the Board, March 2, 12, 23, May 23, 1816; Peter, *Transylvania University*, p. 102.

THE PRINCIPAL BUILDING OF TRANSYLVANIA UNIVERSITY, INSCRIBED TO
PRESIDENT HOLLEY.

The main college building, 1818

Despite this flurry of activity, the trustees could no longer expect to maintain a predominant Presbyterian control without further legislative investigation. At their November 1817, meeting the trustees again elected Horace Holley to the presidency of the University. Though only eleven out of the seventeen trustees present voted for him, the resolution that passed stated Holley was "unanimously elected" at a salary of $2,250. This action was not sufficient to save their heads, however, for in February 1818, the Kentucky legislature, apparently convinced that Holley's position as president would be intolerable without a different Board, passed an act abolishing the old Board and appointing a new one consisting of thirteen men for a two-year term. Among these new men were Henry Clay, Edmund Bullock, Robert Wickliffe, Lewis Sanders and Thomas Bodley — men of distinguished stature who, it was hoped, would avoid sectarian animosities in their attempt to forward the cause of creating a fine university.[18]

It was remarkable that a distant western school should appoint a Boston Unitarian minister to its presidency. Though records do not provide a clear reason, it is likely the Board had asked various individuals for recommendations for candidates. Boston and Cambridge, traditional centers of learning and educational leadership, were natural sources of capable men in this field. It was known that Holley was active in educational affairs in Boston, and he had another major qualification for being a college president — a Yale graduate and minister. Yale and Princeton graduates, particularly clergymen, supplied the bulk of college presidents for the West and South during this period.

In their letter to Holley the trustees described the current status of the institution, financial and otherwise, with special emphasis on the possibility of growth under dynamic leadership. They offered a salary of $2,250, which they pointed out was $250 higher than that of any civil officer in Kentucky, and urged Holley to visit Lexington in the spring of 1818.[19]

Horace Holley was a native of Connecticut, born in 1781 in the quiet farming community of Salisbury. His father and mother were both native New Englanders, the former rising successfully from poor beginnings as a farmer and schoolmaster to the position of well-to-do businessman, the latter the daughter of a Baptist minister. The Holley homelife provided intellectual interests, sound morals, and an unusually mild and liberal religious background. Horace's intellectual interests and capabilities became increasingly evident as he grew older, and his father provided him with an education at an academy in Williamstown, and then at Yale when that college was being guided by the strong hand of Timothy Dwight. President Dwight praised the academic achievements of this promising student who, after a brief tour to New York to investigate the possibilities of a law career, returned to Yale to study divinity

[18] Minutes of the Board, November 15, 1817. "An Act to further regulate the Transylvania University. Approved February 3, 1818," *Acts of the General Assembly*, 1817–1818. It is an extraordinary fact that the minutes of the Holley years have been missing for many years.

[19] John Pope, W. T. Barry, James Prentiss, J. Cabell Breckinridge to Horace Holley, November 18, 1817. Holley Papers, Transylvania University.

under Dwight. Under such tutelage it was not surprising that Holley accepted the most conservative Calvinist theology and began his ministry in Dwight's old pastorate in Fairfield County as an orthodox pastor. However, his theological views began to undergo a substantial change from his Yale days — a change which Mrs. Holley described later as a slow process, beginning in his pastorate and accelerated later by contact with lively minds in Boston. How far his religious views had changed is evidenced by the fact that his next pastorate was at the Unitarian South End Church on Hollis Street in Boston. There he began to develop his oratorical talents which won considerable acclaim for his church (the size of the congregation doubled and a new church had to be built) and fame for him in the surrounding area. He held strong Federalist sympathies at this time (1809–1818) and was on good terms with John Adams, the aging patriarch of Quincy. Later, when the decision to move to Kentucky had been made, John Adams wrote a letter of introduction for Holley to Jefferson, saying that the Virginian would find Holley "frank enough, candid enough, social enough, learned enough, and eloquent enough. He is indeed an important character. . . . I regret his removal from Boston. . . . He is one of the few who give me delight."[20] Holley's interest in community affairs resulted in his becoming a member of the Boston School Committee, a member of the Board of Overseers of Harvard and a member of various literary, scientific and benevolent organizations and institutions. To these causes he gave liberally of his time, money and talents.

Why, then, did Holley give serious consideration to the offer from Kentucky to become president of Transylvania University? His position in Boston was enviable and secure, and his wife Mary, now entering her second pregnancy, was perfectly content with her situation and most disturbed at the prospect of changing it. Yet Holley was attracted to the offer by the challenge it represented, by the sacrifices it demanded, and by the possible rewards it might bring. For Holley was not only a tal-

[20] Biographical data has been largely derived from Charles Caldwell, *A Discourse*, pp. 100–140, and Rebecca Smith Lee, *Mary Austin Holley* (Austin, Texas, 1962), pp. 55–65.

ented man, he was also an ambitious man. He was nearing completion of a decade of service at the Hollis Street Church and may have felt the urge to move out and conquer new worlds. "I did not expect to increase my happiness by taking a more important station, but anticipated some privations and difficulties," he recalled later.[21]

Holley made his first trip to Lexington in the spring of 1818 and was impressed by the town and its hospitality. He wrote his wife that

> the town and the vicinity are very handsome. The streets are broad, straight, paved, clean and have rows of trees on each side. The houses are of brick almost universally, many of them in the midst of fields, and have a very rural and charming appearance. The taste is for low houses, generally two, sometimes even one story high, like English cottages. . . . The town is handsomer than I expected, and has a more comfortable and genteel aspect. It has not the pretension without the reality, that so many of the small towns have through which I have passed.[22]

Henry Clay acted as official host, showing Holley the attractive countryside and introducing him to influential members of the community, including a visit to Frankfort and Governor Slaughter. Holley made a short address to the University's students, professors and trustees and then toured the small campus and buildings. The limited resources did not discourage him. "Everything is to be done, and so much the better, as nothing is to be reformed," he wrote. "Almost the whole is proposed to be left me to arrange."[23]

Holley realized from the beginning that all segments of the community were not equally happy at the prospect of his becoming president. Most suspicious and hostile were the Presbyterian leaders in the area, already distressed at losing control of the Board of Trustees. Holley's Unitarian associations only intensified their suspicion and hostility. While churches of other denominations in the area hastened to invite Holley to speak

[21]Horace Holley to John Tyler, July 18, 1819. L. Gay Papers, Massachusetts Historical Society.

[22]Horace Holley to Mary Holley, May 27, 1818, in Caldwell, *A Discourse*, p. 152.

[23]*Ibid.*, p. 153.

from their pulpits during his exploratory visit, the Presbyterians appeared adamant in refusing him theirs until the elders of one of the most important Presbyterian churches in Lexington voted unanimously to invite him to preach. Large crowds from Lexington and surrounding areas flocked to hear him, for he had become the center of considerable controversy. "Persons came from neighboring towns," Holley reported to his wife, "eager to learn whether I am a heretic or not. As I am no heretic, they went away satisfied, I hope, of the truth."[24] In the exhilaration of the moment, Holley convinced himself that he might prove to be both an educational leader and a uniting force among sectarian differences. Henry Clay warned him wisely against becoming involved in any such activity, however, and for the most part, Holley took his advice. Yet, undoubtedly, Holley underestimated the devastating effect of an unrelenting sectarian hostility.

In April 1818, Holley formally accepted the position of president of Transylvania University. The trustees, more impressed by Holley than ever, guaranteed him a salary of $3,000 — $750 more than they had originally offered him — which made him one of the highest-paid academic officials in the country. He rushed to write his wife of his decision, and knowing her reluctance to leave Boston, tried to be as persuasive as possible.

There can be no doubt that it is my duty as a philanthropist to accept of the station which is offered to me here. I believe it is in my power to do more good in this region than in any other at this moment. My life has not been half so useful in Boston, though it has been of some value there, as I am persuaded it will be in Lexington. . . . For the sole purpose of doing good, I had rather be at the head of this institution than at the head of an Eastern college. The field is wider, the harvest more abundant, and the grain of a most excellent quality. I may become what you call a martyr, but it is not my intention to be one. I shall make sacrifice in many things, but I shall do my duty, and if I meet with success it will be glorious. I am not about to bury myself, nor take my talents, humble as they are, from an active and conspicuous sphere. This whole Western country is to feed my seminary, which will send out lawyers, physicians, and *savans* [sic], who will make the nation feel them.[25]

[24]*Ibid.*, p. 157.
[25]*Ibid.*, p. 162. Schmidt, *The Liberal Arts College*, p. 69.

Years later as Mary Holley reminisced and re-read this letter, she must have thought how prophetic it was, both in the fulfillment of her fears and in the partial achievement of the splendid vision Holley had for his university.

After making arrangements to rent a commodious house on Limestone Street near the campus, Holley set out for Boston, arriving too late for the birth of his second child. This new addition to the family did not increase Mrs. Holley's enthusiasm for packing and moving during the summer heat, but her husband's excitement over his new position conquered her reluctance. Meanwhile, a letter from Henry Clay authorized Holley to hire two tutors in classical languages to replace Professor Sharpe who had resigned. Holley enlisted two young Harvard scholars, one of whom was John Everett, brother of Edward Everett, the latter having already won the reputation as a precocious Greek scholar and orator. Edward Everett developed a life-long interest in the school, visited it in 1829 and gave several volumes to its library.

In the fall of 1818 the Holleys and the two tutors set forth for Kentucky — a distant Western outpost it must have seemed to most of them.[26]

[26]Henry Clay to Horace Holley, September 8, 1818, in James F. Hopkins, ed., *Papers of Henry Clay* (Lexington, 1961), pp. 594–596; Holley to Clay, September 15, 1818, *Ibid*., pp. 597–598.

5

Horace Holley
and the Making of a University

It was in late November 1818, that the travel-weary Bostonians arrived in Lexington. Notice of their coming had been received in time for welcome ceremonies to be arranged. In the evening the graceful three-story main college building was glowing with candles in each of the windows. The proper speeches were made, and the Holleys accepted the invitation of Henry Clay to stay at "Ashland" a few days while their own house was being readied. The *Lexington Reporter* made the proper and flattering gestures in acknowledging Holley's arrival, prophesying a promising new future for Transylvania "under the superintendence of this accomplished scholar and gentleman of talents."[1]

A few weeks later the inauguration of the new president was held on December 19 at the Episcopal Church, the college chapel being too small to hold the crowd. There was a procession and music, and Holley led the people in an "impressive prayer," after which he was presented the keys to the University. Holley then delivered his inaugural address on "literature, science, morals, religion, and civil and religious liberty," which would seem to have covered the field. Already a controversial figure, he may well have been attempting in his first major public appearance to expose his opinions to public view to win support for himself and the University.[2]

President Holley was an impressive figure on the platform. Acknowledged as one of Boston's leading orators and gifted ministers, he quickly established himself as such in this western community. Dr. Charles Caldwell, a member of the medical faculty, described him:

[1]*Lexington Reporter*, November 25, 1818.
[2]*Kentucky Gazette*, December 25, 1818.

Horace Holley by Jouett

In person and general aspect . . . he was not only elegant and imposing, but splendidly beautiful . . . his beauty was as masculine as it was rare and attractive . . . a figure so symmetrical as to be almost faultless, features bold, expressive, and comely, giving strength to a countenance beaming with the brightest intelligence, and animated with the workings of the loftiest sentiments and the most ardent feelings. . . . When to these attributes were added a mellow, rich and silver-toned voice, thrilling at times with the very essence of melody, and of unusual compass, flexibility, and power; an enunciation uncommonly clear, distinct and varied; a manner . . . tasteful and animated, and action the most graceful, expressive and appropriate, the combination to give to elocution all its fascination, and produce the most powerful and indelible effects.[3]

Caldwell, though a friend of Holley's and later his eulogist, was usually hyper-critical of his fellowman and was himself an overweening egotist. Thus his description of Holley, while obviously somewhat exaggerated, would seem to be indicative of

[3]Caldwell, *A Discourse*, pp. 45–46.

this man's remarkable presence. This is further substantiated by the fact that the Reverend Robert Davidson, who as a devout Presbyterian regarded Holley's accession to the presidency as nothing less than a disaster, acknowledged that "Nature had lavishly endowed him [Holley] with her most attractive gifts. . . . He was remarkable for his symmetry of person, mellifluent voice, great vivacity, fascinating manners, splendid conversational powers, and brilliant oratory."[4]

The portraits of Holley by Jouett show him as a strong and vital figure, though not an exceptionally handsome one. He had a bold, bald head with lofty brow, thin eyebrows arching over large, dark brown eyes, and a prominent, thin and long patrician nose. His mouth was rather small, the lips of moderate fullness. His sturdy chin and cheeks, though clean-shaven, still showed a shadow as if no razor was sharp enough to remove his dark beard. One sees in these portraits a man of intellect and character.

There was no doubt as to Holley's goal for Transylvania. It was nothing less than to create in the West an outstanding state university. He saw no reason why this could not be done. At the time there were no major rivals on the horizon. Transylvania's charter established a public, non-denominational school — a state university to serve the state and to be supported by the state. This was in accord with Holley's view of higher education nationally. He believed there should be a federal system of higher education reflecting the American form of government. In agreement with James Madison and John Quincy Adams, Holley thought there should be a national university heading the system, reflecting not only the national and international character of learning but also acting as a unifying agent among the diverse regions of the nation and developing great leaders in the country. Supplementing the national university should be one major university in each state on which the limited state resources might be concentrated. Thus a state might erect a strong institution and counter-act the forces of sectional prejudices and conflicting parties which would undermine the

[4]Davidson, *A History of the Presbyterian Church in the State of Kentucky*, p. 305.

strength of the institution. Holley was convinced that Kentucky was in a remarkably good strategic position to create a strong state university which could influence the entire Mississippi Valley. And falling into the cliché of the time and place, Holley suggested that Kentucky was the Attica and Lexington the Athens of the West. It was this vision that had brought him to Transylvania.[5]

Holley further expounded his educational views at some length in an article he wrote for the *Western Review* entitled "Education in the Western States." His views were marked by flexibility and practicality. He emphasized the importance of adjusting education to the needs and character of different sections of the country, and condemned the tendency of many parents to hurry their sons through their education by sending them to college at too early an age. He also advocated that young students should concentrate on memory disciplines such as languages, and postpone the development of their scientific, speculative and analytical capacities until college. Again, he emphasized the danger of multiplying academies and colleges in the western states, a trend accelerating beyond all reason in these decades. He urged the development of adequate college libraries, pointing out as George Ticknor was doing at the same time in Boston, the vast difference between holdings of American and European university libraries.[6]

His inauguration out of the way, Holley threw himself energetically into the task of solving the host of large and small problems that inevitably crowd the desk of the college administrator. He proved to be an able administrator as well as a talented teacher in Transylvania's classrooms. After creating some order in the college's calendar, organizing students into the traditional four classes, improving the physical facilities and their upkeep, and establishing effective rapport with the community, he concentrated upon recruiting as able a faculty as his personal influence could persuade to come to such an educational outpost. His letters of invitation to men such as John

[5]Caldwell, *A Discourse*, p. 35.
[6]Richard Hofstadter and Wilson Smith, eds., *American Higher Education: A Documentary History* (Chicago, 1961), p. 255.

Warren, Boston's outstanding surgeon, Benjamin Silliman, the cornerstone of Yale's science department, and Edward Livingstone, able New York lawyer and public servant, give evidence of his determination to start with top men. That he had to settle for less than the most famous scholars and professional men in America is understandable, but his success — particularly in the renovated Medical Department — was remarkable. He thus drew to the campus not only many more students, but students of exceptional promise who became the professional, political and business leaders of the Southwest and the nation.[7]

Holley maintained correspondence with friends in the East as he sought distinguished scholars for his staff, spreading the word about the progress and character of the university. He sent Jefferson a copy of a report on common schools and professed admiration for the Virginian's devotion to the new university in Charlottesville. Jared Sparks requested that Holley write a review of Humphrey Marshall's *History of Kentucky* for an issue of the *North American Review*. Benjamin Silliman sent him reports on promising young scientists at Yale and Harvard that Holley might wish to contact. John Adams thanked Holley for his note of condolence on the recent death of Mrs. Adams, saying that of all the notes he had received, none had been "so congenial to my own Sentiments and so consoling to my feelings, as yours. . . ." Dr. John Warren reported that members of the Friday Night Club sorely missed Holley's presence, but if he had to leave Boston then he deserved as distinguished a post as he had accepted. George Ticknor inquired about Transylvania's experiment with enrolling students who were not intending to go on for a degree, and thought Harvard should adopt a similar policy. And Justice Joseph Story waxed poetic to Holley that he looked upon "Transylvania as an institution which must have a very important influence upon the morals & the literature & the taste & the religion & the public feeling of that interesting portion of our country." Here lay the "destinies of an empire," he said, and it was important that people there ac-

[7]Benjamin Silliman to Holley, July 27, 1819; Edward Livingston to Holley, September 12, 1825; Dr. John C. Warren to Holley, July 31, 1824. Holley Papers, Transylvania University.

quire intellectual discipline, eloquence, classical literature, and
"that rational Christianity, which enobles & exalts. . . ." It was
to be expected, he consoled Holley, that opposition would develop "from prejudice & from misrepresentation, & from inno-
cent delusion," but he was confident that in five years Holley's
"perseverance will completely triumph; . . . [and his] fame be
as highly estimated as it deserves." Encouragement from such
a source must have been welcomed by Holley. It was unfortunate that Story's predictions proved to be so wrong.[8]

THE CENTRAL CORE of the University was the Academic
Department, the traditional custodian of the liberal arts, and it
was in this department that Holley himself was most deeply
involved as a teacher and where his chief intellectual interests
were centered. Yet as the administrator of a university, he was
responsible for — and very much interested in — the development of professional departments of law and medicine. In fact
Holley was so successful in recruiting outstanding faculty for
the professional departments that the greatest achievement of
his administration was the creation of a first-rate medical
school establishing such an excellent reputation nationally that
it carried on successfully decades after Holley's departure. To
some lesser extent, this was also true of the Law Department.
But the Academic Department was considered to be the most
sensitive barometer of the University's welfare, and its influence fluctuated wildly, depending on the leadership and popularity of the University at any particular time.

The two major figures in the Academic Department during
Holley's administration were Constantine S. Rafinesque and
Holley himself. The only carry-overs from the former administration were Robert Bishop and Blythe. It was a peculiar and
not very successful decision to keep these men since neither of
them was pleased at Holley's arrival. Blythe, who was trans-

---

[8]Holley to Jefferson, October 10, 1821, Jefferson Papers, Massachusetts
Historical Society. Jared Sparks to Holley, September 14, 1825; Benjamin
Silliman to Holley, July 27, 1819; John Adams to Holley, March 4, 1819;
George Ticknor to Holley, May 5, 1825; Joseph Story to Holley, March 4,
1819. Holley Papers, Transylvania University.

ferred to the chemistry chair in the Medical Department, seems to have accepted his demotion from the acting-presidency with rare stoicism, but he may have secretly encouraged Holley's Presbyterian foes to make his position at Transylvania untenable. Bishop made no secret of his own dissatisfaction. At about the time of Holley's inauguration, he had written an angry note to the trustees, saying

> I am a plain Republican, and therefore speak plainly. Whatever may be the talents and acquirements of our new president, it is a most degrading thought — a thought under which no mind which has any sense of independence can act with vigor — that his services to the institution as compared to mine should be considered by the Board as three to one. The number of students has not as yet been increased on his account. Public opinion is perhaps as strong in my favor as in his.

If he were to stay, he told them, as a contented professor, his salary should be raised immediately to equal that of Holley's. But he neither left nor did he receive the requested pay raise. He was moved from teaching mental and moral philosophy, which Holley took over, to natural science. Some six years later Bishop sided with a student who had been properly disciplined, and the faculty formally expressed its disapproval of Bishop's action to the trustees. This finally provoked him to leave Transylvania, and he was elected shortly thereafter to the presidency of Miami University in Ohio where he made an impressive record as a successful administrator.[9]

By all odds, however, the most extraordinary figure on the campus was Constantine Samuel Rafinesque. Born in 1783 in Constantinople, son of a French merchant and German woman who had been raised in Greece, he led a peripatetic life as his family moved to Leghorn, Italy, and then to Genoa, Pisa and Marseilles. His formal education seems to have been haphazard, but he was intellectually precocious and read voraciously in natural science. Unfortunately for his later career, he never had the careful tutelage of a disciplined scientist who might have inculcated into the aspiring naturalist essential habits of careful and systematic observation, analysis, proper preserva-

[9]Rodabaugh, *Bishop*.

Constantine Rafinesque

tion of specimens and recordkeeping. Richard Call in his *The Life and Writings of Rafinesque* states that

> The record simply discloses that he essayed every branch of natural science, read omnivorously, made copious notes, formed ideas which were often vague and never afterwards matured, and always had before him the travels and work of the great men of his own and preceding decades.[10]

Rafinesque first came to America in 1802 when in company with his brother he visited Philadelphia. He spent most of his

[10]Richard E. Call, *The Life and Writings of Rafinesque* (Filson Club Publication No. 10, Louisville, 1895), pp. 8–9.

time on botanical expeditions in the area, supporting himself by taking various odd jobs until he returned to Sicily in 1805. He stayed for ten years, expanding his natural science interests, doing some writing, and becoming involved in a disastrous marriage. In 1815 he left his muddled marital situation behind and set sail for the United States, never again to return to Europe. He wandered from New York to Philadelphia, continuing his naturalist's pursuits and occasionally earning money as a private tutor. In 1818 John Clifford, whom Rafinesque had met in Philadelphia on his previous trip and who now lived in Lexington, wrote Rafinesque about a possible teaching position at Transylvania under its new president. Across Pennsylvania to Pittsburgh and down the Ohio to Louisville Rafinesque came, and then hearing that John James Audubon was not far away paid the famed painter of wildlife a visit. Audubon's reactions to Rafinesque were ambivalent as the following unforgettable description would indicate.

> A long loose coat of yellow nankeen, much the worse for the many rubs it had got in its time, and stained all over with the juice of plants, hung loosely about him like a sack. A waistcoat of the same, with enormous pockets, and buttoned down to the ancles. His beard was as long as I have known my own to be during some of my peregrinations, and his lank black hair hung loosely over his shoulders. His forehead was so broad and prominent that any tyro in phrenology would instantly have pronounced it the residence of a mind of strong power. His words impressed an assurance of rigid truth, and as he directed the conversation to the study of the natural sciences, I listened to him with as much delight as Telemachus could have listened to his Mentor.

Rafinesque seems to have both intrigued and irritated Audubon, and the former did not help matters any by destroying Audubon's precious violin. Audubon recalled that

> we had all retired to rest. Every person I imagined was in deep slumber, save myself, when of a sudden I heard a great uproar in the naturalist's room. I got up, reached the place in a few moments, and opened the door, when, to my astonishment, I saw my guest running about the room naked, holding the handle of my favorite violin, the body of which he had battered to pieces against the walls in attempting to kill the bats which had entered by an open window. . . . I stood amazed, but he continued run-

ning round and round, until he was fairly exhausted; when he begged me to procure one of the animals for him, as he felt convinced they belonged to a "new species." Although I was convinced to the contrary, I took up the bow of my demolished Cremona, and administering a smart tap to each of the bats as it came up, soon got specimens enough.[11]

Following this memorable encounter with Audubon, Rafinesque meandered toward Lexington, and despite his questionable appearance was hired by Holley to teach natural science, or at least the biological part of the science since Bishop was responsible for the remainder. From the beginning Rafinesque occupied a peculiar position on campus and off. It was not merely that he was of foreign birth — Lexington had many such — but that his absolute absorption in areas of science — which few people academic or otherwise considered to be of much importance — made communication with him difficult. The great emphasis on classical studies at this time gave little status to the laboratory or "collecting" scientist, and though amateur naturalists were plentiful, the regular college curriculum gave slight attention to biology as a respectable area of academic study.

Rafinesque and his colleagues seem to have maintained a cool relationship of mutual forebearance. For doctors and professors of medicine he had little respect. He caught the measles during an epidemic and caustically stated that though he was very sick, he "recovered in spite of the Physicians, by taking none of their poisons, antimony, and opium, while many died at their hands." Considering the state of medicine at that time, he was probably right.

Students regarded Rafinesque as absent-minded, an easy target for their practical jokes. His classes were marked by "the most free and easy behavior, made possible by the total absorption in his subject of the lectures. . . ." But his students may have fared better than they knew, for Rafinesque was a remarkably well-informed man and a real pioneer in his field. He was certainly one of the first science teachers to bring specimens into his classes for teaching purposes.[12]

[11]*Ibid.*, pp. 61, 26–27.
[12] Huntley Dupre, *Rafinesque in Lexington, 1819–1826* (Lexington, 1945) p. 77.

As to his life in Lexington, it was recalled that Rafinesque

> went into society while in Lexington and was a good dancer but
> had no companions, being totally abstracted usually, with his
> own thoughts and having no conversation, although he spoke
> good English, save in his favorite topic of botany. . . .

He found Mrs. Holley to be a considerate and thoughtful friend
who invited him into the Holley home frequently where he
found warm refuge from an indifferent world. He wrote poems
indirectly praising her fine qualities. But for all his tolerance,
Holley became increasingly discomfited by Rafinesque who left
the campus and his classes for days while he combed the
forests and rivers of Kentucky for the specimens to which he
carelessly applied labels and classifications that frequently me-
morialized the discoverer while leaving his fellow scientists in
the dark. The energy and intellectual vitality of the naturalist
were extraordinary. He was secretary to the Kentucky Institute, the first scientific society in the state and one of the first
west of the mountains. (Holley was its president.) Rafinesque
secured community support for a botanical garden and nearly
persuaded the state legislature to pass a law appropriating
funds for the project. He frequently offered public lectures and
courses in Spanish, French and Italian, as well as some on
medical botany and the human mind.[13]

He devised a "patent and Divitial Invention . . . [which] consisted chiefly in rendering Bank stock and Deposits and Savings
circulative by divisible certificates; which [he claimed] will one
day be certainly adopted." In 1825 he hastened to Washington
to secure a patent on this invention. His prolonged absence finally provoked Holley to take disciplinary action against him.
He ordered Rafinesque's effects and botanical collections
which were stored in several of the college rooms to be removed to another place so that a student might be supplied a
much needed room. When Rafinesque returned, he reacted as
an outraged evicted tenant. Despite the fact that Transylvania
had granted him an honorary M.A. degree in 1822, the scientist
was suspicious of Holley's attitude toward him and the

[13]Call, *The Life and Writings of Rafinesque*, pp. 62–63; Lee, *Mary Austin
Holley*, p. 127.

sciences. Rafinesque said

> to evidence his hatred against the sciences and discoveries, [Hol-
> ley] had broken open my rooms, given one to the students, and
> thrown all my effects, books and collections in a heap in the
> other. He had also deprived me of my position as Librarian and
> my board in the College. . . . I had to put up with all this to avoid
> beginning law suits. I took lodgings in town and carried there all
> my effects: thus leaving the College with curses on it and Hol-
> ly[sic]. . . .[14]

Unfortunately for Rafinesque hard times plagued him during his last years after he returned to Philadelphia, for though he was able to get several works published, he lived in abject poverty and obscurity. Finally dying of stomach cancer in a wretched garret, he was buried in a potter's field. Considering the conditions under which he left Transylvania, it is ironic that an enthusiastic group in 1924 should have organized a project nearly a century later to dig up his bones and re-inter them in a crypt on Transylvania's campus. Now Rafinesque, curses and all, lies entombed in the institution he rejected.

It would be an injustice to Rafinesque, and to Transylvania, to leave the impression that he was little more than a charlatan and an eccentric. We have already noted his great energies, ambitions, wide reading and ceaseless acquisition of botanical and zoological specimens in the Ohio Valley. Rafinesque was undoubtedly one of the significant pioneer naturalists in America. One of his most eminent contemporaries, Harvard's Louis Agassiz, assessed the value of his fellow scientist a decade after Rafinesque's death:

> Nothing is more to be regretted for the progress of natural histo-
> ry in this country than that Rafinesque did not put up somewhere
> a collection of all the genera and species he had established, with
> well-authenticated labels, or that his contemporaries did not fol-
> low in his steps. . . . [I]t is plain that he alarmed those with
> whom he had intercourse, by his innovations, and that they pre-
> ferred to lean upon the authority of the great naturalists of the
> age, then residing in Europe, who, however, knew little of the
> special natural history of this country, than to trust a somewhat
> hasty man who was living among them, and who had collected a
> vast amount of information from all parts of the States, upon a
> variety of objects then entirely new to science.[15]

[14]Call, *The Life and Writings of Rafinesque*, p. 41.
[15]*Ibid.*, 93.

It was Agassiz's belief that Rafinesque "was a better man than he appeared." Asa Gray, a colleague of Agassiz's at Harvard, was far more critical of Rafinesque and his work, mostly on the grounds of carelessness and lack of proper technique in examining and classifying specimens.

In October 1940, a symposium was held at Transylvania commemorating the one hundredth anniversary of Rafinesque's death. A group of noted scientists attending delivered a series of papers, later edited and published by Dr. Leland A. Brown, which analyzed Rafinesque's work and his contribution to science. The verdict of today's scientists does not differ greatly from that of Rafinesque's contemporaries — namely, that he was an extraordinary, industrious figure whose irrepressible desire to search out the new, to place his stamp upon it, and then to rush into print overrode the obligation to preserve and identify properly those specimens he so lavishly collected. Failing this, he failed his fellow scientists who were robbed of the only evidence available to them to evaluate Rafinesque's work. One senses the irritation and frustration in their comments about him even as they admired his broad purposes and limitless energies. It is the frustration we would feel in viewing the ruined fragment of a work of art that might have been a masterpiece but for the incredible carelessness of the artist.[16]

WITH THE ACADEMIC DEPARTMENT adequately staffed and organized, Holley turned his attention to the professional departments of the University. Nothing perhaps was more remote from Holley's own interests and competence than medicine, yet he realized how important medical education was for the welfare of society. Medical knowledge and practice was still largely medieval, even as late as the first half of the nineteenth century. Formalized medical education was in its infancy.

As mentioned earlier, a small handful of colleges had initiated some form of medical training beginning with the College of Philadelphia in 1765. Far distant from the eastern seaboard, Transylvania University launched its Medical Department in

[16] L. A. Brown, ed., *Rafinesque Memorial Papers* (Lexington, 1942), *passim*.

1799 with the appointment of Dr. Frederick Ridgely and Dr. Samuel Brown. Virginia-born and trained in medicine at Edinburgh, Brown had moved to Lexington to practice shortly before his appointment at Transylvania. In 1806 he moved to Mississippi, only to return and rejoin the medical faculty at Transylvania in 1819. Impressive in personal appearance, scholarly and eloquent, he made modest contributions to medical literature. He established his reputation as a pioneer doctor by introducing vaccination into the West.[17]

Ridgely had received his medical education at Philadelphia, served as a surgeon in the Revolutionary War and as Surgeon-General in General Wayne's army in 1794, and then settled down in Lexington as a successful practitioner and early teacher of medicine.

Although medicine and medical education were both in process of becoming more scientific, most Americans in the colonial period depended on home remedies, recipes for which were usually handed down from generation to generation. A few European-trained physicians settled in the more populous areas and attempted to improve medical techniques, but many persons clung to the old remedies, or even turned to the clergy for help. The number of amateur medical practitioners increased along with midwives, and even when conditions improved in the East, pioneer conditions in the West discouraged attempts to extend professional medical aid. The pioneer family knew little or nothing about hygiene, sanitation or health precautions. Infant mortality and childbed deaths reached appalling totals. Small cabins and large families made ideal conditions for the spread of contagious diseases. Ague was so common as to be regarded as an inescapable condition of living on the frontier, and work and marriages were scheduled around periods of the "ague shakes" with their chills, racking headaches and aching backs.[18]

[17] William F. Norwood, *Medical Education in the United States Before the Civil War* (Philadelphia, 1944), pp. 27, 58. Henry Shafer, *The American Medical Profession, 1783–1850* (New York, 1936), p. 11. W.P.A., *Medicine and Its Development in Kentucky* (Louisville, 1940), p. 31.

[18] R. Carlyle Buley and Madge Pickard, *The Midwest Pioneer* (Crawfordsville, Indiana, n.d.), p. 16.

These were the conditions confronting doctors, the men with lancet and pillbox, who ventured into the West. The young men who aspired to be doctors knew how desperately training and correct information was needed and how valuable an education at Transylvania would be. For many of them, living in straitened economic circumstances, the medical schools in the East were too far away. Transylvania was accessible and, being in the West, was conscious of the medical needs of the region.

Despite its auspicious start in 1799 the Medical Department at Transylvania limped along for years with various physicians filling in for a year or two and then resigning. Dr. James Fishback assumed the chair of the theory and practice of medicine for the 1805–06 period, gave lectures to a small medical class and then resigned. Three years later Acting-President Blythe attempted to revive the Medical Department by appointing four men — Benjamin Dudley, Elisha Warfield, Joseph Buchanan and James Overton. Due to a lack of facilities, books, cadavers for dissection and students, nothing came of this reorganization even though a number of these men were able and gifted physicians.

Of all these men the most important was Benjamin Dudley who was to become the very mainstay of the Medical Department for many years after this early period of delay and frustration. Born in Virginia in 1785 and brought by his Baptist minister father to the vicinity of Lexington shortly after, he made Lexington his permanent home in 1797. After receiving a rudimentary education, he began his medical apprenticeship under Dr. Ridgely, and then journeyed to Philadelphia in 1804 to study medicine at the University of Pennsylvania with such fellow students as Daniel Drake, John Esten Cooke and William Richardson, all of whom later joined Dudley on the Transylvania medical faculty. He received his M.D. from the University of Pennsylvania in 1806. After a few years of medical practice in Lexington, Dudley went to Europe for four years of additional medical training in some of the notable hospitals under the leading medical authorities in London and Paris. He returned to Lexington in 1814. Shortly after the War of 1812, a new attempt was made to invigorate the Medical Department at Transylvania and five men were appointed to the staff, but only Dudley

Dr. Benjamin Dudley's house at Church & Mill

and James Overton accepted their appointments or taught. In 1815–16 there was a small class of about twenty students, and Dudley lectured to them on anatomy and surgery in Trotter's warehouse on the corner of Mill and Main Streets. The next year Dudley and Overton, joined by Blythe who taught chemistry, instructed a larger class of some sixty students.[19]

Jouett's portrait of Dudley shows a handsome gentleman with fine features, dark eyes and black hair. Robert Peter, a colleague of Dudley's for many years, described the surgeon in his history of the Medical Department as follows:

> As a teacher and lecturer he was admirably clear and impressive. While no attempt at eloquence was ever made by him . . . his terse and impressive sentences . . . were the embodiment of the ideas to be conveyed, in the most lucid and concise language. This, with his great practical skill as a surgeon, his minute and ready knowledge, his great experience, his unequalled success in his numerous operations, his suavity and dignity of manner, the magnanimity and liberality of his character, and his eminent devotedness to his profession, made his students most earnest admirers and followers and aided greatly in the establishment and maintenance of our Medical College.[20]

[19]Peter, *The History of the Medical Department*, pp. 15–26.
[20]*Ibid.*, p. 18.

At a time when there was no anesthesia, it was said that Dudley's hand never faltered in an operation, whatever groans or screams may have come from the patient. Yet he was most sensitive to the patient's pain, and seemed to suffer near nervous prostration after an operation. Dudley established a national, if not international reputation for successfully removing stones from the bladder by lithotomy, an operation he performed two hundred and twenty-five times with the loss of only four or five patients.

Dudley was also expert in the use of the roller bandage in the cure of abcesses, control of inflammation and treatment of fractures, but few of his pupils ever seemed to master the technique as effectively. He also performed the most difficult operation of trephining the skull for relief of epilepsy. Though Dudley did not like to write about his work for the medical journals, he did contribute several extensive and valuable surgical papers for the *Transylvania Journal of Medicine* in the latter period of his career. He remained a devoted teacher at Transylvania until 1850.

At the end of March 1817, a number of medical students formally expressed their gratitude to Dudley, Overton and Blythe for the instruction they had received. The encouraging growth of the department persuaded Daniel Drake and William Richardson to join the other three in late 1817. The first medical degree ever granted by the University was conferred on John L. McCullough of Lexington in 1818. Drake who came as professor of materia medica and medical botany was, along with Dudley, certainly one of the most famous names ever associated with the Transylvania Medical Department. Although he stayed only a year the first time he was appointed, he returned in 1823 for an additional four years. Born in New Jersey in 1785 he had been brought to Kentucky as a young boy and became one of the first medical students in Cincinnati, beginning practice there in 1804. The next year he went to Philadelphia for a year's additional study before returning to the West permanently. He helped to found the Medical College of Ohio at Cincinnati in 1818, but left it for Transylvania after a bitter controversy in 1822. He subsequently held a number of teaching posts at various medical facilities. An inveterate traveller, he toured up and down the Mississippi Valley, writing on the conditions and people of this pioneer region, but especially collecting valuable medical information which he compiled in his major work *Treatise on the Principal Diseases of the Interior Valley of America*. This vigorous, industrious and highly competent physician was an exceptionally able teacher. One of his colleagues wrote of him:

> As a lecturer, Doctor Drake had few equals. He was never dull. His was an alert and masculine mind. His words are full of vitality. His manner was earnest and impressive. His eloquence was fluid.

Another wrote:

> Of all the medical teachers I have ever known he was, all things considered, one of the most able, captivating, and impressive. There was an earnestness, a fiery zeal about him in the lecture-room which encircled him, as it were, with a halo of glory.[21]

Drake's colleague William Richardson came as a professor of obstetrics. While not having the benefit of good early educational training, he was a capable and practical man in his field. Energetic and a man of fine character, Richardson was held in high regard by his students and remained on the medical faculty until his death.

The first year Drake and Richardson were at Transylvania they became involved in a controversy that led to a duel with Dudley. For a variety of reasons, now somewhat obscure, Drake fell out with Dudley over the matter of the former's resignation and some conflict over the post-mortem examination of an Irishman killed in a quarrel. Dudley, who must have been unusually provoked, challenged Drake to a duel, an act quite out of keeping with Dudley's normal behavior. Drake refused the challenge, but Richardson apparently felt compelled to uphold the honor of his friend and acted as his substitute. It is unlikely that either of these men were skilled marksmen, but they confronted one another with pistols and blazed away. Richardson missed Dudley entirely while the surgeon's bullet, somewhat off target, wounded Richardson in the groin, severing the inguinal artery. The young man would rapidly have bled

[21]*Ibid.*, pp. 40–42.

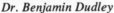

Dr. Benjamin Dudley   *Dr. William Richardson*

to death had Dudley not rushed over and after asking Richardson's permission, placed his thumb over the ilium and thus gave time for a ligature to be applied. The two men were lifelong friends from that moment.[22]

By the time Holley arrived in late 1818, the Medical Department had survived its first duel and was enjoying some success. The new president set about to enhance this promising development by recruiting additional able men for the staff. He persuaded Samuel Brown to resume his post in the theory and practice of medicine, and then used his influence to convince Charles Caldwell to leave his position at the University of Pennsylvania to join his unique talents with those of the present doctors. Holley had met Caldwell earlier on a visit to Philadelphia and had apparently been impressed by the vigor, ambition and intelligence of the man, who at forty-five had reached an impasse at Philadelphia because of differences with his former mentor and the chief medical figure in that city, Benjamin Rush. Self-educated to a large degree, and widely read, this "tall and erect person, with a noble head and piercing black

[22]*Ibid.*, p. 25.

eye" was probably the most egotistical and self-assured man ever to teach in the department. But he was a prodigious worker, pouring out a torrent of the written and spoken word. He loved speculative and theoretical subjects and delighted in debate and argumentation. He tended to be broader and more superficial in his range of interests than Dudley, for instance, but the students learned a solidity of fact and practicality of application from the surgeon they never got from the more eloquent and polished Caldwell. The dogmatic Philadelphian, moreover, filled a valuable role as propagandist and public relations man for the Medical Department. He performed a matchless service for the school in his trip to Europe in 1821 with $11,000 — a combination of funds from the state and the city of Lexington — to purchase books and apparatus. These were to form the core of one of the finest medical libraries in the country.[23]

The effect of these efforts was an amazing increase in enrollment. From a class of thirty-seven in the 1819–20 session, the number had climbed to one hundred thirty-eight only two years later and almost double that in two more years. Seven degrees were awarded during the first of these sessions, sixty-five in the latter. Caldwell acting as dean of the faculty for a number of years successfully welded the doctors into a distinct faculty separate from the academic, with almost absolute control over the policies and operation of the Medical Department and subject only to the president and trustees.

During this period requirements for the degree of doctor of medicine required a student to take two years of lecture courses, unless he had been a practicing physician for four years, in which case he needed to attend only one year. All candidates had to be twenty-one years or older, write a thesis of not less than twelve or more than forty pages on a designated medical subject, and pass two examinations, one before the faculty and one before the president and trustees. The curriculum covered the areas of anatomy and surgery, theory and practice of medicine, materia medica and medical botany, obstetrics, chemistry, and the institutes of medicine. The depart-

[23]*Ibid.*, pp. 47–54.

ment had no building of its own to house its library, apparatus, classrooms and laboratories until 1827. During Holley's day the medical students apparently used some of the main college rooms for these purposes. Dudley, who owned a sizeable house just south of the campus, added an amphitheatre for the teaching of anatomy and surgery. It was probably here that students performed the essential anatomical dissections.

The procurement of "subjects" for dissection had long been a troublesome problem for medical students and medical schools. There was strong public hostility to such use of corpses. Students and professors occasionally engaged in secretive midnight expeditions to graveyards to supply their needs. One Transylvania medical student recalled that

> dead bodies at that day were not articles of commerce, so we, the students, had to disinter them; and we once had a battle . . . at the old Baptist graveyard. . . . We were taken prisoners by an armed guard and hauled up to the court house for trial, but there was no law to make the dead private property, so the declaration of Scriptures that from dust we come and into dust we must return let us off by paying one cent damages for taking that much clay or soil. At another time . . . we were pursued when making our way to our horses hitched outside an orchard fence, and one ball of several fired lodged in the subject, on my back.[24]

In the South bodies of Negro slaves were sometimes made available for anatomical study, if the master approved. Yet as late as 1834, the Kentucky House of Representatives rejected by a 41-34 vote a bill "to authorize and require the Judge of the different Circuit Courts of this state to adjudge and award the corpses of Negroes, executed by sentences of said judges, to the Faculties of the different chartered Colleges in this state, for dissection and experiment." Thus the pressure remained on medical students to secure their own "subjects" by illegal means, or to turn to the commercial "resurrectionists."[25]

Given the best of conditions — and Transylvania was close to providing these — medical education at this time was woefully inadequate because medical knowledge was limited. It was a curious hodge-podge of accurate data, old traditions and

[24]*Ibid.*, p. 33.
[25]*Kentucky House Journal*, 1833–34, p. 104.

superstitions, and experimental techniques such as blood-letting and medicinal dosing without ways of predicting or checking the results. If the patient survived medical prescriptions of the day, then the methods were applauded. If he died, the techniques were not necessarily brought into disrepute.

The terrible cholera epidemic of 1833 showed that the assembled authorities of books, apparatus and faculty of the Transylvania Medical Department — and of every other medical school in the country — stood almost as helpless as medieval physicians did during the Black Plague of the fourteenth century in Europe. Yet some progress had been made, and the students of Dudley and Richardson, Drake and Caldwell, Cooke and Charles Wilkins Short spread out from Lexington through the Mississippi Valley with a degree of competence at least a few levels higher than the pioneer maker of home nostrums. The desperate need for trained medical assistance brought over 6,000 young men to Transylvania by 1859, and most of them stayed for the two-year term, wrote their medical thesis, and headed back to the home towns and the new towns with their M.D. degree, the lancet, pill and scalpel.

The professional quality of the Medical Department was enhanced by publication of the *Transylvania Journal of Medicine*, a quarterly which first appeared in 1828 and continued successfully for a number of years. It solicited contributions not only from the faculty but from medical authorities from all over the region. A second series of the journal was issued from 1849 to 1852.

One reason for the great success of the Transylvania Medical Department was its location. In 1819 a traveller from Nashville listed the advantages of the Lexington school. It was his opinion that the school would make the western people more independent of the East, that costs to the western student would be cut as much as one-half because of the proximity of the school, that Lexington offered "less danger from dissipation, folly, and extravagance," and finally, that the special diseases of the region would receive greater attention here.[26]

[26] Jennings, *Transylvania*, p. 109.

In December 1820, a medical student wrote home that while an epidemic of influenza had temporarily interfered with classes, morale was generally high because the medical students were convinced, as Dr. Caldwell had told them, that theirs was one of the finest medical classes in the country. What he dreaded, however, was the upcoming trial by examination.

> I begin to dread the approaching hour of Spring when I will be put into the green box to stand my examination before the President, Professors, and Trustees. They tell us they will be uncommonly tight and rigid in these examinations of us and they say we shall not pass if we ever miss one question in the examination, for they tell us the whole future prosperity of the University depends upon those they let pass in the Spring.[27]

DURING THE 1800–1820 period, the Law Department had suffered as much as the Medical Department. Mention has already been made of the early appointment of George Nicholas in 1799 as the first law professor, although his death prevented him from ever conducting a class. He was succeeded in turn by James Brown, Henry Clay and John Monroe. After 1808 there occurred a six-year lapse before John Pope assumed the leadership of the department for two years. After another long lapse, Joseph Breckinridge succeeded to the position in 1820, when under the new guidance of Holley the Law Department began its greatest period with William T. Barry, Jesse Bledsoe and Holley himself occupying the faculty positions. Yet even this haphazard record of the early years of Transylvania's Law Department may justly be regarded as a remarkable achievement in the light of the general state of law education in America.

Thomas Jefferson was instrumental in establishing the first distinctive law professorship at William and Mary in 1779. Harvard was blessed with an endowment for a law professorship in 1786 but nothing concrete was done until 1815. The College of Philadelphia started a law department in 1789, but it shortly languished and was not revived until 1817. At Columbia James

[27]*Ibid.*, pp. 110–111.

Kent was appointed the college's first law professor in 1794, but he resigned in 1798 and the school did not reopen until 1824. A law course started at Yale in 1801, but the department there did not get underway until 1826. Brown University claimed at least a nominal law professorship from 1790–1824. Probably the most influential source of legal education in the country was Judge Tapping Reeve's private school in Litchfield, Connecticut, which he opened in 1784 and in which he taught over a thousand students from all over the country for the next half century. Transylvania, therefore, was certainly not very far behind other colleges in the country in establishing its law department in 1799. Considering that Transylvania was far from the eastern centers of learning and commerce, its establishment of a law department was even more remarkable.[28]

It would have seemed that education in law would have been as much in demand as that in medicine, especially since the popularity of politics in America attracted many lawyers into that field. But the old apprenticeship system clung with great tenacity in the field of law, and the lack of any rigid requirements for persons practicing law allowed opportunities for even self-trained novices to try their hand at law. Lawyers who themselves had been trained in the apprenticeship system lacked enthusiasm for the academic method. Then, too, the new law courses at colleges struck the practicing lawyer as being too general and diffuse, not sufficiently practical for a man about to enter the profession. Only gradually was it recognized that academic legal education had advantages over the apprenticeship system.[29]

Law study was even more haphazard on the frontier than it was in the East. As Herman Chroust has pointed out in *The Rise of the Legal Profession in America*:

> Many of the earliest judges or justices — usually wealthy farmers, squires, merchants, or landlords — were uneducated men: some were almost illiterate, and virtually none were grounded in

[28] The most recent and thorough account of the history of legal education in the United States is Anton-Herman Chroust, *The Rise of the Legal Profession in America* (Norman, Oklahoma, 1965), 2 vols. See Vol. I, pp. 189–191.

[29] *Ibid.*, II, p. 92.

the law or versed in its most fundamental technicalities.[30]

These men were usually chosen because they were outstanding in some other field, and were thought by people to have a good deal of common sense and belief in fair play.

License to practice was not difficult to acquire. Before 1820 most states and territories had statutes requiring an applicant to have studied for two or three years under the supervision of a practicing lawyer or judge, at the end of which period the noviate was brought before the bench, vouched for by his supervisor, and granted a license to practice. With the coming of Jacksonian democracy, even this modest requirement was ignored.

In the early decades of Kentucky's existence, the bulk of judges and lawyers practicing in that state were from Virginia. George Nicholas and Henry Clay were two outstanding examples. John Breckinridge clearly stated in 1793 the motivation for lawyers to move into Kentucky:

> I am satisfied with this Country better than with the old, for two substantial reasons. 1. Because my profession is more profitable; and 2ndly, Because I can provide *good* lands here for my children & insure them from *want* which I was not certain of in the old Country. . . .[31]

Breckinridge, who became attorney-general in Jefferson's cabinet in 1805, was one of a number of Kentucky lawyers who rose to the ranks of national prominence.

It was to meet the threat of the frontier's rough indifference to professional standards of law that the Transylvania Law Department was established, and its success in attracting top legal minds to its faculty would seem to indicate that leading lawyers and judges saw a critical need for trained men as lawyers in their western community. One of the striking things about early academic law study was its breadth. This was due in large part to the view of the college and law profession as to what legal training should achieve, and this in turn reflected their opinion of what role the lawyer should play in society. There was, of course, the general goal that education should assist in the

[30]*Ibid.*
[31]*Ibid.*, p. 114.

making of a gentleman, but the gentleman-lawyer had the additional responsibility of being advisor, agent and advocate in American society. The lawyer was always an actual or potential participant in the lawmaking function of his society. To him the voters turned for candidates or for political advice. He was an integral part of the legal and political system. The future lawyer, then, needed more than detailed work in the mechanics of law. He needed depth in political philosophy, a knowledge of man's strengths and weaknesses, a familiarity with politics on the national as well as the local scale. That is why Yale included in its law curriculum such wide-ranging subjects as the law of nature and nations, the general principle of civil government, and a study of the United States Constitution. That is why the curriculum of the Law Department at Transylvania under Holley included lectures on the law of nature and civil law, as well as on common and statute law. In addition, the Transylvania law student participated in moot court exercises and in a mock assembly in which he was to learn the course of legislative business, parliamentary usage and the established rules of legislative procedure.[32]

Holley, who had once thought of becoming a lawyer before turning to the ministry, assisted the Law Department in its less technical aspects. He spoke several times on the role of the lawyer in American society. On November 8, 1823, he addressed students in the University chapel on the subject "Rank, Duties, and Rewards of American Lawyers and Statesmen." He urged the young men to avoid the role of the avaricious, disputatious, cunning lawyer. What the future lawyer should derive from a study of law was knowledge, usefulness and virtue; a knowledge of human nature, society and governmental institutions. Along with this should be development of the lawyer's greatest asset — a cool, impartial, reasoning capacity. A year later Holley spoke on "The Advantages Arising From the Study of Law and Politics in the United States." Law and politics were inseparable in the lawyer's life, the speaker asserted, and for them the gentleman-lawyer must prepare as best he can.[33]

[32]*Ibid.*, p. 115.
[33]Jennings, *Transylvania*, pp. 112–113.

Comprising the law faculty for its November 1822, session were Jesse Bledsoe and William T. Barry with assistance from Holley. Barry was no doubt one of the most energetic and successful men who ever occupied the position of law professor at Transylvania. Born in Virginia in 1784, his family moved to Jessamine County, Kentucky, not long after his birth. Educated at Kentucky Academy and Transylvania University, he completed his law studies at William and Mary and returned to Lexington to practice law in 1805. He was soon appointed Commonwealth's attorney and, when the War of 1812 started, became an officer in the army. In the years following the war he was elected state representative, United States Congressman, speaker of the House of Representatives in Frankfort, United States Senator, Lieutenant-Governor of Kentucky, and circuit court judge — all before he accepted the position to teach law at Transylvania for the 1822–24 period. It was perhaps too much to expect anyone with his penchant for succeeding to prominent positions to stay very long in any one place. Shortly after leaving Transylvania, he was appointed by President Andrew Jackson to be postmaster-general in his cabinet. Barry was described as being

> One of the most brilliant and remarkable men of the age in which he lived, of delicate frame, weighing little, if any, more than one hundred pounds, his mind active and forceful, dominating over all; his oratory was irresistible, imposing and ornate; eloquence marked all his discourse; his gesticulation, though usually violent, was never ungraceful and was always striking.[34]

Jesse Bledsoe, who joined the law faculty the same year as Barry, was also Virginia-born and was, like Barry, brought to Kentucky while quite young. He completed his education at Transylvania and was judged to be one of the finest classical scholars of his time. He studied law and practiced it in Lexington. Governor Scott appointed him Secretary of State in 1808, and he later served as United States Senator, 1813–1815. In 1822 he assumed his post at the University. Six years later he resigned his professorship and resumed private practice, subsequently entering the ministry in the Disciples of Christ.[35]

[34]H. Levin, ed., *The Lawyers and Lawmakers of Kentucky* (Chicago, 1897), pp. 731–784.
[35]*Ibid.*, pp. 587–588.

Stephen F. Austin

Cassius M. Clay

William T. Barry

Jefferson Davis,
Transylvania library bust

The improved quality of the Law Department drew an increasingly large number of students. There had been nine in 1821, but the new faculty attracted forty the next year and forty-four the year after. John Crittenden was one of the outstanding graduates of the 1824 class.

THE STUDENT BODY during the 1820's under Holley's administration, and even later, boasted a number of future notables of whom Jefferson Davis was probably the most famous. His classmates included Albert Sidney Johnston, the able Confederate general who lost his life in the bitter fighting at Shiloh. Davis later recalled how many of his Transylvania classmates showed up in Washington:

> My dear and true friend, George W. Jones, Iowa, was of our class, and with me, also, in this Senate of the United States; S. W. Downs of Louisiana, was a graduate of Transylvania, and so was Edward A. Hannegan, Indiana, both of whom were subsequently United States Senators. When I was serving my first term in the Senate. I was one of six graduates of Transylvania who held seats in that chamber.[36]

Included among them was David Rice Atchison of Missouri and Joseph Underwood of Kentucky. In all, there were seventeen of Jefferson Davis's classmates serving terms in either the House or the Senate when he was in Washington.[37]

In her short biographical sketch of Davis at Transylvania in the 1821–1824 period before he left for West Point, Margaret Newnan Wagers describes student life at that time. Tuition was only $35 a year with an additional $105 to cover board, lodging, fuel, lights and laundry. Students were fed the traditional heavy breakfast of that day consisting of coffee, milk, wheat or corn bread and butter, with a choice of either beef-steak, mutton chops, bacon or salt meat. The midday dinner offered young appetites a choice of wheat or corn bread, two varieties of meat, soup, three kinds of vegetables, and "poultry, when abundant," twice a week. The evening meal was modest, consisting of tea or milk, bread, and corn mush. This was probably not unlike menus given the students who boarded with private families, as Davis did.[38]

[36] Margaret Newnan Wagers, *The Education of a Gentleman: Jefferson Davis at Transylvania, 1821–1824* (Lexington, 1943), p. 11.

[37] Atchison's chief claim to fame was that while he was a senator from Missouri he was president of the United States for a day on Sunday, March 4, 1849, as Zachary Taylor refused to take the oath of office until the next day, Monday, March 5. Since nothing of note occurred in those twenty-four hours, the legality of this position was never established.

[38] Wagers, *The Education of a Gentleman*, p. 7.

Student dress varied according to income and does not seem to have been regulated by college decree at this time, as it would be a few years later. One student recalled:

> I remember that when I was a student at Transylvania University, I was fastidious in the matter of dress — "full dress" consisting of canton crepe trousers, buff-colored buckskin boots, dark blue or black swallow tail coat with brass buttons which were sometimes flat and sometimes bullet-shaped, white waist-coat, shirt ruffled at the bosom and sleeves, very stiff and high standing collars, and the white or black broad silk cloth; I used to beg my laundress, Tiny, to starch my collars so stiff that they would draw blood from my ears.

This, we may assume, was not regular class attire, but doubtless wealthier students, some of whom had Negro servants, dressed very well indeed and pleased the local merchants by their generous purchases. Unfortunately for the image of the school, this led many to identify Transylvania as a rich man's school, and her enemies did not hesitate to level such a charge in this period of growing egalitarianism.[39]

For amusement there was horseracing, of course, and the theatre where such plays as *Macbeth*, *The Weathercock* and *A Cure for Heartache* entertained local audiences. There were dancing schools where the student might polish his dancing technique and perhaps meet a young lady. There were taverns and gaming tables, but these were off-limits to the students.

The University administration, conscious of its responsibility to look out for the welfare of its young charges and sensitive to the criticisms that Lexington and college life might offer temptations to immorality the secluded farm or plantation would not, set up rules and regulations. In addition to those governing conduct in the classroom and on campus, there were rules restricting the movement of students off campus or leaving town. Student monitors kept order in the halls, took attendance and watched student conduct generally. Other regulations have an almost medieval flavor such as those forbidding the students to throw water or slops from the windows lest disease be spread or an unwary passerby doused. Dirks, swords and firearms

[39]*Ibid.*, p. 24.

were prohibited. Special care was to be taken with candles, and a student was not to leave his room in which there was a lighted fire or candle unless another person was in the room. Fire was an everpresent and terrible menace, as the college found to its grief on more than one occasion. By rule Thirty-three the student was prohibited from "possessing or exhibiting licentious pictures and lascivious and immoral books, and lying, swearing, playing unlawful games, and practicing other gross immoralities."[40]

College histories covering institutions operating in the antebellum period present a remarkably uniform picture in the area of student pranks and administrative discipline. Albea Godbold in his *The Church College of the Old South* points out that inter-collegiate or intra-mural sports and other recreational and social activities in the college were almost nonexistent. There were periods of relaxation in the late afternoon, and impromptu ball games, or ice skating, racing, walking, etc., but no gymnasium and no organized and supervised physical education.

> Youthful pranks and practical jokes were a part of the recreation of the students. Perhaps the strict rules, the rigid supervision, and the lack of athletics and physical education made for a situation in which healthy young men were driven to find some way of releasing pent-up energies. Pranks and jokes in the antebellum colleges often served as escape valves. At Davidson College the boys led a ram into chapel which butted a professor out; tied a dressed-up horse in the chapel; burned down the belfrey ... placed a two-horse wagon on the cone of the chapel roof.[41]

At other colleges, geese and calves were placed in the recitation rooms, and a calf attached to the college bell. Transylvania records of the ante-bellum period do not specify what pranks students played on the campus, but there is ample indication the faculty and president had their quota of disciplinary problems.

The more constructive extra-curricular activities of students at Transylvania and other colleges in the ante-bellum period were in the organization of the various student literary socie-

---

[40]Minutes of the Board, April 7, 1810.
[41]Albea Godbold, *The Church College in the Old South* (Durham, 1944), p. 102.

ties. These were run by students, and while some professors were elected as honorary members, they did not influence the affairs of the societies. Most colleges had at least two such societies, for competitive purposes if nothing else. Transylvania had three at one time in the ante-bellum period and even more after the Civil War. Initiation fees ranged from $2 to $10, and dues from 50¢ to $3. The money was used to decorate meeting rooms and accumulate libraries. As can be imagined, rivalry between the societies was intense. Meetings were usually held Friday nights or Saturday mornings. The chief activity of members at these meetings was debating and orating, and many a future lawyer and statesman developed his forensic abilities on this undergraduate testing ground.

Though we find evidence of societies operating almost as early as the establishment of the University itself — the Transylvania Philosophical Society is an example — the best records of student societies at the school date from the Holley period with establishment of the Whig Society in 1821, followed by the Union Philosophical Society in 1829 and the Adelphi Society in 1837. The Whig Society merged with the Adelphi Society in 1842, its members perhaps being more realistic about the Whig future in the United States than their own university trustee, Henry Clay, who made one last try for the presidency on the Whig ticket in 1844.

Though debating was the chief activity of the societies, there were also essay contests. Titles of some of the debates indicate the interests of the day. "Should Kentucky so alter her penal code, as to make Capital punishment inflicted upon White and Blacks for the same offenses?" "Should not the seduction of a female under promise of marriage be punished with imprisonment or death?" (The affirmative team won on this question.) "Do the works of Nature prove the existence of a Deity without the aid of Revelation?" Fear of the country's new immigration policy led students to discuss the desirability of extending the probationary period before naturalization to twenty years. And of perennial interest was "Can the practice of duelling be justified upon any grounds?" Current political partisan issues seem to have been avoided, as were the issues of slavery and secession. These latter issues in particular may have been regarded by students and administration alike as being too sensitive and latent with violence.[42]

In addition to their own society meetings, literary organizations sponsored public meetings, or special ceremonies on national holidays such as Washington's birthday. Short downtown parades frequently preceded the main oration.

Other student organizations included establishment of one of the earliest professional fraternities in the country, Kappa Lambda, a medical fraternity. Founded at the University around 1819 by Dr. Samuel Brown, who envisioned the group as "a truly secret but idealistic brotherhood designed to unite its members against the not inconsiderable dissension then existing in the medical profession," branches were established in Baltimore, Philadelphia and New York.

One of the most unusual societies on the campus was established about 1834. This was the Anti-Gambling Society. Composed of both students and faculty, it reflected the growing reform movement then spreading across the nation. Dr. Caldwell, a famous espouser of causes and one of the school's exponents of phrenology, delivered an address commemorating the first year's existence of this new anti-vice organization. This society, he pointed out, intended to have an effect not only on the campus but on the community and posterity as well. Caldwell stated:

> This is the first anniversary of a solemn compact, in which we pledged to each other and to the world our honour and good faith, not only to refrain ourselves from a certain specified and pernicious practice, but to do all in our power to discountenance and suppress it . . . the first blow of the kind that had been struck in the West [against] the insidious machinations of the BLACKLEG. . . .

As far as he knew, thanks to the existence of this society, there had been no gambling on campus during that college year. Horseracing and Kentucky's popular watering-places were also targets of the anti-gambling crusaders.[43]

[42]Minute books of these various societies may be found in the archives of Transylvania University.

[43]*Lexington Observer & Reporter*, November 4, 1834. Charles Caldwell, *A Discourse on the Vice of Gambling* (Lexington, 1835), pp. 3, 4, 32.

By 1826 Holley had converted the small, struggling University of 1818 into one of the most significant collegiate centers in the country. Concentrated on a modest campus with one handsome main college building and a number of smaller structures clustered about it, were over four hundred students from fourteen states. Drawn mostly from Kentucky, Tennessee, Alabama, Virginia, Louisiana, Mississippi, North and South Carolina, with a smattering from Ohio, Indiana, Illinois and Missouri, the young men had come for traditional academic training, some for legal training, and many for medical education. Transylvania was the educational center of the West and its future prospects were promising. The political and professional leaders of the Mid-West and the South were being educated in its halls. Unfortunately, the prospects were not fulfilled. Forces focusing upon the name and person of Horace Holley were intent on destroying him, if not the institution.

Horace Holley

6

The Making of a Martyr

From the time Horace Holley was being considered for the presidency of Transylvania University, his religious orthodoxy was challenged. During his visit to Lexington in the spring of 1818, he became well aware of the suspicion and hostility of the religiously orthodox toward him. This was particularly true of the Presbyterians who saw in Holley not only a threat to creedal conformism but to their long-held control of Transylvania. In larger perspective, Holley was a symbol of the continuing struggle in Kentucky between the liberal eighteenth century rationalism and Protestant orthodoxy described by Niels Sonne in *Liberal Kentucky, 1780-1828.* It was Holley's misfortune to arrive at a time when the resurgence of religious conservatism was beginning and the leadership of the Virginia elite, which had been so influential in the early decades of Kentucky's history, was waning. It is Sonne's contention that a period of relative religious liberalism prevailed between 1780 and 1820 but that this liberalism was seriously — indeed successfully — challenged in the latter part of this period by Protestant orthodoxy. Intellectual liberalism as well as religious liberalism was placed on the defensive, thus affecting the political and educational issues of the day. The ultimate defeat of liberalism was due as much to the fact that its strength lay mainly among the upper classes and their inability to win support among other classes, as to the conquest of liberal thought by orthodox thought in equal debate. Indeed, the religious hold of churches on the early settlers of Kentucky was so weak that orthodox church leaders had to incorporate into their attack economic, class and political issues, irrelevant to religious dogma, in order to muster sufficient strength to win the battle.[1]

Despite their numerical inferiority Presbyterian leaders led the forces of orthodoxy in Kentucky and other states because of their educational training. They adhered to a strictly-defined Calvinism and concentrated a good deal of their efforts on education and the establishment of educational institutions, not only as a means to provide them with educated ministers but also to provide them with leaders in other fields. The rising intensity of their attacks in the early part of the nineteenth century may have been due to their awareness of their minority position, the challenge of eighteenth-century European thought and the rise of Unitarianism, and the threat of the new, unlettered and powerful revivalism as seen in the Cane Ridge revival of 1801. A growing freedom from the Indian threat provided them with a more secure atmosphere in which to engage in religious controversy.[2]

Since the Baptists and Methodists appealed more to the lower classes, who tended to remain unchurched, battle lines were drawn between the educated and articulate Presbyterians on one side and the educated and articulate "infidels" on the other. Unfortunately for the progress of higher education in this country, schools were frequently the arenas for this contest. Ironically, many of the new schools had to turn to Presbyterians for their faculty and presidents, not so much out of preference but because of the short supply of college-trained men. Richard Hofstadter points out that "of all the churches, the Presbyterians were by far the most vigilant and censorious as men like Jefferson, Thomas Cooper, Horace Holley, and Francis Lieber painfully learned. The history of collegiate education in the South and West is in large measure the history of the struggle in which that church played a central part."[3]

The basis of the struggle between the Presbyterians and Holley, and behind him the reorganized liberal Board of Trustees, was not whether there should be any college chapel services

---

[1] Sonne, *Liberal Kentucky*, Chapter 1. Also, Clement Eaton, *Freedom of Thought in the Old South* (Durham, 1940), Chapter 1.

[2] Thompson, *Presbyterians in the South*, I, pp. 266–267.

[3] Hofstadter and Metzger, *The Development of Academic Freedom in the United States*, p. 244.

and religious instruction at Transylvania, but whether the chapel services and religious instruction would be dominated by a single sect and permeated by its creedal dogma. Except for Thomas Jefferson, and those who shared his views, there were few Americans at the time who believed all religious ceremony or instruction should be divorced from education. The prevalence of Bible classes, daily prayers, compulsory chapel and even some revivalism at most of the early state universities reflected that view. Yet the more militant sects were not content with this situation, and either attacked state universities as dens of iniquity or fought vigorously to bring them under sectarian control. Thus Holley's situation was not unique, but he was more unfortunate than other college presidents in attracting a formidable combination of adversaries.[4]

The usual media used by churches for launching their attacks were letters to the editors of local newspapers, sectarian journals and special pamphlets which could be cheaply printed and widely distributed. Within two weeks after Holley's inauguration as president of Transylvania University, there appeared in the Chillicothe, Ohio, *Weekly Recorder* a series of articles by anonymous authors that levelled at Holley and Transylvania what were to become the all too familiar charges in the years ahead. These centered on Holley's supposed infidelity — a term used by the Presbyterians to define religious deviation and which did not imply sexual impropriety — and his attempts to disseminate his heretical religious views in the classroom and college chapel both by affirmation and by sarcastic ridicule of certain students' orthodox beliefs. It was indicative of the desperation of his critics in their no-quarter attack on Holley that they criticized his private life as well. They condemned the worldly social gatherings at his home where improper conversation was heard (spies apparently had infiltrated these parties), undraped female statuary displayed and carefree songs sung. Holley's occasional attendance at the races and the theatre — the latter a special delight of his — did not go unchallenged. The fact that he watched some plays from the wings revealed his awareness of the delicacy of his position.[5]

---

[4]*Ibid.*, p. 32.
[5] Sonne, *Liberal Kentucky*, pp. 187–190.

A certificate of membership in Kappa Lambda,
the nation's first medical honorary

Holley was a man who enjoyed balancing his periods of serious intellectual work with a lively social schedule. He entertained as much as his financial resources allowed. That he was not exceptionally affluent was indicated by the fact that after his first year in Lexington he moved from his handsome dwelling on Limestone Street to the old building on the college lot just behind the large new college hall. His predecessor, James Blythe, had once lived there. Modest though these quarters were, he entertained many notables including President Monroe and General Andrew Jackson. The most festive and memorable occasion was the visit of old General Lafayette in 1825. The distinguished Frenchman was traveling through America on that grand tour made in commemoration of the fiftieth anniversary of the outbreak of the American Revolution. Transylvania was the scene of special ceremonies for the venerable guest and Holley acted as host.[6]

In March 1819, the first of many defenses of Holley appeared in the *Lexington Reporter*. It was an article written by a committee of students to rebut the accusations against Holley's character in the February issue of the *Weekly Recorder*. A few months later a more vigorous defense of Holley was made in the *Kentucky Gazette*. The unidentified defender wrote in part that

> Mr. Horace Holley, who so deservedly stands high in the literary world, and whose accomplishments have secured to him the esteem of most of those personally known to him, seems to have been marked out, for months past, as an object of the most profligate slander by a writer in a paper printed at Chillicothe, called the *Weekly Recorder*. The style employed by this calumniator in the last number of that paper; the glaring falsehoods that are unblushingly uttered, and the poor and miserable religious bigotry evinced throughout the whole body of the article, is proof, convincive to our minds, that the author resides in Lexington — and that he is one of those stiff-necked, unreflecting, superstitious sectarians who from the pulpit or in conversation would willingly yield up the souls of every individual who differed from him to the writhings and agonies of eternal misery.

The writer went on to state that, while he and many others did not necessarily agree with Holley on everything he said and did, his morality and Christianity could not be questioned. Besides, why did not this Ohio newspaper stick to its own state and business? Most Lexingtonians desired to cultivate Holley's society, the writer concluded, for he was "one of our most exemplary characters."[7]

The war of newspaper columns continued off and on for seven years, except during those welcome moments when editors exerted their prerogative and banished all such communications from their pages. Henry Clay, as one of Holley's staunchest supporters on the Board, had advised Holley to avoid becoming embroiled in sectarian controversies and concentrate on educational matters, and for the most part, Holley restrained himself. His alert critics did not miss a trick, however. In May 1823, when Holley delivered a memorial funeral ora-

[6]Lee, *Mary Austin Holley*, p. 125.
[7]*Kentucky Gazette*, August 13, 1819.

tion for Colonel James Morrison, a wealthy and distinguished Kentuckian and a great benefactor to Transylvania, his words were carefully scanned by hostile critics. There appeared in this oration paragraphs describing Morrison's beliefs which sounded a great deal like a defense of Holley's own views on freedom of thought. In commenting on Morrison's religious views, Holley said that

> Col. Morrison was a Christian in his sentiments and practice, but did not consider the peculiarities of any of the sectarian creeds in religion, whether papal or Protestant, ancient or modern, as necessary, or as useful, or as ornamental to his character. He had large views and philanthropic feelings, and recognized the wisdom, authority, goodness, and impartiality of the Deity in all relations of life. . . . With him a life of virtue was the most suitable homage to the Deity. He knew and felt that the end of all genuine religion is to make men good, useful and happy.[8]

These sentiments reflected the basic religious outlook of Holley himself, and they show why such views irritated the Presbyterians. To the Calvinist such expressions of goodwill as a basis for religious belief were nothing but benevolent banality. It was identified with the whole unhappy, French, enlightened, deistic influence on American thinking. A few months later a number of Presbyterian ministers banded together to issue a special pamphlet known as *The Literary Pamphleteer* to carry the barrage of anti-Holley material that a number of the local newspapers would not print.

In the fall of 1823 a new Presbyterian offensive was launched, using Holley's funeral oration as a starting point. One writer managed to read into the oration that Holley intended that

> such as enjoy the education of a University, and improve it, though there be no knowledge given of Jesus Christ, will not only be saved, but shall be perfectly happy, and most highly exalted in heaven. . . .

The same writer accused Holley of removing the cross from Christianity, placing Jesus on the same level with other religious leaders, and joining together Jew, Greek, Muslim and Christian. Interestingly enough, not only did Holley's religious position come under attack but also his alleged aristocratic

[8] Horace Holley, *A Discourse on the Death of Colonel Morrison* (Lexington, 1823), p. 19.

leanings. Transylvania was indicted as being not only a quagmire of infidelity, but of being the special educational preserve of the rich as well. The introduction of such a tactic at this stage was extremely well-timed, for this was on the eve of the 1824 national election. The age of the Jacksonian common man was emerging in Kentucky politics with the Relief controversy and the demagogy of Joseph Desha.[9]

Harnessed to the religious attacks on Holley and Transylvania were other factors, though perhaps not so obvious. Among these, though difficult to determine statistically, was parochial prejudice. Holley came from Boston which one concerned Presbyterian called "that seat of infidelity, the fountain of that poisonous stream of western Socinianism spreading its baleful influence thro' our State beginning at Lexington." Even Holley noticed that, during the tension aroused by the controversy over Missouri in 1819–1820, "the word Yankee has been used here of late, with a tone of uncommon severity. But it is going down since the compromise, and promises not to do permanent harm."[10]

One thing Holley did not import to Kentucky from New England was abolitionism. In an article he wrote for the American Colonization Society he expressed views on slavery surprisingly similar to those of its long-time president Henry Clay. He condemned the slave trade but condoned humane ownership of Negroes for service in the fields and homes until gradual colonization should again restore them to their original condition. He even purchased a few servants for his own household after coming to Kentucky. His most ardent opponents could certainly never accuse him of New England fanaticism on this score. Ironically, despite the admirable record of Presbyterians on anti-slavery and beginning with the courageous leadership of David Rice who led a vigorous battle in the early Kentucky constitutional conventions to prohibit slavery in the new state, Holley's Presbyterian critics never brought the matter up.[11]

[9] Sonne, *Liberal Kentucky*, pp. 196–199.
[10] S. V. Marshall to Robert Marshall, May 23, 1823. Marshall Papers, Shane Collection. Holley to Willard Phillips, March 26, 1820. Willard Phillips Papers, Massachusetts Historical Society.
[11] Lee, *Mary Austin Holley*, pp. 123–124. Martin, *The Anti-Slavery Movement*, Chapters 1–3.

The most concrete threat the Presbyterians presented to Transylvania was establishment of a competing college not fifty miles away at Danville. Centre College was chartered in 1819, but only after successive tries did the Presbyterians bring the new school under their complete denominational control. The Methodists, meanwhile, had established a school at Augusta, Kentucky in 1822, and the Catholic Church had founded two schools. The familiar pattern of denominational institutional multiplication was already developing. Yet Transylvania had a good lead which it maintained for several years.

Had Holley's opposition been confined to Presbyterians and religious issues, he would not have resigned in despair and left the University to decline. "We are without rival in the West," he confided to a friend in 1820, "and probably shall be for some years. We are hated by a sect, but are out of its power."[12] What religious bigotry could not do, economics and politics could. It must be remembered that despite the religious storm hanging about Transylvania, the school was chartered as a public, non-denominational institution. It was envisioned by its leaders and trustees as a state university. The Kentucky legislature so regarded it. They revised its charter, occasionally appropriated funds for its support, appointed committees to investigate its operations and to make reports to the legislature. One might assume that, if the status of the institution was legally that of a state university, its problems would have been appreciably reduced as public support undergirded it financially and state pride pushed it upward. Unfortunately, no such thing happened. Instead, lively forces of political controversy centered upon the school. During the period of Presbyterian control under James Blythe through the War of 1812, the school was frequently singled out as a Federalist stronghold in this Jeffersonian country of the Kentucky Resolutions. As has been noted, Blythe's condemnation of the War of 1812 did not help the cause. Then in 1818 the legislature rid the school of Presbyterian control. It was not long, however, before Holley and the new Board found themselves in political hot water. As the Jeffersonians became Jacksonians in the 1820's, so Holley, Clay

---

[12] Holley to Willard Phillips, March 26, 1820. Willard Phillips Papers, Massachusetts Historical Society.

and Transylvania became identified as Whig, aristocratic and conservative in both political and financial matters. There was no escaping the Relief controversy, the Old and New Court struggle, and the bitter election of 1824 in which Clay committed the unforgivable act of supporting Adams against the specific direction given to the Kentucky delegation in Congress by the state legislature.

Another factor weakening Kentucky's support of its only state university was that southern states generally had not yet developed a tradition of state support of public education. The state legislatures were willing enough to charter private church-supported academies of all sorts, but this proved nothing except to show they believed education to be beneficial and a private matter. They showed little willingness to support educational institutions financially except by land grants which, though appearing generous in retrospect, were at the time cumbersome and unproductive sources of income. The grants for the most part were inaccessible, unsurveyed, unwanted by affluent purchasers, and plagued by legal entanglements, especially in the case of escheated lands acquired during the Revolution. Like other western states, Kentucky showed a natural tendency to subordinate educational concerns to the priorities of survival in the early years of settlement. Roads, canals and similar public works contributing to the material well-being of the state took precedence over funds for public education, whether of an elementary or collegiate level. It was not until Kentucky's third governor took office in 1804 that any mention of public responsibility for education was even so much as mentioned, and not until twelve years after that was there a suggestion in the governor's message to the legislature proposing some plans for public school education. Finally, a split developed in Governor Adair's administration (1820–1824) between those who supported his position that state support should be given Transylvania and those who wished to funnel state funds to the public or "common" schools.[13]

---

[13]Material on the Kentucky governors and their relation to education is best available in the study by Edsel T. Godbey, "The Governors of Kentucky and Education, 1780–1852," *Bulletin of the Bureau of School Service*, XXXII (June, 1960).

Critics of Transylvania in the legislature said the state had been more than generous in its financial donations to the school. In answer to the question posed by a state committee of inquiry in 1827 "What has been the whole amount received from the State since the institution went into operation?" the Board provided an interesting summary. The total amount was $31,935.95, all of it in Kentucky currency except for $3,299. This amount was given during a period of forty-seven years. The largest item was $20,000 appropriated to Transylvania under the so-called Literary Fund Act of 1821. This Act provided that one-half of the clear profits derived from the operations of the Bank of the Commonwealth of Kentucky should go into a fund "for the establishment and support of a system of general education; to be distributed in just proportions to all the counties of this State. . . ." Under this plan, Transylvania as the state university would be the capstone of the system, and provision was made that it should receive an amount not exceeding $20,000. This was a single grant, however. Had it been established as a permanent feature, the money would have gone a long way toward stabilizing Transylvania's financial condition.[14]

Then in 1820 the General Assembly had made an outright appropriation of $5,000 to the Medical Department for the specific purpose of purchasing books and apparatus. Other items included the bonus from the Farmers and Mechanics Bank of $3,299, the duty on auction sales in Fayette County amounting to $1,977 to be applied to the purchase of books for the law library, and finally, the money received by the courts in Fayette County for fines and forfeitures amounting to $1,659. These acts cover a period from 1818–1822 and show the influence Holley exerted in Frankfort during the early years of his administration, persuading the governor and the General Assembly that Transylvania was the state university and their responsibility.

Prior to his arrival, the state legislature had done nothing to aid the school except for authorizing lotteries and continuing for a few years the policy already established by the Virginia legislature of appropriating to Transylvania one-sixth of the surveyor's fees, not a very sizeable amount. In fact, as Caldwell pointed out, Kentucky had actually deprived the school of its funds, first by

[14] Jennings, *Transylvania*, p. 123.

invalidating the 1783 Virginia grant of 12,000 acres given to
Transylvania of escheatable land by exempting such land from
escheat if legal heirs were known to be resident in foreign countries; and, secondly, by failing to renew the charter of the Bank of
Kentucky in which the University had invested some $30,000
acquired by the sale of land, thus reducing the value of the $30,000
worth of bank stock to about $17,000. By Caldwell's calculations,
the state owed the University about $50,000, but that figure, like
many of Caldwell's pronouncements, could not be taken as very
dependable. Yet there was justice in Caldwell's condemnation of
lukewarm state support.[15]

The monetary honeymoon which characterized the relation
between Holley, Transylvania and the General Assembly in the
1818–1822 period ended with the rise of the Relief controversy,
the Old and New Court struggle, and the ascension of Joseph
Desha to the governor's office. Following a period of unparal-
leled prosperity sparked by the trade restrictions prior to the War
of 1812 and the stimulus of the conflict itself, the Kentucky economy was severely depressed by return to peacetime conditions.
To relieve a money shortage, the Kentucky legislature chartered
forty-six banks in 1818, authorized to issue $26,000,000. Within a
year the drop in the value of such bank notes was disastrous. Only
the two branches of the Second Bank of the United States located
in Louisville and Lexington provided any financial stability and a
dependable currency. The legislature granted brief stays of judgment executions, closed most of the unsound banks, and passed a
replevin law which gave creditors the distasteful choice of either
accepting notes of the Bank of Kentucky in payment of a debt or
granting the debtor a two-year stay. In Governor Adair's administration (1820–1824), growing political polarization around these
controversial economic issues reached its peak as a new Bank of
the Commonwealth was chartered and, even more significant, as
the replevin laws were declared unconstitutional by a number of
the state courts — a position upheld in the state's highest court,
the Court of Appeals.[16]

With the election of Joseph Desha in 1824 as governor and
head of the so-called Relief forces in the state, and backed by a

[15]Caldwell, *A Discourse*, Appendix E.

[16]Thomas D. Clark, *History of Kentucky* (New York, 1937), Chapter 60.
Also Godbey, "The Governors of Kentucky and Education," pp. 30–33.

Relief majority in the legislature, attacks on the Court of Appeals and its decision on the replevin laws began. Failing to impeach the judges, the legislature repealed the law establishing the Court, and set up a New Court manned by supporters of the Relief position. The Old Court would not relinquish its position, the New Court proved to be ineffective and controversial, and the next election for the legislature brought the Old Court forces back into power and legislation establishing the New Court was repealed. The state was thus split between the Relief/New Court forces and the Anti-Relief/Old Court forces. Though Henry Clay tried to avoid embroilment in these state issues in order to preserve bi-partisan support for his presidential hopes in 1824, he was soon identified with the Anti-Relief forces. The situation became embarrassing when Desha and the Relief majority in the legislature, 1824–1825, directed the Kentucky delegation in Congress to cast their votes for Jackson when the election was thrown into the House of Representatives. When Clay and the Kentucky delegation "defected" and cast their support to Adams, Desha and his followers denounced this betrayal and became vigorous opponents of Clay. Clay's friendship with Holley, and his influential role as a trustee of Transylvania, made the New England president and his university tempting targets for Desha.[17]

Governor Desha was a prosperous farmer who had previously served six terms as U.S. Representative, being one of the Kentucky War Hawks during the War of 1812. His political ambitions appeared limitless and his campaign techniques revealed him as a ruthless, wily, effective demagogue. How far he might have gone in politics will never be known, for within two months after his inauguration in the fall of 1824, his son committed a brutal murder and was tried, found guilty and sentenced to hang. Two additional trials only confirmed the first verdict, and Desha resolved this intolerable personal dilemma by commuting his son's death sentence to life imprisonment. The pressure this event placed on Desha, and the handicap it placed on his political future (he went into political retirement after his one term as governor), only intensified his hostility toward persons, institutions and causes he already disliked.

[17] Sonne, *Liberal Kentucky*, pp. 242–247.

Into this category fell Henry Clay, Horace Holley and Transylvania University. To make matters worse, Desha was informed that a student had delivered a vehement denunciation of the Governor and his political principles in the University chapel in the presence of Holley, who had done nothing to stop him. As a matter of fact, Holley had been surprised by the speech and had in no way condoned it. But he had not interrupted the student because it had been his policy to grant students freedom to deliver extemporary speeches on current issues in the chapel, and all shades of political opinion were expressed by the students. The timing of this particular speech was unfortunate, however, and all the arguments mustered in favor of free speech and intellectual debate would not have mollified Desha.[18]

In his message to the legislature in November 1825, Desha delivered charges against Holley and Transylvania effectively designed to arouse the hostility of the Relief, pro-Jacksonian, egalitarian groups in that body. First, he exaggerated the liberality with which the state had appropriated funds to the University and the failure of that institution to make effective use of this money; secondly, he criticized the high salary paid to Holley (it was higher than his own); and thirdly, he condemned the aristocratic character of the student body, inevitable in light of the high costs of attending there. He said that

> this institution has been a favorite of the State, and has drawn with a liberal hand upon the funds of the people. Yet, it is believed, that in its benefits it has not equalled the reasonable expectations of the public; and that for several years its expenditures have been extravagant in amount. . . . A compensation has been allowed to the President, directly and indirectly, two-fold higher than is paid the highest officers of our State government, and wholly disproportional, as well as to the services rendered, as to the resources of the institution. . . . To make up these extravagant allowances, the prices of tuition are raised to a very high rate, which, with the habits of profusion acquired in the society of a large town, effectually shut the door of the University to a large majority of the young men of Kentucky. The only motive a republican government can have to foster such an institution, is to bestow on all, as far as they may desire it, the bless-

[18]Godbey, "The Governors of Kentucky and Education," Chapter 4. Caldwell, *A Discourse*, p. 237. Lee, *Mary Austin Holley*, p. 166.

ings of a liberal education. But as the University is now managed, it seems that the State has lavished her money for the benefit of the rich, to the exclusion of the poor; and that the only result is to add to the aristocracy of wealth, the advantage of superior knowledge.[19]

This official attack was supported by heated denunciations of Transylvania in the administration's mouthpiece, Amos Kendall's *Argus of Western America.*

Holley had gone to Frankfort to see Desha and talk with members of the legislature. What greeted him was Desha's speech and the unveiled hostility of the members of the legislature. He returned to Lexington, and on December 23, 1825, wrote out his resignation and sent it to the Board. The defeat of Holley at Frankfort, placed on top of the constant harassment from other sources he had suffered over the years, was too much to endure. The sectarian attacks were expected, and he was prepared to discount them; he believed Transylvania strong enough to withstand this pressure. But how does a state university succeed when the official agencies of the state belabor it and refuse to support it? In his final report, Holley plainly laid the problem before the trustees and the state:

> Our personal and local jealousies, our political contentions, and our sectarian divisions, have thus far prevented a result which all enlightened men must acknowledge to be eminently desirable. This is a State institution, declared so repeatedly and solemnly by the State itself, assembled in its representatives; and they will doubtless refuse to let it pass out of their hands. What then is the result? Plainly this: the State must endow it amply, and endow it speedily or bear the disgrace of its decline, and perhaps its fall. Individual efforts have heretofore chiefly maintained it, and large subscriptions have been collected from among yourselves and your neighbor. This resource is exhausted, or nearly so; and especially the motives are wanting, which are to rekindle private exertions.[20]

Holley had not fought this battle alone. The Board of Trustees ably defended Holley and the operation of Transylvania. They submitted to repeated legislative investigation, if not

---

[19]*Kentucky House Journal*, 1825. The governor's annual message to the legislature.
[20]Caldwell, *A Discourse*, p. 214.

harassment, and attempted openly and honestly to answer all inquiries and charges. Clay's presence on the Board was perhaps a liability, considering the political tensions existing at the time, but he never wavered in his defense of Holley and tried to persuade him not to resign.

Not all the trustees, however, backed Holley, one of whom was James Fishback. Serving both as trustee and teacher during the New Englander's administration, Fishback had originally been trained as a physician and briefly held a post in the Medical Department in 1805, but he moved from medicine to law, and finally into the Baptist ministry. The break with Holley occurred at the time when Fishback was filling the chapel pulpit several Sundays during the experiment of rotating denominational representatives in the college chapel to avoid the accusation of sectarianism. During a period of public examinations shortly thereafter, Fishback was interrogating one of the students in a manner that apparently irritated the president. Holley then made the mistake of interrupting Fishback and taking him to task for a number of his views presented in the chapel talks. Fishback resigned from the Board in March 1825, to add his weight to the anti-Holley camp.[21]

Not knowing the minds of various legislators hostile to Transylvania, it is difficult to ascertain the real motivations behind their actions. Governor Desha probably reflected some of their motives in his own emphasis on the rich versus the poor, the aristocrat versus the common man. In addition there may have been some rural, pioneer anti-intellectuals, suspicious of the educated classes. The trustees may have symbolized the urban aristocrat to these legislators. Moreover, the Whig affiliations of a number of the trustees may have rendered their influence with a largely pro-Democratic General Assembly ineffectual.

With the exception of Robert Bishop and Rafinesque, the faculty supported Holley, and a number of them signed depositions testifying to Holley's ability and the competence and honesty of his administration. It is difficult to measure the effectiveness of faculty support for Holley as far as influencing public or legislative opinion, particularly as professorial status in Kentucky was probably lower than in New England. Hol-

[21] Sonne, *Liberal Kentucky*, pp. 236–238.

The diploma of Alfred Shelby, son of Kentucky's first governor

ley's critics counter-balanced the faculty influence by stating that while the faculty might be intellectually competent, they could never be accused of being notably religious.

Students were a more complicated factor in this controversy. Some of the more religiously orthodox had unquestionably been offended, or certainly made uneasy on occasion by Holley's sophisticated approach to religious inquiry and light-hearted sarcasm toward the fanatical. They signed affidavits supporting the anti-Holley group. However, the majority of the students found Holley tolerant, well-balanced, sympathetic with diverse views, non-dogmatic, and a challenging and able teacher. In the press and other public statements, they affirmed their support of the besieged president. They denied accusations that Holley "had jested at the sacred Scriptures, or used profane anecdotes, or sneered at Christianity . . . or acted as sovereign or ruler." The students claimed that Holley encouraged freedom, as the student chapel attack on Desha indicated. The accusations against Holley were denounced by these supporters as "false as the kiss by which Judas betrayed his master." There was no attempt to deny that Holley may have attended the races, the theatre, and the ballroom, but students saw no harm in this.[22]

The Lexington elite favored Holley, and the local press proved to be fair during the controversy, even going to the extent of excluding for months articles and letters relating to the controversy. But the newspapers could not maintain a policy of isolation forever, and when their pages were again opened the vituperative attacks and warm rejoinders boiled up in their columns. Editorial opinion generally favored Holley and Transylvania. The business community saw in an expanding and prosperous college a substantial benefit to the town, at a time when the advent of the steamboat and consequent expansion of Louisville and Cincinnati had caused Lexington to suffer a relative loss of population and income. Generous financial support, both public and private, came occasionally from the Lexington community, but it was limited and could never hope to be a substitute for state support.

Holley's personal response to attack was usually a dignified silence. Such a stance was doubtless urged upon him by men like Clay. In retrospect Mrs. Holley disagreed and thought a more vigorous rebuttal on Holley's part would have been more effective. Dr. Caldwell, though himself a most ardent polemicist, believed that had "President Holley been less independent in spirit, less firm and resolute in purpose, and less frank and intrepid in disclosing his sentiments, he would have been more fortunate and Transylvania more prosperous." A greater accommodation to public opinion might have been more judicious, he believed.[23]

It is difficult to see at this distance what tactics could have guaranteed Holley's safety except wholesale surrender. It was only rarely that Holley in public addresses defended his position and the course of Transylvania. Such an occasion was Col. Morrison's funeral address. During the Desha attack, Holley

[22]*Ibid.*, pp. 215–218.
[23]Caldwell, *A Discourse*, pp. 225–226, 72.

became more outspoken, telling the Kentucky Institute that "while my tongue can move, or my pen form its ink in intelligible characters, I will assert and pursue the liberty of philosophical, political, and religious investigation, unawed by civil or ecclesiastical power." But such a defense of liberty, heartening though it was, could seem only futile in the face of legislative and gubernatorial hostility based on other issues.[24]

The trustees reluctantly accepted Holley's resignation but persuaded him to stay for another year. The news of Holley's imminent departure resulted in a sharp drop in enrollment in the fall of 1826, mainly in the Academic Department which always fluctuated severely during various periods of the school's successes and failures. In the spring of 1827 the Holleys left Lexington for New Orleans. Holley's mind was filled with plans for a trip to Europe, perhaps as the educational proctor for a group of young boys, or possibly establishing a new school in Louisiana. They left behind them their daughter Harriette, married to a young Lexington man, William Brand, and a grandson. They auctioned their household furniture in early March, paid off their debts, and made their sad farewells to friends. Mrs. Holley, who at first had not wished to come to Kentucky, now found it hard to leave.

Holley delivered a two-hour valedictory address in the University chapel, ably defending his administration. Then it was all over. Some forty ladies and gentlemen escorted the Holleys a few miles from town and then watched the Holley carriage disappear in the distance. The Holleys went to Louisville to board a steamboat for New Orleans. Plans for a tour to Europe failed to materialize, but the prospects for establishing a new school at New Orleans were most promising.

Holley suffered badly from the heat of the New Orleans' summer, and out of desperation booked passage aboard a ship sailing for New York. On July 22, 1827, Horace and Mary Holley and their young son, Horace, Jr., set sail for New York. A few days later Holley fell ill with yellow fever and died on July 31 at the age of forty-six. He was buried at sea off the Dry Tortugas.

In her fine biography of Mary Austin Holley, Rebecca Smith

[24]*Ibid.*

Lee states that Holley left

> behind him few visible signs of his impact upon Transylvania.
> No building had been erected during his administration; no stone
> was inscribed with his name; only the Jouett portrait in the chap-
> el would bear witness to his personal presence. He had to be
> content that his fame was preserved in the memory of young
> men like William Leavy, and in the continuing opposition of or-
> thodox minds.[25]

This was certainly true, but what he achieved in his few short
years at Transylvania was nothing less than phenomenal. He
showed Kentucky that she could have a first-class university.
The failure to convert this promising beginning into a permanent achievement was the failure of Kentuckians and their state
legislature to overcome the divisive forces of sectarianism,
class jealousies and political rivalries. It showed the lack of a
fundamental commitment to higher education in the form of a
single state university, and the multiplication of small denominational colleges was the result.

What had also gone down to defeat with Holley was liberal
thought and the atmosphere of academic freedom essential to
its existence. Holley's valiant proclamation to "pursue the liberty of philosophical, political, and religious investigation, unawed by civil or ecclesiastical power," appeared quixotic in an
atmosphere increasingly hostile to its fulfillment. To have preserved such liberty at Transylvania, free of denominational
control, would have required a handsome financial endowment,
which it did not have, or generous and consistent state support,
which it did not receive. Holley's lasting contribution in the
history of higher education lies in his role as a pioneer in the
field of liberal university development. His notable achievements and ultimate bitter failure highlight the enormous difficulties such a pioneer faced at that time and place.

[25] Lee, *Mary Austin Holley*, pp. 171–185.

Alva Woods

7
The Phoenix Rises

With Holley's departure the trustees were again confronted with the difficulty of securing an able president. The circumstances surrounding the New Englander's resignation were hardly conducive to encourage a man with goals or beliefs similar to Holley's to assume the responsibility for this institution. Because of his wide contacts, Henry Clay conducted most of the exploratory correspondence. Despite the Holley disaster, New England was again regarded as a possible source for a new man, and Alva Woods, the president pro tem of Brown University, came to the attention of the trustees. Born in Vermont in 1794 into a Baptist family, Woods graduated from Harvard in 1817 with honors. He attended Andover Theological Seminary, spent two years abroad and then assumed the post of professor of mathematics and natural philosophy at Brown in 1824. In 1827 he was acting as president pro tem of that school. When Clay made inquiries about Woods, most of the answers he received were hardly overwhelming in their praise, but all acknowledged his competent if undistinguished scholarship, his amiable character, and the fact that he was a fine Christian gentleman. The most persuasive letter came from J. T. Kirkland of Cambridge, who wrote:

> He is a ripe scholar, well grounded in the several parts of elementary knowledge. He is a good disciplinarian, without any tincture of severity. In manners he is quite gentlemanly. He has as little bigotry as any Baptist I know. In this view I think him the best qualified for the office of President, of any one I am acquainted with in New England, or have heard of in other

States. I think that you can not do better than to choose him.[1]

On the basis of this recommendation the Board elected
Woods on February 7, 1828, at a salary of $2,000 plus a house.
A few months later Woods sent his acceptance, and he arrived
in Lexington the next September to assume his new duties. He
was handsomely housed in one of the finest dwellings in Lexington, the Thomas Bodley house on the northeast corner of
Second and Market Streets — just across from the college
campus.

The Thomas Bodley House

Despite the low enrollment in the Academic Department (it
had dropped to twenty-seven in the fall following Holley's departure) and a slight but not serious drop in the Medical Department, Woods was not discouraged by what he saw. Lexington was an attractive town, physically and socially. The college
campus was small but pleasant. Two blocks southeast of the

[1] Jennings, *Transylvania*, p. 156; Minutes of the Board, February 28,
March 19, July 19, 1828.

The Medical Hall at Church & Market,
Dr. Dudley's house at the rear (beside horse & carriage)

campus was the new Medical Hall, a rather plain brick building erected on the northwest corner of Church and Market Streets at a cost of about $8,000 just a year before. A number of citizens of Lexington and the medical professors had formed a joint-stock company to provide funds necessary for its erection. The building contained a large lecture-room for chemistry classes, a chemical laboratory and a sizeable anatomical amphitheatre with preparing and dissecting rooms. To these new quarters the medical faculty moved the excellent medical library bought by Caldwell abroad in 1821. With its separate quarters the Medical Department became even more distinct and autonomous than ever, but since it was the most consistently prosperous branch of the University, the trustees did not challenge this tendency.[2]

The new president's main task was the resuscitation of the Academic Department. Woods must have sensed the delicacy of his position as successor to the controversial Holley and knew he had to play the role of pacificator. As a Baptist he would not be as religiously suspect as his predecessor, yet he would have to avoid appearing over-solicitous toward his denomination while restoring the impartial religious character of

[2] Peter, *The History of the Medical Department*, pp. 44–46.

the institution. He would have to keep his eye on a variety of publics. In addition to the religiously-concerned, there were the elite groups who had been sending their sons to Transylvania instead of to the East in the belief that at last there was in the West a college of comparable quality. There were those — and their voices could clearly be heard in the legislature — who viewed these elite groups with suspicion and jealousy. Could Woods rid the school of its aristocratic image? Could he persuade those interested in the development of a public school system that Transylvania rightfully occupied a position as the capstone of such a system?

In his inaugural address delivered on October 13, 1828, entitled "Intellectual and Moral Culture," Woods made overtures to these various publics. For the religiously-concerned he stated his belief that the mutually vital relationship between knowledge and Christian virtue had been neglected. This neglect would now be remedied. "The value of religion, both as a principle of action and as an example, depends upon the degree of knowledge with which it is combined." Knowledge without virtue may well be dangerous, he warned, and he could not hope for the prosperity of the school "unless it could be reared on the broad and deep basis of Christian principle."[3]

For those concerned with education for the people, he stated that in popular governments the necessity of an educated and well-balanced electorate was obvious. "Teach the people knowledge, and you teach them to detect the sophistries of the artful demagogue. . . . In proportion to the intelligence of the people will ultimately be their freedom." Therefore, he said, it was essential to support schools from the nursery through college. He deplored the attitude that people "in the lower walks of life" should not be educated. Criminals are products of illitcracy. Then he announced a new departure for Transylvania as it modified its curriculum to meet the needs of the average student. While not derogating the classical languages, he proposed that "for the purpose of political safety and of practical morality, a thorough education in the exact sciences and in English literature is all that is necessary." He concluded his remarks with a personal affirmation that he would not have uprooted

[3] Jennings, *Transylvania*, p. 157.

himself from home and friends to come so far if he had not believed that the people of Kentucky wished to promote higher education. Certainly those who had been first with the axe and the rifle would not be last "in the march of intellectual movement."[4]

Actions of the trustees showed they were anxious to back Woods in giving the University a more democratic image. First they authorized two separate approaches to the college degree: the Department of Ancient Classics and the Department of English Literature. This latter course would be more easily available to the student who had not had sound grounding in ancient languages prior to his entrance to college, and it would be especially valuable for those going into public school teaching. This was the first significant expression of the trustees that the University should be concerned with, or involved in, teacher education. It reflected their growing belief that only as Transylvania could identify itself as being a necessary connection with, or an important contributor to the common school system in Kentucky, would the state legislature open its mind — and hopefully its pocketbook — to the needs of the school. The trustees asked the legislature to appropriate $20,000 from the Literary Fund to establish a chair in English literature at Transylvania to train teachers.[5]

Except for classical languages, the courses taught in the Department of English Literature were almost identical to those taken by all students. These included arithmetic, geography, English grammar, geometry, elocution, history, logic, rhetoric, natural history, intellectual philosophy, bookkeeping, surveying, moral philosophy, political economy, general law, natural and experimental philosophy, chemistry, astronomy, elements of criticism, and the Constitution of the United States. French was also offered. Unlike students applying for the traditional training in ancient classics, the young men applying for admission to the Department of English Literature were not required to have had a previous grounding in the classical languages.

Another interesting response of the trustees to the charge that Transylvania was only for the rich and aristocratic was the

[4]*Ibid*.
[5]Minutes of the Board, November 22, 1828.

adoption of a standard college uniform. The trustees made a point of informing an investigating committee from the legislature that the reason for this was economy and discipline, the avoidance of class distinctions by abolishing differences of dress and rivalry in clothes and, finally, to make it easier for University authorities and local citizens to identify the students. The uniform was described by the trustees in the minutes as consisting of

> coatee [short coat] and pantaloons of blue mixed jeans or cassinette [both were sturdy fabrics] with black cord or binding along with the outter [sic] seams of the pantaloons along the legs with a small black ribbon rose about the size of a half dollar fastened on the collar of the coat in front on the right side; — a plain grey cloth cap with a leathern frontispiece will on all occasions be required to be worn in place of a hat.

The trustees made provision for seasonal change by allowing the clothes to be made of cotton during the summer months and a straw or leghorn hat substituted for the cap. To avoid the aristocratic boot, "the use of shoes or pumps alone will be required during the whole time."[6]

With the arrival of Woods, the condition of the University improved. Enrollment in the Academic Department had immediately risen from thirty to sixty-seven and a few months later to over one hundred. Enrollment in the Medical Department rose from 150 to over 200. In 1829 the Law Department was revived. Yet income remained low, and as an emergency measure some citizens of Lexington had pledged themselves to contribute to a fund of at least $3,500 a year for four years. Persons who contributed to this fund were allowed to send a student to Transylvania tuition-free. A few dollars were still being received from fines collected in Fayette County and from tax on auction sales in Lexington.

The single most important legacy the school received in the 1820's was that of Col. James Morrison. This son of an Irish immigrant had been born in Pennsylvania in 1755, served six years in the Revolutionary army and distinguished himself as one of Morgan's Select Corps of Riflemen. He moved to Lexington in 1792, filling in succession the posts of Land Commis-

[6]Minutes of the Board, October 6, 1828.

sioner, representative to the legislature and supervisor of the revenue under President John Adams. Morrison later became president of the Lexington branch of the Second Bank of the United States and served as chairman of the Board of Trustees of Transylvania for a number of years. Robert Davidson described him as follows:

> Col. Morrison was a man of commanding appearance, stern but courteous; of great decision of character, native talent, wide experience, and considerable reading. He acquired immense wealth, which he disbursed in elegant hospitality, judicious patronage of deserving young men, and the promotion of letters.[7]

A large portrait of Morrison by Jouett reveals a most impressive figure. While on a trip to Washington in April 1823, he fell ill and died at the age of 68. The funeral oration which Holley preached in honor of Morrison has already been mentioned. Long interested in forwarding the cause of education, and having Henry Clay as his lawyer and executor, it was not surprising that Morrison remembered Transylvania handsomely in his will. First, there was an outright gift of $20,000 to establish a professorship at the school. This was done, and in 1828–1829, the interest from this gift brought in $1,200 and was actually used to pay not one, but two professors. In addition Morrison left a residual legacy that fluctuated in value — from $30,000 to $50,000 — according to various estimates placed upon it by the trustees in succeeding reports. Litigation held up the use of this legacy for six years before it became available to the trustees — at a particular moment of great need.[8]

About midnight on May 9, 1829, Woods was awakened by the fearful noise of the crackling of burning wood and shouts of alarm. He rushed to the window overlooking the campus and witnessed the sickening sight of the main college building roof engulfed in flames. The fire had made considerable progress before it was discovered, and the students and professors living on the third story were barely able to escape with their lives and a handful of hastily-grabbed clothes. Fire engines and a large crowd quickly gathered, but the fire, starting on the third

[7]Davidson, *History of the Presbyterian Church in the State of Kentucky*, pp. 306–307.
  [8]*Ibid.*, p. 308.

floor, had already destroyed the roof and the cupola and was rapidly eating its way down to the second and first floors. Most attention was paid to preventing the fire from spreading to the other college buildings immediately adjacent, and to the private homes but a few yards away on Mill and Market Streets. A handful of brave men helped to save part of the college library on the second story, presumably by heaving most of it out of the windows, but the law library of 600 volumes and those of the Union Philosophical and Whig societies, totaling over 1500 volumes, went up in smoke along with the furniture and papers. Most of the scientific apparatus was saved, but Professor Matthews lost several hundred dollars' worth of books and equipment along with his mathematical and scientific manuscripts collected over many years. In two hours the building was a ruin.[9]

Years later Cassius Clay, the famed abolitionist, who was a student living in the college building at the time, recalled:

I was in the old Transylvania Building, 3 or 4 stories high, in the upper story next [to] the steps leading up to the lumber room attic. My black servant stuck a tallow candle to the steps in blacking my boots — went to sleep, & the flames went like powder. I ran down with some clothes in hand in my night shirt. No one was lost as the fire began at the top. The building of red brick stood near the center of the large college grounds . . . on the opposite corner over the Street was the House of the College President. . . .[10]

Had Woods believed in omens, he might have been depressed by an event at the fire later recorded in the local paper. According to this account, a pigeon hovering over the flames, as if trying to recover something from the building, was cheered on by the crowd as a phoenix rising from the fire, holding out new hope for the future of the school. At the last moment, however, the bird overcome by heat fell into this gigantic funeral pyre. Some were overhead to say, "There goes the genius of Transylvania!" Woods was not disheartened by loss of the building, and even later boasted that not a single day of classes was lost because of it. Using the catastrophe to arouse

[9]*Kentucky Reporter*, May 13, 1829.
[10]Cassius Clay's letter dated March 9, 1898, was reprinted in *The Transylvanian*, Vol. XV, No. 9 (June, 1907).

the sympathies and efforts of the townspeople, and later the legislature, he enlisted their support in rebuilding the college.[11]

A month after the disaster Edward Everett, while visiting Lexington during a western tour, received an invitation from Woods to dine. Everett recorded in his diary that "Mr. Woods took me to look at the ruins of the College. Some of the books were saved, as also the principal part of the Philosophical apparatus. A subscription is on foot to rebuild it." Ever since his friend Holley had left Boston (along with John Everett) to assume the presidency of Transylvania, Everett had maintained a keen interest in this pioneer venture in higher education, and after his return to Boston he sent a valuable gift of books. Later when Professor Matthews visited New England to solicit funds for the school, Everett gave him letters of introduction to leading Bostonians such as Harrison Gray Otis and George Ticknor. Everett wrote Woods that he regretted that Matthews' efforts were so uniformly unsuccessful and he blamed the depressed times.[12]

There was $10,000 worth of insurance on the building — about one third of its real value. Morrison's legacy was still tied up in litigation. The trustees appealed to the legislature for help in December 1829, on the grounds that

> it is the present policy of the Institution to render instruction as cheap, as universal, and as profitable as possible. To these ends, simplicity & cheapness of dress is enjoined. Almost all subjects of human learning are taught and the Professors make their lecture-rooms their offices, where they are at all times accessible to each other and to the students.[13]

But the appeal left the legislature unmoved.

Meanwhile Woods continued to proclaim his faith in the future of Transylvania. In his commencement address of July 29, 1829, he stated his satisfaction in the sizeable growth of enrollment in the Academic Department. Should this growth continue, the school would not have to depend on Lexington's charity for income. As for the destruction of the building, he asked

[11]*Kentucky Reporter*, August 12, 1829.

[12]Edward Everett, Diary, June 11, September 7, 1829. Everett Papers, Massachusetts Historical Society.

[13]Minutes of the Board, December 11, 1829. William Townsend, *Lincoln and His Wife's Home Town* (Indianapolis, 1929), p. 14.

Do bricks and mortar compose a literary institution? Is this all that is ethereal or intellectual in its character? Was it brick and mortar which secured to Transylvania the affection of her alumni and the cordial support of its citizens?

It is teachers, books, philosophers, apparatus, and not brick and mortar which make a University.[14]

But in succeeding years either Woods or the trustees became disenchanted with one another. The president may have believed himself unappreciated or underpaid, or the trustees may have been disappointed in the lack of results. In any case, there was a parting of the ways between them in the spring of 1831. Woods moved further south to assume the presidency of the newly-established University of Alabama.

Prior to his departure Woods had worked with the trustees in developing plans for a new college building. In the summer of 1830 the Board appointed a committee to confer with Henry Clay about securing the Morrison legacy. The trustees also arranged to enlarge the campus by acquiring the Castleman lot just north of the old College Lot across Third Street, and requested town authorities to close off this section of the street so the campus would not be bisected by it. In this latter detail the college was only temporarily successful. Third Street proved to be too important a thoroughfare to keep closed for long.[15]

Search for an architect and suitable plans for the new building started. By January 1831, the trustees had found their man. He was Gideon Shryock, only twenty-nine years old. Son of Mathias Shryock, who came to Kentucky from Maryland in 1800, he grew up in a family of builders, carpenters and architects. He was educated in the common schools of Lexington but never attended college. Instructed in the fundamentals of building by his father, Gideon received special training from William Strickland of Philadelphia in 1823. Strickland, one of America's leading architects in this period, had studied with Benjamin Latrobe and had become a disciple of the Greek Revival style, which the latter had introduced in 1798 in his Bank of Philadelphia. It was little wonder, then, that Gideon Shryock

[14]*Kentucky Reporter*, July 29, 1829.
[15]Minutes of the Board, October 30, 1830.

Gideon Shryock   *Col. James Morrison by Jouett*

should have become so enthusiastic about Greek Revival architecture. A few years later after returning to Lexington Shryock secured his first major commission in 1827, winning a competition for the design of the new state Capitol. This building, completed in 1830, was one of the earliest state capital buildings designed in the Greek Revival style, although Jefferson's design for the capitol in Richmond, Virginia, showed how influential the classical style was becoming. Shryock's success with the state Capitol no doubt influenced the trustees in their decision to employ him for the design and construction of Transylvania's new main college building.[16]

The original contract was for $12,500 with the structure to be located on the ruins of the old college building. With the acquisition of higher land north of the college lot, the trustees wisely negotiated a new contract with Shryock in June 1831, moving to this new site overlooking downtown Lexington. This seemed a more appropriate location for the impressive structure. The

[16]Rexford Newcomb, "Transylvania College and Her Century-Old Greek Revival Building," *Art and Archeology*, XXIX, No. 6 (June, 1930), pp. 251–255; Elizabeth S. Field, "Gideon Shryock, His Life and Work," an unpublished manuscript in the archives of Transylvania University; Clay Lancaster, Gideon Shryock and John McMurtry," *The Art Quarterly* (Autumn, 1943), pp. 257–275.

dimensions were likewise enlarged under the new contract, increasing the estimated cost to over $30,000. It was proposed that the center section of the building be forty-eight feet wide with a depth of fifty-eight feet and a height of thirty feet, with a portico in front dominated by four Doric columns, later changed to six. The main section contained the college chapel and was to be flanked by two wings. Prominent antipodia were set before the first and second columns on either end.

Though work had begun on the building in the spring of 1831 on the old site, some delay was involved as the site was changed and a new contract negotiated. The deep excavation for the new cellar was probably done in the fall of that year, but it is doubtful that serious work began before the spring of 1832. The trustees had hoped to see it completed in 1832, but construction dragged into 1833. Shryock had rented a house on the corner of Market and Mechanic Streets and moved his family into it, so that he might keep a constant eye on the project. Delay was not always the contractor's fault as Shryock made very clear in a note to the trustees on August 10, 1832, after the third payment to him of $5,000 had not been paid by the Board.

> In several instances where I had contracted for materials, and agreed to make payments at periods subsequent to 1st of July; the persons after having brought the articles to the place of delivery (and being informed of my inability to comply on my part) have disposed of, and delivered the materials to other persons. Besides this the number of hands in my employment at times requires that I should be enabled to pay them their wages, whenever due, and demanded of me; or else surrender their services which at this time is essentially necessary to enable me to comply with my contract.[17]

Winter always slowed up the work, but Shryock was certainly expecting to finish the building in the summer of 1833 in time for the opening of school in the fall. But a catastrophe hit Lexington which neither he nor anyone else could have prepared for — and against which all were helpless. This was the terrible scourge of the cholera epidemic.

The spread of cholera from Asia and Europe to America can be traced in the newspaper accounts of its arrival at major ports

[17]Gideon Shryock to the Board of Trustees, August 10, 1832. See Shryock File, archives of Transylvania University.

throughout the world, for international commerce not only provided a medium for the exchange of goods from one part of the world to another, but diseases as well. Ineffective quarantine measures did little to prevent its spread. Cholera was reported at Montreal in the spring of 1832, and by fall it had reached Cincinnati, Louisville and Frankfort. Wintertime acted as a damper on its spread, but in June 1833, cholera arrived in Lexington. An estimated one third of the population fled the town. The rest waited, among them Henry Clay who weathered the trial that terrible summer with his fellow citizens. Doctors, including members of the Medical Department of Transylvania, were as ignorant of the cause and cure of cholera as the layman, and offered only the most general and speculative advice which proved to be sadly ineffective. The disease proved to be democratic, for it struck both rich and poor, literate and illiterate alike.

During July and August the local Lexington press reported that over 500 Lexingtonians died out of a population of 6,000. The doctors were overworked, and three of them died. Gravediggers were in short supply, and some of them left town. Only the famous town vagrant "King Solomon" rose to the occasion to help bury the dead and was later immortalized for his efforts in a short story by James Lane Allen. Mathias Shryock died, and it was reported that Gideon, finding no one to help him, had to bury his father himself.

Work on Morrison College — for this was the official name attached to the new structure — was naturally delayed by the epidemic. Not until September 1833, did Lexington return to normal and workmen hurry to finish their task. A building committee of the Board found much left to be done as of November 1, but the trustees were determined to make use of the new facility. On November 4 by arrangement with Shryock, the building was allowed to be used for official dedication. A special procession, formed at the court house to march to Morrison College for the occasion, included the governor of Kentucky, state officials, faculty, students, city officials and clergy. The next day special commencement exercises, delayed by the cholera, were held in the chapel. The day after, a convention of teachers was held, highlighted by a speech by Dr. Lyman Beecher, father of Harriet Beecher Stowe, on the "Dignity and Importance of the Profession of Teaching." Thus was Morrison College launched.

Plasterers and carpenters were still finishing work in May 1834, but the building had been sufficiently completed to be of use that winter. For all the pride he must have felt in designing and building Morrison College, young Shryock must have aged considerably in the nearly three years it took to build it. As late as 1835, Shryock was still seeking payment, and in a pathetic plea to the trustees, he wrote:

> In relation to the balance which is yet owing me on account of the contract; I hope the trustees will make arrangements to pay it to me immediately, as I am in great need of it. Since the Trustees have had possession of the building, and free use of it for their college purposes; — the law suits, perplexities and other difficulties I have been involved in on account of it; have been the means of alienating me from my friends; destroying my credit; agitating my mind, and disqualifying me for all the purposes for which my genius and talents had fitted me.[18]

The turbulence surrounding the building of Morrison College has long since been forgotten. The building remains a lasting tribute to this Kentucky architect. It was one of the most significant achievements of Transylvania in the decade of the 1830's. It may be true, as President Woods pointed out, that bricks and mortar do not make a university, yet it cannot be denied that occasionally a certain structure on a college campus is so distinctive, so effective in capturing the spirit of its age, in centering within itself the collective experience of that academic community, that it assumes historic importance out of all proportion to its cost. Such was, and is, the place of Morrison College in the life of Transylvania University. The title of Morrison College remained the official designation for many decades until replaced in the 20th century with the name of Old Morrison.

[18]Gideon Shryock to the Board of Trustees, February 2, 1835. Shryock File.

8

The Failure of Innovative Education

Benjamin O. Peers

As the construction of Morrison College neared completion, the trustees actively sought a new president. Thomas Matthews, Charles Short and John Lutz had all taken brief turns as acting presidents in the period following the departure of Woods in the spring of 1831. In December 1832, the trustees elected Benjamin O. Peers as Morrison Professor of Moral Philosophy, proctor of Morrison College and Acting-President of Transylvania University. Born in Virginia in 1800 Peers had been brought to Kentucky three years later. He completed his education at Transylvania under Holley who was impressed by Peers' outstanding abilities. After graduation in 1820 he went to Princeton to study theology, but strayed from the path of Presbyterianism to become an Episcopalian. Increasingly interested in education, Peers went to Switzerland to study the novel educational ideas of Pestalozzi, who was then near the end of his life. When he returned to Lexington he taught occasionally at Transylvania, but his real ambition was to open his own school where he might develop his experimental ideas in pedagogy.

This Peers did in 1830 with the establishment of his Eclectic Institute. It was well named, for in it he combined the Rensselearean system of allowing students to be teachers on occasion with the Pestalozzian emphasis on adapting instructions to the capacity of the student. In addition Peers paid unusual attention to the health of pupils, regarding proper exercise as essential to mental as well as physical fitness. The school proved to be remarkably successful, enrolling as many as 100 boys from five states by 1832. A month before his election as acting-president of Transylvania, he had proposed to Transylvania trustees that they take the Eclectic Institute under their care and supervise it as one of the colleges of the University, but the Board believed this to exceed their legal authority and financial resources so they turned the offer down. By the election of Peers to control the educational operation of the University, it might be presumed that the trustees were sympathetic with Peers' educational ideas and would sustain his introduction of novel practices into Transylvania.[1]

It was an excellent time for introducing new techniques. The age of reform was beginning in America, stimulated by the emergence of the common man into political affairs. Andrew Jackson, the people's candidate, was in the White House, just elected for a second term. The cry for more adequate public schooling to meet the needs of the common man was heard widely. The young labor unions incorporated it in their demands for a better society. A few educational leaders were taking up the cause, and as was so often the case, Jefferson was in the vanguard. Near the end of his long life, the famous Virginian had devoted his thought and energies to the new state university in the Old Dominion. He constantly attacked established colleges to which so many young Virginians went, not only because they infected the emerging southern minds with improper political principles but because they seemed to be captives of an outmoded educational philosophy. Indeed this latter defect was evident in colleges everywhere, Jefferson stated,

> that is, the holding of students all to one prescribed course of reading, and disallowing exclusive application to those branches only which are to qualify them for the particular vocations to which they are destined. We shall on the contrary allow them uncontrolled choice in the lectures they shall choose to attend, and require elementary qualification only, and sufficient age.[2]

In 1828 a special committee at Yale issued its famous report on goals and methods. The purpose of the college, the report

---

[1] Jennings, *Transylvania*, pp. 171–172; Alvin F. Lewis, *History of Higher Education in Kentucky* (Washington, 1899), pp. 66–67.

[2] Jefferson to George Ticknor, July 16, 1823, quoted in Hofstadter and Smith, *American Higher Education: A Documentary History*, I, pp. 266–267.

asserted, was "to lay the foundation of a superior education . . . at a period of life when a substitute must be provided for parental superintendence." The Yale committee believed, as did most educators, that education involved the disciplining of the mind as well as storing it with knowledge. The committee even acknowledged the need to provide a college education for more than the privileged or professional classes.

> *Merchants*, *manufacturers*, and *farmers*, as well as professional gentlemen, take their places in our public councils. . . . Can merchants, manufacturers, agriculturists, derive no benefit from high intellectual culture? They are the very classes which, from their situation and business, have the best opportunities for reducing the principles of science to their practical applications.

Despite the democratic echoes in the report, Yale men retreated from experimentation with the old system, for in answer to the question as to which discipline affords the best mental culture, they concluded that "the ancient languages have here a decided advantage."[3]

The most outspoken of college presidents was Francis Wayland, who had assumed the presidency of Brown after Woods had left for Transylvania. In his *Thoughts on the Present Collegiate System in the United States*, Wayland emphasized the importance of the student learning how to study rather than covering a specified range of courses. He also proposed that credit be granted by examination and proficiency rather than by length of residence. Like Jefferson, Wayland believed colleges had been too exclusive in the past. In the face of declining enrollments (Transylvania was not, by far, the only university having problems) Wayland urged that college should be made more inviting to sons of businessmen and mechanics. To deprive them — the very "bone and sinew" of any community — of a collegiate education was to lower the cultural level of the American people. New subjects must replace the old; the elective system must replace the strictly specified curriculum. Ancient languages would have to stand on their own merits and be competitive with other subjects. And on many campuses, the growing influence of the sciences was challenging the monopoly of the classics.[4]

[3]*Ibid.*, p. 287.
[4]*Ibid.*, pp. 352–371.

The new reformers also agreed on the need to change the old cut-and-dried recitation method in classes, to allow the teacher to play a greater role than the conductor of daily rote examinations of the textbook. The status and salary of the college teacher should be upgraded, it was said. Why should he be the poorest-paid professional in the country? Wayland believed most teachers could easily earn more in other professions.

Curiously enough, the move to democratize collegiate education, to attract the sons of manufacturers and especially the sons of mechanics and farmers to college, did not meet with much success. A strain of anti-intellectualism ran through segments of the American public, suspicious of the bookish and the learned. An Illinois legislator in 1835 proudly proclaimed he was "born in a brier thicket, rocked in a hog trough, and had never had his genius cramped by the pestilential air of a college."[5] Similar sentiments must have been present among the rural Kentucky legislators as they continued their adamant opposition to appropriating one cent to Transylvania.

The other force working against reform was the entrenched power of conservatism in the collegiate fortress itself — particularly the faculty and many alumni who regarded the way they were educated as the hallmark of the finished scholar. To open wide the college doors to the common man would threaten to debase the college degree and reduce their elite status in society. And even if these rather egocentric and covetous motives had not been present, there were many convinced that the classical mode of education, received sacrosanct from the Middle Ages, was best.

When Peers addressed the distinguished audience in the chapel of Morrison College on November 4, 1833 — the smell of fresh plaster in his nostrils and bright sunlight pouring through the great, clear-glass windows — he was aglow with the educational reforms he wished to present. His subject was "Intellectual Education." He stated his thesis forthrightly at the very beginning:

> That all rules, expedients, and methods of the intellectual artist, that is, of the educator, should be derived not from tradition or usage; but directly deduced from the laws of the mind; that one

[5] Schmidt, *The Liberal Arts College*, pp. 59–63.

of the greatest defects of the system of instruction ordinarily pursued, is, the giving the pupil too much assistance, or rather, assisting him in the wrong way. . . . The instructor [should] merely
show him *how to work*, but he himself performing the labor; that
in the course of self-education spontaneously followed by very
young children under the instructive guidance of nature, we shall
find the best possible criteria, both as relates to the subjects,
order, and methods of study; by which to regulate our practice in
their subsequent education.

Peers went on to stress the importance of natural science as
having "a greater inherent value than is generally admitted,"
and he thought it should be taught on the Rensselaer system of
practical experimentation and laboratory work. As for ancient
languages, Peers saw some value in their study, not because
they "disciplined" the mind — the favorite jargon of a traditional educator — but because they were useful in helping to
understand present-day English and other modern languages.
Peers pointed out

that the course of education recommended by these principles,
besides being more favorable, both to the extent and accuracy of
knowledge, will ultimately cause a youth to become intellectually, a more original, independent, and efficient man.[6]

This seemed an admirable goal. How receptive his audience,
especially the trustees, to his ideas remained to be seen.

Finally, Peers concluded his inaugural with a necessary appeal to the public that prejudice against Transylvania as a
school for the elite be overcome.

Let us endeavor henceforward to bring the energies of Transylvania into practical alliance with the interests of popular education. Let us make here in reality what she has always professed
to be in theory, a State Institution; the property of the people,
consulting and promoting the intellectual welfare of the entire
people.[7]

With the completion of Morrison College and the inauguration of a man of Peers' vitality and new ideas, one might have
expected that happy days lay ahead. Implementation of Peers'
ideas into the educational program, though undoubtedly encountering some opposition, might well have been the key to

[6] Jennings, *Transylvania*, pp. 172–173.
[7] *Ibid.*

setting the school on a new course as an educational pioneer, attracting a nation-wide constituency. But the vessel of these new hopes went aground before it left the harbor. Strangely, the bone of contention between the Board and Peers was not over dramatic educational reforms. At least the record makes no mention of them.

In the fall and winter of 1833–34, the trustees made a number of faculty appointments without consulting Peers. They had a perfectly legal right to do so. It was part of the unique corporative structure of the American colleges, which placed basic responsibilities such as hiring and firing of the administrative staff and faculty in trustees' hands. Although it had been the practice of the trustees to consult the president on such appointments, they now disregarded Peers' advice on faculty appointments. Either they did not trust his judgment in these matters, or they had become disenchanted with him and used this irritating tactic to encourage him to resign. They did not have to wait long for his counter-attack.

Peers submitted a vigorous report to the Board in January 1834, complaining that he was being deprived of the power to choose faculty while at the same time being expected by the trustees to run the school successfully. He forcefully argued that it was an accepted custom among colleges (he had written to Harvard and Yale to confirm this) to allow the faculty and the president to elect new faculty, even though ultimate confirmation rested with the Board. The president of the United States, the governor of a state, the captain of a ship, all had the right to choose their subordinates. How could he be held responsible for the quality of the institution if he was deprived of the right to determine the quality of the staff?[8]

The trustees did not budge. They spelled out Peers' job as one of supervision, reporting faithfully to the Board the condition of various departments and the progress of the students, and to properly enforce discipline at the school. The entire tone of their rebuttal was insufferably condescending and arrogant, the tones of an aggrieved parent to an obdurate adolescent. No man with any self-esteem would have endured it, and his angry denunciation of the trustees led to their motion — though not

[8]Minutes of the Board, n.d., January, 1834.

unanimous — to dismiss him in February 1834, three short
months after his inauguration.[9]

But this puzzling incident perhaps provides insight into the
fundamental dilemma created by trustee control over academic
matters. Beyond the immediate dramatic confrontation between Peers and the trustees over the issue of faculty appointments was the prospect of a continuing struggle between Board
and president unless some compromise was reached. The president must be able to wield a greater influence, along with the
faculty, in the choice of personnel and the determination of curriculum and teaching methods. Yet as of 1833 the trustees still
clung to the traditional stance of final authority in all academic
matters — the president and faculty being subordinate employ-
ees. Holley had circumvented the trustees successfully, perhaps by diplomatically manipulating them to believe that they
were in control, but following Holley's departure the old practice was resumed.

The institution was small, the campus compact, the student
body young and few in number. It was easy for the trustees to
peer into all areas of the educational operation and, having legitimate authority under the charter, to control things as they
saw fit. A president who did not mind occupying the post of a
subordinate employee, merely fulfilling duties outlined by the
Board, would not have any trouble with the trustees. It was
unlikely, however, that such a president would invigorate the
campus to excell in all its endeavors, nor would he inaugurate
necessary changes or experimental methods. Therefore, to all
of Transylvania's other problems and obstacles to success was
added that of trustee control, at least in this particular period
and on this issue.

Not to be condemned out of hand, many trustees were able
and energetic business and professional men. Their services as
trustees were given voluntarily. They conscientiously assumed
their responsibilities as they saw them delineated in the charter.
Most of them had gone through the traditional educational
process. They met the problems of the institution committed to
their charge with straightforward measures. To their dismay
and puzzlement, special problems of the academic community

[9]*Ibid.*, February 14, 1834. Also see Jennings, *Transylvania*, pp. 176–179.

and environment did not always respond to their solutions. The encounter between Peers and the trustees was but a symptom of this continuing and troubling dilemma.

So Peers left for other educational ventures, and the board appointed John Lutz, a professor of mathematics, as acting president. Another undesirable interregnum prevailed until a new president could be appointed, and this would not be until nearly a year and a half later in July 1835. Meanwhile the Academic Department suffered badly from this administrative fluctuation, an obstacle that not even the new, gleaming walls of Morrison College could overcome. Enrollment in the regular collegiate classes and the preparatory department together ranged between thirty and sixty. However, the Medical Department, independent and aloof it seemed from the ills of the Academic Department, grew in strength and numbers. In the same session that Peers was dismissed, enrollment in the Medical Department rose to 260.

Even the Law Department, resuscitated in 1829 under John Boyle, was continuing to expand under Boyle's successor, Judge Daniel Mayes of Frankfort. Boyle had wisely introduced a system of class discussion of legal principles and cases, but apparently Mayes depended more on the lecture system. He complained to the trustees that as enrollment grew from six to fifty (drawn from seven states) he had to lecture four or five hours a day in a great variety of fields and asked that another man be appointed to assist him.

Mayes divided his law students into two classes. He preferred the beginner with no previous legal reading to one whose mind was cluttered with misconceptions. The price of tuition at the time was $25, which with fifty students would have given Mayes a somewhat larger salary than the members of the Academic Department, but nowhere near the income of medical professors making double that salary. Only in the Academic Department was there a tuition fee for all classes. In both the Medical and Law Departments the admission was by ticket. The larger the enrollment, the larger the salary, which tended to make active recruiters of the faculty.[10]

[10]*Kentucky Reporter*, January 18, 1832.

Some idea of the law course content under Mayes may be derived from his list of textbooks. The Junior Class was assigned Blackstone's *Commentaries* and Kent's *Commentaries*. The Senior Class labored with Chitty's *Pleading*, Maddock's *Chancery*, and Cooper's *Equity Pleading*. To these Mayes later added Starkie's *Law of Evidence*. Daily recitations were scheduled along with what Mayes called "catechetical lecturing" on law and equity. Since a catechetical method is one of teaching by question and answer, it can be assumed that Mayes' method involved something more than a one-way monologue. Classes were held five days a week with a moot court held on Saturdays.[11]

After a session or two, one of Mayes' more enthusiastic students wrote a laudatory letter to the local press, assuring the reader that one could learn in four months under Mayes what it would take twelve months to acquire anywhere else. He noted Mayes' "profound and extensive legal attainments, his urbanity of manners, his power and facility of communication, the ease and perspicuity of his address." Shortly thereafter, the paper reprinted a letter from the *Nashville Herald* in which the writer commented on the growing number of medical schools but the continuing paucity of law schools. "The Western States *can support one Law School*. They should do it." He spoke highly of Transylvania's Law Department and urged the Kentucky legislature to support it.[12]

In the fall of 1834 the trustees made a most significant addition to the faculty of the Law Department. This was the appointment of the Honorable George Robertson, Chief Justice of the Kentucky Court of Appeals, the state's highest court. He was considered to be one of the ablest men to occupy that post. Born near Harrodsburg, Kentucky, in 1790 of parents newly-immigrated from Virginia, he had an elementary education in the area and spent some time in Joshua Fry's school near Danville. After spending a year at Transylvania University, he studied law privately in Frankfort and received his license to practice in 1809. He served in the United States Congress from 1817–21, and later in the Kentucky House between 1822–26,

[11]*Ibid.*, August 4, 1831.
[12]*Ibid.*, June 15, 1831.

occupying the position of Speaker most of the time. He was very much interested in the establishment of a common school system in Kentucky. He fought for the Old Court during that struggle and was appointed to the Court of Appeals in 1828 and Chief Justice in 1829, a post he held until he resigned in 1843. He served as law professor at Transylvania from 1834–57, and once again accepted a position on the Court of Appeals in 1864 until ill health and blindness forced him to resign in 1871.

George Robertson

At the time it was said of him that he was the only American state judge whose opinions had been quoted in the House of Lords. Robertson was a vigorous and inspiring teacher. Known as "Old Buster" in his latter years, this big-boned, stout man had added a hundred pounds to his slender five foot ten-inch frame after he married.[13] He met Abraham Lincoln through Robert Todd, his client and Lincoln's father-in-law, and in the 1850's conducted some litigation for Lincoln in Lexington. Robertson had a firm grasp of principles which made him a good teacher. His son wrote:

> It was by teaching that Judge Robertson refreshed and constantly extended his analytical apprehension of the law. He taught

[13] J. Winston Coleman Jr., "Lincoln and 'Old Buster,' " *The Lincoln Herald*, XLVI, No. 1 (February, 1944), pp. 5–11.

because he loved to teach, and because teaching was one of the best modes of learning. . . . He cheerfully gave his students the use of his library. . . . His mode of instruction was by oral examination and comments upon the text.

Unlike some of his predecessors on the faculty, he was a formidable critic of the Virginia and Kentucky Resolutions, and in 1852 his address to the graduating class was judged by one student to have been the "Most logical, the most unanswerable argument against these Resolutions ever delivered."[14]

In 1837 a third lawyer joined the law faculty. This was Thomas A. Marshall, an associate justice on the Kentucky Court of Appeals. The Transylvania Law Department now consisting of three men was as large as any in the country. Charles Kerr, in his thorough if somewhat over-enthusiastic history of the Law Department, states:

that not withstanding the handicaps encountered by Transylvania because of its remoteness from the more populous centers, with only the elements composing a pioneer population from which to draw support, for nearly half a century it led all its contemporaries.[15]

There is no denying that, from the beginning appointment of George Nicholas, the Law Department established a remarkably fine record in the quality of legal minds it attracted to its faculty.

In the spring of 1835, the Law Department submitted to the trustees a more formal plan of organization. This plan provided for three professorships: one in Civil Law, the Law of Nature and of Nations, and Constitutional Law and Equity; a second in the various branches of the common and statute law; and a third in Pleading and Evidence. Two sessions a year were provided for, and the mode of instruction and textbooks were to be left up to the discretion of the professors. Requirements for the law degree specified attendance at two sessions, or one session if the student had been engaged in the practice of law for two years.

[14]George Robertson, *An Outline of the Life of George Robertson, Written By Himself, With an Introduction and Appendix by His Son* (Lexington, 1876).

[15]Charles Kerr, "Transylvania University's Law Department," *Americana*, XXXI, No. 1 (January, 1937), p. 20.

When Mayes resigned in July 1838, Judge Aaron K. Woolley replaced him. Woolley had earned a reputation as a capable interpreter of the common law, and was especially noted for his conversational and argumentative powers. Madison C. Johnson, another addition to the faculty, had graduated at the head of his class in 1823 at the height of the Holley administration. He studied law privately and by his thoroughness and accuracy became one of the most respected members of the Kentucky bar. Not politically ambitious, he seems to have confined his activities to an admiring Lexington clientele.

In 1839 the Law Department was singled out by Lexington to receive $5,000 for the purchase of an adequate law library. A committee appointed by the trustees to recommend how the funds should be disbursed reported that the principal portion of the funds be used to buy a complete common law library, a complete set of English reports — both common law and chancery, reports of the Supreme Court of the United States and of the principal state courts, and after that the "latest editions of the most valuable treatises both English and American." Woolley was appointed purchasing agent. Students who studied in the Law Department after this purchase had one of the finest law libraries in the country at their disposal.[16]

In the decade of the thirties, law classes ranged from twenty to over fifty students, and the number of graduates averaged about ten each year. As was the case with the Medical Department, so the Transylvania Law Department was one of the chief centers for professional training in the trans-Allegheny region. Hundreds of its graduates became able attorneys and legislators throughout this region. One of its most famous graduates was John Harlan of the class of 1852, appointed by President Hayes as an Associate Justice on the U.S. Supreme Court. He developed into one of the strong liberal nationalists by the end of the century, serving until 1911, a phenomenal term of some thirty-four years. In 1908 he revisited his alma mater to deliver an address in Morrison College. His remarks on the old Transylvania Law Department, mellowed with the years, provide a fitting concluding commentary on that department.

[16]*Lexington Intelligencer*, March 15, 1839.

I remember, when here, of sitting at the feet of some of the greatest judges and lawyers that ever appeared in this country. George Robertson, Thomas A. Marshall, A. K. Woolley, and Madison C. Johnson were the professors or teachers in the law school when I had the honor to be a member of it, and I undertake to say that no law school that has ever existed in this country . . . has had at the same time as professors and teachers of the science of law four greater lawyers. . . . If George Robertson and Thomas A. Marshall had been placed upon the bench of the Supreme Court of the United States in their early years, they would have left a reputation as great as that of Chief Justice Marshall. No greater lawyer, in the largest sense of the word, ever lived in this country, in my judgment, than Madison C. Johnson. He deserves to be ranked by the side of Daniel Webster, Rufus Choate and lawyers of that kind.[17]

[17] Quoted in Ernest W. Delcamp, "Transylvania, the Pioneer College of the Western Wilderness," *Kentucky Progress Magazine*, Vol. II, No. 8 (April, 1930), p. 17.

9

The Crisis in the Medical Department

Thomas Coit   *Robert Davidson*

In the years following Peers' departure, there were long stretches when the University operated under acting presidents. For example, between February 1834, and June 1, 1842, there were only two formally elected presidents: Thomas Coit, who served from July 1835 to September 1837, and Robert Davidson, who served from June 1840 to June 1842. Both these men were ministers, the former an Episcopalian, the latter a Presbyterian. Both men approached their new duties with hope and zeal, but neither of them successfully changed the moribund condition of the Academic Department. Fortunately for Transylvania, the Medical Department maintained its high reputation and large enrollment and the Law Department was moving into the greatest years of its existence. The president, however, was not deeply involved with these departments, nor could he derive much comfort from their prosperity. His primary responsibility was the Academic Department — collegiate and preparatory. If that department did not succeed, neither did he. The president was not only responsible for supervising the teaching in these areas but was himself usually one-third or one-fourth of the faculty. He had to be both an able administrator and teacher.

In their inaugural addresses — those ceremonial barometers of the new president's educational pressure system — both Coit and Davidson indicated a reversal from the innovative proposals of Peers. Such reforms as Peers had proposed had attracted neither the trustees' approval, substantial community support nor new private gifts. They certainly had not secured the approval of the State legislature. Coit, like Holley a native of Connecticut and a graduate of Yale, had taken additional theological training at Andover Theological Seminary and Princeton Theological Seminary. From 1829 to 1835 he was rector of Christ Church in Cambridge, Massachusetts, when he was called to be president of Transylvania at a salary of $2,000. Coit's inaugural address delivered on November 6, 1835, deplored the new theories of education then current and called for a return to the traditional modes. The only novel thing about his plea to restore the old ways was his recognition of the growing tension between science and religion as the former assumed a greater influence in education. In this pre-Darwinian age, Coit was able to say to this audience without seriously endangering his position that more knowledge should not separate man from God. Science, he thought,

> should be but a new tie, to bind us to the great Centre of Creation, the throne of the universal intelligence and love. Science and religion are allies, not aliens. Nay, religion is itself a science, offering wider scope, busier occupation, and intenser pleasure, than any other system which bears this reverend name.[1]

Robert Davidson, son of President Davidson of Dickinson College, was born in Carlisle, Pennsylvania, in 1808 and graduated from Princeton. Unlike his fellow Princetonians and predecessors Peers and Coit, Davidson remained true to his Presbyterian training and did not become an Episcopalian. He assumed the post of pastor of the Second Presbyterian Church in Lexington in 1832 where he served until his election as president of Transylvania in 1840. Coming to office shortly after a major effort of the Lexington community to revive the school, he was impressed by the fact that everything was new — the trustees, teachers, laws, funds, and buildings. Conscious of the rivalry of denominational institutions, especially of the Presbyterian Centre College, he nevertheless saw no reason why Transylvania should not flourish in a new decade of prosperity. Like Coit he noted the educational reform mania, the desire for

---

[1] Thomas W. Coit, *An Inaugural Address Delivered in the Chapel of Morrison College, November 6, 1835.* (Lexington, 1835), p. 18.

practical education, and the criticism of traditional classical education. He believed the mania was now largely dissipated, though there still remained, he feared, a lingering suspicion among many of the public of the "college-bred." The wisdom of traditional curriculum and method was now apparent. There was too little veneration for antiquity in this age, he affirmed.[2]

However, any hope Davidson may have had that his conservative Presbyterian image would bring Presbyterian boys back to Transylvania was soon destroyed. In the last year of his administration enrollment in the Medical Department was 271, in the Law Department 70, in the preparatory school 70, but in Morrison College (the formal designation of the Academic Department) only 28. Davidson commented on his brief stay as he noted that

> this experiment succeeded no better than the former ones. So numerous and vexatious were the embarrassments by which the new President speedily found himself surrounded, that after a vigorous, but ineffectual struggle, he resigned in March, 1842.[3]

THE MOST DRAMATIC EVENT in this decade of the 1830's was the split in the Medical Department, the most serious challenge to its prosperity since its establishment and a frightening omen of the ultimate fate of that branch of the University. The main source of the difficulty was Louisville: the rapid growth of that city since 1818 because of its strategic location on the Ohio River, its accessibility to more students, the availability of a growing hospital, the prospects of a better opportunity for clinical study, the seldom-mentioned supply of cadavers for anatomical study — all were important considerations for a leading medical training center in the West. They were serious issues, needing a cool and impartial investigation and balanced judgment. Instead, the whole affair, centering around the proposal that Transylvania's Medical Department move to Louisville, exploded in an emotional cloudburst which matched in intensity the virulent sectarian controversies of the previous decade.

[2] Robert Davidson, *A Vindication of Colleges and College Endowments. An Inaugural Address Delivered in the Chapel of Morrison College November 2, 1840.* (Lexington, 1841), *passim.*

[3] Davidson, *A History of the Presbyterian Church in Kentucky*, p. 319.

Apparently the subject of a possible removal of the Medical Department to Louisville had been broached in a meeting of the medical faculty some time in 1836 by no less distinguished a member than Benjamin Dudley. He evidently intended the suggestion to be a trial balloon, but the matter got out of hand when half the faculty decided that it was a good idea and recommended action. Dudley backtracked and began to oppose such action, supported by the other half of the faculty, and trouble began. Rumors and counter-rumors spread insidiously, nor did the fact that there was a strong movement in Louisville to establish a medical school there help. Lexingtonians, who regarded the Medical Department as their community's pride and joy, assumed that a dark conspiracy existed to deprive them of it.[4]

As far back as 1833 when the legislature approved a charter establishing a medical institute in Louisville, Dr. Caldwell had published a pamphlet entitled *Thoughts on the Impolicy of Multiplying Schools of Medicine* in which he denounced the move as a threat to quality medical education. The sticky issue seems to have been over the question of whether Transylvania trustees could approve the wholesale physical transfer of the Medical Department to Louisville while maintaining legal control over it. The advantages of being located in Louisville were apparent to the entire medical faculty, but when it became obvious that the trustees had no intention of condoning such a project, and that the Lexington community would fight tooth and nail to prevent it, Dudley and his supporters surrendered possible professional advantages to their loyalty to Transylvania. Unfortunately, other members of the medical faculty were not content to follow their lead and began to take secretive steps to transfer to Louisville.

In January 1837, Dudley asked the Board to investigate the matter, which they refused to do until the end of the current session for fear of disrupting classes. Shortly after commencement in March, the investigation was held. Dudley formally charged that

Caldwell and Yandell have been jointly and severally guilty of

[4]Minutes of the Board, March 15, 1837.

> treacherous & faithless conduct towards Transylvania University
> . . . [having] secretly conspired & personally urged the removal
> of the Medical Department from Lexington & Transylvania Uni-
> versity. They studiously endeavored by artful & improper means
> to conceal the whole plot . . . for many months past until it might
> be too late for you successfully to counteract it.[5]

Dudley further accused these men of writing and publishing li-
belous statements against himself and Richardson because they
stood fast for Transylvania. Dr. Lunsford P. Yandell, professor
of chemistry in the Medical Department, was the only accused
who appeared before the Board since Caldwell was in Louisville on a speaking engagement (in support of the new Louis--
ville Medical School as it turned out), and Cooke was indis-
posed. Yandell claimed that Dudley had on several occasions
criticized the lack of facilities at Lexington and had, indeed,
been the first to suggest a move to Louisville. The trustees,
confronted with a series of charges and counter-charges and an
almost evenly divided faculty, dismissed the entire staff. The
Louisville City Council seized the opportunity presented by
this investigation to act quickly and establish the proposed
medical school. They purchased a site and appropriated
$30,000 for a building. Invitations were extended to the dis-
missed faculty in Lexington, and three of them — Caldwell,
Yandell and Cooke — accepted, forming the core of the faculty
of the new Louisville Medical Institute which opened its doors
in October 1837. Caldwell had apparently changed his mind
about the undesirability of multiplying medical schools.

Establishment of the Louisville school did not, at first,
seriously affect Transylvania. Enrollment dropped only fifteen
in the 1837–38 session, and in the four or five years thereafter
reached record numbers, the highest being 271 in the 1841–42
session. Dudley, Richardson and Short accepted renewed appointments at Transylvania, but the trustees were now faced
with the difficult job of replacing the other men. They tried, but
failed, to secure the services of Benjamin Silliman of Yale for
the chemistry chair, but were more successful raiding the faculty of the Medical College at Cincinnati for three of its
members, James C. Cross, John Eberle and Thomas Mitchell,

[5]*Ibid.*, March 23, 1837.

who filled the chairs of the institutes of medicine and physiology, theory and practice of medicine, and obstetrics respectively. The success of that raid was convincing proof of Transylvania Medical Department's prestige. A fourth member, James Bush, was appointed adjunct professor to Dudley in surgery and anatomy. Bush was an 1833 graduate of the Transylvania Medical Department, a protégé of Dudley's, and a very competent demonstrator in anatomy and surgery who would ably fill his master's shoes when he retired.

The four new faculty members brought energy and ability to the department, though Cross, whose appointment had been only half-heartedly approved, was to prove to be a detriment. The biggest loss to the faculty was suffered a year later when Charles Wilkins Short left for Louisville. Short, a native of Woodford county, Kentucky, had joined the medical staff in 1825 as professor of materia medica and medical botany. "He was a most zealous and industrious botanist, and was possessed of artistic tastes and ability," wrote a colleague. Short wrote numerous articles for the *Transylvania Journal of Medicine* on botanical subjects and other medical topics. He bequeathed his large botanical collection to the Smithsonian Institution, but as there was no appropriate place to display so large a collection there, it was moved to the Academy of Natural Sciences in Philadelphia.[6]

With Short's departure Dr. Mitchell moved into his chair and Robert Peter filled the chair of chemistry. Peter was to become more closely identified with Transylvania in terms of duration, loyalty and service than any other single individual. Born in Cornwall, England, in 1805, young Robert with his family migrated to the United States in 1817, finally settling in Pittsburgh. His work in an apothecary shop generated an intense and life-long devotion to natural science, especially chemistry. He attended the new Rensselaer School in Troy, New York, where he studied under Amos Eaton, the botanist and geologist, who emphasized the practical aspects of science and instituted the famed Rensselaer technique of allowing students to do some of the teaching. Peter returned to Pittsburgh, set up

[6]Peter, *The History of the Medical Department*, p. 79.

his own apothecary shop and promoted scientific interests in the community by public lectures and the organization and support of scientific societies.[7]

In the summer of 1832 Peter moved to Lexington at the invitation of Benjamin O. Peers, whom he met at Rensselaer, to teach chemistry at the Eclectic Institute. He became Yandell's chemical assistant at Transylvania, attended sessions at the Medical Department, and received his M.D. in 1834. He helped Yandell during the cholera plague, but generally finding medical practice unappealing, he devoted his life to chemistry and related fields. He was an able and amazingly industrious man, a lively and effective teacher, instructing classes in Morrison College as early as 1833 and then assuming the more prestigious position with the medical faculty in 1838. Remaining in this position until the Medical Department closed its doors in 1859, he continued to teach chemistry in the Academic Department until 1878 when he joined the staff of the new Agricultural and Mechanical College of Kentucky. Between 1854–60 he was very active as the chemical assistant to the first Kentucky Geological Survey, performing an incredible number of soil analyses to assist farmers, mineralogists and geologists in their study of Kentucky soils. These analyses were a major contribution to the developing field of soil study and the complicated problem of soil fertility. In his later years he devoted much of his time to historical research and writing, publishing the first history of Transylvania entitled, rather gloomily, *Transylvania University: Its Origin, Rise, Decline, and Fall*, which traces the history of the institution up to the Civil War. He also wrote a history of the Medical Department before he died in 1894 at the age of 90.

THERE WAS ONE FINAL major event in the life of Transylvania in the 1830's prior to assumption of control by the Methodists. It was the remarkable effort by the Lexington community to revive and sustain the institution. Letters to the press had been urging the community to rouse itself and launch a crusade to strengthen the school. By 1839 the worst of the 1837 depres-

[7]John D. Wright, Jr., "Robert Peter and Early Science in Kentucky," an unpublished doctoral dissertation, Columbia University, 1955. Chapter 1.

sion had passed and money was becoming available for investment in such worthwhile enterprises as education. In September 1838, there was a meeting of the friends of Morrison
College at the Phoenix Hotel. Among the eleven men present
were General Leslie Combs, one of Lexington's leading citizens; Henry Clay, Jr., who was following in his father's footsteps as a loyal supporter of Transylvania; Dr. Benjamin Dudley, and Dr. Robert Peter. They drew up a plan for a society to
be called The Transylvania Institute of "One Hundred Gentlemen Citizens of Kentucky and Graduates of Transylvania University" to pledge $100 a year for five years for the support of
Morrison College and other literary and charitable institutions.[8]

Founders of the Institute emphasized the need for a permanent endowment to replace the traditional dependence on outstanding personalities of president and faculty to secure funds
and students. Henry Clay was elected president and a series of
lectures was sponsored during the winter to publicize the Institute. Among the donors were Henry Clay, Cassius Clay, Benjamin Dudley, Benjamin Gratz, Madison C. Johnson, William
Leavy and Robert Peter.

Thanks to the activity of Robert Wickliffe, Jr., a lawyer and
graduate of Transylvania, the Kentucky legislature incorporated the Transylvania Institute in February 1839, and changed
the government of Transylvania University by reducing the
number of trustees to eight — two to be appointed by the Institute, three by the City of Lexington, and three by the State. A
Board of twelve overseers was also appointed by the governor
to exercise a watchdog responsibility.[9]

The following spring the Lexington City Council, inspired
and challenged by the action of the Transylvania Institute, appropriated $70,000 to Transylvania. It was donated primarily
for the purpose of enlarging the physical facilities — books,
buildings and apparatus — of all three departments. The City
Council specified that $20,000 should go to Morrison College,
$5,000 to the Law Department for books, and $45,000 to the

[8] Peter, *Transylvania University*, pp. 164–165.

[9] "An Act to incorporate the Transylvania Institute, and for other purposes. Approved February 20, 1839." *Acts of the General Assembly of the
Commonwealth of Kentucky*, December Session, 1838.

Medical Department. Giving the lion's share to the Medical Department was Lexington's answer to the challenge and competition from Louisville. The trustees divided the $45,000 into two parts: $30,000 for a new medical building, and $15,000 for additional books and apparatus.[10]

1846–47 matriculation and library ticket,
showing the new medical building at Second & Broadway

The medical faculty immediately went to work drawing up plans for a new medical building to be located on the northwest corner of Second Street and North Broadway on a site purchased by the faculty itself. The cornerstone was laid in July 1839, in a ceremony highlighted by a speech by Robert Wickliffe, Jr., in which he emphasized the advantages of the location and facilities. The building, completed in 1840, contained three large lecture-rooms, a library, museum, five dissecting rooms, and a private office for each instructor. Into this new building was moved the fine medical library and apparatus accumulated by sizeable purchases here and abroad. No wonder the faculty

[10]*Lexington Intelligencer*, March 15, 1839.

felt justified in proclaiming that "nothing is wanting to make a perfect Medical College."[11]

Meanwhile the faculty sent Bush and Peter to Philadelphia on the first leg of a trip to Europe in the spring of 1839 to purchase $10,000 worth of medical books and apparatus. About half of this was spent purchasing books in Europe that were difficult to obtain at home, and the remaining funds on apparatus impossible to secure in America. Among the books purchased were the works of Buffon, Burton, Cuvier, Lyell, Liebig and Boyle. Apparatus purchased included not only the familiar skeletons, but also a number of so-called "livraisons" secured from Felix Thibert in Paris. These are casts of various types of diseased organs, each framed and identified on the side of the frame similar to a book's title. These frames could be hung on the wall, or placed side by side, presenting the appearance of a set of books. Some forty large drawings of medicinal plants were also purchased. The two doctors bought from Deleuil in Paris some large and impressive pieces of demonstration apparatus to produce those dramatic exhibitions of the basic laws of physics which impressed students. These included such items as an air pump with glass cylinders, a baroscope with a bell-glass, hygrometer to measure atmospheric humidity, magnetic-electricity machine, and a model of Watt's engine with glass cylinders.[12]

But of all the pieces purchased, none produced more interest than a camera. In 1839, the same year Bush and Peter were in Europe, Louis Daguerre had perfected his early photographic process. The two Transylvanians were delighted to bring this brand new invention back to Kentucky. The camera purchased, however, was apparently a Fox Talbot camera, very similar to Daguerre's and one of a number being developed at the time.[13]

The new building and the addition of more books and equipment, all of which were well publicized, acted as an effective drawing power, and enrollment in the Medical Department reached record heights. It seemed that Lexington had saved the

[11]Thomas D. Mitchell, "Valedictory Address," *Annual Announcement of the Medical Department of Transylvania University, 1840*.

[12]John D. Wright, Jr., "Robert Peter," pp. 126–132.

[13]Leland A. Brown, *Early Philosophical Apparatus at Transylvania*. (Lexington, 1959).

Fox Talbot camera and medical apparatus

school from its Louisville competitors, and for another decade medical instruction flourished here.

There was no denying the incomparable quality of the library and equipment of the Transylvania Medical Department. Dr. Nathan Smith, in his letter of resignation from the medical faculty in 1841, called the department the "best endowed medical school in America." William Norwood in his *Medical Education in the United States Before the Civil War* evaluated Transylvania's Medical Department as one that was unusually well-endowed, and its library as "one of the best in the country." In his *Autobiography*, Charles Caldwell, who bore no love for Transylvania after the 1837 controversy, nevertheless admitted the medical library had a "marked and decided superiority . . . in these works, to any other in the West and South, and probably the whole United States — not excepting that of Philadelphia, the parent school of medicine in the Union."[14]

[14]Norwood, *Medical Education*, pp. 292–294; Charles Caldwell, *Autobiography* (Philadelphia, 1855), p. 392; Albert Buck, *The Dawn of Medicine* (New Haven, 1920). Dr. Buck wrote that "the preservation of the unique medical library at Transylvania College, containing several hundred books which have been out of print more than a hundred years and cannot be duplicated in the libraries of Europe or America, cannot be too strongly urged. . . . There are scores of books in the Transylvania library not to be found in the libraries of the Academy of Medicine, New York, or of the Surgeon-General of the United States. . . . This splendid collection was carefully chosen for the most part in Paris and London, at a time when there was a great awakening of scientific men to the history of medicine.

Such resources continued to attract outstanding men to the medical faculty during the 1840's. Among these was Elisha Bartlett, one of the most distinguished teachers the school ever had. He taught the theory and practice of medicine at Transylvania from 1841–43 and again from 1846–48. Dr. William Osler wrote a delightful biographical essay on Bartlett, delivered originally as an address before the Rhode Island Medical Society in 1899, in which he said that in Elisha Bartlett "teacher, philosopher, author . . . you may claim as the most distinguished physician of this state." Bartlett was born in Rhode Island in 1804, studied at the medical department of Brown University shortly before that department closed, and continued his study abroad in Paris and London. Upon his return he settled for nearly 20 years in Lowell, Massachusetts, where he became not only the best-known physician of that city but its first mayor. Next to Daniel Drake, Osler believed Bartlett to be one of the most-traveled medical teachers of that day, having taught in nine schools. Such a schedule was possible because of the short four months' sessions and the theoretical content of the courses.[15]

Soon after his arrival in Lexington Bartlett described some phases of medical education at Transylvania:

> In the school we are getting on very well. The class is of good size, rather larger than last year, worth a little over $2,000, intelligent, attentive, well-behaved. I have given fifty-eight lectures, and we have just six weeks more. My own success has been good enough, I think. . . . My colleague Dudley, you know, is a great man here. . . . He teaches singular doctrines, and follows in many things, a practice very peculiar to himself. . . . Richardson, in obstetrics, boards with me, a plain common-sense man, who fought a duel in early life with Dudley. . . . The style of lecturing here is quite different from what it is in the East — more emphatic, more vehement. It is quite necessary to fall somewhat into the popular style.[16]

At about the same time Bartlett arrived at Transylvania, Crawford W. Long, a former medical student of the institution, made the pioneer effort in the use of ether as anesthesia in an

---

[15]William Osler, *An Alabama Student and Other Biographical Essays* (London, 1908), p. 108.
[16]*Ibid.*, pp. 120–121.

operation performed on March 30, 1842. Four years later the Boston dentist William Morton used ether in cooperation with Dr. John Warren of the Massachusetts General Hospital. Only later, in a welter of claims and counter-claims, was Long's priority recognized. It was testimony to the lack of effective communication in the medical profession of that day that each of these men had no knowledge of the other's works.

The Medical Department flourished during the 1840's, as did the growing Law Department under the able leadership of George Robertson. There was every expectation that the Academic Department would follow suit. New president Robert Davidson had said as much. But after two years of his administration only marginal progress was made, and he resigned a bitter and frustrated man. The trustees, noting the obvious success of denominational competitors at Centre, Georgetown and Augusta — the Presbyterians, Baptists and Methodists respectively — and despairing of ever again receiving state support (despite the pleas of Kentucky governors in their annual messages to the legislature) decided to embark upon a new experiment. If Morrison College could not succeed as a non-denominational state institution, then perhaps a formal denominational affiliation was the only answer.

10

*The Methodists
Take Their Turn*

Henry B. Bascom

At the September Board meeting in 1841, the trustees passed a resolution which offered to the Methodist Episcopal Church of Kentucky the control of Transylvania University "so far as the nomination of the Faculty in the college proper & the preparatory department together with the direction of the course of studies and internal government of the College is concerned. . . ."[1] Thus came to an end the long struggle of Transylvania to remain unattached to any single denomination. It was a poignant confession of failure to persuade the Kentucky legislature and the Kentucky constituency it represented that Transylvania was their school, a state, public, non-denominational institution.

The trustees reported to the legislature in January 1842 the present status of the school and the reasons why control had been offered to the Methodists. While the Medical Department had 271 students and 7 professors and the Law Department had 70 students and 3 professors, the faculty of the Academic Department (Morrison College) consisted of the president and two professors with a student enrollment of 25 of which only 8 were paying students. There were 68 in the preparatory department of which only 17 were paying students. The non-paying students came under the arrangement with the Transylvania Institute to allow shareholders to enroll one student free.

The trustees claimed that low enrollment in Morrison College was not due to a failure to exert themselves, but was caused by

---

[1] Minutes of the Board, September 21, 1841.

the success of competing denominational colleges in Kentucky and the lack of interest in the state university. They listed Transylvania's assets as $70,000 worth of buildings and grounds, and another $70,000 of productive funds for the Academic Department from which they were currently deriving $3,800 interest. All other sources of income, including $440 in tuition fees, brought the annual income of the Academic Department to $5,220. With expenditures of $6,222, including the $2,000 salary for the president and $2,400 for two professors, the annual deficit amounted to about $1,000.[2]

The trustees stated that, unless the state legislature exhibited some interest in the school and aroused public zeal for its future welfare, the school would either have to close or surrender itself to denominational control. In line with the second alternative, the trustees sought legislative approval to offer the control of Transylvania University to the Methodists. President Davidson made a vigorous stand against this action. He claimed that to allow the Methodists to assume control of the University was a breach of faith on the part of the trustees in not giving him more time to reinvigorate the University, a breach of faith with the contributing members of the Transylvania Institute, many of whom belonged to different sects, a breach of faith with the state that had supported the school in the past on the grounds of its non-sectarian character. To submit to the control of one religious sect, Davidson asserted, would drive off support from other sects. Besides, the Methodists already had a college in Augusta, Kentucky. Davidson's arguments might have been more convincing had they not had the appearance of special pleading on the part of a Presbyterian.[3]

There is no record revealing the reasons why the trustees offered the Methodist Church the control of Morrison College, the Academic Department of Transylvania University. The special situation of that church at this time may provide a clue. Early attempts of the Methodist Episcopal Church to establish colleges in the East, such as Cokesbury in Maryland in 1787, had failed so consistently that Bishop Asbury was convinced

[2]"Report of the Joint Committee Appointed to Examine Into the Condition of Transylvania University, January, 1842," *Kentucky Documents*, 1841–1842. (Frankfort, 1842).
[3]*Ibid.*

God had not intended the Methodist Church to involve itself in higher education. In 1820, however, the General Conference decided to try again, and recommended that the various state conferences support new colleges. The next twenty years proved to be extraordinarily fruitful for this endeavor.

The Ohio and Kentucky Methodist Conferences joined together to establish one of the first Methodist colleges at Augusta, Kentucky, in 1822, although classes did not start there until 1825. Despite a promising beginning, Augusta College by 1841 was becoming the victim of the growing split between the slavery and anti-slavery forces within the Methodist Church. In the early 1840's the Kentucky Conference withdrew its support from Augusta College and was therefore in the market for another institution to support. The trustees of Transylvania University were doubtless aware of this situation and offered the school to the Kentucky Conference, which accepted.[4] Henry B. Bascom, professor of moral science and belles lettres at Augusta, was appointed president of Transylvania, and he brought along a number of the college faculty. This blow, on top of the decision of the Kentucky Conference to withdraw support, led to the rapid decline of Augusta College and the end of its brief career in 1849.

WITH THE ARRIVAL of Henry Bidleman Bascom at Transylvania in the fall of 1842, there appeared one of the most capable and vigorous presidents of the University between Holley's departure and the Civil War. He was a ruggedly handsome man, well-built with a commanding presence. There is a determined, bulldog quality in the face in his portrait, with its heavy, square-set face, dark and piercing eyes, thin, firmly-set mouth, and strong chin.

Born in southern New York state in 1796 in a farming family, he had little more than five years of formal schooling.[5] His family moved to Kentucky in 1812, by which time young Henry

---

[4] William Warren Sweet, *Methodism in American History* (New York, 1954); *The History of American Methodism* (New York, 1964), Vol. II; Walter H. Rankins, *Augusta College* (Frankfort, 1957).

[5] Reverend Moses M. Henkle, *The Life of Henry Bidleman Bascom* (Nashville, 1854).

An 1850 magazine view of Lexington from Old Morrison

had undergone a rather intense conversion to Methodism at the age of fourteen, leading to his commitment to the Methodist ministry. He was passionately fond of reading and writing, so that a lifetime of continuing self-education developed a rich resource of knowledge on which he constantly drew in his sermons. He was licensed to preach in 1813 and for the next fourteen years he moved through the Kentucky, Ohio and Tennessee Conferences, being consistently assigned the most primitive and difficult circuits in these areas. The Reverend M. M. Henkle, in his eulogistic biography of Bascom written shortly after Bascom's death, criticized hide-bound Methodist ministers in the various state conferences for being jealous of Bascom's attractive person, his fastidious dress, his worldly air. Bascom was as devout and orthodox as any of them but gifted with a style and voice few of them possessed. Their chief complaint seemed to have been that Bascom did not have the appearance of a Methodist preacher. If they hoped to break Bascom's dedication to the ministry by the arduous circuit assignments, they had mistaken their man. Though his occasional diary accounts of circuit-riding vividly describe conditions which might even have disheartened Saint Paul, Bascom stuck doggedly to his task. Gradually the fame of his oratorical ability spread throughout the Midwest. Henry Clay heard him and was so impressed that he managed to have him appointed chaplain to Congress in 1823. Unfortunately the short limits placed on his speaking apparently unnerved Bascom who was used to warming up in one or two-hour sermons, and he left a poor impression.[6]

He had spoken in Baltimore, Annapolis, New York, and some Pennsylvania cities, all of which reported in glowing terms of his torrential eloquence. By the mid-1820's Bascom was becoming recognized as one of the promising young men in the Methodist Church. He was appointed president of a new Methodist college named after President Madison and located in Uniontown, Pennsylvania. His inaugural address is of some interest since it doubtless reflects opinions he brought with him to the presidency of Transylvania, and exemplifies his rather florid oratorical style. According to Henkle, half of Bascom's magic was in the delivery, so his gestures, commanding presence and thunderous voice must be added to:

> Man is, perhaps, the most singularly constituted being in the high scale of heaven's mysterious workmanship. . . . Man seems to unite in himself the diversities of created nature, and stands forth, not unaptly, to the contemplation of intelligence, as an epitome of being; an abridgment of the universe. . . . As a solitary or a social being, man must be partially wretched, if devoid of proper instruction; but if possessed of the advantages of education, nothing but an evil, an upbraiding conscience, can make him miserable. In the city or the desert; in a palace or a cottage; in robes or in rags; standing on land, or rolling on the ocean; buried amid the snows of Iceland or burning beneath the fervors of the torrid zone; he has resources of which he can be deprived only by the Power that conferred them. Beggared by misfortune, exiled by friends; abjured by society, and deprived of its solace, the interior of the intellectual structure continues unaffected and underanged amid the accumulating wretchedness without.[7]

Bascom's efforts to make a success of Madison College, even introducing such innovations as a professor of agriculture, were to no avail. The familiar fates of non-support and financial penury led him to resign in 1829. He immediately took a posi-

[6]Henkle, *Bascom*, p. 139.
[7]*Ibid.*, p. 185.

tion as agent for the American Colonization Society. This was in keeping with Bascom's conservative views on slavery which had developed rather early in his career and which he never significantly modified. He was not a strong pro-slavery apologist, but he never sympathized with the strong anti-slavery element in the Methodist Church. That is why plans of the American Colonization Society to transfer the problem to Africa appealed to him. He pointed out in his many speeches for the society that the colonization scheme was not only important as a safety valve for the slavery crisis in America but an essential contribution to "the redemption of Africa from her present political and religious degradation and suffering."[8]

Accepting an appointment to the faculty of Augusta College in 1832 and then assuming the presidency of Transylvania, Bascom extended his nationwide reputation as an eloquent speaker and retained his position in the American Colonization Society. Playing an increasingly significant role at the General Conferences on committees wrestling with the intransigent problem of slavery — his voice consistently raised against church involvement in the issue — he defended his southern colleagues in their struggle against the rising tide of abolitionism.

The years from 1842 to 1849 when Bascom occupied the presidency of Transylvania were extremely busy ones for him. First of all, he had to devote his energies to the revitalization of Morrison College. He was remarkably successful in attracting large numbers of students, due primarily to the denominational ties and the use of Methodist churches as recruiting sources for the college. This had proved an effective method for the Catholics, Presbyterians and Baptists, and it now worked for the Methodists. Within a year the student enrollment jumped to 278 in contrast to Davidson's 28. In that same term, 1843–44, the Medical Department enrolled 214 and the Law Department 60. This brought the total enrollment at Transylvania to 552, far exceeding even the peak of the Holley administration. Most students attending Morrison College were from Kentucky, but there was a growing number from southern states. Southern Methodists did not have to fear their children would be infected

[8]*Ibid.*, p. 221.

with undesirable abolitionist sentiments as long as Bascom headed the institution.

The large enrollment justified enlarging the faculty and expanding the curriculum. Bascom carried on the tradition of the college president in teaching intellectual and moral philosophy. Ancient languages and classical literature were, of course, still taught as the essential basis for the educated man, but in addition modern languages and literature were now offered. The latter were taught in the late 1840's by H. Sauveur Bonfils. This was the name printed in the *Lexington Observer & Reporter*, but later accounts of the man call him St. Sauveur Francois Bonfils. From what little we know of him, he was a Corsican who left France during the French Revolution. As did many émigrés he made his living teaching French and French literature. He was teaching at Transylvania when he died in 1849 of cholera, again epidemic in this country, and was buried in the old Episcopal burying-ground on East Third Street.[9]

In addition to the new subjects in modern language and literature, some advances were being made at this time in teaching the sciences, and Transylvania was fortunate in having scientist Robert Peter on its faculty. He not only was well-read in the latest scientific literature, he was as interested in involving the students in laboratory exercises as he was in holding their attention to the theories explained in his lectures. As a member of the medical faculty, Peter was able to use the chemical apparatus from the Medical Department to teach liberal arts undergraduates.

The cost of education still remained amazingly low. The newspaper advertisement claimed that a student could attend a twenty-one week session at Transylvania University for around $100, which included $20 tuition and $52.50 for room and board with a private family.

IN ADDITION TO his daily duties as president and teacher, Bascom found the slavery issue was increasingly absorbing his time and energy. Transylvania was one of many campuses affected by this divisive and heated issue. Hofstadter and

[9] In May, 1939, he was disinterred and placed in the Transylvania crypt in Old Morrison along side of Rafinesque's body which had been brought back from Philadelphia some years before.

Metzger note that in the period 1830–60 "the slavery controversy caused more commotion and more proscriptions on college campuses than any other issue."[10] It soon became impossible to openly discuss slavery on southern campuses without reactions. In border state Kentucky, however, there was wider latitude for differences of opinion. Slavery was unpopular in some of the mountainous areas. Berea College was founded on anti-slavery principles, though its history in early years was a hectic one. At Presbyterian Centre College, but a few miles south of Transylvania, President John C. Young managed to ride out the storm, although he advocated gradual emancipation and introduced a clause in the proposed new state constitution of 1849 providing for gradual emancipation. However, James C. Birney, an abolitionist professor on the same campus, was forced to leave. At nearby Baptist Georgetown College, President Howard Malcolm resigned in the face of growing criticism for having voted for an emancipation candidate to the constitutional convention.[11]

That such incidents were not unusual is substantiated by Clement Eaton in his *Freedom of Thought in the Old South* when he noted that

> a powerful movement developed to sterilize the Southern colleges from antislavery ideas. Not only were attempts made to expurgate dangerous ideas from textbooks used both in colleges and schools, not only was an extensive campaign launched to dissuade wealthy Southerners from sending their sons to Northern colleges, but also a definite effort was made to establish colleges that would be free from the radical teachings of the North.[12]

Northern colleges, presumably freer to tolerate stronger antislavery views, found arguments on the subject frequently disturbing. Schmidt reports that

> at Amherst, after an undergraduate from Tennessee had slugged a classmate from New Hampshire, the faculty "in the present agitated state of the public mind" ordered a student antislavery society to disband.

[10] Hofstadter and Metzger, *The Development of Academic Freedom in the United States*, p. 253.
[11] *Ibid.*, p. 221
[12] Eaton, *Freedom of Thought in the Old South*, pp. 208–209.

Extremist sentiments were criticized at Princeton and Dartmouth. Illinois College, Knox and Oberlin were vigorous centers of antislavery sentiments, however. Generally speaking, northern campuses were not entirely free in allowing discussion of the issue, and the discussion was usually kept on an abstract basis.[13]

Lexington was a major stop-over for slaves being shipped down the Kentucky, Ohio, and Mississippi rivers to Louisiana. Mary Todd, who would later be able to graphically portray what slavery was like to her husband, was distressed by seeing "men, women, and children, manacled two abreast, connected by heavy iron chains that extended the whole length of the line" plod wearily past her door. Transylvania students may have joined crowds that gathered downtown at Cheapside to witness the sale of slaves. In fact it was but a few months after Bascom became president of the University that a sensational sale of a beautiful young girl with only a fraction of Negro blood in her, brought nearly two thousand people to watch a representative of the underground railway outbid a slaveowner to secure the girl's freedom.[14]

Transylvania had never showed any tendency to move into the abolitionist camp. It is true that one of Transylvania's graduates, Cassius M. Clay, became a vehement antislavery advocate by the 1840's, but there is no evidence that he had picked up the doctrine on the campus nor actively campaigned for that cause while a student. Clay's attempt to establish his antislavery newspaper *The True American* in Lexington in 1845 met with immediate hostility and a mob closed the operation of the press a few months after it had begun.

In his annual message to the legislature in December 1838, Governor James Clark devoted more of his time denouncing the vicious threat of abolition than to considering the plight of education in Kentucky. We have every reason to assume that the trustees of Transylvania reflected this Kentuckian viewpoint. After all, Henry Clay was a slave-owner whose ideas of Negro freedom carried him only as far as the program of the American Colonization Society.[15]

[13] Schmidt, *The Liberal Arts College*, p. 39.
[14] William Townsend, *Lincoln and His Wife's Home Town*, p. 81.
[15] *House Journal*, 1838–1839 (Frankfort, 1839).

In May 1844, the Methodist General Conference met in New York City for six weeks, ending in the dissolution of a once-united church. Though the Methodist Church in America had been strongly antislavery during the 1780's because of John Wesley's views and the egalitarian theme of the eighteenth century thought reflected in the Declaration of Independence, this position was substantially altered as cotton became king in the southern economy and slavery its basic labor force. The General Conference wished to avoid the issue and leave it in the hands of the state annual conferences. The increasing determination of northern antislavery Methodists to force the General Conference to adopt strong abolitionist policies was fought vigorously by southern Methodists. After the 1840 General Conference, it appeared for a while as if antislavery forces had been sufficiently muted to allow the church to straddle the issues, or at least to operate on a local-option basis. But a renewed antislavery majority swept into the 1844 General Conference, and the division became inevitable.

Bascom and William Capers of South Carolina were two of the ablest leaders of the southern delegation. The issue which crystallized opposing forces was whether Bishop James O. Andrew, a much-beloved and able churchman, should be released from his office because he was a slave-owner. Various committees were appointed to work out some compromise before a vote on the matter, but to no avail; and the antislavery majority carried the question to suspend Andrew. Though many southern delegates were not proslavery apologists as such, they were opposed to policies dictating their relationship to the peculiar institution. Over this irreconcilable issue the Methodist Church divided, and a call was issued to the southern delegates to meet in Louisville, Kentucky, in May 1845, to establish the Methodist Episcopal Church South.

President Bascom, who had been asked to make a report to the General Conference on Transylvania requesting continued support for the institution, failed to do so under the existing conditions. He explained why to the trustees a month later. He told them that though the signatures of all the southern delegates had been affixed to a paper supporting Transylvania, he thought it unwise to submit it to a body dominated by a majority "whose abolition sentiments and views, expressed not only in word but much more strongly by overbearing, unequal, and oppressive action towards the South." Plans were underway to establish a Methodist Church South, and it seemed wise, thought Bascom, to secure the support of this organization for Transylvania. Indeed, Bascom had persuaded the southern delegates to sign a paper he had prepared pledging their support to Transylvania "as the great and only University proper of the Southern Church." The trustees heartily approved of the action and at the same meeting appointed Bascom as permanent president, his title heretofore having been acting-president.[16]

In September 1844, Kentucky held the first of the southern state conferences to prepare for the Louisville convention. Bascom participated in this meeting, and a few months later was appointed chairman of the Committee on Organization at the Louisville Conference in 1845 when the Methodist Episcopal Church South was formally established. The first General Conference of the new church met in Petersburg, Virginia, a year later. Bascom was also assigned the task of being editor of the newly-created *Southern Methodist Quarterly*.

At the Petersburg General Conference in 1846, a proposal from Transylvania trustees that the Conference assume control and management of the Academic Department of Transylvania University was accepted. The plan provided for a coordinate Board of Curators, appointed by the church, to work with the trustees in running the Academic Department and appointing the faculty. It was suggested that the faculty be representative of the various sections of the South. The present faculty were all discharged to clear the way for the new faculty, although some former teachers were rehired. The Conference requested that Bascom continue as president.

Bascom, meanwhile, entered the ranks of the publishing polemicists in defense of the action of the Southern Methodists. His 165-page treatise *Methodism and Slavery* appeared in March 1845. In it, Bascom examined the history of the Methodist Church in its relation to slavery, denounced the action taken against Bishop Andrew (who was given an honorary degree by Transylvania after the 1844 General Conference), and

[16]Minutes of the Board, July, n.d., 1844.

condemned the northern-controlled General Conference for crippling the effectiveness of the church in the South. It was vehement in style and largely undocumented, which led one of its critical reviewers to comment that the book was marked "by remarkable strength of language and equally remarkable inattention to facts."[17] Three years later Bascom published another exercise in invective, attacking the abolitionist Northern Church. He was fast becoming the best-known spokesman for the Southern Methodist cause.

DESPITE THE AMAZING vitality Bascom and the Methodists had given the Academic Department of the University, the momentum began to taper off by 1847. The previous five years had been extremely exhausting years for Bascom. In addition to his involvement in the affairs of the University and the church, he had had an increasingly large number of personal problems. For one thing, he had not married until 1839 at the age of forty-three, just three years before he came to Transylvania, and he was now the father of a growing family. In January 1846, his seven-weeks-old son died, which saddened the family for months. Another disturbing problem was a growing bronchial trouble which severely limited his oratorical powers. In addition he was burdened with debt, of which, considering how widely he traveled and the expenses of his home and office, a salary of $1,600 was the cause. Finally, his health was breaking down. In February 1846, he confided to his diary:

> My long indisposition has assumed the character of a bilious intermittent, combined with a neuralgic affection involving the nerves of the spine. I have a paroxysm of almost unendurable pain once in each twenty-four hours, usually lasting about six hours.[18]

Whether this was the beginning of the "cancer" that his biographer Henkle mentions is difficult to determine.

Transylvania also struggled with a number of other problems besides those surrounding Bascom. The Mexican War occurred during this period and may have had some effect on student interest and enrollment, but the fact that most of the students

---

[17] Sweet, *History of American Methodism*, II, 155.
[18] Henkle, *Bascom*, p. 288.

were too young to enlist probably reduced the impact of the war on the school. Much more significant was the return of the cholera epidemic in 1849. By July, the disease had spread rapidly through Lexington.

> As many as forty deaths occurred in twenty-four hours, and the terror of the inhabitants was indescribable. Business came to a standstill and many of the stores on Main Street closed altogether, hundreds of the wealthier citizens hastily locked up their houses and fled northward to distant watering places.[19]

Henry Clay and his wife were stricken but recovered, and there was an erroneous report that Bascom had died of the plague. Judge A. K. Woolley, who had taught many law students at Transylvania, was struck down by the cholera and died in August.

Perhaps more critical to the health of Transylvania than any of these factors was the fact that necessary financial support was not forthcoming from the churches. It soon became apparent to many of the southern state conferences that under arrangements made with Transylvania, they did not have a legal control over the whole University. The medical and law departments operated outside of their jurisdiction, and the trustees were still legally free of church control. The church only controlled the operations of Morrison College (the Academic Department) and many of the state conferences were already subsidizing their own colleges. What they had visualized at Transylvania was a major Methodist university to which Methodist students might go for undergraduate and professional training. This expectation frustrated, the motivation for supporting Transylvania was reduced. When the trustees sent out an appeal for $50,000 to the churches in 1847 for the purpose of buying the Blythe property and paying the salaries of faculty and president out of the interest from invested capital, the churches did not respond.

In 1849, weary and ill, Bascom resigned from the presidency. The Methodist Episcopal Church South saw this as a propitious time for severing ties with Transylvania. In June 1850, the committee on education of the General Conference reported to the trustees they were recommending that support of Transylvania

[19]Townsend, *Lincoln and His Wife's Home Town*, p. 199.

be turned over to the Kentucky Conference. The trustees reluctantly recognized the implications of this action and adopted a resolution formally severing their ties with the Methodist Episcopal Church South.

Bascom was elected a bishop at the 1850 General Conference and, as such, presided at the Missouri State Conference a few months later in St. Louis, despite his poor health. On his way back to Lexington he died.

So ended Transylvania's first experiment in denominational support. It might be argued that the dozen years of the Blythe administration were an earlier period of Presbyterian control, but this was never formalized in any agreement with the Presbyterian Church as Davidson pointed out with regret years later. What the Methodist experiment had shown was that denominational support could quickly expand the enrollment of a college. It also showed that, unless the control of the institution was really and not merely nominally in denominational hands, the necessary steady support and financial appropriations would not be forthcoming.

The trustees had certainly seen the impact, short-lived though it was, of denominational support on the vitality of Morrison College. In the light of continuing state indifference towards strengthening Transylvania, it was little wonder that they would become increasingly tempted to keep the door open for future denominational affiliation.

11

The Period
of Decline,
1850–1865

James B. Dodd   *Lewis W. Green*

The period following the end of Methodist support of Transylvania was a dreary one for the institution, marked by futile rearguard actions against the inevitable decline in all departments of the University. Only a brief episode in 1857–1858, when the state gave its momentary approval to the establishment of a state normal school at Transylvania, lightened an otherwise gloomy period. This era, extending through the Civil War, was undoubtedly the nadir of the college's long and fluctuating history, and the prophets of doom who consigned the school to the graveyard of institutional failures were numerous. Even Transylvania's loyal supporters began to wonder seriously if the school could survive.

What made the picture so dark was the decline of the medical and law departments, those bulwarks of Transylvania's strength during critical periods in the past.[1] By 1850 the competition from medical schools in Louisville and Cincinnati was becoming formidable. Those larger cities could provide clinical and hospital facilities unavailable in Lexington for the study of different diseases. Railroad and steamboat facilities also made these cities more easily accessible to students travelling from

[1] Robert L. Sprau and Edward B. Gernert, *History of Kentucky Dentistry* (Louisville, 1960), pp. 43–48. That the Transylvania name still carried considerable prestige was evidenced by the attempt of some dentists of the Bluegrass region to establish a Transylvania School of Dental Surgery. Officially incorporated by the legislature in March, 1850, the school opened its first session in Lexington in December. It had no connection with Transylvania University, and after one session, following which it granted four degrees, it disappeared.

other states, nor was there a shortage of anatomical specimens there.

By the session of 1849–50 the number of students in the Medical Department had dwindled to 92, whereas the average matriculation in past years had been over 200. Robert Peter, who had been dean of the medical faculty since 1847, was especially concerned. He was confronted with the increasingly difficult task of finding new doctors for his faculty. The question as Peter saw it was how to gain access to the resources of Louisville for medical education while still preserving intact the Transylvania Medical Department. He discussed the problem with the medical faculty and in 1850 submitted a proposal to the trustees in which it was suggested that the winter session of the Medical Department be held in Louisville and a new summer session be started in Lexington. The trustees were not enthusiastic about the proposal but by a narrow margin did approve establishing a summer session at Lexington.[2] This action freed the faculty to teach in Louisville, though not as the Transylvania Medical Department. The medical faculty took advantage of this situation to establish a separate entity, the Kentucky School of Medicine in Louisville, and a number of them put in their own money to assist in financing the project. Dr. Bush and Dr. Peter invested $1000 each. They rented a building, sent Peter off to Boston to purchase books and apparatus, and persuaded the Louisville City Council to grant them the right to use the Marine Hospital for clinical purposes, over the objection of the Medical Department of the University of Louisville.[3]

Peter had suggested privately to a few friends that it might be wise if all the medical schools in the area combined to create a great consolidated medical school for the entire West in Louisville, but there were too many competitive vested interests involved to achieve this goal. The Kentucky School of Medicine opened in the fall of 1850 with an enrollment of 101 students from thirteen states and the prospects were promising. But by the spring of 1852, differences arose among the faculty. There

[2] Peter, *The History of the Medical Department*, Appendix, Schedule B; Norwood, *Medical Education*, p. 291; Wright, "Robert Peter, " Ch. 7; Minutes of the Board, May 14, 1850.

[3] Wright, "Robert Peter," Ch. 7.

were accusations that some of the faculty performed their teaching duties half-heartedly. Others were dubious about the school's chances for success. Peter was offered a job teaching chemistry at the University of Louisville but turned it down because he would not desert his colleagues. However, by the end of 1852–1853 session, he decided to withdraw in order to concentrate his efforts at Transylvania and on his local affairs. He was also becoming increasingly interested in a proposed state geological survey, to which he was appointed chemist in 1854. Within a few years the Kentucky School of Medicine became independent of support from the Transylvania medical faculty and continued a reasonably prosperous existence until it was finally merged with the Medical Department of the University of Louisville in 1908.[4]

Peter continued his efforts to keep the Transylvania Medical Department alive, but enrollment continued to decline. Only fifty-three students matriculated for the summer session of the Department in 1854. Costs were cut, but when the session opened in April 1855, only thirty-eight students enrolled. Despite advertisements in various newspapers across the state, the irreversible decline continued until the session of 1858–59 recorded twenty-three students and six graduates. This was the last session of the Medical Department that had taught 6,456 students in its long history and sent out 1,881 graduates to minister to the medical needs of all the nation, especially in the South and West. William Norwood in his *Medical Education in the United States Before the Civil War* made this evaluation of the impact of Transylvania's Medical Department:

> The contribution of the Medical Department of Transylvania University and the other two early Kentucky schools, which were buds broken from the Transylvania stock, can scarcely be estimated. Thousands of physicians were trained in these three schools and went out to subdue the wilderness. Most of them served as general practitioners meeting the compelling demands of a growing society. A few among these practitioners served the duty of the profession to perpetuate its science and art, and pursued academic careers. The influence of Transylvania was felt throughout Transappalachia, and lingered long after Lexington,

[4] H. M. Bullitt to Robert Peter, November 23, 24, 1854, Peter Papers, Transylvania University; Norwood, *Medical Education*, p. 302.

the vaunted Athens of the West, saw its first . . . medical school close its doors.[5]

THE LAW DEPARTMENT likewise caught the contagion of decline. Reasons for this are not as clear as those for the Medical and Academic Departments. There were no other significant competing law schools in the area, and the demand for law training had not declined. George Robertson, pillar of the law faculty, stayed until the end, yet enrollment dropped. Presumably law students continued to depend on the archaic apprenticeship system.

As of 1855 there were still three able teachers conducting classes. George Robertson taught constitutional law, equity, medical jurisprudence and the law of comity. Francis K. Hunt taught the elementary principles of the common law, and criminal, commercial and national law. The third member, George B. Kinkaid, assumed responsibility for covering the practice of law, pleading and evidence, and the law of contract. Two years later only Robertson was left, and he kept the Law Department operating until it closed in 1858.

Statistics on enrollment in the Law Department and the number of graduates are, unfortunately, more fragmentary and unavailable than those for the Medical Department. Even in the minutes of the Board, the clerk would indulge in the infuriating habit of stating that trustees approved granting law degrees to the following, and then left a blank page, expecting, no doubt, to return and write in the names. Nor was any number mentioned. Newspaper accounts occasionally filled the gaps, but even a fair estimate is difficult to make because of the fluctuation in numbers of graduates during periods of reasonable stability. During the Law Department's best decade, classes starting in 1842 averaged sixty students, but the graduates ranged from twenty-four to forty-four. A generous estimate of the total enrollment in the long history of Transylvania's Law Department would be about 1300 students of which 500, at the very most, received law degrees.

With influence similar to the Medical Department, Transyl-

[5] Norwood, *Medical Education*, p. 303.

vania's Law Department was the seedbed for many lawyers practicing in Transappalachia, even though law degrees did not seem as necessary as medical degrees. Formal legal training was not as imperative, for one did not need an anatomical dissecting room, a chemical laboratory or an expensive inventory of apparatus to teach law. The line between amateur and professional was less discernible. Not until after the Civil War would there be a rising insistence on professional training for the aspiring lawyer. Along with its other pioneering efforts, however, Transylvania could justly claim that its Law Department was among the first small handful in the nation, certainly the first in the Transappalachian region, and for a number of years one of the largest and best-staffed departments anywhere in the country.

FINALLY, THE ACADEMIC DEPARTMENT was in decline. Following the departure of Bascom, the trustees appointed James B. Dodd, professor of mathematics and natural philosophy, as acting president. Dodd had been a member of the faculty since 1846 and was the author of several mathematical works. Beyond this, we know very little of the man whose job was mainly to be the caretaker of a very small school for the next six years. Indeed, we know very little of the official actions of the Board of Trustees for the next dozen years since the minute books are missing. One of the last notations, that of August 12, 1850, recorded an astounding proposition made by the trustees to the Grand Lodge of the Independent Order of Odd Fellows of the United States that they be given control of Transylvania in return for guaranteeing $3000 a year to Morrison College for three years, and thereafter $5000 a year for the payment of teachers' salaries in Morrison College and the Preparatory Department. After recovering from their surprise, the Odd Fellows respectfully declined the offer.

Robert Peter even suggested privately to the head of the Western Military Institute in Drennon Springs, Kentucky (located at one of the state's popular watering places), that the Institute, forced to suspend operations temporarily because of a typhoid epidemic, merge with Transylvania. The Military In-

*Henry Clay reviewing troops on the lawn of Old Morrison,
from the cover of a musical composition of 1844*

stitute, Peter argued, would benefit from the healthier surroundings of Lexington, and Transylvania would be aided by a
life-saving increase in enrollment. But the proposal came too
late. The Military Institute moved to Tyree Springs, Tennessee,
and the vision of uniformed students marching across the Transylvania campus never materialized.[6]

One loyal supporter wrote a letter entitled "Our College" to
the local paper in the summer of 1851, appealing to the citizens
of Lexington to aid the college. It was not just money the college needed, the writer said, nor a new president or more professors, but more students.

> We can, if we determine to do so, build up a Yale or a Cam-
> bridge in our midst. Why pay $400 or $500 to send the students
> out of the community? Lexington has always felt a strong inter-
> est in the education of youth, and although her University is not
> now flourishing, her city schools are. . . .

Why not, then, a campaign to back Transylvania?[7]

Robert Peter addressed the YMCA on the subject of education and appealed to the sympathies of his audience to support
the college. He wondered if his hearers were aware of the crisis
facing the school.

> No! You do not know these things; shrewd and liberal people
> that you are are still in a dream of the past years! You talk of the
> days of Holley; and you continue to repeat to yourselves, and to
> others too, the old story — that our College is down! — and
> somehow cannot be resuscitated.[8]

This appeal was not sufficent to arouse the citizens of Lexington to contribute money or send their sons to Transylvania.
They believed that if the University did not prosper after the
generous donation they gave it in 1839, further investment
would be unprofitable. The enrollment continued to decline.

ONE POSSIBLE SOLUTION to Transylvania's difficulties remained to be tried: to convert the University into a normal
school, a state teacher-training institution to supply the desper-

[6] A. J. Williamson to Robert Peter, February 6,1854, Peter Papers, archives
of Transylvania University.
[7] *Lexington Observer & Reporter*, August 13, 1851.
[8] Robert Peter, "On Education," March, 1854, Peter Papers.

ate need for skilled teachers in Kentucky's public schools. Various Kentucky superintendents of public instruction had broached the subject in their annual reports to the legislature during the preceding decade, but as long as the Methodists supported Transylvania there was little chance that a state-financed program would be established. Now the Methodists had severed their connection. In December 1849, the superintendent appealed to the legislature:

> This ancient seat of learning, from the foundation of the State belonging to the whole people . . . ought to be reclaimed by the Commonwealth. . . . No private, local, or sectarian pretensions should be permitted to defeat an object so great and so just.[9]

A year later Governor Helm suggested in his annual message that a plan might be developed to use part of the common school fund to extend educational opportunities to graduates from district schools, particularly with the aim of supplying the state with more teachers. Robert J. Breckinridge, superintendent of public instruction, buttressed this suggestion with a concrete proposal that $8000 be taken from the common school fund to pay eight professors to teach education at Transylvania. By this use of funds a constant supply of good teachers would be guaranteed. Every county and senatorial district and every town having a separate representative in the legislature would have the right to send an outstanding student to Transylvania. This enrollment would be free of charge for a period of time fixed by law, in return for which the student would promise to teach in Kentucky schools for as many years as he was at the University. Such a proposal would not only vastly improve public instruction in Kentucky, he continued, but would also strengthen the state university, "a necessity for any civilized community." A bill incorporating these suggestions never got beyond a second reading at the 1850 session of the legislature.[10]

Nothing was done to further this plan for the next three years. Then, new superintendent John D. Matthews revived the scheme in his annual report of 1855. He laid the groundwork

[9]"Annual Report of the Superintendent of Public Instruction, December 31, 1849," *Kentucky Documents*, 1849–50 (Frankfort, 1850).

[10]*House Journal*, 1850–51; "Report of the Superintendent of Public Instruction to the General Assembly of Kentucky, for the Year 1850," *Kentucky Documents*, 1850–51.

for his crusade carefully. First he persuaded Governor More-
head to come out strongly for the project in his annual message. Secondly, he tried to allay the fears that such a use of the
common school funds was unconstitutional. Thirdly, he presented a memorial from the trustees of Transylvania giving
their consent to any plan or reorganization the legislature might
wish to institute. And lastly, he exploited the troubled conditions of the times. Newspapers were filled with reports of
trouble in "Bleeding Kansas." The Compromise of 1850, constructed by their Kentucky hero Henry Clay, collapsed as the
underground railroad continued to assist runaway slaves to
reach Canada, and aroused northern communities from Boston
to Wisconsin subverted the administration of the Fugitive Slave
Act by mob action and the personal liberty laws. The division
between North and South deepened, and Matthews made the
most of it. Training Kentucky and other southern boys to teach
in Kentucky schools, he argued, would relieve the state's dependence on northern states for teachers. Kentucky was a
border state, a slave state, which needed teachers sympathetic
with her society and institutions. He asked:

> How can we expect men taught from infancy to believe that slav-
> ery is a sin, to refrain from insinuating if not boldly teaching this
> belief? Why, they impart their peculiar accent and pronuncia-
> tion to our children; will they conceal their sentiments from the
> unsolicitous and unsuspecting mind?

Kentucky "is digging her grave," he asserted, by using such
teachers. Lexington, he reported, had had such a teacher in
one of the city schools who caricatured slavery and polluted
the minds of the children, but he was "driven back to the den"
from whence he came.[11]

Before such a concerted campaign, the legislature was finally
stirred to action. On March 10, 1856, an act was passed to reor-
ganize Transylvania University and establish a school for
teachers. A newly-structured Board of Trustees, seven in
number, was appointed including Madison C. Johnson and
Benjamin Gratz, and augmented by a number of *ex officio* trustees, including the governor and the Chief Justice of the Court

[11]"Report of the Superintendent of Public Instruction to the General Assembly for the year 1855," *Kentucky Documents*, 1855–56 (Frankfort, 1856).

of Appeals. Every county and every city having a separate representative could send one student free of charge for a maximum of two years. The student had to be between the ages of seventeen and thirty, of good moral character, and a resident of Kentucky for at least two years. The regular pattern for the student would be to attend Transylvania one year, teach one year, and then return for his final year at the University, followed by another year of teaching. The aim of the entire educational program at Transylvania was to be directed at training teachers. The Law and Medical Departments were in no way to be involved in this program. The superintendent of public instruction was authorized to draw $12,000 from the common fund to pay for the tuition of students and the salaries of staff.

For six years James Dodd had been the conscientious acting president of Transylvania. Now the trustees moved to appoint a permanent president, the Reverend Lewis W. Green. A native of Danville, Kentucky, Green had studied for a time at Transylvania, graudated from Centre College and later studied abroad, establishing a reputation as a teacher and preacher. He was president of Hampden-Sydney College at the time he accepted the position. In his biography of Green, LeRoy J. Halsey states that Green was chosen for the position because his "learning, practical skill, and enthusiasm in the cause of education, all singled him out as the man for the place."[12] As so many before him, Green assumed his new duties with enthusiasm and optimism.

Classes opened in September 1856, with an enrollment of about eighty students. "No school of similar character in this country," reported the superintendent, "ever commenced with that number of pupils, or under such favorable auspices. . . ." He noted that a new normal school in New York had opened with only half that number. There were eight states in the Union that had established normal schools, and Kentucky was now in this vanguard.[13]

[12] LeRoy J. Halsey, *Memoir of the Life and Character of Reverend Lewis Warner Green, D. D., With a Selection From His Sermons* (New York, 1871), p. 52.

[13] "Annual Report of the Superintendent of Public Instruction to the Governor of Kentucky for the year 1856," Legislative Document No. 2, *Kentucky Documents, 1857* (Frankfort, 1857).

The academic structure of Morrison College was not significantly changed except for the addition of an education department. Four other departments in moral science, physical science, mathematics and ancient languages were maintained, and there were other students in attendance besides those enrolled in the new teaching program. This accounted for the combined commencement on June 24, 1857, of Transylvania University and the State Normal School. The chapel of Morrison College was appropriately decorated and a large crowd filled the seats. The local press reported that

> years have passed since a similar exhibition was witnessed in the classic halls of Morrison College, and we sincerely hope that she has met with her last reverse, and may hereafter continue prosperous and powerful. No institution in the country has passed through such vicissitudes and changes.[14]

No truer words had been written, but the troubles were far from over. Yet for a short time the prospects were promising. The inter-locking of Transylvania into the structure of an enlarged and improved common school system made sense. The teacher-training program was part of the national trend toward upgrading public education. The state university character of Transylvania made it a logical choice as the center for a state-supported program.

After the successful first year President Green looked forward to continuing improvement and expansion of the program. Enrollment for the fall of 1857 was 170 in the Academic Department, of which 72 were in the normal school training program. The ladies of Lexington raised money to purchase furniture for the dormitory of twenty-five beds, thus reducing rooming costs of the students. "The studies of the young gentlemen have been conducted with great assiduity under the able faculty of the University," the president reported.[15] It appeared that the Academic Department was becoming stronger even though the Medical and Law Departments were declining.

It was in the 1857–58 winter session of the Kentucky legislature that the bill establishing a normal school at Transylvania

[14]*Lexington Observer & Reporter*, June 27, 1857.
[15]"Report of the Trustees of Transylvania University," Appendix to Legislative Document No. 2, *Kentucky Documents, 1857–58* (Frankfort, 1857), II.

was repealed by large majorities. The repeal was to take effect on June 15, 1858, thus allowing the present session to be completed without disruption. The news hit the campus like a bombshell. The superintendent denounced the action which threatened to scatter students "over the State, without occupations, or certificates as teachers, or means, save those they had sacredly devoted to their education." The hopes of the seventy-five students were blasted. But even worse was the impact on the Kentucky public school system. Superintendent Matthews concluded that "it has given a retrograde movement to State education, which cannot be retracted for at least a quarter of a century." How ironic, he went on, that Kentucky — the pioneer state in establishing free schools among the slave states — was tearing down its normal school while South Carolina was establishing one; was removing any vestige of support for its state university while Virginia was appropriating $100,000 for theirs; was importing teachers with foreign ideas and subversive influences at a time when southern teachers were needed for southern students.[16]

The reasons behind the legislative repeal are clearly seen in the formalized rebuttals made by the trustees. The first argument was that favoritism had been shown by authorized officials who chose the students. The school was impractical because all that was needed to secure qualified teachers was to raise salaries. The most difficult argument to overcome was that which stated it was illegal to divert funds from the common school fund to subsidize a normal school. The law was plain on this, and only by a rather ingenious argument could a normal school be so identified with the common schools as to justify such a diversion of tax monies. Supporters of the normal school recognized this difficulty when they suggested that the legislature levy an additional one-cent tax to enlarge the school fund sufficiently to pay for a normal school. Had the legislature really been committed to the idea of a normal school, solutions to these problems could easily have been found. It obviously was not interested.

[16] "Report of the Superintendent of Public Instruction to the Governor of Kentucky for the year 1857," Legislative Document No. 2, *Kentucky Documents, 1857–58* (Frankfort, 1857), II.

Thus within a year the legislators had reversed themselves, and the plan for a normal school was indefinitely postponed. Indeed, concern for educational projects diminished as the more hysterical cries concerning protection of slavery and fear for the Union dominated the governors' annual messages. In 1859, for instance, Governor Magoffin mentioned common schools only briefly, devoting most of his message to defending slavery and pointing out Kentucky's critical position as a border state. The impact on the quality of public school education was depressing and of long duration. The impact on Transylvania was immediate and even more depressing as indicated by a notice in the paper barely two months after commencement:

TRANSYLVANIA HIGH SCHOOL

The Trustees of Transylvania are enabled to announce that on the 1st of September, or soon thereafter, they will open in the University Building a school in which will be taught the higher branches of a good *English and Classical Education*.[17]

Thus did the University confess its failure. It appeared that the long struggle to survive as a university had ended. The Academic Department lingered on as a high school from 1858 through the Civil War years until 1865, when a new phase of Transylvania's history was to begin.

TRANSYLVANIA HIGH SCHOOL maintained a staff of four to teach students in the major areas of ancient languages, mathematics, English literature, modern languages, chemistry and physiology. Abraham S. Drake, a former professor in the normal school, stayed on as principal for several years until the Civil War began. He was succeeded in 1861 by a man who was to play a major role in higher education in Kentucky — James Kennedy Patterson. Patterson at the time was teaching at Stewart College, Clarksville, Tennessee, but secession was threatening to close its doors and he was looking for a new position. Robert Brank, pastor of the Second Presbyterian Church in Lexington, wrote Patterson to suggest that he apply for the principalship of Transylvania High School, "the attenuated

[17]*Lexington Observer & Reporter*, August 14, 1858.

ghost of Transylvania, which had fallen alas, under the ecclesiastical suspicion of liberalism and for years had ceased from Collegiate or University work."[18]

In August 1861, James Patterson, with his two brothers William and Andrew as assistants, moved into Blythe House on the north end of the Transylvania campus, and the following month began teaching about sixty students.

The overriding concern of everyone during this period was, of course, the Civil War. Kentucky suffered from the embarrassing conspicuousness of being a border state at a time when she wished to be left alone. She did not wish to be militant but neutral. It was difficult and exasperating to be forced to choose between the North or the South. There was certainly strong sympathy with the South among many Kentuckians. The tone of Kentucky life was southern, but the symbol of her political sympathies was Henry Clay, not Calhoun, and the clarion defense of states' rights in the Kentucky Resolutions of 1799 had been mellowed by the nationalism of her favorite son and the American system. Kentucky did not wish to secede nor did she want to war against her southern friends, but the strategic location of this state made it impossible that she should be left alone. Her native sons were presidents of both the Union and the Confederacy. Her citizens were deeply divided, yet most of them voted for the Bell and Everett ticket in 1860 in hopes of avoiding secession. Her official position of neutrality opened her up for ultimate invasion by both the Blue and the Gray. John Hunt Morgan, whose home bordered Transylvania's campus, led his famous raiders time and again through the Bluegrass. Winston Coleman notes in his *Lexington During the Civil War* that

> Lexington and the Bluegrass region, like the rest of Kentucky, was strangely divided. Political sentiments were extreme and mixed. Family ties were rent asunder; father against son, and brother against brother. When they passed on the streets of Lexington men looked askance at each other and said very little.[19]

[18]Mabel Hardy Pollitt, *A Biography of James Kennedy Patterson* (Louisville, 1925), p. 78.

[19]J. Winston Coleman Jr., *Lexington During the Civil War* (Lexington, 1939), p. 9.

Robert Peter, who lived just across the Old College Lot from the home of John Hunt Morgan, was a staunch Unionist. Many Lexingtonians went with Morgan to the Confederacy, but many others joined the Union ranks. Able-bodied men who did not leave the city to join the Union Army volunteered their services to the Home Union Guard which drilled on the Old College Lot in front of Peter's house, commanded by Dr. E. L. Dudley, formerly of the Transylvania Medical Department faculty.

John Hunt Morgan

President Lincoln had treated Kentucky gingerly, knowing full well the immensely important strategic position of this state. He could not afford to allow it to slip into the Confederate camp. There were many powerful Kentucky leaders who were determined their state should remain in the Union. Despite Governor Magoffin's efforts the Kentucky legislature voted to remain neutral. It would not secede. By September 1861, Lincoln was confident enough of Kentucky's loyalty to send Union troops into Lexington, and despite some minor clashes with Confederate sympathizers, Union forces maintained order and control without much difficulty. Lexington remained under the Union flag except for a brief period in the fall of 1862 when the Confederates under Kirby Smith moved into town.

Robert Peter remained associated with the Transylvania High School for the first two years of the war until he received an appointment as Acting-Assistant Surgeon in the U.S. General Hospital in Lexington in the fall of 1862, in time to care for the thousands of Union wounded that poured in from the bloody fields of Perryville. In the fall of 1860, however, he was still listed as professor of physical science and he also offered a "course of Experimental Lectures to the Young Ladies of the Female schools" to be held in the Medical Hall. The building, however, no longer belonged to Transylvania. It had ceased to be a school for medical education after the Medical Department had expired and the City of Lexington claimed it under the agreement of 1839. City authorities gave Peter permission to use it until the Union command in Lexington took it over as a hospital in the fall of 1862, following the battle of Perryville. In May 1862, the Union forces had taken possession of Morrison College, the dormitories and Blythe House for use as hospitals. The trustees of Transylvania surrendered the buildings to the army without opposition, rent-free.[20]

James and Andrew Patterson, teaching in the Transylvania High School, were confronted with the problem of where to hold their classes. Dispossessed from Morrison College, they had moved into the Medical Hall, which in turn was taken over as a hospital. For a time they used the Methodist parsonage on South Mill Street, then moved to the basement of the Second Presbyterian Church. In the 1863-64 school year, classes were held in the building next to Christ Episcopal Church and finally in the old college refectory.

The large medical hall was destroyed by fire on the morning of May 22, 1863. The fire, of undetermined origin, broke out at about 10 a.m. and by noon the building was a blackened ruin. Flames destroyed part of the medical library and some of the chemical apparatus which had not been removed when the Union Army converted the hall into a hospital. The structure had been filled with sick and wounded soldiers, but all were

[20]Wright, "Robert Peter," Ch. 7.

evacuated safely. The destruction of this imposing structure seemed but another somber stroke in the death-knell of this once proud university. Yet the small classes of the high school continued to meet into the spring of 1865. Few would have thought that within months after the Civil War a new effort to create a major state university would be underway on this somnolent campus.[21]

The Civil War, which played havoc with education everywhere, was a fitting period for the apparent demise of Transylvania University. One could have at that time searched its long, eighty-year history to evaluate the achievements of this institution and the reasons for its decline. One such evaluation can be found in Alvin T. Lewis's *History of Higher Education in Kentucky* in which he concludes that a major cause of Transylvania's difficulties was the lack of an adequate initial endowment and the failure of the state to provide adequate appropriations. Part of this lack of whole-hearted state support was no doubt due, Lewis believes, to the denominational influences which hovered about Transylvania even when they did not actually control it. In addition there was not sufficient enthusiasm among local people to support a state university, and educational statesmen were rare among rural legislators. Some may have rationalized their non-support by classifying Transylvania as too denominational to receive public funds while major church denominations criticized the school for straying too far toward secularism.[22]

The school was certainly the loser in this game. Finally, Lewis believes that the independence of the self-perpetuating Board of Trustees made full, efficient state control impossible. The frequency with which the state changed the size and composition of the Board would belie this conclusion, however. The trustees were able and dedicated men, and they must have been some of the most frustrated educational directors in the country. The incredibly fluctuating character of Transylvania's successes and failures in the first sixty years of the nineteenth

[21]Deposition of M. C. Johnson in *City of Lexington vs. Kentucky University* on file in Fayette County Courthouse.
[22]Lewis, *History of Higher Education in Kentucky*, pp. 79–80.

century must have driven them to desperation. How else account for that unbelievable offer they made to hand over the school to the International Order of the Odd Fellows in the early 1850's? Yet with all the frustration, there must have been great pride in the remarkable educational contribution this university had made to higher education in the West. Her alumni filled the halls of Congress, several had been Cabinet members and vice-presidents of the United States, and one became the president of the Confederacy. Graduates from her law school became legal and political leaders in scores of communities throughout the South and West. Her leadership in medical education and that impact on the medical history of this region has already been evaluated. Transylvania was the first significant center of higher education in the Transappalachian region. Under men like Holley, the University attained a stature commensurate with the best colleges in the nation.

12

The Great Experiment: Kentucky University

John B. Bowman

From 1865 to 1878 a remarkable experiment in higher education was undertaken in Lexington: the fusion of two other institutions with Transylvania to form one large university complex under the name of Kentucky University. This achievement was due largely to the educational vision, driving ambition and energy of John Bryan Bowman. This young Mercer County farmer was remarkably aware of the new educational currents in his day and tried, against great odds, to create in Kentucky a state university which could compare with other universities that were beginning to appear in the country. His failure to do so was based on structural rather than conceptual errors; his goals were challenging and progressive, but the institutional base on which he attempted to erect this university contained the fatal flaw of denominationalism that caused its disintegration.

The institutional roots of this new university were laid in the chartering of Bacon College in 1837 in Georgetown, Kentucky. Three faculty members of the strongly-Baptist Georgetown College, founded in 1829, were of the denomination of the Disciples of Christ. They apparently proved to be unacceptable to the faculty and administration, and in the face of threatened dismissal, these three faculty members resigned in 1836. Convinced they would receive adequate support from numerous Disciples in the area, they bravely embarked on an educational venture of their own by securing a charter in 1837 from the state legislature establishing a college named in honor of Francis Bacon. With a president and six faculty members, the school began auspiciously with 203 students, many of whom were attracted by the Department of Civil Engineering which had been transferred along with its professor from Georgetown College. In New Haven, Connecticut, Henry White (later president of Kentucky University) saw an advertisement in the *National Intelligencer* announcing the opening of "A School for Engineers at Georgetown, Kentucky" and came to enroll. He proved to be such an outstanding student that, though only eighteen, he was appointed to the faculty as an instructor in mathematics and civil engineering. He devoted the remainder of his life to Bacon College and Kentucky University.[1]

Bacon College at Harrodsburg

[1]Dwight E. Stevenson, *Lexington Theological Seminary* (St. Louis, 1964). A very thorough account of the founding of Bacon College may be found in Appendix IV. Also, see James F. Hopkins, *The University of Kentucky: Its Origin and Early Years* (Lexington, 1951), pp. 43–50. A. R. Milligan, "Historical Review of Kentucky University Read at the Fortieth Anniversary of Union with Transylvania," unpublished manuscript.

A combination of the nationwide economic depression of 1837 and the hostile environment of Baptist Georgetown reduced both income and students at the new school, the enrollment dropping by one half after the first session. Then, as a number of other schools had done under similar circumstances, Bacon College authorities announced they would move permanently wherever adequate funds from local support were forthcoming. A $50,000 figure was set. In the spring of 1839 Mercer County garnered the necessary funds to meet this specification and Bacon College moved to Harrodsburg. A handsome two-story Georgian colonial structure was erected and in use by 1843, but the necessary financial support failed to materialize. Only a fraction of the originally-pledged $50,000 was ever paid, the salaries of the faculty were cut to sub-survival levels, and the school ceased to function as a college in 1851, having granted only twenty-seven A.B. degrees in the preceding decade. One of them was awarded to John Bowman in 1842.[2]

John Bryan Bowman was born on October 16, 1824, one of four sons of the John Bowman who had studied law under Henry Clay, practiced law in Mercer County and had been one of the founders of Bacon College. As did his father young Bowman studied law after graduation, and in 1855 this thirty-one-year-old alumnus and trustee of Bacon College, now a large landowner and successful farmer, embarked on a remarkable educational and religious venture. Bowman submitted a proposal to the trustees to raise $100,000 as endowment for the college, one-third of which was to be raised in Mercer County. With the invaluable assistance of Major James Taylor who raised over $30,000 in Mercer County, Bowman set out to secure the remainder from surrounding counties.

Bowman interviewed men from all walks of life, infusing them with the contagious enthusiasm of his own educational vision, and in one hundred and fifty days he had accumulated pledges totalling $150,000. Such phenomenal success was a tribute to this man who envisioned not the restoration of a small denominational college but the creation of a new university,

[2] Stevenson, *Lexington Theological Seminary*, p. 406.

an institution [Bowman wrote] which promises to meet in all its arrangements the present crisis in our Church and Society. . . . An institution more liberal in all its appointments — permanent in its nature — and auxiliary to the cause of sound morality and pure Religion in our state.[3]

It was now necessary to secure amendments to the original Bacon College charter to enable the new university to fulfill its goals. Such amendments were submitted to the Kentucky legislature in its 1857–58 session. Among the changes was that of a new name. Bowman's supporters suggested it be named after him, but he demurred. In the absence of alternative suggestions, one representative inserted the name Kentucky University, which proved to be agreeable to all parties.

The legislative act, formally approved on January 15, 1858, noted that the purpose of the petitioners was to establish "a first class university upon a more modern, American and Christian basis." It provided for a Board of thirty curators, of which at least two-thirds "shall always be members of the Christian Church in Kentucky." This was a critical provision because it placed the institution indisputably under the control of this denomination. A devout member of the Christian Church himself, and a graduate of Bacon College established by that denomination, he may have assumed a wider breadth of educational philosophy among his brethren than was justified. In Bowman's mind, educational and moral and spiritual values were interlocked, and to him free inquiry and denominationalism were allies, not enemies.[4]

Kentucky University held its first classes in the old Bacon College building on September 19, 1859. Bethany College, a leader in Disciples' higher education, provided this new Disciples' institution with leadership and faculty. Both the new president of Kentucky University, Robert Milligan, and new vice-president Robert Richardson were recruited from Bethany College, and Robert Graham, a member of the faculty, had been a student there. One hundred ninety-four students enrolled at

[3]John W. Wayland, *The Bowmans* (Staunton, Va., 1943), pp. 143–146; Hopkins, *The University of Kentucky*, pp. 46–47.
[4]"An Act to amend the charter of Bacon College. Approved January 15, 1858." *Acts of the General Assembly, 1857–1858.*

Kentucky University that fall, and Bowman had good reason to anticipate a moderate degree of success for his brain-child. Unfortunately, the Civil War wrecked this new venture. Enrollment plummeted. Only fourteen students graduated in this critical 1859–1865 period. In the fall of 1862 the main college building was commandeered by the Union Army to house the wounded from the Battle of Perryville, and classes continued in the Harrodsburg Christian Church. But the most devastating blow was the fire which destroyed the main college building on February 10, 1864.[5]

In the belief that Harrodsburg could not provide the necessary financial resources for the school's revival, the curators appointed a committee composed of Bowman, Henry White and President Milligan to seek a new location. Transylvania University with its impressive history, imposing Morrison College and a campus conveniently located in a thriving community, caught their attention. The trustees of Transylvania, contemplating the possibility of placing the institution under denominational control, had already secured legislative approval to do so. They viewed the prospect of a union with Kentucky University favorably. Some of the curators of Kentucky University initially opposed the plan, but destruction of the main building forced them to take another look at this opportunity. After long debate, a majority finally favored moving to a community that could provide $100,000 or its equivalent. A committee was authorized to secure an amendment to the charter permitting such a move. The curators also obligated the university to repay the donors in Mercer County upon demand.[6]

Bowman met in Frankfort with Madison C. Johnson, chairman of the Transylvania trustees, to work out a plan for the merger of the two schools during the 1864–65 meeting of the Kentucky legislature. But Bowman had more grandiose plans than the fusion of two small schools. He envisioned a great state university with many different professional colleges. To this end he set his sights on the embryonic Agricultural and

[5]Stevenson, *Lexington Theological Seminary*, pp. 410–412; Also A. R. Milligan, "Historical Review of Kentucky University."

[6]Z. F. Smith, "Recollections," *The Transylvanian*, Vol. VIII, No. 4 (April, 1899). Minutes of the Board of Kentucky University, September 20, 1864.

Mechanical College, laboring into life under the tardy and fumbling hands of the Kentucky legislators. The Morrill Act, signed into law by President Lincoln on July 2, 1862, had committed the United States government to assign parts of its rich endowment of public lands to the states for the purpose of establishing at least one agricultural and mechanical college in each state. The states which wished to accept this donation, which came in the form of land scrip, had to decide to do so within two years, and to establish a college within five years. The Kentucky legislature voted to accept the donation in 1863. The real roadblock was setting up the college. Transylvania had proposed consolidating the new college with itself, but bills authorizing such action failed to make their way through the legislature. A final attempt to consummate this union was tried in February 1865, when it was suddenly put aside to allow a counter proposal engineered by Bowman to be considered.[7]

Ashland

Bowman had appeared before the Committee on Agriculture of the state's House of Representatives and presented a plan to establish the Agricultural and Mechanical College as one of the colleges of an enlarged Kentucky University. He committed himself to raising $100,000 to endow it, and to purchase Henry Clay's estate, Ashland, and the adjoining Woodlands farm as a

[7]Hopkins, *The University of Kentucky*, pp. 62–63; Stevenson, *Lexington Theological Seminary*, pp. 412–413.

Woodlands

campus and experimental farm. In addition, he proposed that
Kentucky students receive free instructions in the Agricultural
and Mechanical College.

A powerfully persuasive man, Bowman won enough legislators to his side to guarantee substantial majorities in both
houses to support the merger with Transylvania, with the inclusion of the Agricultural and Mechanical College as one of the
colleges of Kentucky University, although on an independent
status. According to the act approved February 28, 1865, Kentucky University and Transylvania University were "consolidated into one university and one corporate body, by the name
of Kentucky University. That the curators of Kentucky University shall have all the rights and powers of the trustees of
Transylvania University in regard to all the funds and property
of Transylvania University," bound, of course, by the original
trusts and conditions to which the Transylvania trustees had
been subject. Except as it related to the funds and property of
Transylvania, the charter of Kentucky University was to be the
charter of the consolidated university. It was specified that the
University should be located in Fayette County and that if for
some reason it were to be located elsewhere, Transylvania
would reassume its corporate identity. Donors to Bacon College, and Mercer County donors to Kentucky University, were

to be recompensed if they so desired. The consolidation was to go into effect only after it had been approved by the governing boards of both Transylvania and Kentucky University.

The act that related to the Agricultural and Mechanical College stated that it should become a college of Kentucky University, and that after it was organized the curators should receive the income from funds obtained from the sale of the land scrip donated by Congress. The state was to have the right to send three students from each representative district tuition-free with the additional proviso that these students would have the right to attend classes in the rest of the University except those in medicine and law. The act included specific injunctions against any sectarian influences and prohibited a majority of the professors of the Agricultural and Mechanical College from belonging to a single denomination.[8]

This merger aroused hard feelings and opposition. Major James Taylor, who had so effectively raised funds for Kentucky University in Mercer County, wrote a remonstrance signed by fifty-three people protesting the University's removal from Harrodsburg.[9] Also opposing the connection of the Agricultural and Mechanical College with Kentucky University was former Governor Beriah Magoffin who warned the legislators to "make no union of Church and State in the appropriation of this fund. But I say keep the fund free from the control of the Church."[10]

The dilemma Bowman faced was similar to that of his predecessors as he found the state legislature providing little support or adequate financial appropriations to the University. For these he had to turn to denominational organization and to private individuals. But as soon as he recruited denominational support, he endangered the non-sectarian character of the University and the ideal of academic freedom and the unhampered inquiry essential to its existence. His tremendous desire to erect an outstanding university overrode any qualms he may have had. Good Christian men, he believed, who shared his educational philosophy would not bring to bear on the Univer-

[8]*Acts of the General Assembly, 1864–1865.*
[9]Stevenson, *Lexington Theological Seminary*, p. 414.
[10]*Ibid.*

sity the destructive influence of sectarian bigotry. He was convinced that a university could be both free and Christian, that free inquiry was no threat to God's truth. He wanted to build "an institution peculiarly *modern*, *American*, and *Christian* in its character, free, open, and accessible to the humblest youth of every creed and latitude. . . ." He thought Lexington an ideal location. Bowman told the curators:

> I have but one desire in all this matter, I want to see accomplished the greatest good to the greatest number of our poor, fallen race, thus giving the greatest glory to God. I want to build up a *People's Institution*, a great University eventually open and accessible to the poorest boy in all the land who may come and receive an education practical and suitable for any business or profession in life. . . . Hitherto, our Colleges and Universities have been accessible only to the few, such are the expenses attending them. . . . We want ample grounds and buildings, and libraries and apparatus and museums and endowments and Prize Funds, and Professors of great hearts and heads, men of faith and energy. Indeed, we want everything which will make this Institution eventually equal to any on this continent.[11]

Such was the educational goal of John Bowman. It combined the ideals of Jacksonian democracy with the prevailing tradition of sound Christian training. It struck at the concept of higher education as the prerogative of the elite, and viewed the university as the educational servant of all.

As has been noted earlier, there had been some stirrings even before the Civil War in the field of higher education to develop a more American and democratic education. President Wayland of Brown University had said that collegiate instruction should not be "for the benefit of one class, but for the benefit of all classes."[12] Henry Tappan, who became president of the University of Michigan in 1852, said that the university must become free of sectarian control while continuing its concern with maintaining religious and moral character.[13] Major nationwide educational reform was postponed until after the Civil War which had had a largely negative effect on the colleges. With the coming of peace there was a new willingness on the

[11] Minutes of the Board of Kentucky University, June 20, 1865.
[12] Hofstadter and Smith, eds., *American Higher Education: A Documentary History*, II, p. 478.
[13] *Ibid*., II, 511, 507.

part of educational leaders to adopt new goals, methods, and approaches in higher education, and there was an increasingly large number of wealthy individuals willing to underwrite new educational ventures.

One of the most famous innovators was Charles Eliot, Harvard's new president, who inaugurated the elective system which Wayland had recommended two decades earlier. Such new universities as Cornell and Johns Hopkins challenged older universities, and Eliot did not believe the older institutions should remain in the rear. A growing demand for higher standards approaching those of European universities, the inclusion of more science in the curriculum, the movement toward more specialization and research in the belief that "knowledge must not be merely conserved but also advanced in the universities" — all forced educational leaders to re-examine their philosophies and policies to determine what course their institutions should follow.[14]

The challenge to John Bowman was whether he could create on the charter base of a denominational school a large state university with a variety of professional schools, including an agricultural and mechanical college. According to Bowman's report to the curators in June 1865, the prospects were most promising. Instead of being a "homeless and houseless institution," Kentucky University had acquired $125,000 worth of buildings, libraries and apparatus. Another $65,000 had been subscribed for endowment and an additional $100,000 promised for buildings and grounds. An estimated $200,000 had been raised for the new Agricultural and Mechanical College. Bowman estimated the financial resources of the University as totalling nearly $500,000. In addition, he said,

> you will have a location in or near a city, easy of access, from all directions, just now awakening to a new life and growth under the happy influence of a restored peace and Union, situated in the midst of the richest and most beautiful country perhaps in America, among a people as liberal, refined, and intelligent as any other, in the midst of numerous friends whose sympathies will cluster around it. . . .[15]

The success with which Bowman secured funds for the new

[14]*Ibid.*, p. 593.
[15]Minutes of the Board, June 20, 1865.

university, supported by the editorial opinion of the local press, indicated that the Lexington community seemed ready to embark once more on a campaign to erect a major institution of higher learning. Not since 1839 had there been such evidence of support, and a new generation had grown up with little memory of the dismal outcome of that last crusade. Unfortunately, the same elements for potential discord still remained, waiting only for the proper stimulus to polarize them into opposing forces.

The first ominous note was struck when three curators at the June 1865 meeting of the Board resigned after tabling a resolution to make the Bible a regular textbook and employ a professor for biblical instruction. This resolution reflected the opinion of many sectarians that a university under their auspices should in some way be an instrument for formal religious training. Bowman and his supporters were not of this mind, but they were nevertheless willing to establish a College of the Bible as one of the colleges that opened in October 1865, as part of Kentucky University. The other colleges were the Colleges of Arts and Sciences and the College of Law. The Agricultural and Mechanical College began a year later.

At their June 1865, meeting the curators had appointed a committee to draw up an organizational structure for the University, and a month later they submitted a plan to the Board. It doubtless reflected the ideas of Bowman who conceived of the University as a rather flexible institution, incorporating such colleges as were needed at any particular time for the needs of the students. Formal degree preparation was deemphasized, and students were to be allowed to move rather freely from classes in one college to those in another. Overseeing this operation would be a "Regent who is elected from among the Curators and is ex officio Chairman of the Executive Committee."[16] Not connected with any faculty, the Regent was to see that rules and regulations of the University were carried out. He would be both the chief administrator and a representative of the Board. Each college, in turn, would be governed by its own presiding officer and faculty, the presiding officer himself being a teacher in one of the departments (called schools) in the college. There was to be a university senate composed of

[16]*Ibid.*, July 17, 1865.

the presiding officers and faculty above the rank of instructor and chaired by the Regent. Bowman was selected as the first Regent.

The curriculum devised for the various colleges was hardly revolutionary. Despite Bowman's belief that more was needed "than the everlasting Latin and Greek and Mathematics, whose myths and forms have hung ghost-like so long in the halls of those hoary institutions, and whose slavish worship has crushed the spirit and constitution of many a toil-worn student," departments of Latin, Greek and mathematics were established in the College of Arts and Sciences. However, his desire to emphasize science along with English, modern languages and the fine arts was reflected in the establishment of departments in chemistry, physics, botany, zoology, geology, German, French, Italian, Spanish and English literature.[17]

THE ORIGINAL FACULTY of the College of Arts and Sciences was a mixture of former Transylvania and Kentucky University teachers. Dr. Robert Peter was by far the senior member of this group. This vigorous chemist was now sixty years old and white-haired, but he showed no signs of physical or mental decline. Yet it is doubtful whether any of his colleagues would have predicted that he would be teaching for twenty-two more years. Not only was he to occupy teaching posts at both the College of Arts and Sciences and the Agricultural and Mechanical College for over a decade before he severed ties with the former in 1878, but he also resumed his position as chemist to the Kentucky Geological surveys in the 1870's.[18]

The other Transylvania faculty member to assume a position on the new faculty was James K. Patterson who had kept alive the few small classes offered by the school during the difficult years of the Civil War. Responsible at first for the fields of Latin and History, he later assumed a new role as presiding officer of the Agricultural and Mechanical College in 1869, a position he held until 1910.

Robert Graham was appointed to the Department of English

[17]Quoted in Hopkins, *The University of Kentucky*, p. 79.
[18]John D. Wright, Jr., "Robert Peter," Chapter 8.

Language and Literature and within a year became presiding officer of the College of Arts and Sciences, formerly Morrison College. Born in Liverpool, England, in 1822, he along with his family were brought by their sea-captain father to the United States five years later where they eventually settled down in Pittsburgh. Young Graham was apprenticed to a carpenter, and helped to build the first buildings at Bethany College. His desire to attend the college he helped build was encouraged by Alexander Campbell who advised him to replace the hammer and saw with the Bible. Graham graduated from Bethany in 1847 and went to Fayetteville, Arkansas, to establish a Christian Church and help found Arkansas College, the forerunner of the state university. He accepted an invitation in 1859 to join the faculty at the new Kentucky University in Harrodsburg as a teacher of English, but he stayed only one year before returning to Arkansas. His Unionist sympathies made his position in that Confederate state untenable, however, and he served churches in Cincinnati and California before deciding to return permanently to Kentucky. His students described him as a "solid block of a man" and his portrait shows such solidity. He had a well-shaped, square-set, almost-bald head circled with white hair at the time the portrait was painted. He had lively blue eyes and a pinkish, healthy complexion. In his later years he wore an English walking suit, a standing collar and a white bow tie. He prided himself in controlling his emotions, and was methodical and exacting in his teaching.[19]

Professor Henry White headed the Department of Mathematics. He was also to serve a short term as president of the liberal arts college from 1877–78, and of the entire University from 1878–1880. His main vocation was teaching mathematics until failing eyesight forced him to retire in 1893. Photographs of White show a bald man with bushy white whiskers, wearing small spectacles with hexagonal metal frames. It was said of him that "he was one of those rare mortals who are ever disposed to do much and give much and ask but little of others for themselves."[20]

[19]*The Crimson*, 1898; Stevenson, *Lexington Theological Seminary*, pp. 68–69.

[20]Biographical sketch of White may be found in his obituary printed in *The Crimson*, 1904.

Because of his controversial and significant role in the life of the University in the decades ahead, and his long years of devoted service to and leadership of the College of the Bible, John W. McGarvey was the most significant individual to join the faculty of Kentucky University. Born in Hopkinsville, Kentucky, in 1829, he was raised in a large family by his stepfather, a farmer-physician and a trustee of Bethany College. Entering Bethany College McGarvey came under the powerful influence

John W. McGarvey

of Alexander and Thomas Campbell and decided to commit himself to the ministry. It was here also that he met a number of the men with whom he would later be associated in Lexington: Robert Graham, Charles Louis Loos, and John H. Neville. In 1852 he was ordained and became the minister of the Dover Christian Church in Missouri. It was at this time he began writing for several of the denominational periodicals and taking part in religious debating, both of which activities he was to pursue vigorously for the remainder of his life. He made himself unpopular in Missouri by preaching to Negroes and adopting a strong pacifist position when the Civil War erupted.

In 1862 when Dr. Winthrop Hopson, the pro-southern minister of the large Main Street Christian Church in Lexington,

Kentucky, resigned and the divided opinion of the congregation dictated the recruitment of a man who was not committed to either the Union or Confederate causes, John W. McGarvey was called. McGarvey's dedication to neutrality and his sermons on the New Testament teaching against divisions were remarkably persuasive in keeping the church from following the divisionist examples of the Methodists, Baptists and Presbyterians. Indeed, he remained sufficiently immune to the war fever to be able to work steadily on his first book *The Commentary on Acts* which his biographer, W. C. Morro, has called "McGarvey's most constructive, most original, and most characteristic production."[21]

As a curator of the Harrodsburg Kentucky University, McGarvey was much concerned with the future of the school after the 1864 fire. Bowman's conception of a multi-college university crystallized McGarvey's ideas about a College of the Bible. Aware of his own inadequate training for the ministry at Bethany, he became increasingly concerned about the serious lack of a proper training school for Disciples' ministers. This need, he believed, could best be met by establishing a school specifically tailored to young men going into the ministry. It would not be a typical seminary in which liberal arts and biblical studies were combined, but a course centering exclusively on the Bible. "Only such books as contribute to a complete and practical knowledge of the Scriptures should be put into the student's hands," he said.[22] Whether the subject was church administration, pastoral care, history, theology, biography or literature, the Bible would remain the sole textbook. No man was ever more committed to the all-encompassing role of the Bible as guide for the preacher and his congregation, nor more wedded to the fundamentalist base of the literal truth and completely divinely-inspired character of that book. This was both

[21]The biographical material on McGarvey is derived from W. C. Morro, *Brother McGarvey* (St. Louis, 1940). It is a reasonably fair and well-balanced study of this colorful and controversial figure; and from the prologue to Stevenson, *Lexington Theological Seminary*. Both men benefited by having McGarvey's own notes he had made for his own biography and the additional notes made by his son. Morro had known McGarvey personally during the last nineteen years of McGarvey's life.

[22]Quoted in Stevenson, *Lexington Theological Seminary*, p. 18.

his great strength and his weakness, for it made him self-right-eous and inflexible in his encounters with any who differed from him.

Despite his emphasis on the Bible, McGarvey did not dis-count the value of a liberal arts education; he simply did not believe it to be indispensable. Moreover, considering the need for more preachers, he thought requiring liberal arts training would delay many student-ministers and eliminate others.

McGarvey scarcely looked like the author of violent tirades. Of medium height and weight with erect posture, he had a well-shaped head with blue-gray eyes and a neatly-trimmed beard. The face that looks out from his portrait is pleasant but strong. He was known to be a fine family man, a devoted and kind husband and father. A firm disciplinarian when the occasion required, he was consistently honest, direct and understanding with his students, and performed many acts of thoughtfulness for those who were in trouble. Nothing puzzled his friends and colleagues so much as the inexplicable contrast between this side of his personality and the violent, bitter diatribes he deliv-ered against men with whose opinions he differed — though later encountering them with courtesy and geniality on a social occasion. To McGarvey there was no inconsistency. He loved men and he loved truth, and when men were in error — partic-ularly in matters of faith or doctrine — then there was no room for tolerance. The error must be rooted out and destroyed. Un-fortunately McGarvey frequently could not distinguish between the error of opinion and the man who made it, and both became targets for his denunciation.[23]

The early planning stages for the new Kentucky University

---

[23]Morro, *McGarvey*, p. 48.

In his later years, McGarvey grew increasingly deaf and began to use an ear trumpet which became the subject of a considerable number of student jokes and cartoons, all of which McGarvey took good-naturedly. It became the traditional fearsome trial for the new student in his class to have to march up to McGarvey's desk and recite his lesson into the ear trumpet. There is a famous story that one time a student, seeing that McGarvey had apparently forgotten his ear trumpet, walked up to his desk and said, "Good morning, John, how are you?" To the student's embarrassment and the class's amuse-ment, McGarvey instantly replied, "Very well, Hiram, how are you?" The student had failed to notice a less conspicuous hearing aid McGarvey was wearing.

at Lexington provided McGarvey with the opportunity to present a plan for the kind of seminary he wanted established. In an article entitled "Ministerial Education" published in *Lard's Quarterly* for April 1865, McGarvey sketched the blueprint for a new kind of theological education which would give priority first to a knowledge of the Bible and secondly to moral training. The subjects of homiletics, church administration and pastoral care would use the Bible as their textbook. If a student had the time, money and capacity for additional study in the liberal arts, well and good; but it was not indispensable. This emphasis on Bible study reflected the special character of the Christian Church, whose origins were rooted in the Cane Ridge revival which had emphasized a return to original Christian unity by means of Biblical knowledge. McGarvey believed that a ministry trained with a dedicated and exclusive emphasis on Bible study would provide the kind of leadership best equipped to deal with any sectarian opposition and its possible accompanying perversion of the Scriptures. This training would now be provided in the proposed College of the Bible.[24]

The proposition to establish such a college was accepted by the curators, and Robert Milligan was appointed its first president. Fifty-one at the time and physically frail, Milligan brought with him extensive experience as a teacher and scholar. He had taught at Washington College, Indiana University and Bethany College before accepting the presidency of Kentucky University in 1859, but he refused to serve as president of both the College of Arts and of the College of the Bible in 1865 as the curators intended, indicating to them that he would assume leadership only of the latter institution.[25]

ON OCTOBER 2, 1865, classes began at the new university — but in only three of the many colleges projected. The largest was the College of Arts under its presiding officer Robert Graham with 223 students, followed by the College of the Bible with 37, and the College of Law with 13. In addition a prepara-

[24] Stevenson, *Lexington Theological Seminary*, p. 18.
[25] *Ibid.*, p. 25.

tory school called the Academy was established as an essential co-ordinate agency of the University, since adequate secondary public schools were not yet in existence and many students could not meet the college entrance requirements without assistance. Sixty-three students enrolled this first year in the Academy.

To be admitted to Kentucky University a candidate had to present satisfactory evidence of good moral character. To enter the College of Arts he had to be at least fourteen years old (sixteen years for the other colleges) and pass examinations in English, mathematics, Greek and Latin. When a candidate for admission arrived on campus, he first had to submit testimonials of character to the Regent, procure suitable boarding, submit to examination by the faculty of the college he wished to enter, pay the required fees, read the laws of the University and sign a declaration promising to conform to them, and then find out from his professors the time and place classes were to meet and the textbooks to be used. The session began on the first Monday of October and closed the last Thursday in June. Tuition was a modest $30 a year plus a $5 janitor fee.[26]

Bowman intended to allow as great a flexibility as possible in the student's academic program. Regulations stated that a student might secure a certificate of graduation from any of the various academic departments after having attended one year and satisfactorily completing the requirements of that department. If he wished to secure the degree of Bachelor of Arts he had to complete work in the departments of English language and literature, philosophy, mathematics, Greek, Latin, sacred history, civil history, chemistry and natural history. Two modern languages might be substituted for Greek and Latin, which reflected Bowman's opposition to forcing all candidates into the straightjacket of these ancient languages. A student could qualify for a Bachelor of Science degree by completing his work in the departments of the projected Agricultural and Mechanical College, and in law by similarly fulfilling that department's requirements.

[26]*Ibid.*, p. 52. Also, the *Catalogue of the Officers and Students of Kentucky University for the Academical Year, 1865–1866*, pp. 21–22.

THE STUDENT ARRIVING in Lexington to attend the first classes of Kentucky University might have walked up the hill from Main Street on Mill Street, passing the former home of Dr. Benjamin Dudley, behind which stood the old red brick building once housing the famed Transylvania Medical Department between 1827 and 1840. Stopping for a moment at the corner of Mill and Second streets, he might have admired the handsome house of John Hunt Morgan, the famed "Thunderbolt of the Confederacy," who had been killed by a Union soldier in Greenville, Tennessee, a little over a year before. Glancing along Second Street to Broadway, he might have caught a glimpse of the blackened rubble of the Medical Building — which with its fine colonnaded facade and cupola dominating Broadway had been destroyed by fire in May 1863. The student then would have crossed over the street to stroll through the old College Lot, looking across at the impressive Bodley house where once President Woods had lived and which, more recently, had housed a Union commander. The scene was peaceful now, but vivid memories of the Civil War still filled the air, clustered around the town and stirred in the minds of the people.

The student, pausing in the middle of the old campus, did not realize that under his feet lay buried the rubble of the large college building that had dominated the area during the Holley period. His eye would have been drawn across Mill Street to the well-proportioned brick house with its graceful doorway and palladian window. Here lived Benjamin Gratz, a successful merchant and community leader in Lexington and a longtime supporter and trustee of Transylvania. And here Howard Gratz would live and follow in Benjamin's footsteps, cherishing the memory of old Transylvania, and with the concurrence of the Kentucky University curators gradually convert the old College Lot into a beautiful public park. The only building remaining on the old campus was the long, rectangular, single-storied building that once housed the kitchen and the janitor's quarters. Now it would be used as a classroom for the Academy until a new Academy building was erected close to Morrison. But the student would not pause here long. The echoes of ancient academic battles did not ring in his ears. He would cross Third

Street and head up the path towards Morrison College, towering in its neo-Grecian dignity over all else, dominating the modest but adequate campus of over twenty acres. Behind Morrison College was the remaining dormitory built in 1839, the other having burned down in 1861. Further back were the ramshackle barracks built by the Union army during its brief stay on campus and the old Blythe house, still occasionally housing a college president.

Gratz House

Three of the colleges — Arts, Bible and Law — were crowded into the spacious halls of Morrison College, which had only recently been reconverted to academic use after having served as a hospital for Union troops during the preceding years. Bowman reported that it had been necessary

to make extensive repairs and improvements . . . at a cost of seven thousand dollars, out of moneys paid by the government for rents and damages, and from surplus funds passed over by the Transylvania board. The Libraries, Apparatus, and Museum of the Transylvania University, which had been scattered through the city during the military occupancy, together, and, with that which belonged to Kentucky University, were placed in rooms suitably prepared for the purpose. . . .[27]

Dormitory rooms could take care of only a few men, and mostly these were ministerial students. Other students found room and board in nearby houses, as had been the custom from the earliest days of Transylvania. Some men formed a co-operative dining society and were able to keep their food costs down to $1.50 a week.

The student's life remained tightly-regulated. The college's role as guardian *in loco parentis* was not yet challenged. It must be remembered that boys as young as fourteen might be admitted to the College of Arts. The College of the Bible drew students considerably older, usually in their mid-twenties. Some had already been ministers of churches but, conscious of their deficiencies, welcomed the opportunity offered by the newly-created College of the Bible to overcome them. These young men, longing to involve themselves actively in preaching, frequently grew restive when laboring with traditional liberal arts subjects. One wrote:

> I sometimes think it is almost a sin for us young men who are preparing for the ministry, to stay here conning over dull lessons in mathematics, Latin, and Greek. Like a caged bird, I long to be free of the College-wall cage. I am anxious to go into the world and preach the Gospel.[28]

But the younger men, following the traditional route to the A.B. degree, perhaps still needed the guiding structure of college regulations. Daily chapel attendance was required, as was attendance at public worship on Sunday. The student was expected to be diligent in study, punctual in attendance and respectful of all persons. He was prohibited from attending any "exhibitions of immoral tendency; no race-field, theatre, circus, billiard-saloon, bar-room, or tippling-house." He was forbidden the use of intoxicating beverages, or to use tobacco in the University buildings, or to keep in his possession "fire-arms, a dirk, a bowie-knife, nor any other kind of deadly weapon." He was to abstain from profanity, desecrating the Lord's

[27] Minutes of the Board, June 27, 1866.
[28] Stevenson, *Lexington Theological Seminary*, p. 33.

day, gaming, card-playing, or joining a secret society. Finally, he was muzzled from criticizing the government of the University in any way.[29]

THUS DID KENTUCKY UNIVERSITY begin its new career. Plans were busily made for the opening of the new Agricultural and Mechanical College in 1866 and the establishment of a connection with the local Commercial College. Bowman saw only unbounded progress at this stage, and his year-end report was infused with optimism. What impressed him as much as anything was the fact that though the smoke had hardly settled on the bitter battlefields of the Civil War

> so many who had been foes on the tented field could come together from North and South, and mingle once more in the classic halls, as friends and brothers. It is a beautiful commentary upon our American civilization, and puts to rest the fears of those who predicted political strifes and alienations. And just here, let it be known to all, that Kentucky University knows no North or South, and serves no sectional or political ends; but that it is the only aim and highest duty of all its officers of government and instruction to make it a blessing to the greatest number of every creed and latitude.[30]

To the Disciples church members he reported that the College of the Bible, the first of its kind among the brotherhood and regarded as an experiment by all and with distrust by some, had measured up to expectation. With the Disciples holding the ruling voice on the Board, their attitude towards Bowman's programs would always be crucial.

[29]*Catalogue of the Officers and Students of Kentucky University for the Academical Year, 1865–1866*, pp. 44–45.
[30]*Ibid.*, p. 52.

13

The Embattled Sectarians, 1865–1877

Confronted with a July 1, 1867, deadline of the Morrill Act requiring that at least one agricultural and mechanical college be in operation in the state, Bowman worked feverishly to secure the necessary land and buildings. This vigorous man with his long beard and dark, intense eyes had employed his persuasive powers to convince Lexingtonians to pledge generously to the project, and early in 1866 he purchased the fine home and estate of Henry Clay's "Ashland" for $90,000. Adjoining "Ashland" was the large estate of J. B. Tilford known as "Woodlands," which Bowman also purchased for an additional $40,000. Thus a tract of 433 acres, with assorted buildings of various shapes and sizes, was acquired as an excellent base for the new Agricultural and Mechanical College. Few if any of the new land grant colleges could have boasted of such a favorable site.

With his unified concept of the total university of which the Agricultural and Mechanical College was an integral part, Bowman would have sensed little difference whether the deeds to this property should have been kept by a special arrangement with the agricultural college or vested in Kentucky University as part of its entire holdings. Bowman secured the deeds as part of Kentucky University. At the time, the Board of Curators was responsible for the administration of all the colleges, and in June 1871, when the last payments were made and Kentucky University now owned this great tract in fee simple, the Board praised Bowman for his leadership and accomplishments. Within a few years, however, this point of ownership would prove to be a very hot and controversial issue.[1]

[1] Hopkins, *The University of Kentucky*, p. 67. Minutes of the Board, June 8, 1871.

Meanwhile, Kentucky received 330,000 acres of land scrip from the national government under the land grant act. The proceeds from the sale of this land were to provide the endowment for the new state agricultural college. The future welfare of the college hinged on the success with which this land scrip could be marketed. No worse time for such a sale could have been found. Many other states in the Union were trying to dispose of their public lands at the same time. Those states able to hold their scrip and sell it later received a more satisfactory price. (New York was particularly fortunate in the masterly way Ezra Cornell used part of the state's scrip to invest in Wisconsin land which in later years so increased in value as to provide a handsome endowment for its agricultural college.) But Kentucky neither could nor would wait. It is true that in February 1866, the Kentucky legislature did appropriate $20,000 to finance the initial operations of the Agricultural and Mechanical College until such time as the land scrip could be sold, but this was a one-shot emergency measure. Anyone familiar with the traditional legislative indifference to underwriting a reasonable and consistent program of financing higher education in Kentucky would know that the legislature had no intention of committing itself to annual appropriations of such a size, not as long as the land scrip was there to sell.

In June 1866, the commissioners of the Sinking Fund were instructed to sell the land scrip even though everyone knew that a mere fifty cents an acre could be secured in the current market. Bowman had planned on an anticipated sale of a dollar an acre; now in one sad stroke, the endowment was cut in half. Within six months all the land scrip was sold at a figure of some $165,000 from which an annual income of $9,900 might be expected. The only other income for the college would have to come from student fees and revenue from the farm and shops. Kentucky was not the only state to suffer such a loss. Rhode Island had sold her scrip for forty-one and forty-two cents an acre; North Carolina fifty cents; New Hampshire and Ohio fifty-three cents, and Indiana fifty-four cents.[2]

Of all the colleges of Kentucky University, the Agricultural and Mechanical College held a special spot in John Bowman's

[2] Hopkins, *The University of Kentucky*, pp. 70–71.

affections. He said that Americans were

> not willing to admit that the Law and Medicine and Divinity are
> the only learned professions; but they are determined to exalt
> and dignify labor, and to enoble the professions of the great
> masses of men upon whose shoulders mainly rests the fabric of
> our social and Republican institutions — I mean the *Farmers*
> and *Mechanics*.[3]

This man who still felt the fatigue of farm labor in his own
muscles, who had struggled to secure a college education for
himself at Bacon College and had gone on to become a successful farmer, knew how effectively education and labor could
be woven together. He was the living proof. This was to be the
new indigenous American education, a liberal and practical education for the masses. The ideal of an educated farmer was
certainly as old as Horace, but now it was being democratized
on a scale perhaps Jefferson had dreamed of. This was Bowman's vision as he looked beyond the meagre beginnings of
Kentucky University, beyond the limited resources and legislative parsimony, beyond the narrow view of sectarian control.

Bowman appointed his old friend from Harrodsburg, John
Augustus Williams, as presiding officer of the new Agricultural
and Mechanical College and filled most of the various departments with faculty from the College of Arts. Robert Graham
was assigned to teach English; Henry White, mathematics;
Robert Peter, chemistry and experimental philosophy; Alexander Winchell, natural history; and James K. Patterson, history. What else could Bowman have done? He had no money to
hire an entirely separate faculty. As it was, he had to secure
John Crutcher and A. B. Smith as new instructors for the Commercial and Business Department, and William Arnold for the
area of military tactics — military drill being required by law of
all students in the Agricultural and Mechanical College.[4]

A system of practical labor in the agricultural and mechanical
arts was also introduced as compulsory for all, but more hours
of labor were scheduled for those seeking to work off part of
their expenses. This was the three-fold plan: study, labor and
drill. The emphasis on practical labor was common at many

[3] *Ibid.*, p. 80.

[4] Information is contained in the General Announcement for 1866–1867 attached to the *Catalogue . . . 1865–1866.*

agricultural schools, though it was not generally popular at all of them. Massachusetts State College students struck against such labor on the grounds that it was not educational. But practical labor seems to have had some rationale. What the students at the Kentucky Agricultural and Mechanical College might justifiably have been critical of was the lack of courses in agriculture and mechanics. Not only were these fields new to American education and qualified instructors hard to find, but there was considerable disagreement as to how these courses ought to be taught. The result was that future farmers and mechanics received haphazard suggestions by professors of chemistry, physics and natural history on how to apply theoretical matter to the practical problems they would be facing. Robert Peter, an authority on soil chemistry and its relation to agricultural productivity, was in the minority as a faculty member who could make such practical suggestions.

Despite the difficulties in getting the Agricultural and Mechanical College underway, 120 students had enrolled by January 1867, and 190 by June. The enrollment expanded to 295 by the 1869–1870 school year but dwindled substantially in the next six years due to a severe economic depression and divisive institutional difficulties. Many of the prospective students who arrived had no adequate preparation for college work and had to enter the Academy. A few were expelled for disciplinary causes, but the majority adjusted to the prescribed routine of study, labor and drill.

President Williams resigned the presidency of the Agricultural and Mechanical College after only two years of service to return to Daughters College in Harrodsburg. He continued, however, to influence the fortunes of Kentucky University as an active curator. Professor Joseph Desha Pickett of the English Department served a few unhappy months as acting president until the Board of Curators, unable to secure a qualified member of the Christian Church to serve as president, settled on James Patterson and formally elected him to office in June 1870. He was to remain in that post for the next forty-one years — to endure the years of meagre budgets, inadequate facilities, sectarian hostility — until the twentieth century saw the institution move toward a new future.

The Board of Curators at the July 1866 meeting were so pleased with the progress of the University that they passed a series of resolutions commending John Bowman for his many services, and expressing their confidence "in his integrity and singleness of purpose in all his efforts . . . to build up and endow this institution." In view of the fact that Bowman had refused financial compensation and had made liberal expenditures of his own on behalf of the institution, the curators offered him the free use as his residence Henry Clay's "Ashland." The curators then turned their attention to other matters. They approved the salaries of $2,000 for the presiding officers, $1,750 for professors and $1,200 and $1,000 for adjunct professors.[5] The Board also heard from the committee on the College of Medicine which reported no progress in setting up a medical education program, citing a lack of adequate hospital facilities and competent faculty as the main reasons. No success in the matter of reactivating a medical department was seen until the end of the century.[6]

Also included in the miscellany of business details considered by the curators was an interesting item of $25,000 obtained by John Bowman from the United States government for rent and damage done to Transylvania University buildings during the Civil War. Nothing could really compensate for the loss of the fine medical building, but the grant did help repay money expended restoring Morrison Hall to a suitable condition for classes. In 1871 the Board acceded to a petition from the Lexington Bar Association to move the law library of Kentucky University to the City Library, on condition that the Bar Association assume the responsibility of protecting and maintaining it.[7]

These items, and many others, were the normal grist for the educational mill. The formalized record of these transactions stands like a quiet and undisturbed haven in the growing storm of controversy that was to tear the University apart. From 1869 on, the minutes of the Board meetings reflect the intensifying character of that struggle.

[5] Minutes of the Board, July 12, 1866.
[6] *Ibid.*, June 9, 1869.
[7] *Ibid.*, June 8, 1871.

Morrison Chapel

The rapidity with which Bowman had persuaded Kentucky legislators in the 1864–65 session to endorse his plan to unite Transylvania and Kentucky universities, and attach the Agricultural and Mechanical College to them, undercut any chance for a surprised and startled opposition to organize effectively. Now that Kentucky University was a viable reality, the various elements in the state hostile and suspicious of it began to crystallize their opposition and co-ordinate their attacks.

The Christian Church was a dynamic and growing religious power in Kentucky. The other and older religious denominations regarded this burgeoning native Kentucky church with fear and dismay. The ante-bellum period had already witnessed the way in which denominational rivalry spilled over into educational rivalry as Catholics, Methodists, Baptists, Presbyterians and Christians chartered their own colleges and undercut potential non-denominational support of a state university. Now, suddenly, the Christian Church college Kentucky University had secured legislative endorsement to merge with and almost blot out Transylvania University, and, in addition, had gained consent to operate the new Agricultural and Mechanical College. Other non-denominational critics attacked the action of attaching a state school to a church university.

In view of these external threats from denominational competitors and non-denominational critics, one would have assumed that the Christian Church and Christian curators would have united behind Bowman and supported him and his administration of the University. And for the first few years, they did so. It was ironic that the destruction of Bowman and his plans was rooted in a major schism within the Christian Church congregation in Lexington. It all seemed harmless enough at the beginning. The Lexington Christian Church was bursting at the seams with a vigorous, growing congregation and needed room to expand. In April 1870, the property of the First Presbyterian Church on the southwest corner of North Broadway and Second Street was purchased. There was established the Broadway Christian Church as a branch of the Main Street Church, but the united congregation was to be maintained. The theory had a certain attraction to it, but practically there was a need for a second independent Christian Church. In April 1871, Regent Bowman and Professor J. D. Pickett, who taught English in the College of the Bible, made the mistake of participating in a movement to establish the Second Christian Church. This had apparently been done without the knowledge or approval of the Main Street Church on the correct assumption that they would have opposed such a move. The reaction of the Main Street Church was to condemn the formation of the Second Christian Church, censure its leaders and finally expel them from their congregation.

Nothing could have been worse for Kentucky University. Few contests between human beings are as bitter, vicious and uncompromising as those between dedicated Christians within the same congregation. That the key combatants in this case should have been important members of the University staff was most unfortunate. What normally would have been fought within the confines of the church structure now spilled over into the University with disastrous results. What started as a struggle between the factions in the church ultimately became a tug-of-war between Bowman and his concept of Kentucky University, and John McGarvey and those curators who shared his sectarian concept of the institution. As long as Bowman was able to maintain harmonious relations with the Christian

Church, he was successful in making his educational views prevail. When he made the tactical error of antagonizing church authorities, he risked not only his position within the church but the future of the entire University as well. That some separation between the state-controlled Agricultural and Mechanical College and the church-controlled Kentucky University would ultimately have taken place is very probable. That it would have occurred so soon and under such explosive circumstances, had not the intense fight between Bowman and the McGarvey forces erupted, is most unlikely.

In contrast to Bowman's educational plans for the University, McGarvey's views, according to his biographer, W. C. Morro, were that

> the University was the creature of the church, existed for the church, and should serve the church. . . . From the University he expected two services in the interest of the church, namely, the training of preachers and a Christian education for other students. . . . By the church McGarvey meant the Disciples of Christ.[8]

This view was shared by some of the curators but by no means all of them. For a while the majority of them sided with Bowman and his educational philosophy which consigned Bible teaching to the College of the Bible and to one course in the College of Arts. But the issue kept coming up. In June 1867, the Board adopted a recommendation to instruct the Executive Committee to devise some plan by which "any present difficulties in the study of the Bible in the College of Arts be obviated; and at the same time the Bible be retained as a textbook in the College."[9]

At the November 1871 meeting the curators, subject to increasing pressure from the Christian Church constituency, passed a resolution directing that the faculty be investigated to determine "whether any of the Professors in the University are open and avowed infidels or skeptics and whether any of them are justly chargeable with a want of respect for the word of God." There is no record to indicate whether such an inquisition was conducted, and if so, what the results were. But the

[8] Morro, *McGarvey*, 119.
[9] Minutes of the Board, June 26, 1867.

handwriting on the wall was clear enough. The curators were
moving closer to McGarvey's conception of the church college.

The battle between McGarvey and his supporters and Bowman and his allies was largely conducted in the columns of the
local press, in the *Apostolic Times* — a pro-McGarvey church
publication — and in a variety of pamphlets and broadsides delivered to the church constituency throughout the state. The
Apostolic Times had been founded in 1869 by Robert Graham,
John McGarvey, Moses Lard and L. B. Wilkes. This group
shared a hostile view of Bowman's secession from the Main
Street Church and his administration of the University. In the
days before radio, television and the cinema, the written word
was the main avenue for broadcast of viewpoints. The spoken
word was limited to much smaller audiences. The Holley deba-
cle a half-century earlier had been spawned in the press. Now
Bowman was the target. Intervening years had done little to
mellow journalistic vituperation, and it is hardly a credit to
McGarvey that he became the unquestioned champion in the
use of it. The prevailing practice of using anonymous names to
attach to letters to the press was only partially successful in
obscuring the author's identity and added the tantalizing sport
of ferreting out the secret of authorship.

By October 1871, the letters appearing in the columns of the
Lexington Daily Press, *Kentucky Gazette* and *Kentucky Statesman* indicated the direction of the struggle. First, there were
the battlelines drawn between those persons who had seceded
from the Main Street Church and the leaders of that church
who had led the movement to expel them. A second group centered their attack on John Bowman, not only for being a dis-
contented schismatic in church affairs but also for attempting to
pervert the aim of the charter of Kentucky University by reducing church control of the institution. A third group, of
which Robert Peter was a notable example, came to the defense of Bowman to protect the University and the future of the
Agricultural and Mechanical College. Another group denounced both Bowman and the Disciples of Christ for uniting
the Agricultural and Mechanical College with Kentucky University and wished to separate them. It was a Mad Hatter's
teaparty participated in by characters who would be comic if

the results of their actions had not been so disastrous.

An example of the conflict between individuals representing the first group was the incident involving Professor Pickett when he was prohibited from conducting chapel services in the school. Pickett had sided with Bowman in organizing the secession movement from the Main Street Church and thus created a problem for his colleagues Milligan and McGarvey in the College of the Bible. McGarvey apparently persuaded Milligan to use his presidential office to humble Pickett by not inviting Pickett to conduct chapel. Pickett protested, stating that only the curators could take such action. The curators, however, failed to back him up.

The second group was represented by curator W. T. Withers who attacked Bowman in a letter to the *Louisville Ledger*, saying that

> Regent Bowman is determined to rule or ruin. He is represented as appealing to the Christian Church and the Board of Curators to sustain him in his recent conduct. . . . But it is distinctly announced that if he is "mistaken" in this, then he will rend to pieces the University, and, out of the disjointed fragments, will build up an independent, undenominational institution. . . . If Kentucky University is wrecked through his instrumentality he may rest assured he will never have another opportunity to wreck another.[10]

Withers intimated that Bowman would probably try to detach Transylvania and the Agricultural and Mechanical College from Kentucky University and unite them into a new institution.

Robert Peter, representing the third group, rushed into the fray with an article entitled "Who Owns Kentucky University?" in which he claimed that the Christian Church had in reality contributed less than one-fourth of the money to the total holdings of the University, and therefore, regardless of the charter provisions that two-thirds of the curators had to be members of the Christian Church in Kentucky, the real control of the institution could not justifiably be assumed by that denomination. It was an untenable argument legally, but it had a certain appeal to a sizeable number of donors who had given money to Bowman for land for the Agricultural and Mechanical

[10]*The Louisville Ledger*, November 9, 1871.

College to secure its location in Lexington.

The Board in special session appointed a committee to investigate the charges against Bowman but at the same time unanimously passed a resolution expressing the confidence of the Board in the Regent.[11] The *Apostolic Times* criticized the Board's action in supporting Bowman and asserted that the Christian Church held undisputed control over Kentucky University except for the Agricultural and Mechanical College.[12]

Editors of the local press gingerly side-stepped involvement in a sectarian civil war but were justifiably concerned with threats to the welfare of the University and the Agricultural and Mechanical College. They pointed out that many donors to the University were in no way connected with the Christian Church but merely wished to see a prosperous university in Lexington.

The beginning of 1872 saw no amelioration of the struggle. James Patterson, president of the Agricultural and Mechanical College, rightly feared this tumult would only reinforce a movement in the Kentucky legislature to detach the state school from Kentucky University. He addressed an open letter to the legislature and the people of Kentucky on February 14, 1872, clearly showing that the Agricultural and Mechanical College was in no way unduly loaded with members of the Christian Church. His own staunch Presbyterianism was well-known, and of his nine faculty members three were Presbyterians, two Campbellites (Disciples) and the remaining spread among the Episcopal, Lutheran, Methodist and Congregational denominations. He noted that while the course in Bible history was required in the College of Arts for a degree, none of the A&M students were required to take it. Before the legislature rashly acted to divorce the A&M College from Kentucky University, it had better plan to provide an income of $100,000 at the start, gradually moving to $300,000 a year unless they wished to establish a "half-starved, wretched caricature of a college, with a faculty half-manned and on starving allowances."[13] Whether convinced by Patterson's letter or their own investigations, the

[11] Minutes of the Board, November 24, 1871.
[12] *The Apostolic Times*, November 30, 1871.
[13] *Lexington Daily Press*, February 14, 1872.

legislators appeared content to leave the A&M College under Kentucky University's care.

In mounting crescendo the clash of arms intensified through the spring of 1872. The curators confronted the ugly affair at their June meeting. In a moment of desperation the Board adopted a resolution stating that "hereafter no private or personal difficulty that may exist between Professors, officers, and Curators of Kentucky University shall be introduced into the Board of Curators for settlement."[14] It was a futile gesture. The Board was the court of last resort and they could not dodge their responsibility. At the previous November meeting the Board had appointed a Peace Committee which had been ladened with the task of reconciling differences among the antagonists. Beyond chastising Peter for his newspaper attacks on certain curators and professors, the Peace Committee abandoned any attempt to untangle the controversies. Having given Bowman a vote of confidence, the Board decided to postpone any action for a year, and requested all to refrain from controversy.

The Board doubtless hoped that this would end the affair, but even before their action was made public, speculations on the Board's decisions began to appear in both the Lexington and Cincinnati press. It was in response to these that McGarvey, apparently believing strictures on the curators to preserve peace did not apply to him, let loose a heavy editorial barrage from the office of the *Apostolic Times*. The editors, aware of the significance of the issue, urged their readers to preserve the issue on the grounds that it contained an effective rebuttal to the slanders levelled against them. This issue of the paper so infuriated the Executive Committee that it took the unprecedented action of suspending McGarvey from his post in the College of the Bible when he refused their request to resign.

If any further polarization of the contending forces was needed, this was it. The questionable legality of the Executive Committee's power to dismiss a faculty member, though no one disputed its right to fill a temporary vacancy, forced the Board to convene a special meeting in September. Through the remainder of July and August orthodox forces in the Christian

[14]Minutes of the Board, June 13, 1872.

Churches, who saw the dismissal of McGarvey as the arrogant flinging down of the gauntlet to them by a self-perpetuating board, mustered their forces to resolve once and for all the question "Who Owns Kentucky University?"

Amidst a wave of petitions that flooded them, the curators met on September 16, 1873, in Morrison Hall. With corridors crowded to overflowing by people seeking entrance to the hearing room, the meeting was then opened to the public, and the Board moved from the jammed Board Room to the chapel. There being no lights there, however, they had to adjourn at 8:30 p.m. until the next morning. But the curators tended to ignore the original mass of petitions by sending them to a special committee for evaluation, and the failure of the Board to treat these petitions seriously at this time was a tactical error. It only widened the gap between the churches and the curators.[15]

Having finally heard extensive arguments from all sides — including a three-and-one-half hour defense from McGarvey — the Board adopted a resolution which justified McGarvey's dismissal on the grounds that McGarvey published articles "improper and intemperate in their character and calculated to reopen questions of strife and discord" after the Board had explicitly forbidden such action at its last meeting. McGarvey refused to resign, and therefore the Board removed him from his post.[16]

Now President Milligan was upset. It was reported that tears "streamed down his face" as he sent an urgent message to the Board informing them that the Bible students would leave the University immediately unless the curators took some action to keep them. The majority of students wanted to leave in protest over McGarvey's suspension. Only Milligan's desperate pleas that such action would kill the College of the Bible persuaded about half of them to stay. However, the local press reported that only about six or seven actually left the school and transferred to Bethany.

On the whole McGarvey conducted himself admirably in this defeat, which he no doubt regarded in proper Biblical perspec-

[15]Stevenson, *Lexington Theological Seminary*, p. 52.
[16]Minutes of the Board, September 16, 1873.

tive as only temporary. He told his friends he would now devote more time to his work as editor of the *Apostolic Times* and as minister of the Broadway Christian Church.

Lexingtonians concerned with the prosperity of Kentucky University were justifiably worried that McGarvey's dismissal, wrongly interpreted by the Christian Churches, could be cause for the school's collapse. The *Lexington Herald* said it had not intended to comment on this incident but it feared spread of the belief that only Professor McGarvey represented the Christian Church in the University.

> This is so erroneous [said the editor] it seems hardly worthy of correction. President Milligan and Professor Pickett, both of the Bible College . . . as fully represent the Christian Church in the University as Prof. McGarvey could have done.[17]

Nor, the editor went on, was McGarvey's dismissal an attack on the Christian character of that professor, but an attempt to maintain harmony within the University. The action of certain Bible students to leave on this account was ill-conceived and unjustified.[18]

There was little hope that the churches, especially those who had petitioned the Board to retain McGarvey, would share any such views or heed the editorial counsel. Their sentiment was more accurately represented by the *Apostolic Times*, whose editors spoke of "this foul deed in removing Professor McGarvey" and who denounced the Board for not having "heeded those petitions before the fatal vote was taken."[19]

The rumor mill began to operate. Unsubstantiated reports were spread that Bowman had received a majority of the curator's votes only by distributing among them shares of stock in the Southern Pacific Railroad. The *Apostolic Times* did not support this rumor but offered the effective argument that at least eighteen or nineteen of the twenty-two curators who voted against McGarvey should have disqualified themselves, either because they were members of the Executive Committee, relatives of Bowman or had already made up their minds before the hearing.

[17]*Lexington Herald*, September 26, 1873.
[18]*Ibid*.
[19]*The Apostolic Times*, October 2, 1873.

Meanwhile the special committee, appointed by the Board to examine and report on the petitions of 181 churches and 313 donors opposing McGarvey's dismissal, met and inevitably ended with two reports. The majority report of the curators stated that they administered the University in the interest of the donors, though they were by no means "indifferent to the interests of the Christian Church."[20] Curator Withers drafted the minority report which supported the viewpoint of the petitions that the Christian Church owned Kentucky University.

Students and faculty on Old Morrison steps, circa 1875

McGarvey's supporters viewed the majority report as further evidence of the indifference of the controlling majority of the curators to the true interests of the church. It impelled them to organize a mass movement among Christian Churches to petition the upcoming session of the Kentucky legislature to amend the charter and to sever the Agricultural and Mechanical College from the University. The petition to sever the two institu-

[20] Stevenson, *Lexington Theological Seminary*, p. 54.

tions was based on the inconvenience of the arrangement and the financial burden imposed — inconvenient because the connection of the state college with a sectarian university stirred up widespread distrust and accusations of an improper fusion between church and state, and a financial burden because the $9,000 interest from the state school's endowment was scarcely adequate to cover the expenses of running the college.

Petitions from 250 churches flooded the legislators in the 1873–1874 session, and the House was sufficiently convinced by this appeal to pass a bill by a slim one-vote margin that would have separated the two institutions. The Senate, however, responded to counter-petitions from twenty-four curators and 281 concerned citizens of Fayette County by defeating the bill by four votes. John Bowman's request that the Kentucky University charter be amended to reduce the number of required Christian curators from two-thirds to one-half did not get legislative support and made him even more enemies among Christian Church members.

Nothing had been settled by the legislative action re-affirming the original charter conditions placing the Agricultural and Mechanical College under the direction of Kentucky University. Whether due to the economic depression in the country or to the continuing strife within the institution, however, enrollment dropped drastically between 1870 and 1875 in all colleges of the University. Part of the University funds had been lost with the failure of the "Short Line" Railroad and the Commercial Bank of Kentucky. Professors were being paid in promissory notes. The indebtedness of the University had mushroomed to $120,000 by 1876. Undoubtedly some of the Christian supporters of McGarvey refused to give further financial assistance to the school or even to enroll their sons until the issue of the church's control was decided once and for all.

Such a convergence of negative forces presented Bowman with a dilemma. Either he could penitently return to the church and surrender to sectarian control — an action not only distasteful but impossible for him to take — or he could try to persuade the state legislature to issue a new charter for a University of Kentucky free of any reference to sectarian support. As a last resort he attempted to use the latter approach, but to no avail.

The curators saw no alternative to financial bankruptcy and the collapse of the University but to win back the confidence of the Christian Church. In their 1874 meeting they passed and publicized a series of resolutions submitted by Curator Sloan. They expressed their belief that under the present charter "the Christian Churches of Kentucky do, in a certain sense, real and important, have control of the University," and disclaimed "every purpose to secularize or sectarianize the institution ourselves."[21]

The chief object of concern was the College of the Bible as enrollment continued to decline. On March 20, 1875, the gentle, scholarly Robert Milligan died, and the Board at its next June meeting voted to initiate a drive to endow the college. The curators also offered the Kentucky Christian Education Society an opportunity to nominate two professors if the Society would accept the responsibility for paying their salaries. It came as no surprise to anyone that John McGarvey was selected, along with Robert Graham. With the appearance of these two men in the classrooms of the College of the Bible, the enrollment went up. The Society was reluctant to raise endowment funds for the whole University, however, until Bowman was ousted.

Meanwhile the pressures of a growing indebtedness never let up. The curators in desperation began to sell sizeable sections of "Ashland" and "Woodlands" estates to satisfy the University's creditors, and the rich landed resources of the Agricultural and Mechanical College were thus eroded. Apparently some of Bowman's actions to secure funds for the University, as in the sale of the hemp crop in 1874, had not been approved by the Executive Committee which thereupon demanded that Bowman's accounts be audited. Bowman refused, believing himself accountable only to the full Board. The Executive Committee, irritated by the constant pressure of financial problems and the persistent pressure from the Christian Churches to get rid of Bowman, reacted to Bowman's refusal by suspending him as regent in April 1877. Bowman denounced the action as illegal and said:

So long as I was permitted to devote my attention to my duties

21*The Apostolic Times*, July 9, 1874.

the University prospered. The attacks of enemies alike to the University and myself have impaired temporarily its prosperity, but have not lessened my obligations. The trusts committed to me can be returned only to the board. . . . Undeterred by atrocious calumnies, whether dignified by alleged official endorsement or whispered sedulously in the ear, conscious of my rectitude and of my profound love for the University to which I have given my manhood, I shall lay before the Board of Curators at an early day such vindication of myself as may seem proper.[22]

The annual meeting of the Board in June 1877, turned into a three-day brawl as a concerted effort was made to abolish the regency and expel Bowman. Beyond the bitter contest between Bowman and some of the curators, which took up a good deal of this meeting, was the indisputable financial distress of the University. The Agricultural and Mechanical College was proving to be an impossible financial burden for the University. Despite the seriousness of the crisis, the Board by a 17–7 vote repudiated the action of its Executive Committee and kept Bowman.[23]

For one more year Bowman would try to hold the reins over this ungovernable troika of a university. He must have begun to wonder what mad whimsey had originally persuaded him to attempt to develop a major public university on a denominational base. The greatest priority was to secure adequate financial support, and without the backing of the Christian Church Bowman was not sure he could get it. Yet he would not surrender to the demands of the *Apostolic Times* editors whose effective role as a mouthpiece for thousands of concerned Disciples throughout Kentucky could not be denied. For a while it appeared that Bowman's enormous persuasiveness and energy would accomplish the impossible, but the steady, if narrow, attacks of his opponents began gradually to erode even the commanding position Bowman had occupied as regent.

Increasingly the state legislature became concerned about maintaining the Agricultural and Mechanical College under the supervision of Kentucky University, while many of the curators wished to separate from the state school because of the financial burden. Bowman viewed the possible loss of the A&M

[22]*Lexington Daily Press*, April 16, 1877.
[23]*Ibid.*, June 14, 1877.

College as a major blow to the fulfillment of his educational plans, while many of the brotherhood, worried as to whether Kentucky University belonged to them, kept a close eye on the condition of the College of the Bible. To them, this college was the barometer by which to measure the degree of Christian control.

When it appeared that the actions of the curators in the summer of 1877 would result in a drastic weakening of the College of the Bible and that Bowman had mixed feelings about the desirability of such a college on the University campus, a campaign was launched by the Kentucky Christian Education Society to raise funds for a separate and independent College of the Bible which would have no legal connection with Kentucky University. Fearful this would end once and for all any further significant Christian support of the University, Bowman persuaded his old enemy Moses Lard to assume leadership of the existing College of the Bible, but to no avail. Lard received a volley of criticism from his former associates, and only three students showed up for classes in the fall of 1877 — while forty-one students participated in classwork in the new College of the Bible, meeting in the basement of the Main Street Christian Church. In February 1878, the state legally chartered this new institution, and the University's College of the Bible ceased to function. Robert Graham became the first president of this newly-organized College of the Bible.

In January 1878, a special investigating legislative committee held hearings in Lexington on the condition of Kentucky University. The committee's report based on these hearings was a well-balanced and thoughtful evaluation of the situation. The report concluded that the bitter struggle between Bowman, the curators and the bulk of influential Disciples was a major factor in the deteriorating condition of all components of Kentucky University. It was concerned about the depressed condition of the Agricultural and Mechanical College, and it was recommended that the legislature take necessary action to sever relations between that college and Kentucky University and seek for a suitable spot to relocate it. Nor was it surprising that the committee urgently requested the legislature never again to place the Agricultural and Mechanical College under any form of denominational control.

What did not appear in the report was a secret proposal made by Bowman to the members of the committee at "Ashland" one evening to change the name of the existing institution to the University of Kentucky, repeal the two-thirds clause concerning the Christian curators, and forbid a majority of either professors or curators to be from the same church. He also proposed to reduce the number of curators to twenty-one, take $75,000 of Kentucky University's present endowment and use it as an endowment for a separate College of the Bible and appropriate $25,000 to establish a normal school. What the various members of the committee thought of the proposition we will never know, but they decided to steer clear of it. McGarvey somehow got hold of Bowman's proposals and in the columns of the *Apostolic Times* held them up as proof of Bowman's intention to betray the Christian Church and rob it of its university.[24]

To men who shared McGarvey's views this was all the proof needed, but to accept his verdict on Bowman's intentions would be to surrender historical impartiality to a most prejudiced observer. In retrospect Bowman's last-ditch proposals have a poignant and futile quality about them — the last desperate attempt of this tragic figure to rescue something from the ruins. Nor were they impractical proposals. Unfortunately for him and for the state, they were premature and unacceptable. In the face of an aroused constituency from the Christian Church, it was most unlikely that legislators would have risked battling the church by wresting from it the control of Kentucky University. It was easier to detach the Agricultural and Mechanical College from the controversial institution, though it would mean many long and lean years for the state college. This action was formalized on March 13, 1878, when the college was officially divorced from Kentucky University and set up as an independent institution.

What the curators faced at their June 1878, meeting was the amputated trunk of a university. The state had taken away the Agricultural and Mechanical College and the church had set up

[24]*Louisville Courier-Journal*, February 25, 1870; *The Apostolic Times*, February 15, 1878.

an independent College of the Bible. Left was the College of Arts, a small law department and an informal relationship with the downtown Commercial College to train students in secretarial and bookkeeping arts. And even this reduced core was troubled by rumors that Transylvania might wish to reassume, if it legally could, its own historic identity.

Only John Bowman remained, standing among the shambles to remind the Board of what might have been. It was easy enough to identify him with all their troubles, and now that his educational dreamhouse was crumbling there seemed to be little reason to keep him. Even the arbitration committee authorized by the Board to resolve the difficulties between Bowman and the Executive Committee had failed to materialize, because disputants could not agree on three lawyers to compose a committee. The Board threw up its hands, dismissed the whole affair, and rid themselves of the controversial Bowman by abolishing the office of Regent by a 19–12 vote. This was followed by the election of bespectacled, amenable and devoted Henry White as the first president of Kentucky University. Over the next few months gradual transfer of the financial holdings of Kentucky University from Bowman to other hands took place and by the following year Bowman was requested to vacate the premises at "Ashland."[25]

In order not to cause the Agricultural and Mechanical College undue hardship as a result of its separation from Kentucky University, the curators agreed to continue to operate the college for the next two years while the state selected a permanent location for it. Meanwhile the Board passed a series of resolutions denying any intention to convert Kentucky University into a narrow sectarian institution and vowing to preserve inviolate the trusts and interests of old Transylvania. But the victory, if indeed there was one, was indisputably sectarian as evidenced by the curators' statement in the *Lexington Daily Press:*

> We announce to the Christian brotherhood, the citizens of Lexington and vicinity, and the general public that the protracted struggle to obtain possession and control of Kentucky University for its rightful owners, has at length been crowned with signal

[25] Minutes of the Board, June 13, 1878.

success. The Regency has been abolished, and Prof. H. H. White has been elected President of the University. An Executive Committee has also been elected, all of whom are members of the Christian Church of Kentucky, and are in full sympathy with the Church. The desire of the brotherhood has at length been achieved, and we now appeal to them to rally around the University.[26]

As the years went by, perhaps Bowman could console himself with the thought expressed by Stevenson in his *Lexington Theological Seminary* that in place of Bowman's own shattered plans there now stood "a realization far more resplendent: not one institution but three — a thriving church related college (now Transylvania), a growing state university, and a promising theological seminary. Forces which at the time had appeared so destructive had been truly creative."[27]

Bowman had been naive in his assumption that such diverse elements could be unified under one institutional roof. It was inevitable that at some time the Agricultural and Mechanical College as a strictly state institution would separate from denominational connections. It had been a hazardous attempt at best, made possible only because the Kentucky legislature failed to take full financial and educational responsibility for its own state college from the start. Yet the fact that these three institutions successfully made their own way can hardly hide the defeat that progressive and experimental educational thought and ideals suffered from this struggle. Though there is no guarantee that, had Bowman had his way, a great state university would have emerged (it is hard to see how this could have been done without removing Kentucky University's sectarian connections), there was no man who matched Bowman in educational vision, extraordinary energy and absolute dedication to his cause. Winning instead was a narrower sectarian view of education that influenced the policies of Kentucky University and the College of the Bible for the next several decades, and a continuation of the legislative policy of a reluctant and grudging support for the state college.

[26] Quoted in Hopkins, *The University of Kentucky*, p. 110.
[27] Stevenson, *Lexington Theological Seminary*, p. 59.

14

Apes, Girls, and 'Daddy' Loos

Henry White   *Charles Loos*

The collapse of Bowman's dream of a great state university signaled the second failure of Kentucky within half a century to erect a first-rate institution of higher education. With regard to the first failure, President Patterson once said:

> Transylvania might have been among the great universities of the country had the State managed its interests herself alone. But instead of this, she delegated, from time to time, the duty and business of its management to successive religious denominations, each of which promised great things, but accomplished little.[1]

The second failure resulted from the impossibility of erecting a state institution on a denominational base. The original Transylvania charter had been free of denominational affiliation and would have provided such a foundation, but its fusion with Kentucky University had changed that status; and the legislature bungled the matter in attaching the Agricultural and Mechanical College to it in order to free itself from the responsibility of properly financing and adequately supervising a separate state college. Now the legislators reaped the whirlwind of controversy and failure, and had to face the bitter reality after all. State legislatures elsewhere had avoided making these mistakes — although they made others — and thus other state universities began to move into a period of growth and prosperity that would leave Kentucky far behind. It would take another century to catch up.

[1] Mabel Hardy Pollitt, *James Kennedy Patterson*, p. 14.

Meanwhile Lexington was host to three disparate educational
institutions — Kentucky University, the College of the Bible
and the Agricultural and Mechanical College. The community
wished to remain the site for all three, but with the detachment
of the state school from Kentucky University an intense struggle developed between these two schools that nearly forced the
A&M College to move elsewhere. Many, though not all, of the
Kentucky University curators regarded the independent state
school as an educational rival and wished it elsewhere if, indeed, not obliterated entirely. This ungenerous hostility was
not the monopoly of Kentucky University, but was shared by
the other sectarian colleges in the state, evidenced by the pressure they placed on state legislators not to lay a special tax on
Kentucky property for the special benefit of the state college.

At first it appeared that Kentucky University held only the
most amiable feelings towards the independent Agricultural and
Mechanical College. Arrangements were worked out between
the University and state officials to allow the state college to
remain on the land and in the buildings it had previously occupied. Such an arrangement was to last for two years, 1878–80.
This would give the state time to decide upon a permanent site
for the school and a means of financing it. But when the two
years were up, Lexingtonians were astounded to learn that the
Kentucky University curators had no intention of allowing the
state college to remain on the "Ashland" and "Woodlands"
estates. Hundreds of donors who had given their money to
Bowman for the purpose of buying land and buildings to locate
the Agricultural and Mechanical College in Lexington now discovered that title to the land had been given completely to Kentucky University and not set apart separately for the state college. The curators had an unchallenged legal control over the
property, and they had every intention of selling it, especially
since their financial resources were dwindling. They might have
sold it to the state, but the state had no desire to buy it. Indeed,
the state was willing to wait for bids from various communities
anxious to provide the land and money for the state college.
The Lexington donors felt betrayed and had every right to feel
so. They had given their money in good faith that Lexington
would be the permanent location of the Agricultural and Me-

chanical College. Now, through a legal technicality, they were
being deprived of that. No wonder the citizens and the local
press attacked the University with such virulence. For that
matter, the Board itself was split between those who believed
they had a moral obligation to cede some of the land and buildings to the state college, and those who wished to expel it from
Lexington.

> Curator W. T. Tibbs, who professed to blame the troubles of
> Kentucky University upon its connection with the State school
> went so far as to declare that "the Board of Curators feel that
> the State is under 'moral obligation' to relieve us as far as poss-
> ible by removing the A & M College from the scene of discord
> already occupied permanently by the University in accordance
> with the requirements of the charter."[2]

In the end, there was nothing Lexingtonians could do but
futilely petition the Board and, failing to receive satisfaction
there, invent some other scheme to secure their ends. This they
did by persuading the city and county authorities to put up
$50,000 and a city park of over fifty acres as a campus for the
Agricultural and Mechanical College. The competition from
Bowling Green was not sufficient to overcome the state committee's preference for Lexington, and the state college remained there, much to the chagrin of certain Kentucky University curators.

As critical to the survival of the state college as its location
was the fight over a special tax levied by the state to help finance the institution. Practically all the church colleges combined to question the constitutionality of the tax and to seek its
repeal. President Patterson made an eloquent speech in defense
of the tax, saying that "this crusade against the advancement of
learning would find an appropriate place in the Fourteenth Century, but is strangely out of place in the Nineteenth." He argued that church colleges and state colleges should work co-
operatively rather than competitively; that the church college
educated many students for the ministry, the state college
none. He pointed out that a church college education was more
special in character while that of the state college would be
more general. Church colleges tended to draw their students

[2]Hopkins, *The University of Kentucky*, pp. 119–120.

The faculty, 1886-87

from certain classes, the state college from all classes. Finally, he said that sectarian colleges had had a monopoly on higher education up to now, but that only a small fraction of students wished to go to them. Times had changed. It was time for Kentucky to move ahead in the field of higher education. At present, he concluded, there was not a single educational institution of note existing in the state.[3]

Patterson's view of the situation was an honest one, and it was mean-spirited of denominational schools to seek to hamper development of the state college. Though many Kentucky University curators sided against Patterson, it was to President

[3] Pollitt, *James Kennedy Patterson*, pp. 261–276.

Charles Louis Loos' credit, though he had become president of Kentucky University only two years before, that he disengaged himself from this struggle. He wrote Patterson: "I intend to keep myself entirely free from this controversy. I came here and am here to labour in peace in my vocation. In this purpose I shall abide inflexibly."[4]

Patterson won his fight. The state college remained in Lexington, and the tax necessary for its survival was preserved. Although there were to be many thin years ahead, the dedicated, lean, Scotch Presbyterian with his ever-present crutch guided the school firmly and successfully into the twentieth century.

KENTUCKY UNIVERSITY and its now legally-independent but nevertheless functionally-related sister, the College of the Bible, prepared to go on. What kind of a school would it now become? As a three-dimensional reality with a specific historical identity, it would seem to be an easy matter to describe it, but it did not exist in a vacuum. It was a Kentucky college and its students were largely Kentuckian, though it continued to enroll students from more than a dozen states and from abroad. This meant that there were strong southern influences impinging on it. It was now more than ever a church-related institution with an important theological seminary sharing Morrison Hall until it erected its own building in 1895. The dormitories were used largely as residence halls for the ministerial students. Finally, it was essentially a small, undergraduate institution in the changing American educational scene, sharing the tensions and influences that bore upon hundreds of similar institutions.

It is true that Kentucky University attempted to preserve its university status right up to World War I by maintaining its affiliation with the Commercial College, occasionally reviving the law department and briefly attempting to attach a medical department to itself. But it would be inaccurate to call it a true university in this period. It had neither the resources, leadership, faculty, or even the academic environment to place it in a realistic university status. There were fleeting hopes of recap-

[4]*Ibid.*, p. 136.

turing the status and glory of the Holley decade, but these proved to be illusory, and in the end a practical and wise decision was made to concentrate upon operating a first-rate liberal arts undergraduate college.

The curriculum in 1880 was concentrated in the traditional fields of English language and literature; mental, moral and political philosophy; mathematics; Greek and Latin; sacred history and the evidences of Christianity; natural science, which included physics, chemistry, anatomy and physiology, botany, and zoology; and some basic introduction to the modern languages.[5] To qualify for an A.B. degree, a student had to complete work in all these departments, with occasional modifications such as taking a modern language instead of a fourth year in Latin or Greek.

THERE IS NO DOUBT that the main dynamic force which polarized new and old concepts in higher education and in American thought in the post-Civil War era was Darwinism. Kentucky University shared in this struggle. Intellectual historians have pointed out that Darwinism came at a time in American history when society itself was undergoing a profound change. The years 1865–1900 embraced a period in which industrial and technological advances transformed American society. Urbanization expanded at an unprecedented rate. New cities seemed to spring up overnight. The population was in a state of continual motion as farmers moved to the city, people moved westward into the unoccupied areas of the North American continent, and a growing flood of immigrants poured into the cities, mines, industries and countryside. The rapidity of change in the material environment and mode of living had inevitable social repercussions as well. City living tended to erode family ties, increase the divorce rate and propel women into new roles in the business world. Improved means of communication and transportation facilitated the rapid exchange of new ideas and ways of doing things. Americans were therefore confronted with a serious challenge to the permanence and security in their lives, and the appearance of Darwinism at this

[5]*Catalogue*, 1880.

moment symbolized for many of them the worst threat to accepted values.

Science, which had long occupied an inferior position in the collegiate curriculum, was making a strong and increasingly successful bid to elevate its status. A new form of Biblical criticism, frequently called the higher criticism, had challenged many fundamentalist and literal views of the Bible. Bert Loewenberg has pointed out that

> Darwinism attacked absolutisms whether of species or thought systems. The concepts of change, emergence, and becoming, weighted with scientific dignity, assumed new importance, challenging finalisms in whatever guise.[6]

The age-old and continuing search for reality and permanence, still very much alive in the nineteenth century, was now being threatened by a theory of mutability in the realm of life. Colleges and churches were the main arenas for this intellectual warfare. The scientific community was far from being united behind Darwin's theory, as the split in the Harvard faculty between Louis Agassiz and Asa Gray demonstrated. Nor was the clergy united against it, as the actions and writings of men like James McCosh, leading Presbyterian theologian and president of Princeton University, Henry Ward Beecher and Lyman Abbot attested. As Hofstadter and Metzger have discovered:

> Determined efforts were made in the sixties, seventies, and early eighties to hold the line of education by the tactics of exclusion where possible, by threats and tirades where necessary. Synods gave warnings to trustees and trustees instructed presidents to reject the applications of Darwinians. Attacks in the local pulpits, alarms in the religious press, were employed to make colleges toe the mark and professors mend their ways. Once again, a battle of ideas became a battle for the schools.[7]

For southern colleges in particular, Darwin's theories became identified with northern Yankee subversive thought — a kind of intellectual carpetbagging. Southern society, only gradually recovering from the trauma of Radical Reconstruc-

---

[6]Bert James Loewenberg, "Darwinism Comes to America, 1859–1900." *Mississippi Valley Historical Review*, Vol. XXVIII, No. 3 (December, 1941), p. 358.

[7]Hofstadter and Metzger, *The Development of Academic Freedom in the United States*, p. 326.

tion, closed its ranks against any ideas or actions that would disturb the status quo in race relations. A young Yankee professor at Vanderbilt University was summarily dismissed for entertaining ideas contrary to those of Biblical creation.

> He was informed that "our people are of the opinion that such views are contrary to the plan of redemption," stripped of his office, and sent home to his native Michigan with the Tennessee Methodist Conference's denunciation of himself as an emissary of "scientific atheism" and "untamed speculation" ringing in his ears.[8]

Those who wished to teach Darwinism tended to move North, and although some instructors were dismissed in northern colleges as well, northern colleges tended to accept the teaching of evolution more rapidly than southern colleges. However by the end of the nineteenth century, outspoken exponents of Darwinism began to appear and to survive on some southern campuses. What is important to understand in studying this struggle is that it was not simply a war between a single biological hypothesis and certain religious dogma, or even between science and religion, since many evolutionists wished to strengthen both fields. Hofstadter and Metzger conclude that

> in consequence there was not a war, but many particular wars: a war between two kinds of knowledge — the clerical and the scientific; between two sorts of educational control — the sectarian and the secular; between two fundamental ways of knowing — the authoritarian and the empiricist; between two basic approaches to instruction — the doctrinal and the natural. . . .[9]

The long-range, constructive outcome of the fight over Darwinism was the slow establishment of a positive concept of academic freedom, emphasizing the scientific concept of truth and developing a formula for tolerating error. Academic freedom assumed "an affirmative moral position, and not merely a negative condition, the absence of overt restraint."[10]

It was not surprising that Kentucky University as a sectarian school in a southern atmosphere should have reflected the attitudes of southern colleges generally. Though legally indepen-

[8] W. J. Cash, *The Mind of the South* (New York, 1941), p. 148.

[9] Hofstadter and Metzger, *The Development of Academic Freedom in the United States*, p. 346.

[10] *Ibid.*

dent from the University, the College of the Bible was a functional component of the campus and the influence of its
faculty — especially men such as John McGarvey — and the
presence of many ministerial students reinforced the religious
and educational orthodoxy of the school. As far as can be
ascertained, the anti-Darwinian attitude prevailed among the
faculty at Kentucky University. In 1887 President Charles
Loos, who was also professor of Greek language and literature,
expressed this viewpoint in an article in the campus periodical
The Tablet, noting that the thirst for knowledge was "one of
the noblest qualities and manifestations of the human soul." It
was this quality that lifted man above the beasts, and not even
the most gifted anthropoid, "the Darwinian progenitor of
man," has it. Then, continuing in a satiric vein, Loos asked:

> Imagine for a moment the superior serious monkey, the ape, the
> forest-devil, the baboon, the huge gorilla, coming solitary, or in
> groups, to Darwin or to Haeckle with the light of passion of
> knowledge in their shagging winking eyes: Why has this idea
> never yet struck these learned zealous professors of anthropolo-
> gy to establish schools for the incipient intellectural culture of
> these primitive brothers of man?[11]

In 1894 Alfred Fairhurst, professor of natural science, delivered a chapel address on the "Origins of Man" in which he
energetically attacked the Darwinian thesis, and was enthusiastically applauded by the students for his efforts.[12] One of the
most popular professors at Kentucky University, Fairhurst was
a man of deep religious conviction, intensely loyal to the Christian Church, and was the pastor of a number of different
churches in Kentucky. This in itself would not necessarily have
made him an opponent of Darwinism, because many Christians
had reached a satisfactory compromise with the new concept.
But apparently the devout faculty members at Kentucky University shared the more fundamentalist orthodoxy of John
McGarvey, who remained a lifetime foe of Darwinism. The curators had already satisfied their consciences in the matter of
faculty conformity by authorizing an investigation in 1871 to
find "whether any of the Professors in the University are open
and avowed infidels or skeptics for the word of God."[13] Noth-

[11]*The Tablet*, Vol. I, No. 1 (February, 1887).
[12]*Kentucky Leader*, January 13, 1894.
[13]Minutes of the Board, November 23, 1871.

ing in the record indicates that such a faculty member was uncovered. It is puzzling, however, that Robert Peter, the most outspoken and argumentative faculty member in the sciences, never voiced his opinion one way or another on Darwinism.

The most dramatic revelation of the prevalence of religious orthodoxy and anti-Darwinism on the campus in this period was the publication in 1900 of James Lane Allen's novel *The Reign of Law*. Allen, one of the most popular novelists of his day, was a native of Lexington and had enrolled in Kentucky University in 1868. Here he met William Benjamin Smith, a brilliant student, who was deeply involved in philosophical and religious speculation. Doubtless Allen's interest in the conflict between Darwinism and the Biblical account of creation was greatly stimulated by his conversations with Smith. After his graduation in 1871, Smith was appointed a tutor, later an assistant professor, and finally an adjunct professor in the natural sciences at Kentucky University. His wide reading in the literature of higher criticism and Darwinism deepened his skepticism of the authenticity of the Biblical account, and arriving at the conclusion that a literal belief in the Bible was impossible, he decided that orthodox Christianity was completely false. Had he been prudent and wished only to keep his teaching position, regardless of what this might have cost in intellectual honesty, he might have stayed at Kentucky University. This he could not and would not do. In 1874 Smith sent a letter of resignation to his church and another to the University. He then published an article entitled "Are We Christians?" in which he expressed his belief that most professed Christians did not follow the precepts of Christ. His actions and his views brought down upon his head a storm of criticism from most of the faculty, except for "Jack" Neville (whom he always regarded as one of the finest teachers he ever knew) and Patterson. These men remained his friends even though they disagreed with him.[14]

[14]Warren Browne, *Titan vs. Taboo: The Life of William Benjamin Smith* (Tucson, 1961), pp. 25–26. See also Grant C. Knight, *James Lane Allen and the Genteel Tradition* (Chapel Hill, 1935), and the chapter on "The Reign of Law" in Stevenson, *Lexington Theological Seminary*.

Smith left Lexington and went to Germany where he made a brilliant record at Göttingen and there received his Ph.D. Returning to the United States, he taught mathematics and later philosophy at Tulane University.

Smith's collision with the established orthodoxy of the church and campus in Lexington made a profound impression on James Lane Allen, and years later in the 1890's when he began to turn to more philosophical and somber themes for his novels, he used this incident as the plot for *The Reign of Law*. Using Smith as the intellectual prototype for the novel's hero, Allen completely transformed the details of Smith's life and compressed events to fit the pattern of his novel. The story is based on the experiences of David, a poor farm boy from the Lexington area, who attends Kentucky University, or more precisely the College of the Bible, to study for the ministry. The intense intellectual narrowness of his professors, and especially the denunciations of modern infidelity (Darwinism) from the pulpit of the local church he attends, repels him and drives him to examine for himself the very books and ideas so vigorously condemned by the voices of orthodoxy. He finds these books to be provocative and convincing. The espousal of these ideas on campus makes David unacceptable to the academic authorities and he is expelled. The book ends on a more positive note as the hero marries Gabriella, the attractive local school teacher, and heads north to study science in a northern university.

Despite the statement by some historians that by 1900 the fight for Darwinism had been won, one would never have guessed it by the violent criticism Allen's new novel received, especially in Lexington. It was not surprising that John McGarvey, College of the Bible president, should have made the most publicized denunciation of it. After all, there was no other person who qualified so well as the living model for Allen's narrow-minded and fanatical pastor and professor in *The Reign of Law*. This fact only intensified the old man's hatred for the book and the views expressed in it. As was his custom, McGarvey always disclaimed any personal animosity for Allen, or any of his opponents.

Before a packed house at the Broadway Christian Church, McGarvey delivered an address later printed in the *Lexington Morning Herald* of October 8, 1900. He expressed surprise that an honored alumnus (Allen had received an honorary degree from Kentucky University in 1898) should make such an attack upon his alma mater and declare that sectarianism had ruined its usefulness. McGarvey declared the chief aim of the book was to degrade Christianity and place it on a level with Asiatic religions. The title of the book was a misnomer, McGarvey said, because the law of nature did not reign, and cited the resurrection and other miracles to upset the theory. He also ridiculed the idea that a young boy not knowing the meaning of "matriculate" in September should be able to read and understand Darwin's work by the following January. Moreover, young readers of this book might well become infidels, for if one believed in Allen's views "then the Bible is false from beginning to end."[15] McGarvey denied Allen's contention that sectarianism had ruined whatever prospects Kentucky University might have had to become a first-rate school, and he attempted to refute the implication that a student had ever been expelled for his religious views.

Allen might well have ignored these attacks. After all, he was a novelist who had a strong, popular national reputation. But McGarvey's comments irritated him. He replied to the College of the Bible president in a letter published in the Lexington press in which he admitted that in general his own religious beliefs were similar to David's, the novel's hero. Allen claimed that such men as McGarvey drove intelligent, searching young students out of the church. Nor did Allen retract his belief that sectarianism had played a negative if not disastrous role in the history of the school. He felt with considerable justification that the history of Transylvania and Kentucky University would support that view.

The writer for the *Lexington Morning Herald* who reviewed both Allen's book and McGarvey's condemnation of it, ended this rebuttal article with an eloquent defense of Allen. It was tragic, he wrote, that McGarvey in his criticism of Allen ignored "the great depths of the book — those life questions that came to David.

Then, after all, how plain Mr. Allen makes it, something not mentioned in the address on Sunday morning, that there was a

[15]*Lexington Morning Herald*, October 8, 1900, Knight, *James Lane Allen*, pp. 134–137.

faith possible for David that knew nothing of tuning forks, organs, and a certain mode of baptism, being a violation of the Word of God. This faith the College of the Bible destroyed. During this process his reason was awakened, and he asked for this higher faith, the faith that can believe in God and evolution too.[16]

That Allen, perhaps, and many other students at Kentucky University, were not alone in questioning religious orthodoxy was affirmed in a statement by the Reverend David Utter of Denver, Colorado. In a letter to the editor of the *Atlantic Monthly* in September, 1900, Mr. Utter, who had been a student at Kentucky University during the controversial period, confessed it had been his experience as a student, as well as in observations of other campuses in Kentucky and Indiana, that the academic atmosphere was such as Allen described it.

THOUGH THE INTELLECTUAL struggle over Darwinism provided some dramatic interest in the academic life of Kentucky University in the half-century before World War I, the general tenor of college life was stable, conservative and traditional. Student life was normal, vigorous and typical of hundreds of other similar campuses. There were probably fewer cases of deliquency calling for faculty or administrative discipline than on some campuses because of the presence of the College of the Bible and the number of ministerial students. The curriculum was traditional. The presidential leadership was provided by men of scholarship and piety, but none of them could match the energy and vision of John Bowman.

Following Bowman's removal from the regency and the abolition of that office, Professor Henry H. White was elected to fill the office of president of the University. It had been forty years since the seventeen-year-old youth had come from Connecticut to Georgetown, Kentucky, to enroll as a student in the engineering course at Bacon College and had stayed on as a mathematics instructor. He had come to Lexington along with some of the other faculty when Kentucky University merged with Transylvania. Despite his plain, modest and unassuming

[16]*Ibid.*, October 14, 1900.

manner he exhibited qualities of administrative capacity which impressed the curators sufficiently to lead them to appoint him to positions of leadership. It was White who was originally scheduled to be the presiding officer of the Agricultural and Mechanical College, but when J. A. Williams, who had been appointed head of the College of Arts resigned, White was appointed presiding officer to replace him and James Patterson took over the leadership of the state school. White served for over ten years as presiding officer of the College of Arts until he was appointed president of Kentucky University. As far as can be ascertained he performed his duties as president ably and responsibly, but one gets the impression that his first love was the classroom. In 1880 he resigned his position and turned exclusively to his teaching duties as professor of mathematics and astronomy. He did assume the additional task of being college treasurer, however, ably handling that task until 1901. His failing eyesight finally forced him to give up his classroom activities, and he died in 1903 at the age of 82. Charles Loos, a longtime friend and colleague, spoke of him as

> a man of more than common intellectual ability. He was an earnest student from his boyhood to his maturest age. His reading was large, and in the best fields of literature. He was a careful and deeply interested observer of current events . . . a man of the strictest rectitude of motives and actions. . . . He was a profoundly pious man. In his judgment of right and wrong he was as firm and unyielding as a rock. But kindliness, gentleness, and unselfishness marked all his conduct towards his fellow beings.[17]

White's successor was a remarkable Alsatian scholar by the name of Charles Louis Loos (pronounced Lows). Born in 1823 in Woerth-sur-Sauer, France, of a French father and German mother, young Charles was bilingual from his earliest years. When his family migrated to the United States in 1834 Charles added English to his vocabulary. Though confirmed a Lutheran he later joined the Disciples of Christ, much to the dismay of his pious Lutheran grandmother. This move to the Disciples apparently influenced his choice of a college, for he decided to attend Bethany College from which he graduated in 1846. In

[17]A Tribute to Henry White by Charles Loos in *The Transylvanian*, Vol. XIII, No. 3 (December, 1903).

1849 Loos was ordained to work in the ministry and served in a number of churches in Virginia, Pennsylvania and Cincinnati, assuming the added burden of editing some of the denominational periodicals as well. In 1857 he accepted an appointment to the presidency of Eureka College in Illinois but held this post for only one year before returning to his alma mater at Bethany to teach ancient languages and literature. In May 1880, he resigned his position to assume the presidency of Kentucky University, continuing to teach Greek as well. It was said of him that

> the personal appearance and manner of President Loos indicate his French origin, while his speech is German. The influence of these two races is still more marked in his mental characteristics. The studious thoughtfulness, the philosophical acumen, the plodding industry and generous hospitality of the German are happily blended with the volatile spirit, the fire and enthusiasm of the French.[18]

He was blessed with a rugged and vigorous constitution. Even after he resigned from the presidency at the age of seventy-four he continued to teach Greek until his eighty-sixth year. Known as the "Grand Old Man" of the campus, his faculties remained undimmed. Fascinating students by the way he kept removing and replacing his pinch-nez glasses while he taught, he successfully infused into them his own profound love of Greek classics. One of his students later recalled that Loos

> was one of the great minds on the campus. He seemed to be just as much at home walking around in Euripides' *Medea* or Sophocles' *Antigone* in the original Greek as he would be reading the King James version of the Bible or in a contemporary textbook.[19]

As a friend and instructor to the students he was preeminent. They called him "Daddy Loos" and they meant it.

DURING THE SEVENTEEN YEARS of Loos' presidency, the curriculum remained almost unchanged. To the B.S. and B.A. degrees a Bachelor of Literature degree was added in

[18] Stevenson, *Lexington Theological Seminary*, p. 125.
[19] *The Transylvanian*, Vol. II, No. 5 (February, 1893).

1893, enabling a student to replace Greek with French and German, and reducing the requirement in Latin and mathematics. The candidate for the B.A. degree, however, was still confronted with a formidable amount of Greek and Latin. In 1893 an experiment was made to add civil engineering, but it did not prove successful.

The Law Department, which had been operating with modest enrollments since 1865, closed its doors at the time Loos became president. An attempt to reopen it in 1889 failed, but a law class was enrolled in the fall of 1892. However, the small classes of about a dozen students made it uneconomical to function, and the Department was closed again in 1895.

The stability of the institution was likewise reflected in the very few changes in faculty. During Loos' nearly two decades as president, the core of the faculty consisted of Robert Graham, professor of the English language and literature and for some years the president of the College of the Bible; Henry White in mathematics; Alexander Milligan in Latin; John McGarvey in sacred history; Alfred Fairhurst in the natural sciences, and the amazingly successful operators of the Commercial College — Wilbur and Ephraim Smith.

Enrollment in the College of Arts, the basic core of Kentucky University, had dropped to eighty when Loos became president in 1880. Slowly through the next decade it increased to over 150. The College of the Bible had enrolled fifty-one in 1880, and the totals ranged from fifty to a hundred in the following decade. The Academy enrollment hovered between thirty and forty students. Though enrollment in the Commercial College downtown was always faithfully reported in the catalogue, dramatically expanding the total figure as registration in that school expanded from 200 to 783 in 1887, it cannot be said in any realistic appraisal that the Commercial College was an integral part of Kentucky University. Though it had been part of Bowman's scheme to provide as an adjunct to the University a practical vocational school in business and secretarial arts, the Commercial College was, in reality, a separate operation, conducting its own financial and personnel affairs entirely apart from the University.

The most significant change in the character and composition of the student body occurred in the fall of 1889 when twenty-seven girls officially matriculated in Kentucky University. In this matter as well as some others, Loos proved to be open-minded and willing to take the initiative. The example set by the state college in admitting women to its new Normal Department in the 1880–1881 session may well have influenced Loos and the curators to consider seriously the admission of women to Kentucky University.

Precipitating this change was the action of Miss Laura Clay, daughter of Cassius M. Clay and noted leader in Lexington of the expanding national women's rights movement. In January 1888, the Fayette Equal Rights Association was organized, one of its purposes being to open Kentucky University to women. Miss Clay was appointed to a committee to visit professors and obtain a hearing before the curators. She later recalled that President Loos had been cordial and cooperative during the debate on this issue. At the meeting of the Board on June 12, 1888, a petition was presented by Miss Clay's committee urging the admission of young ladies to classes in the University. The Board said it would give the matter careful consideration and appointed a committee to work with Loos to study the question. Presidents of eight to ten major coeducational universities and colleges were asked their opinion and advice. All expressed themselves in favor of coeducation and said experience confirmed their opinion.[20]

At a special meeting on April 27, 1889, the curators considered the committee's report recommending admission of women to the University, and the Board approved the recommendation unanimously. The faculty was given the responsibility of deciding what conditions should be set up to implement this decision. The 1889 catalogue announced that

> the College of Arts is now open to students of both sexes. It is the policy of the university to receive only such young ladies as students as are ready for the Freshman Class and are of suitable age; this will not preclude them from attending also some classes in the Academy.

The minimum age of fourteen years was not changed. The girls

[20]Minutes of the Board, June 12, 1888.

were warned that the University had no dormitory accommodations for them and that they would be admitted as students only if they could find a home in the city or vicinity "where they can be under protecting and controlling family care." The rules of conduct remained the same as they had been since 1865, which either indicated unusual conservatism or a remarkable degree of consistency and stability in the student environment and perhaps the society at large.

Not until four years later was male reaction to coeducation expressed in the campus publication *The Transylvanian*. The author pointed out the practical advantages of coeducation by noting it was an economical way to operate educational institutions by reducing the number of colleges and improving the remaining. By diminishing the number of teachers needed, better ones might be secured.

> And then, when the sexes are educated together, by the presence of each other they are stimulated to their best endeavors. The young man has too much pride and self-respect to fail or blunder in the presence of young ladies with whom he keeps company.[21]

Such were the happy expectations of another day! Yet the writer did make a valid point in stating that coeducation offered each sex the opportunity to find out what the other was like, to grant the student trust and responsibility. Finally, in a country with a democratic philosophy, coeducation meant equal education.

The College of the Bible, however, remained a male sanctuary. President John McGarvey would not allow women in this exclusive male reserve. Loos, challenged by this defiance, concocted a scheme to breach the wall. Since the classes of the College of the Bible were freely open to Kentucky University students, he registered a girl for McGarvey's course in sacred history. McGarvey refused to admit her at first, but retreated from that position by allowing her to attend only if she observed certain conditions. She would be allowed to enter the classroom only after all the men had arrived; she would sit on the back row and speak to none of the men; she would leave first on a nod by the instructor, and on days when McGarvey

[21]*The Transylvanian*, Vol. IV, No. 1 (October, 1894).

felt the material to be discussed was unfit for female ears, he would leave a note on her desk requesting that she absent herself from class that day.[22]

In due time McGarvey's resistance to admitting women was eroded and in 1904 women were permitted to enter the College of the Bible. But as for women being preachers, McGarvey believed the Bible had once and for all forbidden them that vocation.

IT HAD BEEN MANY decades since any significant construction had been undertaken on the Transylvania campus. Now under President Loos several major projects were initiated, and during the 1880's two projects were completed: necessary repair work on Morrison Hall and erection of a new academy building. Loos told the curators in 1884 that Morrison Hall was "beyond all doubt the most dilapidated and forlorn looking edifice in all our land."[23] The building committee had been reporting the same thing to the Board for years, but failure to repair the structure was always due to lack of funds. And indeed, the University was running on a shoestring budget. For the school year 1883–1884, the income had been $19,452. Expenses had totaled $18,600 but this rigorous thrift had been possible only by keeping the salaries of the president and staff at pathetic levels. President Loos was paid $1,925 a year. Over sixty years earlier Holley was earning well over $3,000. Faculty salaries ranged from $1,500 to $1,675 for the senior permanent teachers. Foreign language teachers, a highly mobile and transient group, received $300 for each language taught.

Tuition was low and income from invested funds was modest, for the total university funds invested were only $213,574. Yet Morrison Hall had to be repaired. And the old academy building, the only college structure left on the former college lot now called Gratz Park, was inadequate. Loos reported that it was "altogether unfit for the work, the comfort, and the character of this branch of our university. It is too small, is old and decaying . . . and looks very sad and is unworthy to be the

[22] Stevenson, *Lexington Theological Seminary*, p. 126.
[23] Minutes of the Board, June 10, 1884.

Ella Jones Hall

nursery of the young men who are prepared there."[24]

In 1886 the Board appropriated the money to repair Morrison Hall and Loos was proud to report a year later that the improved condition of the classic structure "has done much to give the institution the character before the public it deserves, and to inspire all . . . with new hopes."[25] The curators then appropriated $5,000 for the construction of a new academy building. When completed this building, a plain two-story brick structure, contained four or five classrooms and a few faculty offices. It was located a short distance east of Morrison Hall and served the needs of the preparatory students until this particular function of the University was discontinued in 1913. Overflow classes from Morrison Hall were also held here as the number of academy students declined. About the turn of the century the building was known as East Hall.

One other building — a gymnasium — was constructed

[24]*Ibid.*, June 7, 1887.
[25]*Ibid.*

under Loos' administration. Though various forms of extra-curricular athletics existed on campus, there was neither a systematic physical education program nor any building for it. In 1892 an editorial in *The Transylvanian* criticized the lack of concern in college education for developing the body as well as the mind. Heavy emphasis on classical studies in the curriculum did not seem to be accompanied by the Graeco-Roman concern for the health of the body and physical training. The editors of

Alumni Gymnasium, 1894

The Transylvanian urged that a gymnasium be built. They believed that one could be erected for $6,000 and made suggestions as to how the money might be raised. The curators responded by appointing some of their members to work cooperatively with an alumni committee to select a site and make plans for a gymnasium. A year later at their June 1893, meeting the gymnasium committee recommended to the Board "a site fronting Broadway, near and a little west of where the Barracks stood."[26] The old barracks built by the Union army during its occupation of the campus had only recently been torn down.

It was estimated that the new gymnasium would cost $8,500

---

[26]*Ibid*., July 1, 1892; June 2, 1893.

The students near the rear dormitory, circa 1897

excluding equipment. The alumni had accumulated $2,800 and had an additional $974 in pledges, while students themselves had contributed $1,095. On the basis of this support, the curators moved ahead on construction and authorized the Executive Committee to borrow the additional money needed to complete the building. Bids were opened and accepted in September 1893, and the structure was completed in time for the fall session, 1894. *The Transylvanian* reported that

> the interest in athletics this year in the University is greater than during any other year in the institution's history, and this can easily be accounted for. The fact that we now have a well-equipped gymnasium and a competent instructor at the head of it is the cause of the increased interest. To say that Prof. Frew is a competent instructor is a mild way of putting it. In the gymnasium, as well as on the football field, he is, to use a slang expression, just simply "out of sight."[27]

Not only had the University been busy building, but the College of the Bible, long in need of its own home, erected in 1895 an imposing brick structure dominated by a massive tower that

[27]*The Transylvanian*,Vol. IV, No. 2 (November, 1894).

The College of the Bible building, 1895

overlooked Morrison Hall and afforded a fine view of the entire town. With its own chapel, classrooms and offices the new College of the Bible building greatly relieved overcrowding of the limited space in Morrison Hall and the academy building. There was now sufficient room in Morrison Hall to store the law library — which for many years had been housed at the public library and, lacking adequate supervision, had lost 200 volumes. The location of the new College of the Bible building adjacent to Morrison Hall reaffirmed the continuing close relationship of these two legally independent institutions. It was President Loos' belief that the number of Bible students taking courses at the University shows to you [how] rooted the life of the College of the Bible is in the University. . . . The College of the Bible could not exist without the College of Arts, and the College of Arts ought not to exist without the College of the Bible, for the latter embodies in itself one of the chief motives of the founders of the University. . . . This University must cherish as a supreme interest, the welfare of the church, in giving it a well-educated ministry, and able to furnish a Christian education of the best order to its members who are not preachers.[28]

Loos saw the College of the Bible and the College of Arts as one unit in the University. Though he emphasized that Kentucky University was not sectarian and that nothing was taught to offend the convictions of any Christian believer, "yet the spirit and morality of the religion of Christ are maintained as the law of life and conduct within it." The Bible was a textbook, the professors were all good Christians and every recitation day was opened with religious services in the chapel which students were obliged to attend.

In June 1897, Loos submitted his resignation as president. He had persevered at the job for seventeen years, and wanted a rest and the chance to devote himself fulltime to teaching his beloved Greek. *The Crimson* of 1906 was dedicated to him, noting that

although he has already passed his eighty-second year, he is second to none on the University faculty in the regular and conscientious and efficient discharge of his duties. . . . As Kentucky University's "Grand Old Man," he is a striking figure in the life of the institution. With faculties unimpaired, with eyes undimmed, and with step unimpeded, he becomes the companion for those sixty years his junior. . . . Although he is continually admonishing the students against unrestrained enthusiasm at the inter-collegiate contests, he is generally found in a more prominent place on such occasions warmly supporting the efforts of ambitious youth.[29]

In 1918 Loos was made professor emeritus, and he died two years later.

[28] President Loos' Report to the Board, June 9, 1897.
[29] *The Crimson*, 1906.

15

The Creative Administration
of Burris Jenkins

Reuben Lin Cave   *Alexander Milligan*   *Burris Jenkins*

Between 1897 and 1901 two men filled the presidential chair for brief terms. The first was Reuben Lin Cave. Five times wounded while serving in the Confederate army and one of the famous 8,000 of General Lee's army at Appomattox Court House, this native Virginian had gone into business after the War. Having decided to enter the ministry, he enrolled in the College of the Bible in 1869. He served a number of churches over the next few decades, interrupted by a few years as a faculty member and later president of Christian University, Canton, Missouri. He had made a notable record at the First Christian Church at Nashville before being offered the presidency of Kentucky University. Cave entered the office in September 1897, and resigned in February 1900. There is little or no evidence to indicate why he occupied the office for so short a time. No special crisis developed and no clash between Cave and the Board occurred. Perhaps the job was not to his liking, or the future of the school not sufficiently promising. Yet nothing in Cave's annual reports to the curators reveals such discontent. He had nothing but praise for his predecessor and satisfaction with the condition of the University.

The most interesting achievement of Cave's administration was the re-establishment of the Medical Department under the aegis of Kentucky University. The doors of the old Transylvania Medical Department had closed in 1859. Though Bowman had hoped to establish a Medical Department as part of the broad structure of Kentucky University, nothing beyond words, reports and hopes ever materialized. There was never adequate leadership, sufficient funds or the necessary faith that such a school could succeed in Lexington. Shadows of the 1837 dispute that split the Transylvania Medical Department and led to half of it migrating to Louisville had not quite been dispersed, and factors that contributed to the decline of medical education in Lexington at that time were still present.

Nevertheless the idea of attaching a medical department to the University never quite died. In the 1890's circumstances in Louisville medical circles created the opportunity for its fulfillment. Stimulus for this action came from the Kentucky School of Medicine in Louisville, the offspring of the Transylvania Medical Department whose faculty in 1850 was convinced there was no future for medical education in Lexington and established a branch in Louisville. The branch was independently chartered and continued to prosper long after the parent Transylvania Medical Department closed. Reasons for the Kentucky School of Medicine wishing to establish relations with Kentucky University were revealed in the words of one writer who stated that

> several years ago it began to be evident that this constant growth could be better accommodated, the invested capital better protected and greater permanency assured by a connection with a greater university — a connection necessary for the establishment of the associated colleges already projected for dentistry, pharmacy, veterinary medicine and other collateral branches of the healing art.[1]

The Kentucky School of Medicine had thirty-six faculty members plus an additional ten instructors on the hospital staff. It was well-equipped with buildings and apparatus.

It appears that the Kentucky School of Medicine initiated the proposal to operate as the Medical Department of Kentucky

[1]*The Crimson*, 1898, pp. 23–24.

University. Since the medical school offered to function autonomously, having complete control over its own property and faculty and taking full responsibility for financing its operations, there would be little or no burden on the University. It had nothing to lose, and the University image would be greatly strengthened by the addition of a Medical Department to its structure. At a specially-called meeting of the curators on November 4, 1897, the contract with the Kentucky School of Medicine was approved. Except that the diplomas awarded graduates of the medical school would now be signed by the president of the University, little change in either the medical school or the University took place. It was a liaison of convenience. Being located in Louisville, the campus of the medical school was remote from the University and certainly medical students could have felt little connection with the Lexington school or its students.

It is interesting to compare the requirements for an M.D. in 1897 to those prevailing a half-century before at Transylvania. Admission requirements were not too different. The applicant must have good moral character, attested to by two physicians who knew him. He must have graduated from "some literary or scientific institution of learning, or received a certificate from some legally constituted and reputable university, college, academy, high school, or normal school." The significant difference is seen in the requirements for the degree. Instead of only two years in the medical school, the second year being really a repetition of the first, the requirement was now four years. The graduate had to have two years of clinical instruction, two courses of practical work in chemistry and anatomy, courses in histology, pathology, bacteriology and operative surgery, in addition to practical work in physical diagnosis and obstetrical manipulations.

Beginning with the session in January 1898, Kentucky University had a functioning medical department in Louisville. Apparently this new arrangement, however, did not work out satisfactorily for in May 1898, the contractual relationship with the Kentucky School of Medicine was abolished. The reasons were not recorded. The curators wished to continue this new Medical Department if at all possible. Thus when a number of

Louisville physicians proposed establishing a new medical school to be known as the "Medical College" of Kentucky University, the curators were more than willing to approve a new contract with them. Again, it must be admitted that the appealing aspect of the arrangement as far as the curators were concerned was the assumption by the Louisville doctors of full legal and financial responsibility for the project. In addition they agreed to pay Kentucky University five dollars for each diploma granted by the new medical college, all diplomas being signed by the University president and affixed with the University seal. One free scholarship would be awarded each year to a deserving Kentucky University graduate. In a moment of optimism, a provision was included to continue the contract in force for fifty years unless cancelled by mutual consent.[2]

The new medical school was apparently a success. It enrolled over two hundred students a year from as many as twenty-six states and six foreign countries. Adequate physical facilities were acquired. Each year a picture of the medical classes appeared in *The Crimson*, the annual of Kentucky University, and one edition showed the students clustered around a partially dissected corpse.

On February 19, 1907, the Dean of the Medical School notified the curators that twelve months from that date the school wished to cancel its contract with Kentucky University and would cease to use the name of Kentucky University Medical Department. The curators, having little choice in the matter, concurred. No reasons were given, but there was a movement to consolidate medical education in Louisville under the aegis of the University of Louisville, on the justifiable grounds that an outstanding medical school would better meet the needs of contemporary medical education than the existing half-dozen competing schools. There were no further attempts of Kentucky University to associate medical education with its other programs, and not until the University of Kentucky added a new major medical school in the 1950's did medical education again return to Lexington.

It was during President Cave's administration that the Board

[2]Minutes of the Executive Committee, December 2, 1898.

moved to establish a normal school in the fall of 1899. Courses in the history of education, psychology, school management, advanced method, advanced management and advanced psychology were offered. The University, being somewhat in a financial bind at the time, may have been convinced that they could attract a larger number of students by offering courses in teacher preparation. The State College had long been engaged in this area, and the curators may have wished to offer similar opportunities to its students. The experiment was short-lived, however, for in 1906 the normal school was discontinued.

The need for the preparatory academy was also diminishing as public school education improved, and the Academy was gradually phased out. An attempt was made in 1902 to close it, but some preparatory classes were taught until the eve of World War I when it finally disappeared.

The question of what to do with Gratz Park, the old College Lot, perennially occupied the curators who on various occasions considered selling or leasing the land. President Cave suggested that faculty housing be erected on the land, and President Jenkins made the same suggestion some years later. The project might have produced some rental income, though at a very modest level considering the faculty salaries at the time, and it would have created a rather unusual community of faculty members. Not only would faculty members have been close neighbors to one another but their homes would have been as much a part of the campus as the dormitories and easily accessible to the students. What the faculty thought of this proposal is not known, but the question remained hypothetical for the plan never materialized. Beyond approving H. H. Gratz's plans for beautifying the park, the Board did not make final disposition of the land until World War I.

The Spanish-American War, that "splendid little war" as Secretary of State John Hay and his fellow Americans thought of it, took place during Cave's administration, but the war was so brief and so limited in its demands on the United States' financial resources and manpower that its impact on college campuses was mild, if Kentucky was any example. In the fall of 1897, a few months before the battleship *Maine* blew up in Havana harbor, the campus monthly *The Transylvanian* took notice of the critical events in Cuba. In a column on current events the writer said he thought the United States government might recognize the Cubans as belligerents and issue an ultimatum to Spain to end the military activities against the rebels. He believed public opinion endorsed such a policy but the wisest and most conservative statesmen opposed it. The student writer regretted the fact that a jingoistic spirit was growing in the country, fueled in part by the United States confrontation with Britain over Venezuela, and the Hawaiian question.[3]

In the same vein, another Transylvania journalist attacked the growing power of the "yellow press."

> We have no purpose of discussing any feature of the MAINE disaster, or of hoisting upon the bewildered public mind another report or theory of the calamity. But we should like to call attention to some of the gross abuses of their power which the newspapers are indulging. Sometimes a man becomes tired of the sensational journalism of the present time and seeks for a paper in whose news he can place some confidence. . . .[4]

The writer said he expected that the United States would be at war before the next issue appeared. For all the war fever abroad in the land, there seemed to be little intense patriotism on the campus. Examinations in psychology and English created more excitement than the blowing up of the *Maine*. There was only a dim prospect that a Kentucky University company would be organized in case of war.

Once the war began there was ample display of patriotic fervor. Some students enlisted in the Kentucky contingent of troops drilling at the Fair Grounds. The boys in the dormitory organized their own company and drilled on campus. Flags floated from the rooms of professors and students, and the editors of *The Transylvanian* urged the administration to raise a large flag over the campus. The war was the subject of the commencement address. Some students wanted to learn Spanish, and Charles Loos undertook the job of opening a class for sixteen of them, but enthusiasm soon waned and the class was discontinued.

The climax of President Cave's administration was the cen-

[3]*The Transylvanian*, VII (October, 1897).
[4]*Ibid.*, (March, 1898).

tennial celebration of the creation of Transylvania University. There had been little or no centennial celebration in 1880 of the original chartering of Transylvania. The crisis through which the school had just passed overshadowed everything else, and there was little enthusiasm among staff or curators to indulge in festivities. But 1899 presented a different picture. The school had survived, had preserved the character of the educational institution the curators intended and had maintained a close and vital relationship with the College of the Bible. Though Kentucky University was in reality a fusion of two distinct institutions, it now proudly celebrated the long history and tradition of one of these schools.

The Executive Committee had appointed a special committee in November 1898, to prepare a program for January 1899, to commemorate the event. It was decided to schedule the program for January 1, a Sunday. Snow fell the day before but it was clear, cold and white on New Year's day. According to a reporter, a "large and representative assemblage of Lexington's best people" gathered in Morrison Hall at 8 p.m. The building had been lavishly decorated. A large electric star had been placed in the pediment, lighting the campus in front of Morrison Hall and assisting guests in finding their way up the paths. The stately Doric columns were festooned with evergreens. Inside, the chapel doorways, gallery, windows, platform and even the frames of the portraits were tastefully decorated with evergreen. Above the large portrait of Colonel Morrison, which occupied the center of the wall over the speaker's platform, was a crimson shield from which hung crimson drapery. The words "100 Years Old" were spelled out in electric lights over the shield.

Everyone of importance had been invited, including Governor Bradley who made one of the numerous addresses given that evening. Those — such as James Lane Allen and Mrs. Jefferson Davis — who could not be there in person sent letters of felicitation and congratulations. Mrs. Davis said her husband always spoke of his alma mater with "pride and pleasure." There was a letter from John Hay, the Secretary of State, who said his father graduated from the Transylvania Medical Department.[5]

[5]*Ibid.*, VIII (January, 1899).

THE SECOND CENTURY of the University began no easier than the first. A shortage of funds continued to plague the governing board. Just a few weeks after the centennial celebration, the Executive Committee voted to cancel the proposed plans for a June celebration, as the cost of the January festivities had been twice as much as had been set aside for both occasions.[6] Some of the University's land in Fayette county was sold. The treasurer was forced to borrow on short term notes to meet the current expenses. The Executive Committee even proposed reducing professors' salaries for the next academic year but this suggestion was wisely rejected by the Board.

President Cave, who had wished to resign in the summer of 1899, stayed for a few more months on the urging of the curators to act as a financial agent to raise money. The preparatory department was temporarily incorporated into the new normal school to consolidate departments and save money, and the old cottage in Gratz Park was again pressed into service to house the normal school. The treasurer predicted a deficit of over $3,500, which from this distance would hardly qualify as a crisis, but, of course, the total annual operating budget was small and the anticipated deficit would comprise a significant percentage of it. Whether financial stringency inspired it or not, the curators appointed a three-man committee to visit the classes that they might recommend to the Board measures "for the better government and general welfare of the institution as may from their observation be deemed expedient."[7] There is no record of what the faculty thought of this proposal. If such class visitation by curators took place, no specific recommendations or Board actions seem to have been based on it.

Following the departure of Reuben Cave the Board appointed Professor Alexander Milligan as acting president. Son of Robert Milligan, the first president of Kentucky University, he had graduated from that institution in 1861 and remained with the University in various teaching capacities. From 1870 he had occupied the chair of Latin language and literature. The job of acting president was not to his liking, and within a few months he was complaining about his poor health, the difficulties of the

[6]Minutes of the Executive Committee, February 3, 1899.
[7]Minutes of the Board, June 7, 1899.

position and the need for a new permanent president to strengthen the University. The most dramatic event he had to report to the annual meeting of the Board in June 1900, was the terrible typhoid epidemic that swept through the student body living in the dormitories. The villain seems to have been the college water supply, since students boarding in town and drinking water from the town's sources were not affected. The epidemic broke out in October 1899. Milligan said it "cast a gloom over the campus not known even during the Civil War."[8] Bible students, most of whom lived in the dormitories, suffered the worst. The epidemic which lasted for almost two months took the lives of four students, the most outstanding of whom was Lloyd Morris Ford, editor of *The Transylvanian*. A memorial service was held for him in Milligan Chapel in the College of the Bible.

It is remarkable that few students quit the school to escape the threat. Milligan remarked that the "steadiness with which the entire student body bore themselves through these dark months deserves official recognition and commendation."[9] Closing the college cisterns and connecting the college with the town's water supply solved the problem. Milligan believed the epidemic perhaps accounted for a drop in enrollment the following year, and he accused other colleges of exploiting the incident to draw students away from Kentucky University to bolster their own enrollments.

ON MILLIGAN'S URGING, the curators set out to recruit a new president. By May 1901, they were in contact with Burris Jenkins, then living in Buffalo, and in June it was announced that he had accepted the post. At thirty-two, Jenkins was the youngest president the University had ever had. He had been born in frontier conditions near Kansas City in 1869. In his autobiography *Where My Caravan Has Rested* Jenkins recalled many of the incidents of that frontier life which he believed strengthened the character of those who experienced it. His early schooling was desultory, and his education was as much

[8] Report of Acting-President A. R. Milligan, June 13, 1900.
[9] *Ibid.*

the result of avid reading as formal training. He rather early became fascinated by amateur dramatics and public speaking to which he devoted much time and energy. This was how he laid the basis for his mature oratorical ability. Home influences, particularly those of his deeply religious mother, and church influence, especially that of noted preacher Alexander Proctor of Independence, Missouri, sent him to Bethany College and into the ministry. At Bethany, nestled in the isolation of the West Virginia hills, he lived and learned in this "little Waterbury watch of a college, numbering not over two hundred and fifty, containing the whole universe for those who belonged to it."[10]

He was editor of the college monthly magazine, participated in college dramatics, and had his first taste of preaching in nearby churches. Yet in looking back, he could not remember a single outstanding teacher, and blamed the lack of adequate resources to bring first-rate persons there. The new president of Kentucky University recalled:

> I did learn to work for grades, to prepare lessons in such a way as to recite them perfectly and examinations in such fashion as to "knock out" the best marks. Memorization played the greatest part in all preparation. No single professor opened my mind to an inrush of enthusiasm for any subject.[11]

He had heard of great teachers such as William Rainey Harper of Yale — teachers who could rouse the student's curiosity, interest and enthusiasm. Such great teachers were born, he believed, and fortunate was the university that could secure them. It was Jenkins' conclusion that

> colleges too often crystallize and fossilize along conventional lines and squeeze out the originality, the verve, the electric energy of the men in their chairs, until they cannot communicate to the student their own enthusiams. Why must examinations always be conducted according to a pattern? Why examinations at all? They seem designed only to find out how little a student knows, and the real teacher has already found that out. Colleges, for the most part, seem dry as dust, instead of throbbing with life, as they should if only the teachers could be found.[12]

[10] Burris Jenkins, *Where My Caravan Has Rested* (New York, 1939), 60.
[11] *Ibid.*, p. 68.
[12] *Ibid.*, p. 69.

Such was the attitude of the man about to take over the presidency of Kentucky University. He would now have the opportunity to interject into the ongoing, historic and tradition-laden institution the fresh vigor of his unorthodox ideas. Behind him were years of graduate work at Yale and Harvard and years of practical labor as a journalist, pastor and teacher, and later president of Butler College in Indianapolis. From there he went to Buffalo to accept a pastorate, and then accepted the offer from Kentucky University to come to Lexington — where ten years before he had been married to his Kentucky wife by Robert Graham, then president of the College of the Bible.

A photo of Jenkins taken at the time of his inauguration shows a young and good-looking face, an open, direct look and a hint of humor about the lips. There is no evidence here of the physical pain he had suffered, and would increasingly suffer as the years went by, from an injury to his knee incurred on the playing field years before. The bone disease ultimately required amputation of the right leg above the knee. He suffered from many bouts of paralyzing pain from that leg before the operation and never knew when the pain would strike. One of the students recalled Jenkins:

> He was tall, handsome, the last word in physical build. Those were the days when they wore morning coats — cutaways. He soon donned a white vest, and he had a way of putting his thumb in his vest pocket. In six weeks fifty-nine students had on white vests and had their thumbs in their left pockets. He was a charming speaker; he was in his prime. He was breaking into new territory and a new order.[13]

Jenkins approached his new responsibilities with enthusiasm. For one thing, he enjoyed the delightful atmosphere of Lexington and the Blue Grass region. He liked the age and tradition of the college, the sense of lingering greatness created by memories of the famous men who had been educated here. He "liked the main building, huge, frowning Old Morrison Chapel, Greek in architecture." His home from which he could view the campus was in the spacious, white-columned mansion on the southwest corner of Mill and Third streets, later known as the

[13] Quoted in Stevenson, *Lexington Theological Seminary*, p. 134.

Prewitt house. His wife Martha gave teas and receptions to students and faculty for which Jenkins acted as the genial host. And he delighted in entertaining such noted alumni as the novelist John Fox, Jr.[14]

In the fall of 1901 Burris Jenkins was inaugurated as president of Kentucky University and took the opportunity to present his views in the inaugural address. "It is a grave responsibility," he said, "that one assumes in coming into the administration of so old, so conservative, so dignified an institution as Kentucky University . . . [but it has] two of the most essential requisites of a seat of learning — a history and traditions."[15] The school had a cherished classical architectural atmosphere in Morrison Chapel. Safety, soundness and an equilibrium come from its history and traditions, and in the process of change the University should be as careful of what it eliminated as what it added. He did not fear competition from the state college or other colleges in the area. Lexington was in a fine location for colleges, and the success of one college would be beneficial to others.

However there was room for change, he said, and perhaps this was the time to consider it. The requirements for the A.B. degree had long been "stationary and conventional." Might it not be wise to evaluate those requirements from the viewpoint of today? The classical ideal had taken a long time to make its influence felt, and the same might hold true for the modern ideal. "The principle of election is one of the surest means of meeting the need of the hour," he said.

> The day calls for liberty of choice in the course of study to be pursued, according to the predelictions of the aims of the students. While the path of learning is never to be made a royal road . . . while no student can avoid what is difficult, nevertheless he ought to be allowed to avoid what is impossible to him or what he can never perform with profit and pleasure. . . . After all, it is not so much what one studies — within certain established bounds, always, bear in mind — not so much what he studies as how one studies.[16]

[14] Jenkins, *Where My Caravan Has Rested*, p. 146.
[15] Burris Jenkins, "Inaugural Address," *The Transylvanian*, XI (October, 1901).
[16] *Ibid.*

Jenkins believed the A.B. degree ought to give the student two invaluable possessions: suspended judgment and the sense that there is more beyond. He would look to the faculty to keep abreast of current educational trends, and to provide movement, reform and advancement. He saw the role of the president as being a channel of communication between the governing board and the faculty. He also wished to communicate with the alumni, and to tell them of the needs of the college. He would not wish the role of president to be one primarily of a money-raiser. The outstanding needs of the college as he saw them were adequate library facilities, adequate scientific equipment and endowment, expansion into the areas of political science and other social sciences, better accommodations for women, more funds to assist poor students, and more adequate compensation for the faculty.

JENKINS BROUGHT BOTH theological liberalism and educational innovation to Kentucky University, and it is not surprising that he ran into opposition in both areas. In the educational area he proposed the normal school, recently initiated by his predecessor, should be integrated into the liberal arts college structure as an educational department rather than operate as a separate and competing branch. The Academy whose preparatory functions had been taken over by the normal school was reestablished on its own independent footing. In the second year of Jenkin's presidency enrollment stood at 264 in the College of Liberal Arts and 81 in the Academy. This dropped somewhat in succeeding years but rarely went below 200 in the College.

A new course in sociology was offered by Jenkins himself in the department of philosophy. It consisted of lectures on the problems of modern society such as charity, labor, liquor legislation, marriage and divorce. A new department in civil history had been introduced into the curriculum in 1896, concentrating on ancient, medieval and modern European history. Jenkins revamped the department somewhat in 1902, stating that courses in history would emphasize the idea of the unity of mankind, and expanded offerings to include United States history. He removed Professor Anna Bourne, who had been teaching history courses, and replaced her with Dr. Irene Myers, a Yale Ph.D. Professor Bourne protested to the Board about this action but the curators upheld Jenkins' action.

The new president also introduced a department of Biblical history and literature, a rearrangement of the former sacred history and evidences of Christianity courses. These changes, though significant, did not alter fundamentally the traditional curriculum. The student applying for admission, besides having to be fifteen years old and of good moral character, had to offer substantial preparation in Latin, English, mathematics, history and science.

Carnegie Science Building

"The faculty looked upon me with some suspicion," Jenkins later recalled. He thought the faculty needed some modernization and he had exacted a promise from the curators to support him in his nomination of new faculty. Trimming out the dead wood was a ticklish task, as he soon found out, for in replacing the tired veterans he "made enemies among the wide circle of friends which most of these old-time teachers possessed."[17] Absence in those days of academic tenure made his task a little easier.

One of these old-timers was Charles Louis Loos. Whether the octogenerian resisted the suggestion to retire we do not know, but retire he did, and Jenkins carefully searched for an able man to replace him. He found such a person in Thomas B. McCartney, Jr. This new assistant professor in Greek, who also assumed the post of Academy principal, had been born and reared in Newcastle, Virginia. He graduated from Milligan College in 1895 and stayed on there for a few years as instructor until he moved to the University of Virginia in 1898, where he acquired an M.A. and a Ph.D. While at the University of Virginia as instructor in Latin, he was recruited for Kentucky University. This slender young man with the sprightly moustache (Jenkins said he looked like Robert Louis Stevenson) became an immediate favorite among students, faculty and administration. He had a lively and probing intellect, an effective teaching technique and a warm personality. He was remembered by many as a courteous and sensitive gentleman. He contributed significantly to the University in many ways and on two occasions served as acting president.

The robust and vigorous Irene T. Myers, mentioned earlier, was another Jenkins recruit. A graduate of Bethany College she went on to Yale to earn a Ph.D. in history in the days when female Ph.D.'s were rare. She had taken a position in the Floyd Training School for teachers in Boston before Jenkins brought her to the University as the new dean of women and professor of history. In addition to her duties as dean and history professor, she found time to write *A Study in Epic Development*, a report on the archives of the state of Kentucky for the American Historical Association, and numerous magazine and news-

[17]Jenkins, *Where My Caravan Has Rested*, p. 148.

paper articles. Her students praised her teaching highly, stating that she not only knew the facts of history

> but she knows how to interpret them in terms of life, particularly in terms of *our* life. . . . She has the power to make history live over again in the lives of her students. Her classes are required to do hard work, but she so directs that work that the results obtained are a sufficient recompense for the labor.[18]

Another faculty member providing years of long and effective service during this period was Samuel Mitchell Jefferson who taught philosophy. The breadth of the subject matter encompassed in that field in those days demanded the teacher be a person of wide reading and culture. Jefferson was such a teacher. A later president of the University once said of him that "few equalled him in genuine culture. . . . He was a full man, ready and exact."[19]

In addition to liberalizing the curriculum and improving the faculty, Jenkins heartily approved of the Board's action in selling the lower half of Gratz Park to the city for $9,000 as a site for the proposed Carnegie Public Library. A proviso was included that should such a building be used as anything but a library, title would revert to the trustees of Transylvania University and the curators of Kentucky University. To have such a library resource so near the campus and easily available to students was a great boost to the educational program. Jenkins renewed Reuben Cave's suggestion that the rest of the park be converted to faculty housing, but nothing came of that idea.

Jenkins also enthusiastically endorsed the honor system for examinations started by the students. He won Board approval for the introduction of a program known as special honors. This would permit students with a grade of ninety or better in the department in which they wished to take honors, and with the consent of the faculty, to undertake independent study, write a thesis, and be examined on their honors work.

In 1905 Jenkins encouraged the curators to consider reviving the Law Department. This Department had closed in 1895 after a spasmodic and haphazard career of thirty years during which the Department was operating about half the time. There being

[18]*The Crimson*, 1913.
[19]*The Crimson*, 1914.

no law department at the Agricultural and Mechanical College (State College), it was believed that a respectable law program at Kentucky University would be successful. Judge Lyman J. Chalkley, who was appointed the new law dean, had studied law and history both in the United States and Germany. He received his law degree from Washington and Lee in 1889, and had occupied judgeships in several Virginia counties. Recruiting the best legal talent in Lexington and Frankfort for his faculty, Dean Chalkley started classes in Morrison Hall in the fall of 1905. There were nine men on the faculty, including Charles Kerr who later was to write a history of the old Transylvania Law Department. The University law library, moved sometime earlier to the county courthouse as part of the Lexington law library, was available to the law students. The course for law students was to run two years. No specific admission requirements were listed, but applicants were advised to attend courses in the College of Liberal Arts in English, Latin, logic, history, civics, economics and Biblical history and literature. The catalogue stated that "while holding to the landmarks and preserving the priceless traditions and precedents, it is proposed to present a course of law studies that will fit the student to practice the profession wherever he may be located. It will be sufficiently broad to provide a comprehensive view of the American law as practiced and enforced today."[20] Indicative of the purpose to maintain old traditions was the inclusion of Blackstone's *Commentaries* as a text in the course. The point was also made that the old system of practical apprenticeship was now being discontinued as inadequate for effective legal training. The case, lecture and textbook systems were used in combination.

Twenty-five students enrolled the first year and *The Crimson* boasted that far from leading a scholarly monastic existence, law students had contributed four star players to the football team, two debaters to the literary societies, and representatives to Kentucky intercollegiate and southern oratorical contests.

In the fall of 1908 State College established its own law school with a three-year program prescribed. It had at first been proposed that the University's law school be merged with

[20]*Kentucky University Catalogue*, 1905.

this new school, but there was sufficient opposition from alumni, friends and curators to prevent it. Despite competition from across town, the University's Law Department prospered for a few years. Dean Chalkley resigned in 1907 to accept a similar position with the University of the South, and was succeeded by Butler T. Southgate and, later, Matthew Walton. Enrollment never increased after the first year and had declined to about a dozen students by 1911. Six or seven students received the LL.B. each year, except for 1912 when the number of graduates dropped to three and the Law Department was discontinued.

An unusual opportunity to upgrade the science department at Kentucky University came in 1905 when Andrew Carnegie agreed to give the school $25,000 if an equal matching sum could be raised for the erection of a science building. The curators accepted the proposal and expressed the belief they could raise the matching funds among themselves. Jenkins left before construction began, but the money was raised, thanks to a special gift from B. A. Thomas of Shelbyville. The building completed in the fall of 1908 was an imposing brick structure of three stories with an attic and a deep basement. It was well-equipped with chemical, physical and biological laboratories, and a museum for the display of geological, archeological and zoological specimens.

Jenkins was also responsible for taking over Hamilton College and restructuring it as a junior college for women. The

Hamilton Hall

impressive structure on North Broadway just north of the University had been erected originally to house the Hocker Female College, established in 1869. The first president was Robert Graham, who held the position between appointments on the faculty at Kentucky University and the College of the Bible. In 1877 Hocker sold the school to a board of fifteen who continued to operate the institution under the name of Hamilton Female College. In 1889 through a stock transfer Kentucky University became a major stockholder in the college, and in 1903 assumed complete charge of the college. Jenkins recruited a very able woman by the name of Luella Wilcox St. Clair from Christian College, Missouri, to administer the affairs of the school as a junior college for women. There was no intention of making Hamilton College co-educational or of creating a rival institution to Kentucky University. In fact, many girls who completed two years at Hamilton transferred to Kentucky University for their A.B. degrees. Basically it served a useful function as a two-year terminal educational institution. The two-year college movement was then in its infancy, and it was indicative of Jenkins' innovative educational philosophy that he established Hamilton College as the first two-year college in Kentucky.

Property adjoining the Hamilton College campus, on which stood an attractive dwelling once the home of President Graham, was bought by the trustees and used as a dormitory for seniors. It was given the name of Graham Cottage and later served as the home of several Transylvania presidents.

Though President Jenkins did not introduce football into Kentucky University as he claimed in his autobiography, he did recruit an excellent football coach in 1905. Curtis G. Redden of Michigan guided the team through the incredibly successful season of the fall of 1905 during which Kentucky University tied Northwestern and defeated the University of Texas, Texas A&M and the University of Arkansas. Jenkins was irritated at McGarvey's prohibition against College of the Bible students playing football because there were some rugged men enrolled in the seminary, but occasionally regulations were circumvented by enrolling the young men in Kentucky University since they enjoyed the privilege of attending any class in the College of the Bible.

This was not the only issue over which Jenkins and McGarvey clashed. McGarvey had long entertained serious doubts as to Jenkin's orthodoxy, and in 1906 his worst fears were confirmed. Jenkins had been asked his opinion of textbooks written

Graham Cottage

by Charles Foster Kent of Yale, which were in tune with the latest historical criticism of the Bible. Jenkins said that he approved of Kent's books, that he thought they reflected the view of leading educators and ministers regarding the historical method of Biblical study, and that historical criticism did not undermine faith in the Bible, God or Christ. McGarvey would have none of it. Jenkins, he said was "a young man with almost no experience as an educator, and who, though a brilliant speaker, is scarcely a leading minister."[21] The gap between McGarvey and the new generation of Biblical scholars was clearly revealed in McGarvey's view of Biblical historical criticism. The contention, he said, that historical criticism would not endanger one's faith was

[21] Stevenson, *Lexington Theological Seminary*, pp. 130–134.

a most marvelous unbelief. To teach that the Bible's account of creation is not true; that its account of the flood is not true; that its accounts of Abraham, Isaac, Jacob, and Joseph are unhistorical . . . and its accounts of a multitude of other events recorded as sober history are legends, myths or romances — that all this cannot endanger anybody's faith in the Bible, is a proposition too absurd to argue. . . . Continued faith in the Bible is as incompatible with the acceptance of such teaching as light with darkness.[22]

Other comments of a similar nature flowed from McGarvey's pen, and Jenkins now joined a sizeable fraternity of the misguided who had suffered from his attacks. It proved to Jenkins that though McGarvey "in private conversation and relationships could be the sweetest old gentleman in the world, when he began to write in what he considered to be the defence of the faith, he dipped his pen in gall and blotted his paper with asbestos."[23]

All-in-all these were lively progressive years for the University under Jenkins' leadership. There were failures along with successes. The University deficit continued to plague him — despite a growing endowment — and there was some decrease in enrollment. But Jenkins felt he could explain these setbacks and worked for their solution. What finally defeated him and forced him to leave Lexington was a terrible recurrence of his knee and leg-bone ailment. It struck with paralyzing intensity in the spring of 1906, on the eve of the Conference for Education in the South, which he had been responsible for bringing to the campus. He was prevented from participating except at the opening session in Morrison Chapel when he insisted on welcoming the distinguished guests including the governor of Missouri. The students who attended never forgot the occasion.

How bitter was that fight, how intense the physical suffering, only his most intimate friends may know. We, the students, saw him come on crutches into Morrison Chapel last May, and with face pale and intense from suffering, introduce, in the graceful manner of which he alone is master, the noted visitors of the Educational Conference.[24]

[22]*Ibid.*
[23]*Ibid.*
[24]*The Transylvanian*, XVI (November, 1906).

This enhanced his popularity among the students "for the college man likes nothing better than grit."

Jenkins went to Europe that summer to consult medical experts in Berlin and elsewhere, but none was able to diagnose his illness or prescribe an effective cure. Nothing but morphine could make the pain endurable, but after weeks on the drug he realized he was becoming addicted to it and had to take precautionary steps against that. Gradually he improved and was able to return to the campus in the fall of 1906, only to suffer a setback in late September. He journeyed to San Antonio, Texas, searching for a change of climate which might alleviate his condition. It was hopeless to attempt to continue as president. On October 22, 1906, he sent in his resignation to the curators:

> I tender to you my resignation as President of Kentucky University. I do this for only one reason, viz: my certainty that I cannot, on account of my rheumatism, live in the climate of Kentucky. There I suffered repeated attacks, which were growing more frequent. Here I find relief. I regret this necessity more than I can say as I had come to love the state more than any place in which I had ever lived; and I had hoped to remain with the University long enough to assist in solving some of its difficult problems.[25]

Despite continuing difficulties with his leg — which necessitated first an operation on the knee which left the leg completely stiff and later amputation of the leg above the knee — Jenkins led a vigorous and productive life after he left Lexington. At various times a journalist, a war correspondent in France during World War I, and the pastor of such active churches as that in Kansas City, he was in the forefront of liberal causes, whether in politics or religion. He loved to write and he turned out a respectable number of novels, none of which were especially distinguished.

What he might have achieved at Kentucky University had he been able to remain is debatable. He accomplished perhaps as much in five years as he might have done in ten. Though never articulating a complete educational philosophy, he was the instigator of change and experimentation within the old structure.

[25]Minutes of the Executive Committee, November 2, 1906.

He brought vigor and excitement to the campus and the students regretted his departure. The student editor of *The Transylvanian* said:

It is doubtful whether any one man since the days of John B. Bowman, has worked harder or accomplished more for Kentucky University than President Jenkins. . . . He infused new life into the student body, aroused the alumni to renewed interest, brought us into the notice of large educational bodies, and materially bettered our financial standing. . . .[26]

[26]*The Transylvanian*, XVI (November, 1906).

16

Student Life from the Civil War to World War I

Nothing more strongly supports the contention that human nature has changed very little over the past millenium than a historic survey of student life in educational institutions in western civilization. Whether one delves into the ancient records of a medieval European university or those of colleges in America from the colonial period to the present, one is struck by the similarity of attitudes and behavior patterns of the students. The perennial struggle between the dynamic, rebellious spirit of adolescence challenging the entrenched discipline of the educational institution is ever present. The sheer exuberance of animal spirits as expressed in a colorful variety of practical jokes on faculty, townspeople and fellow students is a constant factor. The formation, disintegration and reformation of extracurricular activities, rituals, holidays and organizations are part of the familiar pattern.

Historically the major difference between the European university student body and the American was that of age and independence. The university student in Europe was traditionally older and freer of institutional discipline as it related to the details of his personal life. The university frequently occupied a distinct, separate and sometimes hostile posture in relation to the town or city in which it was located. Student rampages through the streets or attacks on the persons and property of the townspeople sometimes resulted in bloody encounters.

IN AMERICA WHERE THE STUDENT was much younger, the academic authorities had assumed, though reluctantly, the *in loco parentis* role. This inevitably centered upon themselves the accumulating and rebellious hostilities previously reserved for students' parents. Dormitories became necessary for colleges located in areas where adequate housing in nearby private homes was not available. Concentrating such young energies in a limited space under autocratic and highly restrictive rules produced problems of disciplinary control and punishment that have plagued college administrations from the seventeenth century to the present.

In the ante-bellum period, wide use was made of off-campus housing at Transylvania University. Institutional regulations were still strictly enforced on all students regardless of where they lived, but splitting them up among families anxious to co-operate with the school authorities in regulating student lives made the job easier. Adequate dormitory space was not available for all students enrolled in Kentucky University in the latter half of the nineteenth century, and ministerial students were given priority to those rooms which were provided. Tracing the history of student housing at Transylvania is occasionally difficult because the records during this period as to when and where dormitories were built, altered, torn down or replaced are maddeningly vague.

A few students may have lived with the president as boarders in the original two-story brick building that housed the University on the northwest corner of Gratz Park in the early days. Certainly a sizeable number were housed in the imposing main college building erected in 1818 and destroyed by fire in 1829. Student housing was specifically excluded from the new Morrison College as a fire prevention measure. Thus the bulk of the student body was again thrown upon the town's resources. In 1839, when the University received a sizeable financial boost from the Lexington community, provision was made for the erection of dormitories. One dormitory was built, but as to its precise appearance, capacity and location there is some doubt. It may have been the structure later called Logan Hall, a three-story brick building containing twenty-two double rooms and a large reception room.

During the Union army's occupation of the campus, rambling wooden barracks were erected on the northwest corner of the campus, and for many decades these were used as dormitories. In the 1880's Craig Hall was built as an attachment to Logan Hall, these two dormitories being located immediately behind Morrison Hall. In addition to bedrooms, the new dormitory provided a dining room for about two hundred men. Meanwhile, the old Blythe house, built on the northeast corner of the campus and occupied for many years by that staunch Presbyterian president of Transylvania, was turned over to the College of the Bible in the 1890's to be used as additional dormitory space. All three of these buildings were demolished in 1914 to make way for a spacious, modern men's dormitory — Ewing Hall. The girls were parcelled out among a group of rented structures along North Broadway.

Throughout the decades following the Civil War expenses were modest. A student in 1896 was charged $10 a semester for tuition, $7.50 for a room and $85 for meals. It was estimated that $15 would cover books and stationery. Life in the dormitories was plain and simple. The rooms were heated by small coal stoves and illuminated by kerosene lamps.

THE RULES GOVERNING student discipline changed little in the last forty years of the nineteenth century. There was the usual list of prohibitions against attending the races, theaters, circuses or barrooms; or drinking intoxicating beverages, or keeping deadly weapons in the rooms. Students were compelled to attend church on Sundays, though they could choose which church they would attend. Chapel services were compulsory on other days. No student could leave the University or Lexington without permission. He was to cooperate with the faculty for the good of the University and to refrain from criticizing the administration. By the end of the nineteenth century, these specific prohibitions and rules were dropped and a more general statement replaced them.

The government of the University, directed by the presiding officers and professors, who treat the students as friends, aims to maintain such a discipline as will conduce to the good order and prosperity of the institution. Every matriculate is required to abstain from whatever is inconsistent with good order, good taste, and good morals. . . . The discipline is parental and is administered not with severity but strictness.[1]

President Jenkins recalled that discipline was not a significant problem in the University. He always maintained that only two rules were necessary: no student shall burn down any of the college buildings, and no student should murder any member of the faculty. He once had to break up a fight between sophomores and freshmen in the attic of Morrison Hall, but he did so with good nature and a few blows from a slender cane he carried.[2] Generally speaking, Kentucky University was remarkably free from excessive horseplay. The presence of many ministerial students, who tended to be older and less rambunctious than the average undergraduate, undoubtedly contributed to this situation.

The years immediately after the Civil War were apparently more marked by student disciplinary problems than later. There being neither a dean of the college nor a dean of students, the disciplinary agent on campus was the faculty backed up by the president. The minutes of the faculty meetings reveal that the faculty was on continual call to handle breaches of discipline. On occasion they met as often as twice a day, or every other day, or every week. There was no set pattern. In the very first fall of Kentucky University's opening on the Transylvania campus in 1865, one student was dismissed for attending a theater, another for the use of liquor, and a third for visiting the Phoenix Hotel Billiard Saloon. One student in 1870 seemed intent to encompass all the sins. He was dismissed for "carrying a concealed weapon, of engaging in an angry controversy with a fellow student, and of visiting in company with a fellow student, a house of ill-fame near the College premises, this visit having been made in open day in the view of many of his classmates."[3]

What was probably the most famous and dramatic incident of this time involved Champ Clark, who later became the famous

[1] *Catalog of Kentucky University*, 1900, p. 15.
[2] Jenkins, *Where My Caravan Has Rested*, p. 147.
[3] Faculty Minutes, November 10, December 1, 1865; November 5, 1870.

Champ Clark

Missouri politician dominating the United States House of Representatives for a number of years from the speaker's chair. Clark later recalled:

After attending the university for three years and two months, I was, in October, 1870 expelled for shooting at a fellow student named Webb from Ohio. I would not mention it save for the fact that it was greatly magnified in the Presidential campaign of 1912 very much to my detriment. We fell out about what time we should have supper in our Barracks' mess. Webb and I were both of unusual strength. . . . The conversation, warm from the first, developed into a quarrel. He called me a liar, whereupon I cracked him over the head with a small piece of plank and we clinched. Nothing more serious would have grown out of it, most probably, than blackened eyes and bloody noses had not one of my room-mates, a young giant named Thomson, grabbed me backholds and pinned my arms to my body. Webb squared off and hit me a jolt between the eyes and another on my mouth. I kept telling Thomson either to let me loose or to knock Webb down. He was so excited that he did neither. Wild with rage, I finally threw him off, Webb still pounding me. Under the head of the bed I had an old revolver, whose cylinder would not revolve except by hand manipulation, for which I had swapped a German grammar and a French grammar. I got that and fired at Webb. Thomson knocked up my pistol hand and the bullet went about an inch above Webb's head and lodged in the door-casing. That ended the fight.[4]

[4]*The Crimson Rambler*, March 7, 1918.
In June, 1917, Transylvania awarded him an honorary Doctor of Laws.

COLLEGE OF THE BIBLE   POWER HOUSE   GYMNASIUM   MORRISON HALL

OFFERS STANDARD COURSES IN CLASSICS, MODERN
LANGUAGE, SCIENCE, EDUCATION AND THEOLOGY.

TRANSYLVA

LEXINGTO

A campus scene from a promotional poster

Clark went immediately to President White to explain what had happened, hoping that his excellent academic record would save him from expulsion. White said there had been "so much fighting, carousing, and violation of the rules among the students" that the patience of the faculty was exhausted. It was decided to make an example of Clark, and he was expelled. A few years later he went to Bethany College to finish his work and get his degree, which he did with such distinction that he was made president of Marshall College at the age of twenty-three.

The presence of girls on campus intensified the problem of discipline, and the college authorities undertook the job of guarding the persons and morals of the girls with great diligence. The daily contact between the men and women in the classroom on the Kentucky University campus after 1889 created a less rigid relationship between the sexes than was maintained at Hamilton College, the girls' junior college. Hamilton College, under the jurisdiction of the University beginning with Jenkins' administration, was but a half a block north of the campus. It was not surprising that it should receive careful attention from the male students. Regarding their college as a female sanctuary in a gross masculine and dangerous world, the Hamilton College authorities in the 1880's erected a barbed-wire entanglement of restrictions guaranteed to daunt the most dedicated infiltrator. Calls on the girls were generally discouraged, but if parents must visit their daughters, they had to do so outside of school and study hours. Strangely, there were to be no visitors on Sunday. "Brothers, having sisters in the college, must call on Saturday afternoon, call singly, and never protract a visit over one hour. Lengthy visits from friends and relations are injurious to the progress of students, and, not infrequently, a source of great annoyance to the college."[5] Strangers had to present proper letters from parents and state the object of their visit "before a young lady will be called into the parlor." All mail had to pass through the president's office. Clandestine correspondence was forbidden. And sending boxes of cake and confectionery was discouraged as being a useless expense and inimical to the health of the girls.

[5] Article by Annette Mayer in *Lexington Herald-Leader*, May 19, 1963.

The years from the Civil War to the beginning of World War I seem in retrospect to be fairly stable ones on college campuses such as Kentucky University. The major educational reforms were not taking place here, and student life seemed to have moved from generation to generation with amazing continuity and the acceptance of the American traditional value structure. Students were generally willing to accept the orthodox as being applicable to the needs of the graduate moving into a rapidly changing society. Thus in 1903 the salutatorian of Kentucky University, in his commencement address, defended the classical regimen of Greek and Latin as being the fountainheads of our culture which should "form the basis of classical education, with only so much of the philological study as may best serve in the attaining of this knowledge." Art, literature and history were the great fundamentals which would give mental poise and discipline to their possessor wherever he went. Nor was there any need to neglect science. These standards had to be maintained, he said, in the face of a gross popular culture, symbolized by the great circulation of ephemeral fiction at the Lexington Public Library.[6]

Despite the fact that Kentucky University was strongly church-related, the student body was not free from traditional problems of cheating and rebellion against compulsory chapel. In 1886 a student article in *The Atlantis*, a short-lived campus publication, decried the widespread practice of cheating and the unfortunate situation created by the success of the dishonest, clever student in acquiring better grades than the honest, hard-working plodder. What made matters worse was the unfortunate example set by the Bible students in this practice. It was time, said the writer, for the moral part of the college to rise and get rid of cheating, and for the students to do their own policing. It took a few years for that moral part to rise, but rise it did. In 1903 a faculty ruling initiated the honor system whereby a student was placed on his honor during an examination and required to write a pledge on his paper that he had "neither given nor received aid to this examination." A year later the students reenforced the honor system with rules of their own. "Probably the most significant action ever taken by

[6]*The Transylvanian*, XIII (October, 1903).

the students of Kentucky University was the adoption of the honor system," *The Transylvanian* said with pride.[7] The honor system was maintained until World War II.

In 1895 a student complained about student conduct in chapel.

> We deplore the fact that some few students in the Art College seem to have no ability to distinguish between what is smart and funny, and what is coarse and disgraceful. . . . With no excuse whatever they begin a rattling of the feet that can be plainly heard over the room, doing this in direct violation of the rules of the college.[8]

Another problem was the singing. It was "lifeless, spiritless, and very bad in every way."[9] This was not due exclusively to student inertia, however, but because many of the songs were outdated and unfamiliar. A decade later a complaint was voiced that the chapel periods had become increasingly perfunctory and dull. The students wandered in and straggled out, singing the hymns in any manner they chose. More dynamic speakers and programs were asked for, although there yet was no widespread demand that compulsory chapel be abolished.

CONCERN WITH MORAL VALUES, spiritual goals and the evils of tobacco seems to have been more intense on this church-related campus than at state universities or non-church-related colleges. As early as 1872 a student editorial in *The Collegian*, another ephemeral campus publication, stated that the object in life was not to gain wealth, power, military distinction or scientific mastery, but to seek celestial honor, glory and immortality. Other articles in the same issue denounced political corruption and declared alcohol to be a terrible evil.[10]

The editor of *The Focus* believed the magazine had a special responsibility as it represented a college with such a wide reputation for good morals. "It would be clearly unprincipled for the organ of Kentucky University to countenance and support that which the faculty of the university would deem injurious to

[7]*Ibid.*, (May, 1904).
[8]*Ibid.*, IV (January, 1895).
[9]*Ibid.*
[10]*The Collegian*, I (September, 1872).

the morals of the students."[11] Therefore the first rule was not to support or even advertise intoxicating liquor, cigars, cigarettes or tobacco in any form. In 1892 *The Transylvanian* was recommending that a Prohibition Party be supported since neither major political party was dedicated to temperance. Eight years later a Kentucky University Prohibition Club was organized for the purpose of affording students an opportunity to study the different aspects of liquor traffic. The club had a sizeable membership, and when the national Prohibition Party's candidate for president spoke at Cheapside, two blocks south of the campus, the club escorted the distinguished guests to and from the depot in a specially-decorated car. Later the Prohibition Party's candidate for governor addressed the club at its regular meeting. When the Intercollegiate Prohibition Association was organized, local chapters were established on campuses across the land, and in 1903 Kentucky University students who were enthusiastic about supporting the movement set up the Kentucky University Prohibition League. It met every two weeks to discuss phases of the temperance question.[12]

Enthusiasm for this cause was sporadic, for the prohibition group disappeared shortly thereafter, not to reappear until 1917 when the temperance question was sweeping the country, culminating in the passage of the Eighteenth Amendment to the Constitution.

If the college publications are any guide, national issues occasionally discussed were involved with greed, corruption and materialism in American life, or the destiny of the United States, or its role in the Cuban controversy, or the destiny of the Anglo-Saxon race. One isolated manifesto for the Populist Party appeared at the height of the 1892 presidential campaign, but that was all.

Student opinion on the Negro in American society or in higher education was predictably traditional and prejudiced. Stirring up one editorial writer in *The Transylvanian* in 1894 was an article in a New York newspaper praising the integrated educational program at Berea College, soon to be prohibited by

[11]*The Focus*, II (May, 1891).
[12]*The Crimson*, 1913.

state law. "We do not decry the education of the negro," he wrote, "although it is of doubtful propriety and expediency, but we say let him be educated by *himself*." He believed it would lower the self-respecting white student's dignity to be associated with Negroes "upon a plane of *assumed* equality." The effect would be to lower the standard of refinement, culture and social standing. He would have nothing to do with "amalgamated" education.[13] But for the most part the issue was not even discussed.

ANOTHER FEATURE of student life in previous generations which strikes the contemporary reader today as unusual, protected as he is by the marvels of modern medicine, was the number of student deaths due to diseases such as typhoid and tuberculosis. Sanitary protection of water supplies was rather haphazard, and there were reports of typhoid outbreaks in the 1890's which culminated in the terrible siege of the fall of 1899. Campus publications carried eulogistic obituaries of those who died. One in *The Transylvanian* of October 1896, captured the flavor of that time:

> He was an able, manly boy. He was a gentleman in the classroom. He was a gentleman on the playground. He was a prince in feeling. He loved the beautiful, and at the feet of the true and tender he was a worshipper. He has passed out of his life like a soldier, and the majesty of his living will never change.

Accidental deaths of students remain a common factor; only the mode changes. In 1896 it was reported that a student was accidentally drowned when his buggy was swept downstream as he tried to ford a creek. In 1897 two girls barely escaped a serious accident when, while out driving, their horse was frightened by the electric cars, and in his fright nearly trampled two other girls.

AS FOR EXTRACURRICULAR activities on college campuses in the half century following the Civil War, there was remarkably little novelty, although there was a growing proliferation of them near the end of the period. The predominant organizations remained the literary societies. The role they

[13] *The Transylvanian*, III (March, 1894).

played in developing the literary, oratorical and social skills of the individual indicated the remarkable tenacity of the educational tradition that a college education was intended to produce something more than disciplined intelligence. It was to produce a gentleman as well as a scholar, a person whose poise, speaking ability and erudition would make him a leader wherever he went. The editor of *The Transylvanian* in 1892 spoke out in praise of the literary societies

> whose aim and object is to cultivate their literary tastes and add to their attainments. . . . It is in the society hall that the modest and unassuming young man from "way back," who is invariably very bashful comes to wear off that outer coating of bashfulness and reticence and learns to face any kind of an audience on any subject and express himself clearly and forcibly and creditably to himself.

It was the writer's belief that a literary society member got as much from the society as he might from his studies.

Old Transylvania societies which had died off in the 1830's and 1840's were replaced by new Kentucky University organizations. The faculty had recommended that, when Kentucky University moved to Lexington and merged with Transylvania, former literary societies of both institutions be dissolved except for the Philothean Society. This would allow for the establishment of new societies for the new University. On the evening of November 17, 1865, committees appointed to write the constitutions of two new societies met in an old hall in Morrison. They accomplished their task and adopted the names of Periclean for one and Cecropian for the other. George W. Ranck, who later wrote a history of Lexington, became the president of the Cecropian Society, and William Garrard became the first president of the Periclean. The students dug into their classical training for these names, "Cecropia" being derived from Cecrops, the reputed founder of Athens, and "Periclean" after Pericles, Athen's most famous leader. The Philothean Society, founded by Robert Milligan in the early days of Kentucky University while still at Harrodsburg, had a somewhat more ministerial orientation — combining "intellectuality with spirituality" according to its members. It became the society of the College of the Bible, and continued its career even after that institution became legally independent of the University. A companion organization, the Christomathean Society, was organized in 1870 but was not carried over into the independent College of the Bible. The Philothean Society remained the only one in the College of the Bible until the Phileseubian Society began its career in November, 1886.

The girls were not to be outdone. A year after Kentucky University became coeducational they organized the Ossolian Society, replaced in 1896 by the Cornelia Society "in honor of a certain dame in ancient Rome, who won distinction by her womanly qualities."[14] This society published a semi-monthly publication known as *The Jewel*. It received help from the older male societies, and was probably offered the use of their halls since at first it had no place to meet. Inevitably a competing girls' literary society appeared. This was the Alethea Society organized in 1900.

Literary societies, prior to the appearance of the Greek letter fraternities, served a multiple purpose by providing a sense of fraternity while polishing manners, developing poise, encouraging literary endeavors and, above all, involving the members in debating and oratorical contests. The faculty was frequently called upon to judge these contests, which were occasionally long and tedious. Morrison Chapel was usually the setting with townspeople as well as the University family invited to attend. For example, at the fall meeting of the Cecropian Society in 1891, an essay on the study of the dead languages was read, followed by two orations and a debate on the topic "Ancient Oratory is Superior to that of Modern." A gold medal was awarded to the winner of an essay contest on the early history of Kentucky, and music for the occasion was furnished by the University orchestra. A few weeks later the Philothean Society interlarded their verbal presentations with vocal solos with guitar accompaniment, a quartet and a duet. Such songs as "Moonlight on the Lake" and "She is Fooling Thee" were especially popular.

THE WANING OF INTEREST in programs of the local societies by the turn of the century was offset by the establishment of intercollegiate oratorical contests. At first the contests were

[14]*The Crimson*, 1898.

confined to five Kentucky colleges. By 1901 Kentucky University had won three out of twelve contests. In the Kentucky Chautauqua Oratorical Contests, a six-college competition, Kentucky University won four times out of eleven. In 1901 the University withdrew from the Kentucky Intercollegiate Oratorical Association and joined the Southern Inter-State Association, comprising some of the outstanding universities of the South. R. E. Moss of Kentucky University participated in the finals in Austin, Texas, on May 15, 1901, and won by a unanimous decision. The news hit the campus the following morning, and cheering and celebrating continued all day. In the evening a victory parade formed outside Hamilton College, marked by the singing of songs and yelling. Students then marched down to the Phoenix Hotel. Morning recitations were suspended on the morning of May 20th.

> Professors, students, and citizens went out in decorated street cars to welcome Mr. Moss. Young ladies wearing crimson colors and waving crimson pennants and umbrellas, young men with horns, flags, banners, megaphones; the "carrying-on-shoulders committee" seizing upon poor Moss by arms and heels and raising him high in the air, dashing furiously, plunging recklessly through the cheering crowd toward the long line of street cars waiting . . . the triumphal trolley tour around the city, the concluding addresses of welcome at Morrison Chapel . . . the response of Mr. Moss, consumed the rest of the morning. . . .[15]

But the days of full-blown oratory were numbered. "The day of Clay, Webster, and Blaine have gone," commented an editor of *The Crimson* in 1914, "and with them the style of oratory associated with them. The trend is toward the extemporaneous, the newly-thought and sincere style of address." Debating was now replacing oratory, and he hoped the small college would train students for the new style. Other societies were emphasizing creative writing, and social fraternities were taking over the social functions of the traditional literary societies. *The Transylvanian* suggested in 1913 that the literary societies disband: "When the branch becomes withered the husbandman casts it away. When anything has fulfilled its usefulness, it must give place to that which can and will serve progressive ends."

Although the societies lingered on through World War I, all

[15] *Ibid.*, 1903.

but the Periclean had disbanded by 1920, and this society gave
up the ghost in 1925. The societies had served a useful function, and the Periclean and others boasted proudly of such distinguished alumni as John Fox, Jr., and James Lane Allen.

INTEREST IN CREATIVE WRITING resulted in the organization of several clubs dedicated to that specific literary activity. In the winter of 1907 Dr. Shearin, professor of English, and
a handful of students met to establish such a society. They
called it the Boar's Head after a famous old London tavern,
once the meeting place of literary figures. Membership was to
be selective, based upon the student's literary contributions to
The Transylvanian. The Boar's Head being an all male organization found itself faced with a competitor in 1909 when the
girls organized The Mermaid Club. And up the street in Hamilton College, the girls established the Blackfriars Club. Creative
writing clubs were apparently all the rage. Later, the Boar's
Head became a chapter of the Sigma Upsilon fraternity, founded at the University of the South in 1905, and was still active in
the 1930's even though the others had largely disappeared by
then.

Certain other campus organizations also began to appear in
this period. Sometime before the turn of the century, a YMCA
chapter was established to be followed shortly by the YWCA.
A glee club and quartet appeared along with an early dramatic
organization called the Mask and Wig Club, and various state
and foreign groups such as the Missouri Club and the Australia Club. There was a continuous coming and going of non-
sense clubs or organizations with ephemeral interests, among
them the Peterrinctum Club devoted to promoting athletic interest among the members, reforming society, raising class
standing and promoting temperance. Also appearing were the
Divinity Doctors' Socialistic Society of Prestidigitatical Gour-
mands and the Kosmopolitan Konfraternity of Koatless Kom-
fort Konnoisseurs. There was a Bachelor's Club and a Married
Men's Club — all exhibiting a bumptuous innocence. A more
serious group organized the "Living Link" organization in

1905, dedicated to supporting a foreign missionary, and doing so successfully for a number of years.

One of the most significant organizations founded at this time (and one which continues to play an important role on the campus to this day) was Lampas, founded in the 1904–05 school year. It took for its models the Golden Bear Society of the University of California, the Hasty Pudding Club of Harvard, and the Skull and Bones of Yale. Its purpose was

> to promote in every legitimate way possible, the general welfare of Kentucky University — to help onward every good movement; to stop as quickly as possible every bad movement. . . . The members are presumed to have some ability and some influence to be used in a quiet, unassuming manner in backing up all movements which will lead to a truer college spirit or will in any way lead to the further enrichment of college life at Kentucky University.[16]

Membership in Lampas was confined to junior and senior men who displayed some leadership in campus affairs, such as athletics or student publications. Among the original members were Thomas Young, Clinton Harbison, H. T. Myers, H. W. Carpenter, and E. B. Bourland. Lampas remained exclusively a male honorary for thirty years until Women's Lampas was established. The two organizations were combined in 1959, but the original purpose has remained basically the same.

Another organization which had a long and successful life was the Book and Bones senior society, established in 1911. It remained small with a highly selective membership, and died out during the World War II years. The students in the Law Department formed the Harlan Law Society named after its most famous graduate, but of course this disappeared along with the Law Department in 1912.

STUDENT PUBLICATIONS have had a rather sporadic career on the Transylvania and Kentucky University campuses. The earliest campus publication, apart from the professional journals such as the *Transylvania Medical Journal*, was *The Transylvanian*. It appeared in the winter of 1829 with a verbose

[16]*Ibid.*, 1905.

prospectus in the local press announcing its publication, and stating its purpose as the diffusion of useful knowledge, cultural uplift and literary improvement. Its first editor was Thomas J. Matthews, the Morrison professor of mathematics and natural philosophy. Its aim was somewhat more pretentious than the average college magazine today, but it lasted only two years as Matthews moved to Cincinnati; and although it was revived momentarily in 1837, it soon disappeared again.

John Harlan

A few years after the opening of Kentucky University on the old Transylvania campus in 1865, a new campus periodical appeared entitled *The Collegian*. This and similar publications such as *The Atlantis*, *The Tablet* and *The Focus* were produced as monthly or quarterly issues in the following decades. Then in October, 1891, the long buried *The Transylvanian* was successfully resurrected, to enjoy an unbroken, if sometimes perilous career, since that time. *The Crimson* college annual began its career in 1897, and in May 1915, the first campus newspaper *The Crimson Rambler* was published. News material, formerly printed in *The Transylvanian* was taken over by the new publication, and *The Transylvanian* became increasingly a repository for literary work.

A CATALOGUING of every organization that existed in these prolific years would serve little purpose. There was one for every activity, if not every whim. However, there was one new major area in which permanent organizations began to appear — the Greek fraternity. College regulations had generally prohibited their existence until the late 1890's, when a growing student pressure in their favor and a changing attitude on the part of the administration and faculty lowered the barrier.

College fraternities date as far back as Phi Beta Kappa at William and Mary in 1776, but these early fraternities tended to be more honorary societies than social. Professional fraternities likewise were among the earliest. In fact, it was in the Transylvania University Medical Department in 1819 that Dr. Samuel Brown organized Kappa Lambda, the first professional Greek letter fraternity in America.[17] It was his hope that the society would foster the idealism necessary to unite the profession against the prevailing dissension among doctors. Other chapters were later formed in Philadelphia, New York, Baltimore and other cities.

National social fraternities began to appear in the second decade of the nineteenth century. Union College was responsible for establishing three of the earliest. The burgeoning popularity of these organizations on campuses, especially in the South and the Midwest was due to a variety of social and economic causes. Socially, they reflected the characteristic adolescent American trait for secret societies with all the excitement of oaths, rituals, secrecy, drama and exclusiveness. Economically, they provided room and board for many students, especially the affluent, when there was an inadequate supply of dormitory housing. Institutions such as Harvard and Yale countered the invasion of social fraternities with a structure of their own honor societies and social clubs. In the earlier part of the nineteenth century, students, faculty and administration — perhaps sharing in the Jacksonian antipathy to secret organizations as undemocratic — formed a considerable barrier to the spread of the Greek fraternities, but by the end of the century this

---

[17]Frederick Eberson, *Portraits: Kentucky Pioneers in Community Health and Medicine* (Lexington, 1968), p. 35.

opposition had largely been eroded, and the movement showed great strength and increasing popularity.[18]

Since 1865 there had been a Kentucky University regulation forbidding students from joining secret organizations without faculty permission, and the only approved organizations were the traditional non-secret literary societies. Bowman had always insisted that the University was for the masses, especially the poor young man from the farm. Fraternity organization found uncongenial soil here; literary societies had a monopoly on campus until the 1890's. But a marked change occurred in 1896 when the curators expressed a favorable opinion that Greek fraternities should be added to Kentucky University. The faculty had previously been approached by the students for its approval, and the reply was that since the statutes of the University prohibited such activities, the decision lay with the curators.

Despite some delay and opposition from other student organizations, the first fraternities were established. The first was Kappa Alpha. The Alpha Theta chapter was actually chartered in 1891 but had to operate *sub rosa* until it became safe to emerge publicly. Kappa chapter of Pi Kappa Alpha was chartered in the fall of 1900. The girls, not to be left behind, secured a chapter of Chi Omega. Though Chi chapter was founded in 1899 at the Jessamine Institute near Lexington, it was not transferred to the University campus until 1903. The other permanent addition to sorority circles in the period before World War I was Beta Zeta chapter of Delta Delta Delta, established in 1908. A fraternity, probably local, called Phi Pi Chi, appeared in 1912, but disappeared five years later.

By 1915 *The Crimson* could say that the "college fraternity has come to be looked upon as a dominant factor in college life. The time was when a fraternity was looked upon as a bunch of snobs . . . [but] now recognized to be composed of men and women of high ideals, bound by fraternal ties in the interest of the college." As will be noted later, the number of fraternities and sororities doubled after World War I and have remained a significant part of the campus life. The fact that fraternity housing did not become permanently located off campus, and

[18] Schmidt, *The Liberal Arts College*, pp. 195–197.

chapter rooms frequently were located in the dormitories, may have contributed to the interdependence of college and fraternity, and the Greek membership did not seem isolated from central concerns and activities of the campus.

IN ADDITION TO THE ARRIVAL of Greek fraternities on campus, there was another novel and significant feature that appeared in the post Civil War period. This was the development of both intramural and intercollegiate sports. The totality of college life that centered around intellectual discipline in the classroom and spiritual discipline in the chapel was becoming somewhat fragmented as the concept of what a college education should be began to change. The proliferation of extracurricular activities and organizations was one evidence of the change. The growth of athletics was another.

At first most college administrators welcomed the appearance of campus athletics. Competitive sports and gymnastics promised a solution to the problem of discipline. All that excess energy, those animal spirits, would be safely channeled into athletic activity. The boy, tired from participating in sports, was less likely to use his energies in horseplay and practical jokes. At first there was little supervision. Given enough room on campus, or a nearby pasture, the boys could regulate their own activities.[19]

Between 1855 and 1895 the most popular sports nationally in order of their appearance were rowing, baseball, football and basketball. The order of their development at Kentucky University was almost the reverse of this. Rowing was never contemplated. Football came first, to be followed by baseball and basketball. Football, which began to arrive on college campuses right after the Civil War, was at first nothing more than a rowdy soccer game with teams composed of as many as twenty men. Games might run from noon to dark. Harvard and Yale began to standardize the game by creating a hybrid of soccer and English rugby. By the early 1870's the team size had become limited to eleven men, and intercollegiate contests began to shift into high gear. Some writers believe it was the competitive element that gave athletics its status and prestige. It was a

[19]*Ibid*., pp. 198–199.

form of competition, unlike intellectual excellence, that could be precisely measured. As George P. Schmidt says,

> when you could put the best nine or eleven men against your rival's best, under conditions agreed upon in advance and subject to the judgment of an impartial arbiter, superiority was clearly established. . . . Competitive sports became an oversimplified symbol and fetish of excellence. All the self-effacing loyalties of campus life, the pride of achievement, the nostalgia of alumni, were channeled into this one direction and in a flood of sentiment swept other values before it.[20]

Combine with this the great appeal to a large potential spectator public — and implied increased revenue — and intercollegiate athletics were hard to resist. There was talk of body and character building, and the philosophy of a healthy mind in a healthy body, but in the matter of intercollegiate competition these philosophical platitudes were soon shunted aside by a hard-nosed professionalism and the figure of the coach as a man to be reckoned with.

In the South, this new national fad caught on somewhat more slowly. Eastern colleges had been hammering at one another on the football field for over a decade before the first recorded intercollegiate football match was played in the South. Kentucky University was one of the participants in this match. Two students, Miles Dawson and Charles Thurgood, the latter from Melbourne, Australia, sent to Australia for a ball and a set of rules, and began practicing their team. They challenged Centre College to a game, and on the afternoon of April 9, 1880,

> the two teams met in a cow pasture, belonging to Hubert McGoodwin near Lexington, the present site of the University of Kentucky's Stoll Field. . . . There were fifteen players on each team and a player once injured or removed for other reasons could not re-enter the game. At the end of much scuffling and butting of scholarly foreheads, Transylvania was declared the winner by the score of 13-3/4 points to 0. . . . The team members were older men, a good many of them having whiskers. And they wore extremely heavy shoes and heavily padded apparel.[21]

The crowd paid fifty cents to see the game, and the presence of a good many ladies "induced the boys to exert themselves

[20]*Ibid.*

[21]*Lexington Herald-Leader*, Special Section, n.d., circa 1941–42.

more." The Centre boys, smarting from a loss they would more than adequately revenge years later, protested that Kentucky University had misled them by sending them rules for rugby and a round ball, while Kentucky University decided to play by Princeton rules and used an oval ball.

Though the game between Kentucky University and Centre College marked the beginning, it was a long time before organized athletics appeared on the campuses. It was not for lack of student interest, however. In 1887, a student writer for *The Atlantis* pointed out the need for athletics to balance the training of the mind with that of the body. There was no need for a student to be a physical weakling when he could participate in various sports and exercises. He saw no reason why Kentucky University should not have a first-rate football team and gymnasium. If friends of the University would provide the building, students would purchase the necessary equipment.

The girl's basketball team in the gymnasium

The plea of students for a gymnasium did not fall on deaf ears. Alumni became involved, and a special committee to assist in financing a gymnasium was created with which members of the Board cooperated. In 1892 work on a site and plans for the building were underway. At the June 1893 meeting of the Board the special committee recommended a site for the building fronting on North Broadway "near and a little west of where the Barracks stood."[22] Bids were opened in September, construction started, and by April 1894, the rather impressive, spacious brick building was completed at a cost of about $10,000. A new physical education department was added in the fall of 1894 with James Frew as the first instructor.

In 1900 student editors were not content with the situation. They felt students were not making sufficient use of the gymnasium. There was a need for a good football team, but the program lacked money, and some of the students were too poor to contribute financially. Faculty members did not support the team the way they should, and it was hard to get a good coach. Some of the students physically able to be good football players would not bother to show up for the team.[23]

An even greater threat to football was the growing hostility toward it from faculty, administration and even some of the public and state and national political figures. The reason was the game's brutality. Inadequately trained and improperly equipped, the players were subject to extensive and dangerous injuries. A number of deaths had occurred on the playing fields across the nation. Looking at photographs of the early football uniforms, one can understand why injuries were so frequent. The earliest uniforms were hardly more than padded track suits and heavy shoes. By 1900 the players were wearing heavily padded pants, shin guards and nose protectors, and by 1904, helmets and shoulder pads, incredibly thin and ineffective by today's standards, began to appear.

In 1897 the Georgia legislature passed a law prohibiting football playing because of an accidental death of a player, but the governor vetoed it. He said the matter should be left up to the individual faculties. *The Transylvanian* probably reflected wide-

[22]Minutes of the Board, June 2, 1893.
[23]*The Transylvanian*, X (November, 1900).

spread student sentiment in its criticism of actions similar to those of the Georgia legislature. The game had been played for decades, the writers said, and was the legislature only now realizing its brutality? Did not the legislators have something better to do?[24] The sport was here to stay. Its worst aspects were increasingly eliminated as better protection of the players through better equipment and officiating was provided.

The football team of 1892

In 1892 Kentucky University invited representatives from Central University in Richmond and State College to a meeting on its campus to form the Kentucky Intercollegiate Football League. A constitution was adopted and regulations written for the governing of all contests.[25]

Despite Kentucky University's interest in football, her showing on the playing field in the 1890's was pitiful. The team was so bad in 1895 that it was disbanded before the season was

[24]*Ibid.*, VII (December, 1897).

[25]*History of Football at Transylvania College.* Data compiled by Joseph Fitch and other WPA workers under the direction of Tate C. "Piney" Page. (Lexington, 1941).

over. Students blamed the faculty for its opposition to college athletics. Yet each season saw another team organized, though in 1896 only one game was played. In fact, until President Jenkins came, most of the seasons posted winless records. Though Jenkins did not, as he claimed, introduce football to the University, he was right in saying that he brought

> in as instructor a young Yale man who knew the game and coached the first winning team in the history of the college; made up of young natural athletes from mountains and bluegrass, it swept away everything in Kentucky and some things outside. I went to see all the games and cheered our own lads; so it was only natural that they approved of me and my conduct.[26]

The young Yale coach was William Edward Selin, who had graduated from Yale in 1898 at the age of twenty-five, having been an outstanding track man while there. With remarkable skill he moulded the young men of Kentucky University into a winning combination with the help of the brilliant running backs Hogan and Worth Yancey. In the very first year, Selin chalked up a 7-1-1 record, followed by a 7-win, 2-loss record the next year. And these were substantial victories, such as the 70–0 win over Georgetown, the 57–0 win over Butler University, and the 27–0 win over State College. The season to end all seasons, however, came in the fall of 1905, even without the help of the Yancey boys. It was a 7-win, 3-tie record, that included victories over the University of Texas, Texas A&M and the University of Arkansas, and a tie with Northwestern. The boys at Texas A&M were so peeved at losing that they threw rocks at the Kentucky players all the way to the railroad station.

It seems incredible that after such a season the Board of Curators voted the following March to withdraw from all intercollegiate athletics. Finance was the main reason. The University did not have enough money to adequately maintain the program. Lack of support from students and Lexingtonians, strange as it may seem, was also cited. But with most of the games played away from home, it is difficult to see what more support they could give except outright financial contributions. The editor of *The Transylvanian* said, not surprisingly, that no

[26]Jenkins, *Where My Caravan Has Rested*, p. 147.

more unpopular decision by the Board had ever been made. He complained that there was no reason to drop baseball, basketball and track just because football was expensive. He was sure students would be willing to pay higher matriculation fees to maintain football. Withdrawing from intercollegiate athletics would hurt the school and probably result in a loss of students. Meanwhile the students conducted a mock burial of a football on a corner of the practice field.[27]

At their annual meeting in June 1906, the curators stuck to their decision but created a loophole by authorizing the Executive Committee to restore intercollegiate athletics during the next school year if it saw fit. In October the Executive Committee did so, starting with basketball in the winter. It is ironic that at the time the curators were doing away with football, they had acquired an excellent athletic field on North Broadway, three blocks north of the campus, which became known as Thomas Field. A grandstand was erected to seat several hundred spectators.

Though football was revived in the fall of 1907, Kentucky University teams were never again as successful as they had been for those few brief years. There was difficulty in securing good coaches. For a few years, Hogan Yancey, the famous back of the Kentucky University team a short time before, tried his hand at coaching with only fair results. One explanation is that University opponents were becoming stronger as their institutions became larger, while the base for the Kentucky University teams remained the same. Thus in 1910 when the University team played the University of Texas and Texas A&M teams, both of whom it had previously defeated, it was soundly beaten by both. Kentucky University now began to change its schedule to play teams more within its own capacities. When Cincinnati beat it in 1912 by a score of 124–0, Cincinnati was scratched from the list of contenders. The University played seventy games in the decade 1911–1920, of which it won thirty-one and tied six. The golden era of 1901–1906 was never again equalled on the football field.

Baseball had probably been played informally by students years before the first team was organized in the spring of 1892.

[27] *The Transylvanian*, XV (March, 1906).

Though apparently without the benefit of formal coaching, the new team launched a victorious season by beating State College 16–7 and Georgetown 23–3. The records of succeeding seasons, where available, reveal a less consistent pattern. However, a team was fielded every year. What coaching they received was provided by the physical education director. A regular intercollegiate schedule was maintained through these years, varying in number and variety of competitors. In the 1907–1908 season, for instance, the team faced Centre, the University of Cincinnati, State College, Georgetown, Berea, University of Nashville and Vanderbilt.

The women's basketball team of 1903

The first intercollegiate basketball season in which Kentucky University participated was in the 1902–1903 school year. In fact, it was the first season in which Kentucky colleges competed against one another, because basketball was comparatively new as a college game. It quickly became popular, perhaps for the reasons suggested by the editors of *The Crimson:*

The game catches alike the man who says that baseball is too slow and uninteresting, and the man who says that football is too dangerous and exciting. Basketball strikes a happy medium and there is no game in which one can display more science and at the same time be in such need of absolute control of his head and muscles.[28]

And it was convenient to have basketball come in the empty season between football and baseball!

Kentucky University won the basketball title that first year by beating State College once and Georgetown twice. It was not an exhausting schedule. Remarkably there was an immediate appearance of a girls' basketball team. The girls played regularly during these years, participated in a regular intercollegiate schedule in the World War I period, and won the state championship in 1920.

One problem confronting basketball teams was that many of the games were played at night. There was no problem with the floor, for the gymnasium was practically new, but there was a problem with lighting. In December 1906, *The Transylvanian* was complaining that the lighting was atrocious. "The gas jets which adorn our beautiful gymnasium went on strike years ago, and a reconciliation has not yet been effected," the journal said. The lights burned fitfully and undependably. Some of the burners were located so close to the baskets they were frequently hit. What was needed was electrical lighting. Meanwhile, it was suggested that the students bring candles to the next game.

Kentucky University had a track team participating in field day contests as early as 1894. For a time the school must have provided training facilities, for *The Crimson* noted that "early in the spring Gratz Park becomes the scene of vigorous training when the bare-legged sprinters begin to harden their muscles on the cinder track." The track team had participants in all categories including the 100, 220, 440 yard dashes, the half-mile and mile runs, shot putting, throwing the hammer and even a two-mile bicycle race. There were track teams on campus in most years up to World War I, and then, for no obvious reason,

[28]*The Crimson*, 1903.

they disappeared in the 1920's. Track apparently never achieved the popularity among students the other sports did, so it lacked both participants and spectators.

By 1905 the University had provided tennis courts on campus and the Clover Leaf Tennis Club was organized. This, and similar clubs, were short-lived. There does not seem to have been any systematic intercollegiate tennis competition in which Kentucky University participated. The tennis courts were used mainly by students for recreation.

As the years went by, there was increasing recognition of the need for establishing basic regulations governing eligibility for participants in intercollegiate competition. The semi-professional hardened bruiser who showed up every now and then in college football, having little or no academic connection with a college or university, was to be eliminated. In 1909 the Kentucky Intercollegiate Athletic Association set some rules. A student participating in contests involving members of the association must be a bona fide student, taking at least twelve hours of courses per week or its equivalent, and maintaining passing grades. There were to be no professionals on the team, and no financial bonuses were to be paid for playing.

Such were the early years of athletics at Kentucky University, and hundreds of other colleges, some four generations ago. A great deal of human history has passed since those days, and the old annuals and their precious photographs of the teams have an amateur and archaic flavor about them. But the clear-eyed, broad-shouldered, determined-chinned faces of the athletes do not look strange or faded. They look much like the athletes of today. Yet the differences of dress and manners may amuse us — hair parted in the middle, the big, heavy, turtle-necked sweaters with large KU numerals emblazoned on the front; managers proudly standing in their suits and vests and stiff, high collars. The basketball players look slightly ridiculous in their plain jerseys and long, baggy short pants that come to the knees. The flashy styles, the tailored uniforms, the semi-professional polish are missing. Collegiate athletics was still an amateur activity. And the girls' basketball team — what a formidable looking group! It may be the bulky, formless sweaters or shirtwaists, the long, full skirts reaching to the floor. Or is it

Students in the new library

the turn of the century hair, waved and piled high for combat? Styles, dress, make-up, hair styles must make the difference, for in some respects the girls seem more distant from the contemporary college student than do the boys.

There seems little doubt that student life on the college campuses between the Civil War and World War I underwent considerable transformation. The more rigid rules of conduct were modified. Heavy emphasis on classroom work and study diminished with the rise of a host of extracurricular activities engaging students' interests and time. Whether it was a literary society, a fraternity, a debating contest, dramatics or athletics, there was now a greater variety of alternatives to study than ever before. There was more play in campus life. Traditionalists who believed that schools were the workshops in which a rebellious and malleable youthful spirit was to be tempered and disciplined were dismayed at the change. College presidents such as Burris Jenkins fostered the change. It was the direction in which American higher education would move in the twentieth century.

17

The Beginning
Struggle
for Identity

Thomas B. McCartney, Jr.   *Richard Crossfield*

The period from the departure of Burris Jenkins to the end of Andrew Harmon's administration was a challenging and critical one for both Kentucky University (or as it reassumed the name Transylvania University in 1908) and the College of the Bible. From 1912–1928 these two institutions became increasingly integrated — sharing the same president, faculty and financial resources. After Harmon's departure in 1928 the process of disentanglement began, although not until 1938 did the College of the Bible have its own president, the first since the death of McGarvey in 1911. The interlocking of fortunes of these two schools raised serious problems of identity for each, and on occasion threatened the survival of both. The crisis confronting them was both financial and ideological. The changing American society of the twentieth century was placing a great strain on traditional values, customs and modes of living.

The public school system was expanding at a remarkable rate, and higher education was feeling the impact of the rise of great universities and the influence of new ideas on the goals and methods of collegiate education. As the Progressive Movement sought to cleanse the archaic and corrupt aspects from American political and economic life, to raise the quality and expand the scope of citizens' participation in local and national politics, and to regulate the unbridled excesses of an immensely energetic, but too frequently exploitive American industry, so men such as John Dewey introduced novel concepts of education into the American school system as a manifestation of a progressive spirit in the learning process. The ferment resulting from the collision of Dewey and his followers and the traditionalists still bubbles today. Colleges and universities had been debating the radical revision of the curriculum and requirements for the A.B. degree ever since Charles Eliot forced it on their attention by brow-beating Harvard into accepting his elective system in the 1870's. Now Dewey came along to undergird the elective system with a broader and more profound philosophical basis.

Until Burris Jenkins arrived on the campus, there was little indication that either faculty or administration was seriously considering a fundamental reordering of the goals and methods of Kentucky University. Even Jenkins did not attempt a major overhaul of the university curriculum or degree requirements. But he did introduce a far more liberal influence into the university structure and improve the faculty, and he gave a much needed surge of new energy to the institution.

The problem of maintaining two institutions on the same campus, each legally a corporate and independent body with distinctive purposes and traditions, was an increasingly perplexing one. The giant tower of the new College of the Bible building, erected in 1895, challenged the physical, if not institutional prominence that Transylvania's Morrison Hall had for so long occupied. For those persons who had always viewed the creation of Kentucky University as a sectarian training ground for Christian citizens and a preparatory school for ministers, and the College of the Bible as a collateral nursery for future church leaders of these citizens, there was no conflict in having these two institutions side by side. But for those who viewed the University as a non-sectarian enterprise, with broad educational goals, and which only incidentally provided the essential liberal arts basis for the future seminary student, the interlocking of the two institutions not only confused the distinct purpose of the University but also hampered the development of the College of the Bible into a fully mature graduate seminary. The study of this crisis of identity and survival is our concern for these next few chapters.

FOLLOWING THE DEPARTURE of Burris Jenkins in 1906 the curators named Thomas B. McCartney, Jr., as acting president. McCartney had been one of Jenkins' proudest faculty acquisitions. Every inch the Virginia gentleman, he was a favorite among students and faculty alike, but administrative work was not his cup of tea. He told the curators as much, but they were too impressed by his obvious abilities to listen to him. They even wanted him to accept the presidency, but McCartney refused. Greek and Latin were his loves, and the classroom and teaching were the place and mode of his expression of this love. Yet he did perform manfully as acting president until a new leader was secured. He engaged in no fund raising but concentrated on administering the ongoing campus program.

It was during this interim period that the institution reassumed the name of Transylvania University. It might seem a perfunctory matter, this changing of a name. It was far from it. A rose might smell as sweet by any other name, but would a university? Many believed not. The subject was emotional dynamite. The name of Kentucky University had now for over forty years been accumulating a cluster of associations and memories, a staunch alumni, an historic identity that could not easily be sloughed off. And what of Transylvania? For its alumni and for the community of Lexington, the campus on the hill north of Main Street dominated by the chaste, classic structure of Morrison Hall and its six Doric columns, was Transylvania. Calling it Kentucky University had not changed that.

What brought matters to a head was not a dialogue among the curators about institutional identity. It was the threat by the school across town, the Agricultural and Mechanical College — known for years as State College — to change its name to State University, Lexington, Kentucky. It was a logical step as the state school more clearly developed into a university. There was nothing to prevent the State College from changing its name except the embarrassing existence of another institution in Lexington called Kentucky University. The possibilities for confusion were endless, but the matter could not remain unresolved forever. The State College had decided to change its name. Would Kentucky University consider changing its name? The matter had been discussed years before 1908. In 1897 Maury Kemper, class of 1893, informed the editors of *The Transylvanian* that he polled a number of the alumni on the subject of changing the school's name from Kentucky University to Transylvania and found them in favor of the change. The local community press endorsed the proposal. The name Transylvania was associated nationally with the noted historic university situated on the Lexington campus, and it would resolve the problem of confusion with State College. The editors agreed that "there can be no question but that it ought to be changed to Transylvania, a name so beautiful and euphonious, and so intimately connected with the early history of the Commonwealth. . . ."[1]

The University's governing board was of a different mind. In January 1898, the Executive Committee was alarmed to hear that a bill had been presented to the legislature proposing the name "State University" be applied to the Agricultural and Mechanical College. Members of the Committee took steps to thwart its passage and were successful. A few months later one of the curators had the temerity to suggest at a Board meeting that the institution reassume the name of Transylvania. This was rejected by an overwhelming vote. Seven years later, President Jenkins proposed to the curators that a special committee be established to sample alumni sentiment on changing the name. The curators were so excited about this proposal that they ordered it be officially expunged from the minutes.[2]

They could not sweep back the tide forever. In 1908 when the legislature was in session, the Agricultural and Mechanical College (State College) indicated that it would postpone making the change no longer. A special committee from the Kentucky University Board met with officials of State College and reluctantly agreed to give up the name of Kentucky University. The Board was informed that no other action was feasible or wise. State College had an indisputable and legitimate claim to the title of State University. To keep the name Kentucky University would be detrimental to both institutions. Circumstances

[1] *The Transylvanian*, VII (October, 1897).
[2] Minutes of the Board, January 7, 1905.

thus made a painful decision necessary, and the committee recommended the name Transylvania University be assumed with
the provision

> that the State of Kentucky will grant to Kentucky University all
> legislation necessary to change its name to Transylvania Univer-
> sity under the control and management of the present Board of
> Curators of Kentucky University and enjoying all the rights and
> privileges of the Board of Trustees of old Transylvania Universi-
> ty, and that the trustees of the Agricultural and Mechanical Col-
> lege will assist in all possible ways in securing such legislation.[3]

The name change would become effective upon passage of such
legislation, and the State College would pay Transylvania a
sum sufficient to defray the costs involved. The report was approved by the curators with a 15 to 2 vote, the legislature formalized the change, and in the spring of 1908 the name Transylvania University proudly was reassumed. "The return to
TRANSYLVANIA, the name of the University from 1780 to
the Civil War, was received with almost universal approval,"
wrote an editor of *The Transylvanian*. It certainly made sense
to that publication!

Appropriations were made for a special issue of *The Transylvanian* to be printed, informing readers of the name change and
incorporating articles on Transylvania history to celebrate the
occasion. A special feature was to be included in *The Crimson*,
and news stories were to be sent to newspapers and journals.
Special mailings to alumni, friends and all those involved in the
recruitment of students were made.[4] In 1909 a new seal was
created for the University with the motto "In Lumine illo Tra-
dimus Lumen."

The transition to assuming another name was not as traumatic as many curators had anticipated. The experience might
have been different had an entirely new name been chosen.
Transylvania University has remained the legal title of the institution to the present, but with the dissolution of the Law Department in 1912, Transylvania no longer maintained any graduate or professional programs. There was only the liberal arts

[3]*Ibid.*, January 7, 1908.
[4]*Ibid.*, March 10, 1908.

college. In 1915 the Board decided to use the name Transylvania College for this main nucleus of the University, and for over fifty years the school was referred to as Transylvania College.

Another significant change in the governing structure of the University occurred at about this same time. It was proposed at the March 1908, meeting of the curators that a special committee of three be appointed to consider the advisability of changing Section 8 of the charter of Kentucky University to eliminate the provision that "at least two-thirds of the Board of Curators shall always be members of the Christian Church in Kentucky" and to report at the June meeting. The appointed committee recommended in June that the charter be amended to eliminate this provision, and McCartney fortified the recommendation in his annual report when he stated that dropping the membership clause would make the University eligible to receive the benefits of the Carnegie Foundation for retiring professors and would show no disloyalty to the people who had largely made the school what it was. Two other Disciples' institutions, Drake University and Butler, had eliminated such provisions from their charters. The curators appeared convinced and adopted the recommendation, and the chairman was instructed to appoint a committee to see that this recommendation was put into effect.[5]

Considering the controversial role this provision had played in the great struggle with John Bowman decades earlier, it is remarkable that the elimination of the clause caused such little comment at the time. While it was true that control by the Disciples of Christ was so unchallenged and complete at this time there seemed little need to guarantee it by charter rights, it certainly opened up the possibility of electing a Board who were not church members or who indeed might question the desirability of maintaining such close ties with the church. But in reality, the question was academic — at least for the next several decades.

One other change in the Board was made when in 1910 it was decided to divide the thirty-five members into five distinct classes of seven, each with a five-year term of office.

[5]*Ibid.*, March 6, 1908; June 10, 1908.

THE BOARD FOUND a replacement for Jenkins in Richard Crossfield, a Disciples minister. The tradition of placing Disciples ministers in the presidential office began with the appointment of Charles Loos. Though Kentucky University was chartered as a Disciples institution, neither John Bowman, its creator and regent for many years, nor Henry White who succeeded him were ministers. The fact that the curators offered the position to McCartney, who was not a minister, indicated the tradition was not a hard and fast one. Yet from 1880 to the present, all occupants of the position other than acting presidents have been ministers of that denomination. Combining both the College of the Bible and Transylvania under a single president was thus made easier.

Born in Lawrenceburg, Kentucky, in 1868 and educated in the public schools in his native county, Richard Crossfield came to Lexington for his college work, graduating with an A.B. degree from Kentucky University in 1889 and receiving his ministerial degree from the College of the Bible in 1892. Later he secured his M.A. and Ph.D. from the University of Wooster. He served successful pastorates in Kentucky at Glasgow and Owensboro before accepting the presidency of Transylvania in 1908.

This strong, vigorous, fine-looking man brought a rich background of study, travel, practical experience and boundless enthusiasm to the job. His energy was prodigious. His secretary, the remarkable Miss Ledridge, said of him that "he could accomplish more each 24 hours and keep it up longer than any other mortal I ever knew."[6] And she had been amanuensis to many presidents. He not only performed the duties of president but also what today would be done by an assistant to the president, a public relations man, a financial agent and a student recruiter. As a student in the College of the Bible he had written an essay entitled "The Hero of the Future" in which he expressed his own view on the importance which the active man, especially the active Christian, can have in society. His own life exemplified that ideal.

[6] Quote from a statement by Ernest Delcamp, June 7, 1943, in the Crossfield file, Transylvania University archives.

Crossfield traveled widely, speaking at alumni banquets, visiting other campuses, and even attending the inauguration of President Taft in 1909. These experiences he shared with an enthusiastic student body in a series of chapel talks. He also possessed a valuable talent of choosing the right man for the job, picking his faculty with great care and then demanding their best. His faculty must not only be interested in their subject matter but in the campus as a whole, in the community, and in contributing towards the development of a Christian society. And he defended his faculty against all assaults.

THE TRANSYLVANIA CAMPUS in 1908 was a modest one. The old college lot, for years known as Gratz Park, was no longer a part of the campus. The lower quarter had already been sold to the Lexington Public Library trustees for the erection of an imposing new city library. The long, low brick structure on the northeast corner, dating from at least 1818 (perhaps even the 1790's) drowsed quietly under the weight of its memories — first as a janitor's house, then a kitchen and dining room for the students, and finally a preparatory school where once James Lane Allen taught young, reluctant minds the fundamentals of Latin and English. But the new Academy building northeast of Morrison Hall, known at various times as East Hall, and later Ella Jones Hall, had replaced the older building's function. The city would one day take over the old cottage to house its park and recreation office.

The remainder of Gratz Park north of the library was leased in perpetuity to the City of Lexington in 1915 for use as a park by a grant of $20,000 from Anderson Gratz of St. Louis, who submitted the proposal.[7]

On the main campus the two towering structures of Morrison Hall and the College of the Bible jostled one another for domination of the campus. To the east of Morrison rose the impressive new Carnegie Science Building, finished just before Crossfield's arrival, and a few yards north of it, East Hall. Behind Morrison and the College of the Bible were the old dormitories and the gymnasium. Photographs of that period reveal only a

[7]Minutes of the Board, November 4, 1915.

few young trees in the whole wide sweep of the campus, and not a bush or a shrub to soften the buildings' hard, stark lines. The late nineteenth-century and early twentieth-century American structures were sturdy but not especially gracious or appealing. Morrison Hall stood strangely independent of the others, a dignified visitor from another age.

A block north stood Hamilton College, run by Transylvania as a girls' junior college, and ultimately destined to become a large dormitory for Transylvania girls.

There were 225 students in the college in Crossfield's first year, 18 in the Law Department and 101 in the preparatory department. In his thirteen years on campus, Crossfield saw the enrollment fluctuate in the college to a low of 166 and a high of 306. The Law Department closed in 1912 and the preparatory department was phased out in 1915. The College of the Bible's enrollment during this same period ranged from 71 to 140.

THE FACULTY WAS rather sharply divided in age between a handful of senior members and a majority of younger men and women who had joined the staff since 1900. Charles Loos, a phenomenal eighty-five years old in the days when retirement was not determined by age but by fitness, shortly became professor emeritus, as did Alexander Milligan in 1911. Alfred Fairhurst, who taught physics and chemistry, had been at Kentucky University since 1881. He retired in 1914 but returned briefly to the campus to speak out against the liberals and evolutionists in the famous 1917 investigations of the College of the Bible faculty. *The Crimson* of 1904 had been dedicated to Fairhurst "in grateful remembrance of his genial and generous spirit, and in recognition of his undaunted courage and profound ability in the defense of the Bible, from the stand-point of a well-equipped scientist."

The last of the oldtimers was Samuel Jefferson, who had come to the campus in 1900 to teach philosophy in both the University and the College of the Bible. Dr. William C. Bower, his younger colleague, characterized him as "a great-hearted, broad-minded, and tolerant scholar . . . the continuing link between the old and the new."[8] He died from a heart attack in 1914.

These are fine, distinguished faces that stare so steadily from photographs of the annuals. Bearded and mustached, they gaze with an air of wisdom and detachment on their younger, clean-shaven, and more intense colleagues. The nucleus of the new faculty who would devote decades, if not their whole teaching lives to the college, was beginning to form. Henry Lloyd in mathematics and astronomy; the imposing Irene T. Myers, a Yale Ph.D. who served so vigorously as both professor of history and dean of women for fifteen years; Thomas B. McCartney, who gave his life to the institution; and young, energetic, multi-talented Ernest Woodruff Delcamp, who, after a distinguished record as a student at Kentucky University, stayed on to teach Latin at his alma mater, securing his Ph.D. later in that subject at the University of Chicago. This fine scholar and excellent musician was to give unstinting service to Transylvania for half a century. Also there was Clarence Freeman, pillar of the English department for many years. This group remained through the World War I period and into the Twenties.

None of these faculty appointments provoked the controversy that resulted from Crossfield's engagement of Alonzo Fortune and William Clayton Bower to the faculty of the College of the Bible. In 1912 Crossfield had accepted the presidency of the College of the Bible much to the dismay of Dean Hall Laurie Calhoun. A Harvard Ph.D. who paradoxically clung to a conservative and orthodox theology despite his liberal training, Calhoun was acting president of the College of the Bible following McGarvey's death in 1911 and may have been anticipating election to the presidency himself. Crossfield, now wearing two crowns, was interested in updating the College of the Bible as well as Transylvania. McGarvey's death marked the end of an era and opened the opportunity for a profound change of stance as the seminary entered a new age. Some years before Jenkins had expressed his disapproval of the seminary, its methods of teaching and its unyielding traditionalism, but his leverage was insufficient to change it. He crossed

[8] William Clayton Bower, *Though the Years* (Lexington, 1957), p. 38.

swords with McGarvey, but that duel ended in a draw. Now Crossfield was in a position to initiate the long-overdue change. He was extremely conscientious in his recruitment methods, polling the leading figures in education and the denomination. As the field of nominees narrowed, he exhaustively examined their qualifications as scholars, teachers and Christians. He finally selected Alonzo Fortune in April 1912, to teach church history and New Testament theology and William Clayton Bower to occupy the chair of Bible School Pedagogy.

Fortune, a graduate of Hiram College, had continued his advanced work at Colgate-Rochester Divinity School and was about to receive his Ph.D. from the University of Chicago. The announcement of his appointment through the public press aroused a storm of protest among conservative brethren. The editor of *The Christian Standard*, S. S. Lappin, wrote Crossfield: "I may say to you privately and personally that I regard this as a great calamity for the school. . . . I would not for the world permit my son to be in his classroom."[9] A Louisville evangelist by the name of John T. Brown led the fight against Fortune, both in private letters to Crossfield and in public protests in the pages of *The Christian Standard*. Fortune, a product of the new Biblical scholarship and associated with the modernist University of Chicago, told Crossfield that he had no intention of coming to Lexington if it could injure the school, involve him in endless harassment or embarrass Crossfield. For the new president, stakes were high. The future of the seminary was involved, as well as his own reputation both as president and as a pastor in the denomination. Convinced by the best advice he could obtain that his decision to hire Fortune was a wise and necessary one, he decided to fight it out on the barricades.

Ashley S. Johnson, president of Johnson Bible College in Tennessee, exploited the situation in hopes of strengthening his own school. Evil was abroad in the land, he said, and when the subversive influence of a Chicago critic was now to be exercised in the good old College of the Bible, the men of true faith needed to cling together to the remaining citadels of righteous-

[9] Quoted in Stevenson, *Lexington Theological Seminary*, p. 140.

ness. The Board of Trustees of the College of the Bible conducted its own investigation after examining the accusations of critics, and came to the conclusion Fortune was eminently acceptable as a new member of the faculty. The disgruntled opposition never acquiesced in this decision, and many went their separate ways. It was, perhaps, an irreconcilable division, for, as Stevenson has so well stated:

> The issue, of course, was not between fidelity and infidelity, as Brown had thought, but between two opposing sets of assumptions within Christianity, one conservative, the other progressive; one legalistic and literalistic, the other bent upon an open-minded inquiry into the spirit of the Bible; one closed to the scientific attitude, the other openly welcoming it.[10]

Professor Bower represented the new trend as well, but perhaps because the subject matter he taught seemed less controversial and his educational training less tinged with heretical associations, he did not attract as much of the orthodox fire as had Fortune. A few years later, however, would find both Bower and Fortune along with Crossfield under a new assault.

One other noted figure, Elmer Ellsworth Snoddy, joined the faculty before World War I. He was appointed to teach philosophy in the college and practical theology in the seminary. By all accounts this man who taught from 1914 to 1936 was one of the most remarkable and gifted teachers ever to appear on the Transylvania campus. Coming from the sod-house frontier of the Dakota territory, Snoddy was twenty-eight when he started his education in the preparatory department of Hiram College. After completing work for his A.B. degree he stayed on to teach Greek language and literature. He then shifted to philosophy, taking time off to secure his M.A. in this field at Yale. At the age of fifty-one he left Hiram to join the faculty at the Lexington schools. Stevenson says that "armed with homely wisdom of the common people, with wit and a quick, germinal mind, E. E. Snoddy was undoubtedly one of the most stimulating teachers ever to come to Lexington."[11]

Testimony from his many students reveals a man who was truly a gifted and rare teacher. Men who later studied under the

[10]*Ibid.*, p. 149.
[11]*Ibid.*, p. 150.

Elmer E. Snoddy

finest scholars in major universities across the land rated Snoddy the best teacher of them all, although it was acknowledged that he never wrote a book and but a few articles. What little he wrote does not illuminate the man. His reading assignments to his students were relatively light and undemanding. He apparently made little formal preparation for class by way of written lectures or outline notes. His was the dialectical method, and like some rough-hewn Socrates he brought the dynamic functioning of the ancient but timeless academy into the worn classrooms, which wearily exuded the stale air of endless old-style rote recitations. What mattered to him was the fresh encounter with students and the constantly renewed intellectual quest. The blackboard was his sounding board, bearing the hurried chalkmarks of his thoughts as he elaborated them into complex diagrams, then sweeping them away with his chalk-smudged hands as one thought tumbled over another. "Ah, young theologue, what do you think of that?" he would ask as he swooped down on an entranced student, clapping him on the shoulder and leaving behind the telltale mark of his chalky hand. When he became excited he furiously massaged a prominent wart on his bald head, or "would curl and uncurl a loose strand of hair."[12] He had the gift of homely illustration, and

[12]*Ibid.* See the delightful pages on Snoddy, pp. 254–257.

was a delight to hundreds of laymen who attended his Wednesday evening class at Central Christian Church.

The noted psychic Arthur Ford later recalled from his Transylvania student experience that the only teacher who truly stimulated him and who did not immediately denigrate his lonely quest and unorthodox ideas in the field of psychic phenomena was Snoddy.[13] Herndon Wagers recalled that Snoddy

> had the Socratic mind, the kind of mind that delights in discourse and philosophizing, and knows fraud when he sees it, without being hard.[14]

Crossfield was hampered somewhat in his recruitment of new faculty by the abysmally low salaries he had to offer. Financial resources being limited as they were, Transylvania had never paid satisfactory salaries throughout its long career. Jenkins had come in 1901 for a salary of $2,500, and the rest of the faculty were averaging $1,500 a year. By the time Crossfield came, they had edged up to $1,600, although the president's salary was only $3,000 and all fees from his lecturing had to be turned into the college treasury. In 1912 he urged the Board to raise faculty salaries to $1,800 within two years and to $2,000 in five. Although salaries had risen to $2,500 by 1921, Crossfield argued that these low salaries forced the faculty to seek additional employment to raise their income, much to the detriment of their scholarship and writing.

Such low salaries made it difficult to attract any of the growing number of Ph.D.'s coming from new universities. Until the 1890's no major university in the country had more than a handful of Ph.D.'s, but within two decades this situation changed drastically. For the smaller college, the doctorate remained rare among its faculty. Not until President Jenkins recruited Irene Myers and Thomas McCartney could Kentucky University boast having any Ph.D.'s. When Crossfield came there were six doctorates among a faculty of twenty-one, an enviable percentage which dropped slightly during the next two decades. Not until the mid-1930's was there a gradual improvement in the situation.

[13]Ruth Montgomery, *A World Beyond* (Greenwich, Conn., 1971), p. 22.
[14]Stevenson, *Lexington Theological Seminary*, pp. 254–257.

THE CURRICULUM DURING this period expanded to incorporate more of the new disciplines. The basic philosophy concerning requirements for the A.B. degree remained about the same. Transylvania did not adopt the complete elective system, and the fundamental pillars of the traditional curriculum stood fast. There was the continuing requirement in Latin, but a choice was given between Greek or German for the second language. In addition, there were required courses in English, mathematics or astronomy, a year of laboratory science, a year either of history or philosophy, and a few required hours of physical education. This basic concept of requiring students to take some courses in each of the major academic areas was, and still is, widespread, for the educational goal of the well-rounded person is an acquaintance with all these areas. What was gradually diminishing was the central role of Greek and Latin in the curriculum. Alternatives to Greek were already offered, and by the mid-1920's the Latin requirement had also disappeared. Some of the older prestigious schools clung to it

The president's home at Fourth & Broadway

for a decade or two more, but eventually the classical languages moved into the elective category almost everywhere, meaning the end for many classical departments on smaller campuses. President Crossfield noted the factors influencing the change in emphasis in the curriculum in his 1920 report:

> With the changes in the social and industrial order there has been a shifting of emphasis in education. The classics, the basis of Transylvania glory, have yielded first place to social, physical, biological, and chemical sciences, so that while it will be necessary for Transylvania to maintain her classical traditions, the increasing interest in other departments is calling for additional teachers and enlarged equipment.

Science departments began to expand, as did those of the social sciences. On the eve of World War I, Transylvania offered courses in Greek, Latin, German, French, Spanish, English, Biblical literature, history, philosophy, sociology, economics, education, mathematics, astronomy, physics, chemistry, biology and geology. Conspicuously missing was the whole area of the fine arts, psychology and political science. A music department first appeared in 1930, and a course in the fine arts in 1926. Psychology and political science were also added at about the same time.

PRESIDENT CROSSFIELD manfully tackled the problems of strengthening financial resources of the college and expanding and improving the physical plant. Having received a provisional gift from the General Education Board of New York of $50,000 if an additional $150,000 could be raised, Crossfield embarked on a whirlwind tour. He announced in 1912 that a two-year campaign had ended successfully with the accumulation of $250,000 in pledges. It was hoped the annual deficits would be wiped out. "We have made the discovery that Transylvania has the staunchest supporters in every part of the nation," Crossfield said.[15] His next goal was a joint campaign for $300,000 for the two colleges. The money was to go toward the construction of a new men's dormitory and a heating plant.

[15]Minutes of the Board, June 8, 1910; *The Crimson*, 1912.

The new dormitory, named for John M. Ewing of Morgan, Kentucky, who contributed $15,000 to the project, was begun in late 1913 and completed in time for the opening of school in September 1914. Housing between 130–140 men, Ewing Hall also boasted a dining room capable of seating 240 persons. The brick structure, composed of three sections, was built in what one writer called the classical renaissance style. There was certainly nothing elaborate about it; it was plain and serviceable. Compared to the historic rigor of life in Craig, Logan, and Davies Hall — all of which were torn down to make way for the new building — Ewing Hall was a giant step towards adequate and comfortable rooming for students. As one student described it:

Ewing Hall

Ewing Hall, a modern up-to-date hotel, with hot and cold water in every room. . . . And the heat, what an improvement! No one will deny that a person would much prefer to leave his warm blankets to the musical tune of a steam radiator than the harsh jangle of an old-fashioned alarm clock. "Licorish lights?" Yes, sir, two of them in every room and they aren't turned off at nine o'clock either.[16]

In addition to the new dormitory, a much-needed heating plant was constructed at the same time. The students called it

[16]*The Crimson*, 1915.

the new department of combustion. "It will supersede the old course in Thermology," they said, "so long conducted by Professor William Hunt [the janitor] with his meager equipment of stoves, coal boxes and scuttles, which have graced the halls and classrooms of our Alma Mater since the year 1798."[17]

Money also was appropriated in 1916 to remodel Morrison Chapel. A new gallery was constructed with a seating capacity of two hundred and an entire new ceiling was installed. The old plain glass windows were replaced by large, art glass windows given as memorials to such men as Alexander Milligan, John McGarvey, Samuel Jefferson and Henry White.

Meanwhile, Crossfield was urging the Disciples brotherhood to organize a more systematic plan for the financial undergirding of its educational institutions. He helped to establish and became the first president of the Association of Colleges of the Disciples of Christ, later called the Board of Higher Education. An Education Day had been designated some years earlier to dramatize the need for financial assistance and Crossfield sought to make the most of this observance. Few funds were derived from this source, however. In 1913 the Disciples launched the Men and Millions movement "to recruit 1,000 men and women for service at home and abroad and $6,000,000 for missions and colleges."[18] Of this, Transylvania and the College of the Bible hoped to secure $350,000. However, because of the controversy concerning the questionable orthodoxy of the College of the Bible and its faculty, intensified by the so-called heresy trial of 1917, there was considerable difficulty in securing any of this. Crossfield did announce in 1921 that Transylvania's endowment had been increased to $474,359, almost twice what it was when he arrived but woefully short of anything that might be termed adequate. In that same year the total income from all sources was only $65,637 while expenditures amounted to $84,624. The deficit of almost $15,000 seems miniscule by today's standards, but in the light of Transylvania's total resources at that time and the fact that annual deficits have a way of accumulating to impressive totals, the deficits were symptomatic of serious financial trouble.

[17]Ibid.
[18]Stevenson, *Lexington Theological Seminary*, p. 157.

One other item of interest in the area of financial and property transactions should be noted. This was the acquisition in 1914 of the property of McLean College located in Hopkinsville, Kentucky. This institution had in 1908 become the successor of South Kentucky College, chartered in 1851. The college had confronted difficult financial problems, and even the generosity of such persons as Ella Jones was insufficient to preserve it. As it closed its doors Transylvania seized the opportunity to purchase at a bargain price the entire assets and property of the school along with certain property in Hopkinsville belonging to H. D. Smith. This property was then subdivided into house lots and the modest income derived from such sales placed in Transylvania's treasury. The only visible memorial to this whole transaction is a bronze plaque honoring Mrs. Ella Jones, which had been placed in a new college building on the McLean College campus, built in part with her money. The plaque was brought to the Transylvania campus, and placed in East Hall, the old academy building, which was then renamed Ella Jones Hall.

During these years college spirit remained high, encouraged by the vigorous leadership of Crossfield. In 1911 the college finally acquired its alma mater song. Entitled "Hail, Transylvania!" the words were written by W. C. McCallum of the class of 1909 and set to the music of the Russian national anthem. Who chose this music for the Transylvania school song, or why, remains something of a mystery.

18

World War I and the Heresy Trial

Outside political events interfered only rarely in students' interests. The college campus can become a rather isolated, self-centered community in which academic and social activities of the student wrap him in a protective screen of circumscribed interests and actions. Against this, editors of student publications have energetically fought in a frequently futile attempt to awaken the student body to an awareness and concern for realities beyond the campus. In March 1913, the editor of *The Transylvanian* spoke of the significance of Wilson's inauguration, warned against possible United States intervention in the Mexican imbroglio a few months later and in December 1914, expressed his opinion of World War I.

> Commercialism, imperialism, what not, who not — perhaps all conspired with German philosophy and the lamented Nietzsche, and it just happened. . . . Maybe we wouldn't know there was a war over here if it weren't for the campfollowers. But there's cotton we can't forget, and all those books on the war.[1]

Months would go by with no mention of the war. Such sensational events as the torpedoing of the *Lusitania* received no notice. Every now and then the editor would try again. What about Christianity and the present war, he asked? At another time the question was raised whether actions and ideas of college men had any significant impact on national policy:

> No, Harvard cannot stop the war . . . but Columbia advances a project for the organization of college men to oppose "militarism in general and an increase of our army and navy in particular," which she believes will be effective, in some measure, at least, before Congress.[2]

[1]*The Transylvanian*, XXIII (December, 1914), p. 97.
[2]*Ibid.*, (February, 1915).

Such sentiments were closely in tune with prevailing public opinion, still strongly neutralist at the time. Wilson won re-election in November 1916, on a "he kept us out of war" platform. A few months before that election, President Crossfield polled the student body in chapel and found a majority favored Wilson's preparedness policy.

The fight for prohibition was apparently as significant an issue as the war, for in February 1917, right on the eve of America's entrance into the war, the students and faculty voted unanimously to send telegrams to their Congressmen and Senators urging them to support "dry" measures before Congress.

Once war was declared, all fell before it. The editor of *The Transylvanian* wrote:

> The present crisis of our nation calls for the earnest considera-
> tion and ardent patriotism of every American. We are glad to say
> that Transylvania has responded nobly to the call of duty. At the
> chapel service on Tuesday, March 20, President Crossfield gave
> a short talk in which he expressed his desire that every able-
> bodied Transylvanian would equip himself for service in case of
> need. He announced that a company would be formed to begin
> drilling in order that they might be ready for service when need-
> ed. The call for volunteers was first extended to the faculty, and
> eight of that body rose to their feet amidst the wild applause of
> the student body. When he asked for volunteers from the student
> body, nearly everyone responded.[3]

Crossfield urged that soldiers should enter this conflict with idealism and not hatred, a theme reiterated by President Wilson in his creation of the Great Crusade.

A Transylvania company of 120 men was organized. It was drilled by John Barclay who had recently returned from active duty on the Mexican border. Once war was a fact there seemed to be few remaining reservations about either its justice or its beneficial effects. *The Transylvanian* acknowledged that war brings wrack and ruin and death, but it also brings heightened energies, patriotism and efficiency. It imposed a much-needed discipline for an American generation lacking reverence and patriotism.[4]

[3]*The Crimson Rambler*, November 22, 1917.
[4]*The Transylvanian*, XXV (April, 1917).

The campus had not been so militarized since the Civil War. College men knew they would be prime conscripts to provide leadership, both in military and non-military duties. Classes began to thin as men left every day to enlist. It was estimated that within less than two months after war was declared, one hundred Transylvania men signed up, seventy-five of them waiting for officer-training at Fort Benjamin Harrison. Despite the loss, enrollment in the fall of 1917 was close to 95 percent of what it had been the previous year. It was rumored that other colleges had suffered a 50 percent loss of students. President Crossfield met with the college men in the chapel to organize the military drill for the year. All were required to participate in the drill who had not previously had two years of gymnasium work or were not involved in football practice or suffered from a physical disability.

A huge bonfire was kindled one night in front of Morrison Hall to celebrate the war effort and to encourage the sale of Liberty Bonds. A rally was held in the chapel to raise money for relief work. President Crossfield loyally echoed the government's war themes, but unlike President Wilson, he was not willing to separate the German people from their government. The Germans, Crossfield said, were infected with the virus of Nietzchean philosophy and cultural superiority and they supported their government. One could not make war on one without attacking the other. "We can easily understand the terror and frightfulness of the present conflict," he said, "a war of rapine and plunder and outrage without parallel in the reign of Nero, or the invasion of the Goths and Huns."[5] He then went on to list without qualification fearsome and terrible atrocities attributed to the Germans. These were the modern Huns against which a crusading America would fling the strength of its young men and great material resources. December 1917, was "the darkest hour" said Crossfield. England was reaching the end of her resources, France was losing her morale, Italy was close to collapse and Russia had just had a revolution that would take her out of the war. It was a moment requiring stout hearts, he told the students in chapel. Certainly Transylvania

[5]*The Crimson Rambler*, November 22, 1917.

A page of military snapshots from the 1918 Crimson

was doing her part. This was symbolized by the enormous service flag presented by the girls with its one hundred stars representing the college boys in service.

The war ruined the football team. Most of the veteran players enlisted. Coach Willis T. Stewart did his best with untried raw material, but Vanderbilt defeated Transylvania 41–0 and Sewanee whipped her 72–0. In November 1917, Stewart left to join the U. S. Engineering Corps. Perhaps he wanted to join the winning team.

The cost of the war was soon felt on campus. In March 1918, Wilson Donaldson of Aberdeen, Mississippi, was the first Transylvania man to die in the service, killed in a flying accident at Kelly Field, near San Antonio, Texas. In the fall of 1918 the toll mounted. Bob McLachland lost his life in a raiding party in France, Fielding V. Meeks died of wounds in France and Captain Reuben Hutchcraft was killed in action. Others lost their lives to the terrible influenza epidemic that swept the army camps and the nation as well. The 1919 *Crimson* listed twelve names of Transylvania men who lost their lives in the service.

In October 1918, the campus took on a realistic army atmosphere as eighty-five Transylvanians were voluntarily inducted into the Students Army Training Corps. Ewing Hall was converted into a barracks. Several lieutenants and a handful of non-commissioned officers ran the corps. Despite the flu ban which closed the college for a few weeks in the fall of 1918, the corps kept active with drills, inspections, signalling, athletics, bayonet work and fatigue duty. Uniforms and rifles eventually arrived, and even a band was organized which played the national anthem every afternoon at retreat. The life of the corps was short, however, for in November came the news of the armistice, and in December the unit was demobilized.

Influenza and the establishment of the Students Army Training Corps had effectively wrecked the fall semester of 1918, but both were short-lived and by June 1919, activities had nearly returned to normal. Many Transylvanians had returned. The coming of peace quieted most fears, but the uneasiness over the Communist threat was still widespread. The college administration thought it was a bad joke when the editors of *The*

Crimson flew a red flag from the pole in front of Morrison Hall. The Bolshevik threat was not a thing the American public was taking lightly at the time.

Transylvania's experience during World War I was probably typical of most colleges. The themes of neutrality, pacifism and detachment heard on campuses before the U.S. entry into the war were suddenly and effectively muted. Loyalty, patriotism and war fever swept over all. Church-related colleges, even those with seminaries on the campus, acted no differently. Crossfield was a Christian minister, but he spoke the vocabulary of war as intensely as a military man. Apparently there was no dissenting voice among the administration, curators, faculty or students in converting the campus into an army camp. This was not the first nor last time the campus was thus affected.

The old yearbooks of this period are filled with photographs of students standing proudly and self-consciously in those strange-looking uniforms with the riding pants, leather or cloth puttees and broad-brimmed hats. There is a strange and unreal quality about the whole affair, intruding as it did abruptly and roughly into the tranquil scheme of things with vivid excitement and drama. Suddenly it was all over. The trappings disappeared, and only the bronze plaque remains with names of the dead.

FOR TRANSYLVANIA AND the College of the Bible there was another event that exploded on the campus during the same months the U.S. was declaring war on Germany. This was the so-called "heresy trial" of 1917. It all began as a small tempest in a teapot. Ben F. Battenfield, a student in the College of the Bible, sent out on March 12, 1917, 300 copies of a letter asking recipients to help him rescue the College of the Bible from "the control of destructive critics. It is commonly acknowledged by the students [the letter went on] that President Crossfield and the four professors [Bower, Fortune, Henry and Snoddy] he has been instrumental in placing on the faculty hold advanced critical views and stand opposed to Professors Calhoun and Deweese, who hold to the old principles of the college.''[6] Quotes from so-called heretical statements attributed to the professors were included.

Nine other students signed the petition along with Battenfield, although five of them withdrew their support within five days; and of the remaining four, one had been in the college for only six weeks and another for six months. It was apparent that Battenfield was among a small minority of students who found Dean Calhoun's rigid orthodoxy and rote teaching much to their liking. In fact it was the growing criticism against Calhoun among the majority of students that motivated Battenfield to come to that professor's defense by a crude and wholesale assault on the rest of the faculty. Battenfield's circular was immediately contradicted by Crossfield and the other professors involved who effectively revealed its distortions and falsehoods. Battenfield's attack appeared to be effectively blunted, and the whole attempt to intimidate the faculty and administration seemed to be a failure. However, there were those who saw in this incident a rich opportunity to even old scores and to resurrect the campaign against Crossfield, Fortune and Bower that had started in 1912.

The agency that thrust this controversy into nation-wide prominence among the Disciples brotherhood was *The Christian Standard*. Yet even this militant crusader for orthodoxy would have had little influence if there had not existed at the time an intellectual and social milieu from which a strong response could be expected. America was on the verge of entering World War I, and before the various hearings on Battenfield's accusations were over, she had declared war on Germany. This military conflict polarized certain elements in this country and intensified latent tensions. The rapidly changing character of American society, the challenge to old traditions and values and the appearance of new problems for which there seemed to be no answers created fear and insecurity in the country. Many people sought security in the familiar pattern of traditional religious beliefs, and for them the Bible was

[6] Stevenson, *Lexington Theological Seminary*, p. 169. Chapter 13 of this book has a thorough and detailed account of this whole affair. Professor Bower's *Through the Years* richly supplements it. In addition, there are two boxes in the Transylvania archives loaded with material pertaining to the controversy.

the unshakeable, unchangeable and unchallenged source of these beliefs. To criticize the Bible, to modify its statements not only confused people but angered them. Their response was a fierce demand for unwavering conformity and a literal acceptance of Biblical text. The church, they believed, should be the mouthpiece of this Biblical orthodoxy. But what if the spokesmen in the pulpit were infected with unsound views during their training in seminary? Then the church itself became the agency of their undoing. It was obvious that the faculty of these seminaries should be of unquestioned soundness.

What gave the critics of Crossfield and his innovative policies in the College of the Bible the ammunition they needed for this battle was the position of Dean Hall Laurie Calhoun. In retrospect Calhoun appears in a somewhat sad and tragic role. He held no personal grudges against his colleagues, but confessed his love for them. As Dr. Bower recalls: "The result was a split personality, in which his intelligence reached out toward a rationally supported position while his loyalties and emotions remained firmly attached to his conservative past."[7] Add to this his disappointment at not having been appointed McGarvey's successor as president of the College of the Bible and his ineffectiveness as a teacher, and the result was a deeply troubled man. The temptation to release his frustrations by supporting Battenfield's crusade proved irresistible. As dean of the faculty his accusations could not be ignored. When *The Christian Standard* quoted him as saying on March 24, 1917, "candor compels me to state that for more than a year I have been fully convinced that destructive criticism was being taught in the College of the Bible," the constituency of this institution could not fail to be aroused. A formal investigation was inevitable.

Although this crisis primarily involved the College of the Bible, it could not but seriously affect Transylvania College. Once again problems created by the interlocking of these two institutions became apparent. Crossfield was president of both colleges, and Bower and Snoddy were on both faculties. The schools were to be mutual recipients of a proposed $350,000 from the Men and Millions campaign of the Disciples of Christ. An attack on one hurt both. In fact editorial critics of *The*

[7]Bower, *Through the Years*, p. 39.

Christian Standard demanded that an impartial investigation of Calhoun's and Battenfield's charges be conducted by a committee whose members would in no way be connected with either institution, although it was not suggested that Disciples' members likewise be excluded.

If the opinions of the editors of the local campus newspaper *The Crimson Rambler* reflected the majority student viewpoint, then the majority was heartily behind Crossfield and the accused professors. The editor wrote on April 5, 1917:

> There is only one issue, only one. It is this. *Shall President Crossfield and Professors Fortune, Bower, Snoddy, and Henry be dismissed from the College of the Bible because certain persons disapprove of their teaching?* This editor can see no evidence of destructive influence of either Crossfield or any of the other professors, but only their powerfully constructive influence on students and the institutions. Shall these men be tried, condemned, and executed on the hypothesis of a professor who admits that he has never heard them teach, and a few students who have known them but a short time, and some outsiders who do not know them at all?

The Christian Century, a periodical considered heretical by *The Christian Standard*, came to support the accused, an action which confirmed guilt in the eyes of fundamentalists. *The Christian Century* saw three points at issue: academic freedom, whether modern concepts must be excluded from instruction in a college of the Disciples of Christ, and the jurisdiction of the Board of Trustees. The issue of academic freedom was a familiar one to this school. It had risen repeatedly in Transylvania's history. From the days of Harry Toulmin and Horace Holley through the era of John Bowman and James Lane Allen, the battle between intellectual freedom and religious orthodoxy with intellectual conformity had been fought vigorously time and again. Each side could claim its victories, but the war never seemed to be permanently over. On the issue of the trustees' jurisdiction, the Board of Trustees of the College of the Bible decided to conduct the investigation themselves. Again, some of the trustees were also members of the Board of Curators of Transylvania.

The trustees met on May 1, 1917. The campus meanwhile had been in a turmoil in which supporters of both sides sought to strengthen their positions. The press had broadcast the conflict sufficiently to create widespread public interest, although war news must have overshadowed it in all but the denominational journals. The trustees met for six days and held seventeen sessions in a room in Morrison Hall. Calhoun had insisted on arrangements that would have converted the hearing into a formal legal arraignment against the accused on charges of unorthodoxy. Professor Bower, surveying the arrangements, arose and protested that this had all the trappings of a heresy trial, something entirely at odds with the basic conceptions of the Disciples of Christ. The trustees, impressed by the argument, immediately disbanded the meeting, and the next day, disclaiming any intention to conduct a heresy trial, arranged for a more private and informal hearing.

Dean Calhoun was upset by this decision and continued only under protest. He presented only one witness who was so thoroughly cross-examined by Fortune and Bower that Calhoun protested the whole proceedings, submitted his resignation and withdrew, threatening to take his case to the public, which in this case, meant using the friendly columns of *The Christian Standard*. The Board accepted his resignation and continued the investigation. They listened to six students who testified their faith had been strengthened under the teaching of the accused professors. They listened to statements read by Bower and Fortune and questioned the two men exhaustively. They heard Crossfield present resolutions from official boards of the various churches with which the accused were associated. All of this testimony was largely affirmative for the accused.

One incident lightened the proceedings. When Professor Snoddy appeared before the trustees he was interrogated at great length by Alfred Fairhurst, professor emeritus of biology at Transylvania and now a trustee. According to Bower's account, the interrogation

> developed into a somewhat lengthy argument over evolution. After some time, Professor Snoddy said that, anticipating that something like this might happen, he had gone to the pains of writing out some statements concerning evolution which, if Professor Fairhurst was willing, he would like to read and ask Pro-

fessor Fairhurst wherein he could not accept them. After Professor Snoddy had finished reading, Professor Fairhurst said he could not accept such statements without serious modification, and launched upon a somewhat lengthy discourse pointing out the specific points of his objections. Whereupon Professor Snoddy said, "The statements I have just read are verbatim excerpts from your own book!" The Board broke into applause, and Professor Fairhurst sank into his chair in devastating confusion. If there was any vestige of an investigation remaining, this episode ended it.[8]

Despite the fact that Board chairman Mark Collis, minister of the Broadway Christian Church, was a staunch conservative, he did not attempt during the trial to swing the trustees to Calhoun, and he participated in the report which exonerated Crossfield and the accused faculty. The report, released to the local press on May 10, read in part as follows:

> The Board has found no teaching in this College by any member of the faculty that is out of harmony with the fundamental conceptions and convictions of our brotherhood which relate to the inspiration of the Bible as the divine word of God, divinely given, and of divine authority, or to the divinity of Jesus Christ or to the plea of our people.[9]

The trial was over but not the controversy. *The Christian Standard* ran columns by Calhoun and his sympathizers through the summer of 1917 which contained the familiar charges and urged readers to demand that a new investigation be made. What gave the fight an ugly character was the editorial use of the intensifying hatred against Germans to injure the opponents by identifying them with German culture and critical rationalism.

When it appeared they had lost in their attempt to win control of the College of the Bible, the fundamentalists did all in their power to injure it. Once again narrow sectarianism struck out against this weary but courageous institution in its struggle to preserve a degree of academic freedom and liberal thought. Once again some of its supporters turned away. Financial contributions diminished. Students were discouraged from attending. A Christian Bible College League was formed in Sep-

[8]*Ibid.*, p. 42.
[9]Stevenson, *Lexington Theological Seminary*, p. 183.

tember 1917, to establish orthodox sanctuaries which the devout might attend instead of the College of the Bible.

When a potential gift of $125,000 to the Men and Millions movement was in jeopardy because the donor was unsure whether any of it should go to Transylvania or the College of the Bible, the editor of *The Christian Evangelist* was sent as an informal investigator to the campus. He concluded that everything was satisfactory, and Transylvania and the College of the Bible were not excluded from the financial campaign. This compensated only partly for the loss of support from other sources, however. The defense of principle was not inexpensive.[10]

Following the so-called "heresy trial," Calhoun went to Bethany College as part of the faculty of the newly-established Graduate School of Religion, but the program soon failed and he then went to Tennessee to join a conservative group known as the Church of Christ. The College of the Bible continued to combat the lingering suspicion and hostility towards the school

[10]*Ibid.*, p. 191.

Lyons Hall

by publishing several quarterly bulletins emphasizing the positive features of the school's educational program. This was later supplanted by the creation of the *College of the Bible Quarterly* which was dedicated to a policy of educational enrichment.

President Crossfield participated in a campaign to defend the College and the seminary, but the controversy had created divisions too deep to ever be successfully reconciled. Friends of Calhoun and what he stood for created their own schools, publications and what was for all practical purposes a separate sect. Even the Disciples' churches in Lexington identified themselves with one side or the other.

What happened on the small campus at Lexington in the spring of 1917 was symptomatic of a national malaise that was to intensify as the decade of the twenties unrolled. The fundamentalist crusade burgeoned. The golden-voiced orator from Nebraska, that now weary but undaunted crusader William Jennings Bryan, was at the forefront until he collapsed following the notorious Scopes trial in Tennessee. The evolution issue, so vehemently debated in the late nineteenth century and once thought to be quietly dwindling away, was resurrected in this period as a number of state legislatures sought to follow Tennessee in enacting prohibitions against the teaching of the theory of evolution in tax-supported schools, Such a bill was introduced into the Kentucky legislature in January 1922, and its supporters prevailed upon Bryan to campaign for it across the state. The University of Kentucky would have been one of the main victims of this legislation, and its president, Frank L. McVey, courageously placed his career and program on the block by vigorously opposing it. The bill lost by only one vote. By such a precarious margin was academic freedom preserved in the state. Though only public institutions would have been legally affected by such legislation, every school in the state would have felt the oppressive pressure of this prohibition.

President Crossfield and the faculty who stood with him may well have felt some pride at this time in that they had stood fast against the attacking forces of hysteria and bigotry and thus strengthened the hands of a man like President McVey in his struggle with the state legislature.

19
Transylvania Survives the Twenties

Andrew D. Harmon

The problem of survival and identity became critical in the decade of the twenties. This was not immediately apparent as the University recovered with vitality from the temporary intrusion of the war. In November 1919, the boards of Transylvania and the College of the Bible agreed to launch a drive for over a million dollars for the immediate needs of Transylvania, the College of the Bible and Hamilton College, plus an additional two million dollars over the following five years. The money was to be spent in part on increasing faculty salaries by 50 percent, thoroughly repairing Morrison Hall, erecting a new science building and constructing a new library. Students and faculty pledged over $13,000 to this campaign. An impressive parade marched through downtown Lexington to dramatize the needs of the institution. Yet with all the enthusiasm with which it was launched, very little came of this campaign. In his June 1921 annual report, Crossfield made no mention of it.

There were other optimistic omens as the decade began. Enrollment was expanding. The year 1920–21 showed a class of 268, representing twenty-two states and four foreign countries, but the fact that 208 students were affiliated with the Disciples Church pointed out the heavily denominational character of the institution. The faculty had expanded to twenty-seven, of which eight held Ph.D.'s or its equivalent.

It was no surprise to anyone conscious of the national trends in education that enrollment in Greek courses had sharply declined. It was no longer required for graduation, and although it was taught by one of the most popular teachers on campus, Thomas McCartney, even this did not guarantee its success. Enrollment in Greek classes dropped so radically that McCartney had to adapt in 1925 by taking a semester at Columbia University in economics and sociology to be able to teach courses in those areas. Latin still remained fairly popular, but six times as many students studied French. As was happening everywhere, students were now concentrating on the natural and social sciences. The Carnegie Science Building, not twenty years old, was proving to be inadequate. Courses in history, economics, psychology and sociology were very popular, although the latter two disciplines were just emerging as scholarly and respectable areas of study.[1]

As early as 1921 Transylvania could boast of a radio station on campus, installed with the cooperation of the physics department. The physical plant was improved, the library expanded and thanks to a $10,000 gift from the Thomases of Shelbyville, the athletic field on North Broadway, to be named Thomas Field, was graded and prepared for use with plans for a grandstand being studied.

President Crossfield stated in June 1921, that "it is not extravagant to say today that Transylvania more nearly approaches the ideals of an institution of its class established by the various standardizing agencies than at any time in its recent history."[2] Yet the total indebtedness, if the various loans and mortgages on the College buildings are included, was $122,242, and the accumulated operating deficit was $25,000. Shortly after making this statement, Crossfield resigned to accept a position as comptroller of the Federal Council of Churches of Christ in America, a job he evidently disliked, for he left it to become president of William Woods College in Missouri. Why he decided to move at this particular time is not quite clear, although the recent financial drive failure may have been one reason. He had made an admirable record, and he did not publicly express any doubts as to the successful future of the institutions he had presided over. The curators deeply regretted his

[1] President Crossfield's annual report, June 6, 1921. Transylvania University archives.
[2] Ibid.

going. "We truly recognize our utter inability to suitably express in words the great loss entailed upon this institution by reasons of the severance of his connection with it."[3]

AS WAS THE CUSTOM, the curators appointed an acting president, this time Thomas McCartney, to administer the institution while they sought a new president. By the end of January 1922, the executive committees of the College of the Bible and Transylvania voted unanimously to recommend to their respective boards the election of Andrew D. Harmon to the presidency. Born in Nebraska in 1871 of pioneer Virginia and Tennessee stock, Harmon was raised "amid the hardships of a western rural community."[4] His early education was in country schools before he entered Cotner College near Lincoln, Nebraska. Following his graduation he was made head of the Greek department at Cotner, was ordained a Disciples minister in 1893, and a few years later became pastor of the First Christian Church in St. Paul, Minnesota, for fourteen years. He then moved to the First Christian Church in Omaha, Nebraska, but left there after a year and a half to become president of Cotner College. He occupied this post for six years before being called to Transylvania.

Dr. Harmon (he received the D.D. from several Disciples colleges) had as a pastor been increasingly convinced of the need for effective Christian education, which led him to move from the church to the college campus. It was noted that "as a public speaker Dr. Harmon possesses an ease of manner, a fluency of speech, and a conciseness of diction. . . ."[5] A year before his appointment at Transylvania, he had been a guest speaker at the Ohio State Convention of Christian churches and one of the audience, the editor of *The Christian Evangelist*, commented:

Many of us had never heard of A. D. Harmon, but for breadth of view, clearness and decisiveness of utterance and soundness of

[3] Minutes of the Board, June 6, 1921.
[4] *The Crimson Rambler*, September 29, 1926.
[5] *Ibid.*

position, his two addresses established him not only as a leader of marked distinction but a coming man among our people.[6]

President Harmon was immediately confronted with the continuing financial crisis of the interlocked institutions. Transylvania, the College of the Bible and Hamilton College formed an ill-matched troika, each with its own problems and resources, with the prosperity of each dependent on the prosperity of all. Hamilton College became a financial albatross which hung heavily on the necks of her sister institutions in the decade of the twenties. Like his predecessor, Harmon bravely initiated a bold financial campaign to raise a half million dollars, inspired in part by the offer of the General Education Board in New York City of a $80,000 grant to Transylvania if she could match it with double that amount. Two years later it was reported that $587,464 had been raised, but this was largely composed of ephemeral pledges. Harmon had to urge each curator to personally raise $11,000 to take advantage of the foundation offer.[7]

Despite the growing financial burden that would create a crisis for Harmon before the decade was over, the campus appeared vigorous and normal. Enrollment continued to climb, jumping to 354 in 1924–25 over the previous year's 295. The growth was made possible, in part, by the excessive number of scholarships which Transylvania and the College of the Bible gave and which they could ill afford. In addition, the cost per student was reduced to $212, against $460 in most colleges of Transylvania's type. Such economy was at the expense of the low faculty salaries and large faculty teaching loads.[8]

OCCASIONALLY STUDENTS gave evidence of interest and concern for issues beyond the limits of the campus. For example they held a referendum on ratifying the Treaty of Versailles and joining the League of Nations. In January 1920, when President Woodrow Wilson's hope of having the treaty ratified without reservations was fast waning, the majority of Transylvania students supported the president's position, though a national poll showed a slight majority of college students favored

[6]Stevenson, *Lexington Theological Seminary*, p. 219.
[7]Minutes of the Board, October 10, 1922; August 1, 1924; May, 1925.
[8]*Ibid.*, June 2, 1925.

some compromise between Lodge and the Democrats in order to secure ratification. The Red Scare that swept the nation as the decade of the twenties began, and dramatized by Attorney-General J. Mitchell Palmer's raids on January 1, 1920, to round up thousands of suspicious aliens as Bolshevik suspects, was viewed with relative calm by editors of *The Crimson Rambler*. They believed there was a modified form of Bolshevism in America manifested in occasional mob violence, but they were not convinced that it justified mass hysteria or massive repression. What was needed, they said, was an increase of college-educated people who could confront Bolshevism with calm reason and faith in the democratic principles.[9] They urged moderation on Americans to maintain justice as a middle road between the radical laborer and the arch capitalist. They saw no justice in the expulsion of socialists from state legislatures, as New York had done, or deporting them for no other reason than they held unpopular beliefs. To this extent, the college students expressed a welcome sanity in this period of extremism.

Students were also conscious of their changing times:

> Truly ours is a fast and fussy age. It is a furious time. . . . Perhaps it was never easy for Americans to be still, but it is particularly difficult now. . . . Our activities are numerous . . . on the college campus. There are meetings or organizations for every day or night of the week . . . speed is at a premium. . . . The use of the horse and buggy as a means of traveling has, in most places, become practically obsolete. The method is too slow. It takes too much time. . . . Traveling by automobile is fast becoming too slow a process for us. Speed limits are exceeded on every hand. Little heed is paid to intersections of streets. . . . When traveling on the ground becomes too wearing upon our nerves, we resort to the aeroplane.[10]

SOME OF THE TRADITIONAL student organizations began to disappear as the age that bred them slipped into history. Such was the fate of the literary societies. Indeed, they had long outlived their usefulness, and even before World War I

[9]*The Crimson Rambler*, January 13, 1920.
[10]George V. Moore, "Speed at a Premium," *The Transylvanian*, XXIX (April, 1920), pp. 20–21.

questions had been raised as to their continued existence. In the fall of 1919 Cecropia disappeared from view and the Ossalia Society postponed its oblivion only by uniting with the Periclean. This society, in addition to other organizational activities, sponsored the annual Washington's birthday festivities, consisting of a large number of student orations in Morrison Chapel. For some inexplicable reason, the Cecropian reappeared briefly in 1925 but by 1927 all the literary societies were disbanded except for the honorary literary sorority, the Mermaid Chapter of Sigma Theta, and the men's Boars Head Chapter of Sigma Upsilon. In 1928 the Mermaid Chapter became Alpha Iota Chapter of Chi Delta Phi, another woman's honorary literary society. World War II saw the end of all these literary organizations, and they were never revived.

Most of the other campus organizations continued from the pre-World War I period, although a few new ones appeared. The Crooks and Crones, a new senior society for girls was founded in 1925 to compete with the boys' Books and Bones senior honorary which dated from 1911. Senior honorary fraternities were popular on many campuses, and these two enjoyed healthy careers until they disappeared during World War II.

Pi Kappa Delta, a new honorary forensic fraternity was organized in 1925. Debating had become increasingly popular as the old-style oratorical style and contests began to disappear. This group enjoyed a vigorous career through the twenties and thirties. Though World War II saw the end of this fraternity, college debating was revived very strongly in the post-war period, and debating clubs of various sorts have been active through to the present.

The basic dramatic, musical and publishing organizations provided the central core of student activities. Names of the groups might change; their functions did not. Student chapters of the YWCA and the YMCA were also active, and remained so through World War II until the early 1950's when the organization of the Student Christian Association absorbed them both, though not claiming to be a substitute for them.

The years between the two world wars were years of growth for the Greek letter fraternities and sororities. At the end of

World War I there were but two fraternities, Kappa Alpha and Pi Kappa Alpha, and two sororities, Chi Omega and Delta Delta Delta, with memberships ranging from seven to sixteen. As postwar normalcy returned to the campus and the enrollment grew, so did the number of fraternities and their membership. In the 1919–1920 school year, the Phi Kappa Tau fraternity and Alpha Delta Theta sorority were established with twenty-five men and eleven women respectively. In 1922 the men's Pan-Hellenic Council was instituted. During the 1924–1925 year, the Kappa chapter of Sigma Sigma Omicron sorority was founded, followed the next year by Alpha Gamma Chi fraternity. The women likewise created a Pan-Hellenic Council. By 1928 the Sigma Sigma Omicron national changed its name to Sigma Phi Beta, and in 1934, the Kappa chapter stated that it was now affiliated with Phi Omega Pi as a result of a merger between Sigma Phi Beta and Phi Omega Pi. A local Greek maverick organization by the name of Lambda Omega had been founded in the fall of 1920 by a group of girls. It never was affiliated with a national organization and thus was never represented on the Pan-Hellenic Council, but it played an active role on campus until replaced by Delta Zeta sorority in 1954. In 1929 the Omicron chapter of Alpha Lambda Tau was established, having previously been active on the campus as Alpha Gamma Chi.

ATHLETICS AT TRANSYLVANIA during the twenties allowed for plenty of team spirit and pep rallies by the students, but with the exception of one or two years, the record in intercollegiate athletics was a dismal one. The war had been a hindrance, but even with the return of larger enrollments and more normal circumstances, teams lacked both good material and good coaching. Financially, Transylvania was in no position to do much about either need. Football coaches came and went with monotonous regularity, rarely staying longer than two years. Centre College, meanwhile, had a phenomenal football team known as the "praying colonels" in the early twenties that swept everything before it, including Harvard — then ranked among the top in the country. It was that team that trounced Transylvania by a score of 98–0 in 1921.

Coach Willis T. Stewart, who had made an enviable record at Transylvania just before the war, was hired back for a short while in the mid-twenties, and the picture brightened. In fact, in the fall of 1924 the football team won six out of eight games, including wins over St. Xavier, Kentucky Wesleyan, Louisville, Eastern and Western Kentucky, and Marshall. Stewart left in 1926 and his successor James Elam provided a successful substitution, giving the student rooters the sweetest of prizes — a 6–0 win over Centre in 1928. Coach Elam is also credited with introducing night football to Kentucky. In 1929 Centre and Transylvania celebrated their fiftieth anniversary of the first game which had brought football to the South. Coach Elam left after that season and his successor, Coach Pyle, had a gloomy record of only one win in the following year.

The record of the varsity basketball team during the twenties was an unrelieved tale of woe, with many seasons showing only one or two wins out of fourteen or fifteen games played. Much to the chagrin of the boys, the girls' basketball team made excellent records year after year during the decade, winning the state championship several times. The baseball teams were erratic, sometimes winning only one game a season, and then capturing most of them the following year. One of the most colorful, totally devoted and able players on many of these teams in the 1917–1921 period was the irrepressible Albert Benjamin "Happy" Chandler, who was later twice governor of Kentucky, U.S. Senator and Baseball Commissioner. The yearbook fondly stated that

> when the Lord made "Hap" he used up the end of the piece so that there can never be another like him, and then sent him to the Class of 1921, for the singing athlete to make good. . . . His "rep" on every team is best explained by a young Wesleyan rooter: "Kill 'Hap' Chandler; the rest of them won't hurt you; kill 'Hap.' "[11]

The athletic program at Transylvania was given a considerable boost upon implementation of plans for a new gymnasium. When the need for a new basketball floor became desperate, loyal students organized a financial drive. Professor Ernest Del-

[11]*The Crimson*, 1921.

camp and Coach Webb organized two teams to canvass the student body, and students and faculty pledged $25,000. In the fall of 1928 ground was broken on the corner of North Broadway and Fourth streets. Since there was enough money for only the first unit, the walls of the structure were to be temporary until they could be replaced with brick. It was planned ultimately to have a gymnasium seating 4500 persons and a 40 by 90 foot swimming pool. These plans had to be severely modified later. Meanwhile students made the best .of the situation. *The Rambler* said that "there has been a lot of foolish criticism of the new gym. Of course, we admit, that at the present time it looks a lot more like a tobacco barn than like a gym; but that isn't the way it is to look permanently."[12]

Who then would have believed that it would be twenty years before a new unit was added, and that not until 1957 would the old "tobacco barn" itself be torn down and replaced with a permanent brick structure. For in the very year the new gymnasium was started the great stock market crash occurred, followed by years of depression and another war.

THROUGH THE DECADE, events and personalities created the special institutional fabric that made Transylvania unique to its students and alumni. Times changed, and with them customs and traditions. *The Rambler* editor bemoaned in 1922 the disappearance of such customs as raising hats to the professors and of not wearing sweaters to chapel or the dining-hall except for those boasting a "T" sweater. One freshman was seen coming to chapel in his shirtsleeves, and many neglected to wear their freshman caps.

On May 10, 1923, the first Transylvania Day was celebrated on campus. It had been the custom in preceding years to set aside one day in the spring for a kind of no-classes, festive day of spring cleaning of the campus. Now the informality was being converted into a more highly programmed holiday occasion. This day, the originators hoped, would be "one of vast opportunities toward the development of a unified student spirit and a college consciousness. All Transylvania mingling in a real

[12]*The Crimson Rambler*, February 1, 1929.

'get-together' for the sole express purpose of having a good time is something novel. It should be a true Circus Day for all of us.''[13]

In the fall of 1923, plans were made for the next Transylvania Day to include the election of a Mr. Pioneer and a Miss Transylvania. Ryan Thompson and Thelma Shephard were the elected royalty, the first in a long list that has come down to the present as Transylvania Day has remained one of the high points of the school year. Dances, circuses, olympics and downtown parades have all, on one Transylvania Day or another, been part of the festivities. Some years the steps of Old Morrison (as it was now being called) were the setting for a dramatic and colorful pageant culminating with the crowning of Miss Transylvania and Mr. Pioneer.

T-Day, 1924

In the spring of 1924 a rather bizarre event took place on campus. The body of Constantine Rafinesque was shipped from

---

[13]*Ibid.*, April 26, 1923.

Philadelphia, where it had lain for nearly a century, to the campus he once had cursed. It was the original plan to place the body in the new library when it should be built, but meanwhile it was stored in a stone vault in the south antepodia of Old Morrison. This strange project resulted from the rediscovery of Rafinesque's grave in 1919 by Henry C. Mercer, a Doylestown, Pennsylvania scientist and philanthropist whose interest in the nineteenth century eccentric led him to search out his burial place. He found it in Ronaldson's cemetery, a private burial lot, and had placed over the grave a large stone marker bearing the inscription

Honor to whom honor is overdue.
Constantine S. Rafinesque
Born Constantinople 1785
Died Philadelphia Sept. 18, 1840.
To do good to mankind has
Often been an ungrateful task
The works of God to Study and Explain
Is happy toil and not to live in vain.
This tablet placed here September, 1919.

In the fall of 1923 Robert Spencer, the nephew of Transylvania's librarian Mrs. Charles Norton, made a visit to the grave which he reported to his aunt. In the same letter he informed her the graveyard was soon to be converted into a public park and urged Mrs. Norton to ask the Transylvania authorities if they would consider removing Rafinesque's body to the college campus where it could be prominently marked and honored. To the surprise of everyone the idea caught fire. Dean McCartney was sent to Philadelphia in February 1924, to work with James Spencer, Mrs. Norton's brother, and the various necessary authorities to secure permission to disinter the remains and ship them to Lexington, and by March 1, the body had reached its final resting place in Old Morrison.

An interesting footnote to this event was the notice given to it by David Starr Jordan, the eminent botanist, zoologist and president of Indiana University and later Stanford. He was chancellor emeritus of the latter institution at the time of the Rafinesque incident. He wrote Mrs. Norton that it would be a pleasure for him to visit Transylvania "for Rafinesque was the

Rafinesque's tomb in Old Morrison

first teacher of Natural Science in the west, and there were not many anywhere in his time. . . . As you doubtless know, I have been one of the men who have restored Rafinesque to his place in Science. He was a very remarkable and very gifted man, highly eccentric, full of activity, with large insight and endlessly careless in regard to details."[14] No other institution had any

[14]David Starr Jordan to Mrs. Charles F. Norton, April 3, April 23, 1924. Rafinesque Scrapbook File, Transylvania University archives.

historic connection with the man, and certainly no other cared whether Rafinesque rested in honor or oblivion.

Traditions such as the honor system were preserved. That system, apparently originating at the University of Virginia "whereby a student's pledge as a gentleman of honest performance rendered proctoring and penalties unnecessary," was successfully adopted in only a few colleges.[15] Oberlin and Ohio Wesleyan tried it for twenty years and then gave it up. It worked better in girls' colleges, which may say something for that sex's principles. It apparently was effective at Transylvania for a time as the faculty and older students impressed upon the new students the principle of honesty. Begun in the 1902–03 school year the honor system, initiated "to foster manly and womanly sentiments among its students," lasted for forty years when it was suspended during World War II and never re-established.[16]

Compulsory chapel was another tradition. Nearly every collegiate institution had once firmly believed in the necessity and virtues of compulsory chapel. When colleges were smaller and enrollments low, and the student body and its values and traditions more homogeneous, the validity of compulsory chapel could be effectively argued. But with the expansion of colleges and universities in the post-Civil War period, and with a changing concept of the nature and purpose of higher education, the role of compulsory chapel was viewed differently. The newer state universities were the first to abolish it, followed by others such as Wisconsin, Cornell and Johns Hopkins, the latter institution maintaining chapel regularly every morning at 8:45 but stating that "no notice will be taken of the presence or absence of anybody."[17] Among the older and more prestigious institutions, Harvard gave up the requirement in 1886, Columbia in 1891. Yale, playing its historic role as the religious counterbalance to Harvard's infidelity, clung to compulsory chapel until 1926, and Princeton even longer.

The smaller, tight-knit and traditionally more conservative church-related colleges such as Transylvania might naturally

[15]Schmidt, *The Liberal Arts College*, p. 194.

[16]*Kentucky University Catalogue*, 1903; *The Crimson Rambler*, February 13, 1942.

[17]Schmidt, *The Liberal Arts College*, p. 191.

have been expected to follow Yale's example. It is rather striking, therefore, to notice that compulsory chapel came under attack in 1926. Taking note of Yale's abolition of the requirement that year, the editor of *The Rambler* wrote in a strongly ironic tone:

It is almost unbelievable that colleges ranking with Yale, whose standards are already low enough, should be so near-sighted and disrespectful as to discontinue this time-honored rite. . . . Thank goodness, Transylvania is outstanding in the ranks of those forward moving universities who still recognize the necessity of "compulsory chapel."[18]

A year later the paper advocated the abolition of compulsory chapel. In the fall of 1926 the administration, recognizing a rapidly growing absenteeism from chapel, reduced the number of meetings from four to three and slightly enlarged the number of cuts. The number of compulsory chapels, or convocations as they came to be called, was reduced more and more over the next few decades, but the compulsory policy was not surrendered until the 1960's. The problem of compulsion thus was solved, but the problem of replacing an occasion when the entire student body was brought together in a shared experience was not solved, nor, perhaps, can it be.

The tradition of practical jokes was waning, too, although recurrences were not unknown. In January 1926, *The Rambler* reported that

Jimmy Wyker's Ford went on another trip Wednesday night. Thursday morning, students going into chapel were confronted by the startling spectacle of the now famous yellow flivver, sitting nonchalantly on the chapel platform. It was rather funny — a good joke for the moment. But, on second thought, it seemed a little stale. . . . As Dean Bower pointed out in chapel this kind of stuff has become passe in the colleges of today.[19]

In succeeding decades Rafinesque's coffin made a similar trip to the chapel platform, a goat was discovered browsing on the roof of Haupt Humanities building, and the locks of the doors of Old Morrison were jammed. But the frequency of these events had been greatly reduced.

[18]*The Crimson Rambler*, March 4, 1926.
[19]*Ibid.*, January 23, 1926.

Nor was it to be expected that the type of student who came to Transylvania would dramatically symbolize the flaming youth of the Roaring Twenties. Most of them had neither the money, temperament nor background to do so. They were not immune to style, however. Girls wore their hair bobbed and dressed in those dismal flat-chested, shapeless fashions that gradually crept up to the knee. But if campus publications reflected student attitudes, then the majority of students preserved their youthful idealism in the face of the growing cynicism among intellectuals and the conservative patterns of behavior in the midst of all kinds of challenges being thrown at such patterns by many Americans. There was a lot of foolish talk about "The Revolt of Youth," one student wrote, "but it is also true that behind the so-called revolt is an ideal, and in that ideal, a few young spirited souls can see a bigger, happier, and more truthful world."[20] Students on other college campuses might brandish the pocket flask in this prohibition society, but at Transylvania most students supported prohibition.

Yet the religious attitudes of the majority of students were not fundamentalist. In February 1926, when a new attempt was being made to pass a bill in the Kentucky legislature to forbid the teaching of evolution in the schools and colleges of the state, the editor of *The Rambler* wrote a long editorial condemning the action. "Quite a lot of misguided zealots," he said, "are still under the delusion that it is possible and desirable to pass laws regulating the channels of thought and investigation in our institutions of higher learning."[21]

THERE IS SOME QUESTION as to how close the attitudes of President Harmon and the Board of Curators were to students on the nature of the education they should be receiving at Transylvania. As financial troubles increased and church support became critical, President Harmon appeared to become more conservative than Crossfield who had fought so long and well against the stifling pressures of excessive orthodoxy. In November 1923, an advisory committee appointed to assist the Executive Committee in a $500,000 campaign submitted a state-

[20]*The Transylvanian*, XXVI (Summer, 1927), pp. 24–25.
[21]*The Crimson Rambler*, February 9, 1926.

ment that they wished to have used as part of the campaign "to establish Transylvania and Hamilton College in the confidence of all members of the Churches of Christ in Kentucky."[22] The main emphasis of the statement was that these schools would take special pains to employ as teachers only those persons "whose moral and Christian character is unquestioned," and then gave a list of orthodox Christian principles to which these teachers must adhere. Harmon incorporated these suggestions in his own statement to the Executive Committee a few months later.

> A church college must be intensely Christian but not sectarian. It must be loyal to the recognized fundamentals of the Christian faith. It must hold to the existence of a personal God possessing will and intelligence. Otherwise it propagates a mechanistic and pantheistic conception of the universe. It must, therefore, regard the Scriptures as the word of the Eternal God. . . . This faith must be made vital in the youth. . . . That which makes this faith vital in a college is that the men and women who teach upon its faculties are themselves the embodiment of the spirit and the life of the Christian faith. In the search for faculty members of high scholarship in recent years many church colleges have sacrificed real Christian culture for academic standardization.[23]

Whether this statement secured greater support from the Christian Churches is debatable. It may have encouraged some parents to send their children, but it certainly did not garner enough support to solve the financial problems of the institutions involved. Students who attended Transylvania believed the small Christian college had a significant role to play in higher education and should not be squeezed out of existence by the larger universities. But, said the editor of *The Rambler*, if the Christian college was to have a future and to grip the youth, it must "relentlessly throw away the old, though sometimes the accepted, the outworn, unproofworthy religious phrases, interpretations, atmospheres, standards, and methods."[24] The young student would not accept them. Everything on the modern campus must be submitted to rigorous examination and be accepted or rejected through the minds and hearts

[22] Minutes of the Executive Committee, November 2, 1923.
[23] *Ibid.*, January 4, 1924.
[24] *The Crimson Rambler*, October 12, 1928.

of youth. "Here," he said, "your iconoclastic hammer becomes constructively necessary."[25]

IT WAS EVIDENT that some tension and differences of viewpoint existed between conservative, traditionalist curators and the faculty and students. The college president was confronted with the difficult task of mediating between these groups and of interpreting one to the other, while keeping the major issue of the health and existence of the institution before the eyes of all. It was to the task of rescuing Transylvania, the College of the Bible and Hamilton College from a three-way disaster that Harmon had to apply himself.

In 1924 Harmon appointed F. W. Reeves of Transylvania's Department of Education to the project of surveying the financial condition of the respective schools and proposing solutions. Reeves was so impressed by the dismal conclusions of his survey that he resigned, and Harmon took his findings and wrote up his own recommendations. In essence he proposed that the operation of all three be unified, with the College of the Bible and Hamilton College filling subordinate roles to Transylvania. This would have had the girls' college offering courses in home economics and music and the seminary responsible for teaching all the courses in religion while surrendering its present main function of offering degrees of Bachelor of Divinity and Master of Religious Education. A Master of Arts in Religion would replace them. Dean Bower was given the task of creating a new curriculum to implement these recommendations in which the freshman and sophomore years would be devoted to general culture and the latter two years to specialized majors.

Seminary students, most of the seminary faculty and even Sarah McGarvey, daughter of John McGarvey, rose in unified protest against this proposal which they believed would destroy the integrity and future of the College of the Bible. The alumnae of Hamilton College protested against the subordination of their alma mater in the plan. Within a year, Harmon's integration plan was a shambles, but a solution to the problem still had to be found.

[25]*Ibid*., December 15, 1928.

Though the Hamilton College alumnae fought to maintain that college's independence, they could not provide the funds to stave off the ever worsening financial condition of the institution as each year added a larger accumulated operating deficit. In March 1928, the curators approved the action of the Executive Committee not to renew the lease with Hamilton College whose indebtedness at the time amounted to well over $82,000. In addition they voted to offer the college $5,000 a year for the next two years until Hamilton trustees could come up with a plan to solve the school's financial problems.[26]

The trustees never did secure the necessary money essential to the survival of Hamilton College. In June 1932, Transylvania assumed the responsibility of operating Hamilton College and decided to use the building as a dormitory for the Transylvania girls. By 1934 Transylvania had paid most of Hamilton's debts and held a mortgage of $140,000 on the property. It had charge of the building and controlled the dormitories and dining room but permitted Hamilton College to use the classrooms and to conduct a day school. Transylvania gave Hamilton a five-year option to redeem the property and earnest efforts were made to contact alumnae and raise the money, but all the appeals to Hamilton's "glorious history" and the fact that there was a place for a good junior college in the region were not sufficient.[27] The depression years merely compounded the problem of securing adequate financial support. Hamilton College had served effectively as a high-quality girls' school for over sixty years. Now its service was ended. The buildings became integrated into Transylvania's operations as dormitories and classrooms.

Meanwhile, President Harmon sought desperately for a solution to the troubled status of Transylvania and the College of the Bible. He reported to the Board in March 1928, that he expected to balance the budget that year but anticipated a deficit of between $20,000 and $25,000 for the next year. Mounting costs continued to eat away at the financial resources, even though these resources had been substantially increased over

[26] Minutes of the Board, March 23, 1928.
[27] Mary E. Hughes, Promotion Director, to Hamilton College alumni, August 3, 1934. Hamilton File, T.U. archives.

the past years. In looking about for other causes for Transylvania's difficulties, Harmon was struck by the fact that there were ten other colleges within a fifty-mile radius of Lexington and, most crucial to Transylvania, was the presence of the inexpensive, tax-supported state university. He stated that "the place that Transylvania is to occupy educationally in the future is uncertain. The trend of education today puts the small church college in a precarious situation."[28] The tax-supported junior college system was expanding. The small four-year college offering a general undergraduate program faced a doubtful future unless strategically located. Harmon was not convinced that Transylvania was so located.

What special role, he asked, could Transylvania play that would not be duplicated by the University of Kentucky? Education in the field of religion, he concluded. The state university must of necessity avoid this area. Harmon proposed to "recenter the program of Transylvania College" by avoiding the pre-professional courses now taught at the College and train an adequate leadership for the church. Since there were at the time about twice as many students from Disciples churches in the University of Kentucky than at Transylvania, the latter could hardly claim to be the main source of higher education for its church youth. But it could function as a specialized religious training institution with the College of the Bible giving specific graduate training. Arrangements might even be made with the University of Kentucky to take over the instruction of Transylvania's freshmen and sophomores.

Harmon presented this plan at a called meeting of the curators in March 1928, but they decided to postpone action until June. News of the proposal spread rapidly through the College community. Students, faculty and alumni reacted unfavorably to the program. To them the plan spelled the end of Transylvania as a historic, traditional four-year liberal arts college and made it nothing more than a training ground for leaders for the Christian Church. It placed the College in a subordinate position to the University of Kentucky and spelled a lingering decline for this proud institution. Petitions from these various

[28]*Lexington Leader*, April 24, 1928.

groups were sent to the Board, and there was a rising demand for Harmon's resignation. There was even a rumor that Harmon had tried to sell the invaluable old medical library to raise funds. The besieged and bewildered man, conscientiously seeking a solution to the educational crisis he confronted, threw up his hands and submitted his resignation on April 9. It was to have taken effect July 14, but the hue and cry against Harmon was so intense that the desperate man requested a special-called meeting of the Board on April 27 and asked for an immediate leave of absence, which was granted, and Harmon left town that very day.[29]

The Board formally rejected Harmon's "recentering" plan and provided that a committee should be appointed to nominate a new president. In the meantime, the Board directed Transylvania to continue operating as a four-year liberal arts college. In retrospect it is difficult to judge whether the condition of Transylvania at that time justified the radical solutions proposed by Harmon. The ability of the College to survive through the nation's worse depression and greatest international conflict would seem to indicate that it possessed the resilience necessary to continue.

[29]Stevenson, Lexington Theological Seminary, pp. 235–236.

Elmer Campbell   *Arthur Braden*

20

Depression and War

Raymond F. McLain   *Leland A. Brown*

Following the tempestuous climax of Harmon's administration, Transylvania desperately needed a period of calm evaluation of its position. This was provided by the serene and reasonable leadership of Thomas McCartney while the Board searched for a new president. It was not so much that McCartney had the solutions to all of Transylvania's problems, but that the search for such solutions under his guidance proceeded in an atmosphere of thoughtful deliberation. His health, as always, was in precarious balance. This was one reason he would not assume the presidency permanently. His restatement of Transylvania's purpose and nature in the fall of 1928 was succinct:

> It believes that sound learning should be indissolubly connected with integrity of personal character and a social outlook on life. It believes that the best type of education centers in personal, intellectual and spiritual values. It assumes . . . that these values

can best be secured in a small college through the responsible participation of students and faculty in a small social community. . . .[1]

The one new major change on campus in which McCartney participated was groundbreaking for the first unit of the new gymnasium. At this occasion in November 1928, the acting president said the new building would realize plans made the previous spring when curators decided to reject the plan for recentering the college. By the spring of 1929 McCartney's health worsened, and on September 11 he died in his home on Market Street. His premature death — he was but in his mid-fifties — was a real loss to the college. Elmer Campbell, who succeeded him as acting president, said that

> in our spirits we shall ever see him and marvel at his wisdom and versatility, follow him in his leadership, smile and laugh at his wholesome wit, and rejoice fervently that it has been an honor to know him.

His colleagues spoke of him as a "versatile and accomplished scholar, a wise administrator and a supremely good teacher."[2]

It was almost two years before a new president was found. The Great Crash which struck the country in October 1929, did not make the search any easier, although the full effects of the depression were not to be felt for another year or two. At a called meeting in January 1930, the boards accepted the recommendation of their nominating committee to appoint Dr. Arthur Braden as president of Transylvania College and the College of the Bible at a salary of $7,500. Braden, born in England in 1881, had been reared and educated in the United States, securing his A.B. at Hiram College, his theological degree from Auburn Theological Seminary in New York, and a Ph.D. from Syracuse University. He served churches in Ohio and New York, was president of Keuka College for a year, Dean of the School of Religion at the University of Kansas, and finally president of California Christian College (Chapman College) in Los Angeles from 1922–1930 before coming to Lexington with his wife and five children.

[1]*The Crimson Rambler*, October 12, 1928.
[2]*Transylvania College Bulletin*, October, 1929.

Braden was pleasant in appearance with a scholarly air emphasized by his pince-nez glasses and the attached long black ribbon. Personable and energetic, he was fortunately optimistic as he approached the problem of running a school with as many problems as Transylvania had during the depression years. He was realistic in performing the tasks essential to survival but idealistic in his view of what Transylvania could become. Although he assumed his duties in the spring of 1930, his formal inauguration was postponed until June in order to incorporate it in the elaborate plans for the sesquicentennial celebration. Such a commemoration doubtless added an inspiring atmosphere to the inauguration as the new president had occasion to review the long and checkered history of the institution. It was inspiring not merely because so many famous men graduated from the school, or that an outstanding medical and law school had once existed here, but that despite repeated adversities the University had survived.

As early as April 1930, Braden had drawn up future plans for the next ten years for Transylvania and the College of the Bible. These included an enrollment of 500 as soon as possible with a much larger number in the future, an enlarged faculty, an able department of music and fine arts, a completed gymnasium, a girls' dormitory, a fireproof library and a million-dollar endowment. He envisioned the College of the Bible as developing into an outstanding graduate school of religion.[3]

The symphony orchestra

[3]*Lexington Herald*, August 15, 1930.

WHEN BRADEN ARRIVED on campus he found the dominant extra-curricular interest was intercollegiate football, a situation that "was demoralizing to the academic and moral and spiritual life of Transylvania."[4] It created all kinds of disciplin-

The band

ary problems. Having just left Chapman College which had a vigorous musical program, Braden was determined to introduce such a program at Transylvania so that the extra-curricular program would take on new balance. This he did in 1931 by creating fifty scholarships of varying amounts to students of musical ability. First a band was organized, and then by offering more scholarships a symphony orchestra was established. During these depression years an effective recruitment program using these scholarships brought top-notch musical talent from the mid-West to the campus to occupy the first chairs in these organizations. The multi-talented and immensely energetic Ernest Delcamp plunged into this program in addition to his task as English teacher (the classics in which he had his Ph.D. were now rapidly disappearing). Having already conducted various choral groups during previous decades, he now conducted the band and orchestra until his gifted and equally energetic assistant John Bryden helped to shoulder the burden.

Under such stimulus, both financial and personal, the music program at Transylvania became an important part of the

[4]Letter to the *Etude* magazine, October, 1935.

campus life and attracted many of the townspeople to the concerts. Musical comedies, symphony, band and choir concerts all became traditional features of these years. The musical organizations also toured widely throughout the region. As to the effect of this new music program on intercollegiate football, it is hard to assess. But there is certainly a marked change between the successful season of 1929 and the dismal records of the next few years. That the two programs were not incompatible is evidenced by the fact that in 1936, the football team made an impressive record — the best in twenty years — under the coaching of Claude "Monk" Simons, a former Tulane All-American half-back. Whatever the effect on football, Braden was convinced the new music program had obviated many of the evils that formerly had plagued the campus.

ONE OF THE TOUGHEST decisions Braden had to make within a year after he became president was to dismiss seven faculty members, some of whom had taught here for years. The reason was not hard to find. It was the deepening depression combined with the terrible drought in Kentucky that confronted Transylvania with "one of the greatest emergencies in all her long history," according to Braden. Considering the disaster-laden character of that history this was saying a great deal. For several years faculty salaries were sharply cut, and the College of the Bible faculty volunteered to give back 10 percent of their salary with the proviso that should there be a substantial surplus at the end of the fiscal year, some compensation would be made.

The curators gambled on expanding the program at Transylvania by enlarging the number of scholarships. This had paid off in terms of enrollment (494), one of the largest in the college's history, but it had not wiped out the deficit. This Braden tried to correct by reorganizing departments and reducing staff. He had only praise for the dismissed faculty, and said that only economic stringency could justify this action. Even this was not a popular explanation — first of all to the faculty members affected, but also to devoted students and alumni who knew and admired these teachers.

As conditions improved with the passing years, and especially as enrollment continued to grow thanks to the College's generous scholarship support, Braden began thinking in more expansive terms about the future. He proposed that the concept of "Transylvania University" be restored. If a university was an association of colleges, then Transylvania already had a liberal arts college and the College of the Bible. The new music department might be converted into a Fine Arts College. The spirit of John Bowman permeated these proposals, but the times were not suitable for their implementation. Considering the existence of the University of Kentucky across town and the limited resources of Transylvania, it is doubtful the scheme was either feasible or desirable.

Despite these innovative proposals for a restructuring of the University and the introduction of a major music and fine arts program, the curriculum remained remarkably unchanged. Most colleges changed their programs slowly and reluctantly, but a middle ground between the traditional nineteenth century concepts of the liberal arts education and Harvard's free elective system was the curriculum stance by the time of World War I. Even before this, Harvard's new president, Abbott Lawrence Lowell, had signalled a retreat from Eliot's system. The college, he asserted, must assume a greater responsibility for guiding the young student in his education by requiring him to study certain basic disciplines or academic areas in his freshman and sophomore years before concentrating on a narrower major subject in his junior and senior years. Outside the major, there would still remain considerable latitude for electives.

Not until 1926 under Professor Bower was this kind of program described, programmed and put into operation at Transylvania. The first two years were to be committed to a General Culture Unit with two objectives in mind:

> The first is the securing of appreciation . . . of the natural and social world in which he is to live, of the spirit, movement, and achievements of civilization, and of the instruments by which mankind had evolved his ideas, his institutions, his culture, and his purposes. . . . The second objective is self-discovery on the part of the student, especially with reference to the work which

he will do in life and by which he will make his contribution to society.[5]

The last two years were to be spent in specialization. Thus Transylvania had moved belatedly but surely into the main stream of collegiate curricular practices.

At the time Braden took office, Transylvania specified that in order to graduate a student must take certain courses which included one on "The Bible and Civilization," in which an effort was made to interpret civilization and progress from the Christian viewpoint. Braden taught this course himself for sev-

The choir

eral years. Other prerequisites included English, a mathematics survey course in which "the relationship of quantitative thinking to modern material civilization and to scientific progress generally" was emphasized.[6] The student was allowed some choice in the selection of which foreign language, natural science, fine arts course, or social science he preferred, but he was required to touch upon all these fields. What was new with Braden's arrival was the establishment of a new department of music with sixteen different semester courses offered. Considering the agitation in the 1920's created by the teaching of evolution, it is noteworthy that a course on evolution was now included among the biology courses. The catalogue stated that "this course deals with the facts of organic development, and

[5]*Catalogue*, 1926.
[6]*Ibid.*, 1930.

the main evidences used by modern scientists in support of their confidence in evolution as a fact."[7]

The growing de-emphasis on classical languages was symbolized by merging the Greek and Latin departments into a Classical Languages and Literature Department with Delcamp and Pyatt sharing the teaching duties. This was only a temporary holding operation. In the summer of 1932 Braden wrote Dean Pyatt that

> it has become obvious to the faculty of Transylvania as it has with most other colleges of liberal arts, that Latin and Greek are gradually fading from the curriculum. This is true whether we like it or not. . . . There is very little demand, and there is going to be less in the future. . . . Transylvania is in no position, with a hundred and fifty thousand dollars indebtedness, to provide classes for three or four students. . . .[8]

When Clarence Freeman, long-time head of the English Department, retired, Braden appointed Delcamp to fill the vacancy. The Classical Languages and Literature Department disappeared, and the foreign languages department took over the few Latin courses still being offered. Only the ministerial students interested in New Testament Greek would be affected, and they could study this subject either in the College of the Bible or at the University of Kentucky.

In the fall of 1935 a limited experiment in a new teaching approach was undertaken in education, psychology and English. Emphasis was to be placed on group-conference study. Small departmental libraries were installed. Students were allowed to proceed with their studies at their own pace under the guidance of the professor. It was a form of tutorial education, but for some reason it did not work and the project was abandoned.

Though there were some changes in course offerings among various departments during the depression years, the basic framework remained unchanged until 1941, when under the prodding of new president Raymond McLain major changes were initiated. These changes were more methodological than substantial, however. The College calendar was divided into

[7]*Ibid.*

[8]Braden to Pyatt, August 22, 1932. Pyatt File, Box N-R, Transylvania University archives.

four quarters; the academic offerings were organized into units known as "full courses" and "half courses"; and classes were to meet six days a week for seventy-five minutes each day. A student would take two, or at most three, full courses in a single quarter, thus allowing him to concentrate more fully on a single subject area. World War II interrupted further change, and it was not until after the war that a significant experiment in curricular innovation was undertaken.

Despite depression conditions, it was necessary to raise tuition and other costs. When Braden took office, tuition was $125 a year. In 1932 it was raised to $150, in 1936 to $170, and in 1941 to $200. Rent for a single room went from $90 in 1930 to $110 in 1932, and for a double from $75 to $90. These rates then remained fairly stable for some time.

THE MAJORITY OF THE FACULTY under Braden had been appointed in the 1920's, but a few, such as Delcamp, Freeman, Saxon and Snoddy, had been serving the College since before World War I, and they had long been rated as among the best. Time, diminishing energies, and death would remove some of these men in the 1930's, but the phenomenal Ernest Delcamp would successfully survive another world war. There were five Ph.D.'s in 1931, including Braden himself, Elmer Campbell, Virgil Payne, Delcamp and Dingus. A few years later Braden was fortunate to be able to recruit more Ph.D.'s — men such as Leland Brown, Harvey Wright, A. B. Crawford, Garvin Davenport, and Scott Hall — who would provide a new strength and vitality to the curriculum and stimulus in the classroom, as well as able and devoted leadership for the College for more than three decades. Also serving faithfully and effectively during this period were James Leggett, Howard Groves, James Saunders, and Winona Stevens Jones. Promising young instructors added to the vitality of the campus: Walter Greenwood, Jack Bryden, Aubrey Bradshaw, Alfred Reece and Jasper Shannon. Roemol Henry began her apprenticeship under Mrs. Norton in the library in preparation for her important role as librarian and archivist for Transylvania.

Doubtless the depression years made it easier for Transylvania to secure such capable men and women. Salaries were modest, ranging around $2,500 a year for the professors. They added greatly to the quality of education here and provided invaluable leadership, not only during the bleak years of World War II when the survival of the College was again at stake, but especially in the creation of a new curriculum in the post-war years. Braden's relations with the faculty were, with a few exceptions, amiable and harmonious.

Interest in Transylvania's history had been stimulated by the sesquicentennial celebration in 1930. The Bryan Station Chapter of the DAR placed a granite marker on the northwest corner of Gratz Park to note the site of Transylvania's first building. In October 1931, the United Daughters of the Confederacy presented a handsome bronze bust of Jefferson Davis to Transylvania. The governor of Kentucky was present for the occasion, and Senator Alben Barkley delivered an address on Davis.[9] In June 1939, the old Robert Patterson cabin, reputed to be one of the earliest structures erected in Lexington, was moved from its temporary residence in Dayton, Ohio, to the college campus. That same spring, the body of Professor St. Sauveur Bonfils was exhumed from the old Episcopal cemetery on Third Street and moved to Old Morrison to share the crypt with Rafinesque. This action was apparently taken in response to a request of his great-grandaughter, Mrs. Helen Bonfils Somnes, of Denver, Colorado. Bonfils had been a professor of modern languages at Transylvania when he became a victim of the cholera epidemic of 1849.

The optimism of the early period of Braden's administration was reflected in the launching of a nation-wide drive to secure funds for the erection of a new library to be named in memory of Thomas McCartney, but the depression ended all hopes for the fulfillment of this project. Despite his disappointment in not securing these funds, Braden nevertheless inaugurated a campaign in the fall of 1936 for $35,000 to convert the old gymnasium into a little theater building and student center. In this case

[9]Program of ceremonies on the occasion, October 19, 1931. Transylvania University archives.

he was more successful. Mrs. Fannie H. Graves of Georgetown provided a substantial part of the funds for the project, and during 1937–1938 the old structure was rebuilt to contain a 600-seat auditorium, a spacious stage, a student center on the basement level and assorted smoking-rooms, club rooms, publication offices and some faculty offices. It was opened for use in October 1938.[10]

Graves Hall

The imposing building which had once housed Hamilton College was now converted into the girls' dormitory, a long-felt need as the girls for years had been rooming in a variety of houses along North Broadway. The dining hall in Ewing Hall was closed, and all students now dined in Lyons-Hamilton Hall, so named for a generous donor who had earlier provided funds for a girls' dormitory.

IN ADDITION TO MEETING the fundamental problems of funding, enrollment, curriculum and physical plant for Transyl-

[10]*Catalogue*, 1939.

vania, Braden worked closely with Dean Pyatt of the College of the Bible to achieve the goal Pyatt had long sought and with which Braden agreed: to detach the College of the Bible from Transylvania and make it a fully-accredited, independent graduate seminary. Not all the trustees of the two institutions were in accord with this goal, and for a variety of reasons it seemed impractical at first. Since Crossfield had become president of both institutions in 1912, the two appeared to be indissolubly connected and functionally inter-related. The faculty of the College of the Bible taught the religion courses in Transylvania, and many of the seminary classes were largely constituted of Transylvania students. Library resources were combined, recruitment programs were jointly operated, and the two institutions had the same treasurer. They both supported the inter-collegiate program, yet legally they still remained distinct corporate entities.

By stages, progress towards the goal of separation was achieved during the 1930's. First, the contribution of the College of the Bible to the intercollegiate athletic program was stopped. This action caused no problem for it coincided with Braden's aim to de-emphasize football and build up the music program. The $77,000 loan made by the College of the Bible to Transylvania with Hamilton College stock as dubious collateral (in order for Harmon to secure the $80,000 gift from the Rockefeller Foundation) was paid back. The College of the Bible gave over to Transylvania its half ownership in the dormitory, cafeteria and heating plant while agreeing to pay an annual rental instead. The offices of the business manager, treasurer and registrar were separated. Even the joint recruitment program was re-examined, and the amount of money contributed by the College of the Bible for recruiting Transylvania students was reduced.

Despite the national depression, the College of the Bible undertook a financial campaign to secure funds to pay a graduate faculty that would not be dependent on Transylvania salaries or students. The campaign was remarkably productive. Meanwhile the seminary applied for accreditation from the American Association of Theological Schools and received it in 1938. The resignation of Braden ended the joint presidency. The doubts of some of the seminary trustees about electing their own president were quieted when they found they could secure the services of Stephen J. Corey for that post. Corey, a man of eminence as a national executive for the Disciples of Christ, had just reached retirement age and saw in the presidency of the College of the Bible an opportunity for continued service. He was inaugurated as the seminary's president in September, 1938.

The seminary faculty no longer taught the religion courses in Transylvania. A new department of religion and philosophy was created, and for a year or two, the College of the Bible paid the salary of the man teaching in this department. Also discontinued was the annual appropriation for recruitment of Transylvania students from which the seminary had for so long received its main supply. Separate commencements were held.

As long as the College of the Bible shared the same campus with Transylvania, however, the two institutions were identified with one another in the public mind. If the seminary was to draw a larger number of students from a wider national constituency, as it must, then a separate campus was essential. The necessity for this action was not acknowledged by the seminary trustees. That more room was needed by the seminary was indisputable, but some of the trustees hoped this might be provided on the Transylvania campus. When the Transylvania curators understandably refused to part with any of their already-restricted campus area, the seminary trustees were forced to consider a new campus site. The alternatives were to build on acquired property on North Broadway across from Transylvania or on a site opposite the University of Kentucky on South Limestone, the latter site being chosen. A handsome bequest of $300,000 left by Mrs. Henry Bosworth to the seminary in 1946 enabled the school to buy the property, and in the spring of 1949 work on the new buildings was begun. In the fall of 1950, the completed structures were dedicated and occupied. The College of the Bible, later named the Lexington Theological Seminary, was now a truly independent institution, although it would take the public some time to fully comprehend this fact.

The last physical vestige of the longtime residence of the College of the Bible on the Transylvania campus disappeared in the spring of 1960 when the massive old building the seminary had occupied for over fifty years was torn down to make way for the erection of the Haupt Humanities building. Now both the seminary and the College could move more freely and independently of one another, cherishing their historic evolution and cooperative careers but now unhampered by the confusion caused by cross-purposes, conflicting goals and lack of clearly-defined faculty responsibility and administrative control. Despite some difficulties at the beginning, ultimately the health and prosperity of both the College and the seminary benefited.

The demands upon Braden during these trying years finally proved too much for his physical well-being, and in December 1937, Braden informed the Executive Committee that he wished to resign the presidency in June 1938. In his resignation, Braden expressed his satisfaction with the job and his belief that the future of Transylvania was bright. He said that

Mrs. Braden and I shall always look back on these eight years of service in Lexington with gratitude, for while they have been blood-letting years of worry and toil, they have also been years of friendship, understanding, co-operation, and, we trust, of modest achievement. I am resigning for one reason and only one, namely the burden of these two colleges is too great for me any longer to bear without serious impairment of my physical health.[11]

He had decided to accept a call to the pastorate of the First Christian Church in Los Angeles.

The Crimsom Rambler praised Braden highly for restoring Transylvania to a position of prosperity and prestige. It pointed out Braden's remarkable achievement in increasing enrollment and income during the critical depression years, and in developing such new programs as those in intramural activities and music. There were new buildings, new ideas and new people contributing to the College's growth.[12]

Braden had indeed overcome serious obstacles as he eliminated the annual deficits and increased enrollment, introducing

[11] Minutes of the Executive Committee, December 8, 1937.
[12] *The Crimson Rambler*, December 11, 1937.

new programs at the same time he was reducing or eliminating old ones. In meeting the financial problems during these difficult years, he had the invaluable assistance of Spence Carrick who had assumed his duties as business manager of the College at about the time Braden came. This hard-working, conscientious and toughly realistic man was absolutely dedicated to Transylvania's welfare and especially its economic survival. Braden wrote Carrick a warm letter of thanks at the time of Braden's resignation in which he said:

> . . . your wisdom, oversight and care, involving sometimes almost brutal frankness in matters of finance, have been a large factor in whatever success Transylvania has had down through these years in paying her bills and in making her way.[13]

Carrick was able to see the College as a whole, conscious of the complex interlocking of factors that weakened or strengthened the College. At various times he would suggest plans for strengthening alumni relations or involving the faculty more effectively in administration, in order to cut down on the number of staff, raise faculty salaries and broaden their information and perspective on all phases of the college's operations. He drew up plans for financial campaigns and provided field workers with a digest of Transylvania's past, present and future, pointing out that

> perhaps it is not too much to say that no acreage of equal size on this continent has contributed more helpful influences to the various channels of this nation than has Transylvania in the past one hundred and fifty-four years.[14]

STUDENT LIFE DURING THE 1930's maintained a degree of regularity, normality and tradition despite the depression. Everyone and every organization worked on severely limited budgets, but the programs continued to function. The musical organizations, especially the band and orchestra, were among the newer and more active organizations. Student drama, debate and publications were varied and active. The sororities and fraternities were as popular as ever. Somehow, despite the

[13] Braden to Carrick, December 11, 1937. Box: Spence Carrick, 1934–50. Transylvania University archives.
[14] Box: Spence Carrick.

economic trauma, college life flourished. Editors of the campus newspaper berated the students, as had been their custom and responsibility from time immemorial, for their indifference to world affairs and national affairs. During the decade of the thirties this editorial tongue-lashing centered on the need for Transylvanians to support the Inter-collegiate Disarmament Council; to back an economic boycott against Japan because she invaded Manchuria, and to be more concerned with the disarmament conferences, the Sino-Japanese War, and Hindenburg's presidential campaign against Hitler. There was the usual editorial despair at lack of intellectual atmosphere on campus, although it was acknowledged that the crowded schedule was partly to blame. There was no intelligent conversation at mealtimes. Even many of the courses did not stimulate thought. There was too much noise in the library reading-room. The editor complained further that

> the dormitory with its varied and frequent programs of singing, clog dances, whining saxophones, and howling radios does not encourage deep thought. The literary societies have now been replaced by the fraternities and the show. The student who takes time to think is usually classed as a "bookworm" or a "dumb-bell" and is considered either "queer" or "slow."[15]

The Rambler condemned the rise of new dictatorships in Italy and Germany and bemoaned the fact as Armistice Day was to be honored in November 1935 that

> in these last few months it has often seemed that it was in vain that those millions died during the Great War, and in vain were our assurances that "it would never happen again." We see no longer a world in reconstruction but a world rearming; and we hear talk not of peace, but of preparedness. . . . Only by arousing the will against war, by a program of enlightenment as to the folly of it, can we ever hope to attain permanent peace. If the student youth of the land do not take the initiative then who will?[16]

While this view represented widespread national student sentiment, active student protest was not forthcoming — at least on the Transylvania campus. The prevailing campus apathy

[15] *The Crimson Rambler*, March 4, 1932.
[16] *Ibid.*, November 8, 1935.

with regard to the growing international crisis reflected the indifference of most Americans toward these matters. *The Rambler* editors spoke of the obvious inertia, the complacency induced by a sense of secure isolationism.

Dick Godfrey's columns in *The Rambler* in 1937 on international affairs were remarkably well-informed and, indeed, prophetic. Doubtless his views reflected wide reading among professional commentators, but it is striking to see them show up in a modest newspaper on a small college campus. On April 9, 1937, he wrote that another world war was inevitable, perhaps within five years. He wondered why it had not broken out over the re-occupation of the Rhineland, the attack on Ethiopia, or the Spanish Civil War. When war comes, he said, the U.S. will be drawn into it, not because it wishes to get involved but because it cannot stay out. It is questionable how many students read Godfrey's columns, discussed them, worried about the issues or even seriously considered the possibility of being involved in a war. It all seemed so remote. The clamor of campus activities drowned out most outside issues and concerns.

The students were certainly very much interested in the selection of a new Transylvania president, however. In the six months after Braden had announced his resignation, the search for a new president had been fruitless. The Board prevailed upon the seventy-year-old Richard Crossfield to come out of retirement and fill in for a year until a permanent president could be found. Crossfield graciously accepted this thankless task and returned in 1938 to the campus he had left some seventeen years before. Physically the campus had changed very little except for the beginnings of a new gymnasium and the conversion of the old one into a little theater and student center. However, the value of the physical plant had grown from $477,000 to $763,000, the endowment from $319,000 to $740,000, the enrollment from a little over 300 to 540, the faculty from 22 fulltime and 2 part-time to 28 fulltime and 12 part-time, and the number of books from 21,108 to 39,324. The number of students from Disciples' homes was dropping along with a sharp reduction in the number of pre-ministerial students. There was also the changed curriculum and Braden's new music program. The nagging $150,000 indebtedness hung on tenaciously despite Braden's success in reducing annual deficits.

One disturbing factor was a warning from the Southern Association of Colleges that Transylvania could be risking its accreditation by paying the faculty too little, employing too many with inadequate training and by making them teach too many students. For instance in the matter of student load, Dr. Garvin Davenport, who taught all the history and political science classes at Transylvania in 1936–37, had 212 students in six different courses in one semester at an annual salary of $2,700. It is not surprising the Southern Association was raising questions. Nor could there be any doubt the faculty was substantially subsidizing the college by being underpaid and overworked. Yet, these were desperate years, and the faculty accepted their meager salaries with a good spirit and a sense of strong dedication to the college. These conditions were not improved until after World War II and the Southern Association was placated.

By the spring of 1939 a new president, Raymond F. McLain, had been appointed. Only thirty-four years old, Dr. McLain was one of the youngest presidents in Transylvania's history. Educated at Bethany College, Mount Union College, the University of Chicago and Western Reserve University, he had become well-known in the Disciples brotherhood in the field of religious education. His excellent record as president of Eureka College had caught the attention of the curators who persuaded him to give up his post there to assume the leadership at Transylvania. The young, energetic good-looking president had a remarkably creative mind in the area of education and was an exceptionally gifted speaker. There were few men who could match his eloquence and persuasiveness whether in small or large groups.

WITHIN A FEW MONTHS after McLain's arrival, World War II began. There was not much student comment in the campus publications about the event at first, but by January 1940, the editor of *The Rambler* stated that while editorials and news stories so far had been confined to campus activities, it was obvious that the war would intrude more and more into student lives and concerns. This was dramatically demonstrated in the fall of 1940 when 89 Transylvania students and 13 of their professors registered in the gymnasium for the first peacetime draft in United States history. Among the registrants was the new young president of the college.

There was a faculty forum on the war's effects on various aspects of American life, but none of these comments were picked up by campus publications. Some special courses were offered and an information center on the draft was established. *The Crimson* for 1940–41 admitted that some students had listened to the air raids on London, joined in the singing of "God Bless America" during the halves of the football games and learned a great deal about democracy from chapel speakers. Many men worried about the draft, and bull sessions included such topics as Roosevelt's third term and national defense. But these things had to compete with the football victory over Georgetown, the renovation of Old Morrison and the girls' changing hair styles.

For the seniors who graduated in June 1941, before Pearl Harbor brought the era of the Roaring Twenties, the depression and the New Deal to a close, the college years were filled with memories of the hard times and the good times. One girl summed up these memories in *The Transylvanian:*

> All of us in the present generation are depression babies, I suppose. We lived through the roaring twenties. . . . Depression is far more realistic. . . . I hated it. . . . Wearing made-over clothes and not going to camp and reading everything I could find, especially how the war was responsible and how the munitions makers got wealthy. . . . I still remember the Freshman Icebreaker, when you played kid games in the gym under the supercilious gaze of the upperclassmen, and ate ice cream out of paper cups. There was the Arcadia, where you danced, and the Den, where you ate your breakfast doughnuts standing, because of the crowd that surged in between seven-thirty and eight. And there was the old bookstore where you loafed after chapel and between classes. . . .
>
> In spring, couples under the trees, moonlight and shadowy figures on the steps of Morrison, and radio music from Ewing Hall . . . the dances when you remember Bagwell singing "Basin Street Blues," and Couf's clarinet rides, and Crumbaugh with

his trombone playing "Gettin' Sentimental". . . . The way J. T. Beale clattered chairs at nine o'clock in the library to remind you that it was closing time. . . . The inevitable stop at the corner for a coke, and the nickelodeon playing the pieces you loved. Glen Gray's "Sunrise Serenade" was one . . . Artie Shaw's "Begin the Beguine." The Inkspots singing "If I Didn't Care."

Pearl Harbor ended normal times for the College, but not the need to keep an eye on the main goal. Now that the U.S. was in the war, college leadership for the future was even more critical. McLain emphasized this in speaking to the student body in Morrison chapel soon after the news of the attack on Pearl Harbor had been received. He urged students and faculty to maintain a balanced judgment and rational attitude in this crisis, the seriousness of which should not be underestimated. Transylvania had successfully survived other crises and he expected it would survive this one. The main task of the College was now to train a group of thinkers ready to deal with the profound issues of the post-war world, to "lead the way toward a recovery of wisdom and happiness" and find solutions to difficulties arising between "spheres of selfishness."[17]

A few weeks later in his Christmas message to the students, McLain said:

> Remember that the present moment is not all there is of time. Remember that the present marshalling of facts is not all there is to reality . . . a saner order can be built. Here lies the purpose of the college; to so inform students as to banish provincialism; to so transform selfish desires as to provide a broader basis for human relationships; to so enrich the individual life as to make living infinitely precious. Surely a college cannot counsel an escape from the present moment. It is impossible and ethically undesirable. We are part of the titanic struggle, and in his own way, each of us will see it through.[18]

The crisis for the College was not slow in coming. By the fall of 1942 the faculty had been cut by a third, student enrollment had dropped 30 percent as the number of men was reduced radically and McLain was appealing to the alumni for $40,000 to balance the budget by June 1943. He appealed to the churches for money and students, and made a whirlwind tour

[17]*Ibid.*, December 12, 1941.
[18]*The Transylvanian*, LII (December, 1941).

of the eastern United States in the spring of 1943 to visit alumni groups and enlist their support for the College. Being a young man McLain was subject to military duty, so he accepted a commission in the U.S. Navy and left the campus in late July 1943, to be trained as an administrator for occupied countries. For some months in 1944 he served as an education officer for about 18,000 civilians in Saipan.

The vacant presidential chair was left in the very capable hands of Dr. Leland Brown, who had assumed the responsibilities of being academic dean some years before. He maintained his office as dean while adding the duties of acting president, though of necessity he gave up his teaching. For this new task, Dean Brown was paid an additional $50 a month, which gives some indication of the financial condition of the college. Expenses were cut wherever possible. In February 1942, the Board voted to discontinue the intercollegiate football program. This saved money, but it would have been impossible to continue in any case due to the lack of men. Few at this time would have prophesied that this was the end of intercollegiate football at Transylvania, but such proved to be the case.

It was during this period of wartime economic stringency that a proposal designed to increase income and enrollment was submitted by Hume Logan of Louisville, who had resigned as chairman of the Board of Curators in May 1942, after having served on the Board for twenty-seven years. Logan, wealthy and successful head of a Louisville metal works, was convinced that the growing separation of the College of the Bible and Transylvania was reducing church support for the College. He revived the old idea, dating back to John Bowman and the beginnings of Kentucky University in 1865, that Transylvania have its own College of the Bible. After all, he said, it was a university and could legally establish such a college. It was his belief that the present College of the Bible was moving away from training young men for the ministry and merely offering a super seminary education to men already in the ministry. As a purely liberal arts college, Logan said, Transylvania had no claim on the resources of the brotherhood. He was ready to finance the salaries for a Bible faculty. What irritated him was the fact that he heard from the dean about faculty objections to his proposal which "in some mysterious way would contaminate the lily-white purity of the Liberal Arts College."[19] He thought these objections bunk. Logan was a staunch traditionalist in these matters as evidenced by his hope of recruiting many young men from the Cincinnati Bible College, a strongly conservative Disciples school hostile to Transylvania and the College of the Bible.

McLain had already called Logan's proposal "an absolute negation of the liberal principles on which we are trying to build the college."[20] Logan was ready to give $28,000 to Transylvania in the form of an annuity note, but even this was not sufficient to override objections for establishing a separate Bible college. A compromise was eventually worked out by which the Department of Religion would be expanded to include a program of education for the ministry for which a full-time faculty member would be hired who would be a member of the Disciples Church. The proposal of Hume Logan was one of the last major efforts to pull Transylvania back into the conservative camp and it had failed. Transylvania had no intention of cutting itself off from the Church, however.

The Executive Committee was conscious of the dilemma in which Transylvania found itself. In the minutes of the September 12, 1944, meeting it was stated that the college must decide either to strengthen its ties with the church or assert its independence on a non-sectarian basis. "Transylvania will not remain a standard accredited college in the decade after the war in its present anomalous relationship to the public on one hand and the church on the other."

Acting-president Brown, motivated in part by the critical economic crisis of the college at the time, spoke to this issue in November 1944. After pointing out that since 1865 Transylvania had been dependent on Disciples' resources for finances, students, capital investments, while the college provided the church with a significant amount of lay and ministerial leadership, he said that

it is imperative that Transylvania re-establish herself in the confidence and recognition of the Disciples of Christ for her own life

[19]Minutes of the Board, May 26, 1942.

[20]McLain to Clinton Harbison, December 8, 1941. Box H–I, Transylvania University archives.

destiny and chartered mission. It is imperative that the churches reinstate Transylvania in their interest, financial, moral support, and student patronage. It is imperative that the campus administration re-establish a definite and working active church relationship.[21]

This theme was reiterated by succeeding Transylvania presidents in the decades after World War II.

The problem of how to keep the College operating during the war years was the major one. By the fall of 1943 enrollment had plummeted to 132, of which 105 were women, and by the following spring the total had been reduced to 115. Recruitment of women was vigorously pursued for they were the key to continued operation. The temptation to close during the war was strong, but the Board and administration thought the negative effect of such an action could be disastrous and the difficulties in reopening the College after the war might be insurmountable.

Fortunately for Transylvania, the armed forces helped out in several ways. The Army Signal Corps rented Ella Jones Hall in the summer of 1942 for a year as a radio training center. In March 1943, a contract was signed with the U.S. Air Force to house, feed and train a group of air corps cadets. A month later 200 air force cadets, known as a College Training Detachment, appeared on campus for a five-months pre-flight course in preparation for pilot training. Ewing Hall, now practically emptied of all male students, was easily converted into the cadets' quarters. McLain greeted them:

> Your presence here is a constant reminder that our nation is at war. This is the greatest fact of our day. You provide the college with a direct opportunity to meet the demands of the fact of war. . . . You are an invigorating challenge to us. . . . War is no stranger to these halls.[22]

The unit was commanded by three army lieutenants. Some of the Transylvania faculty recently released for financial reasons were now employed in teaching cadets physics, mathematics, geography, English and physical training. Dean Brown served as the director of the army's academic program, while Dr.

---

[21]Statement by L. A. Brown, November, 1944, for distribution to the churches. Box TC, 1940–48. Transylvania University archives.

[22]*The Transylvanian*, LIII (December, 1942).

Scott Hall acted as coordinator among the programs of the regular college, the "war" college and governmental agencies. The academic program was to occupy the first four months. The last month would be devoted largely to flight instruction at the Lexington airport. At the end of the program the cadets would be assigned elsewhere for further flight training.

The early morning quiet of the campus was now rudely disturbed by the 6:30 reveille, the singing of cadets in Ewing Hall and the marching in formation across the campus and up to Hamilton Hall for breakfast. There was the rhythmic sound of the marching cadence, the crowding into classrooms, the drills and inspections on the campus, the gathering in the student center after dinner to talk with the girls and arrange for dates. There were informal dances in the student center and more formal dances in Hamilton Hall. There were special variety shows, such as the one on Halloween to which students and cadets contributed their talents. There were the expected administrative headaches, too, of trying to meet army requirements of proper sanitation, food and medical services.

Students occasionally complained that war and presence of cadets were all very disturbing and disruptive to a college education. Yet they had to admit that the war did make them think more seriously about the fundamentals in life. Rationing of food, gasoline, tires and many other items did restrict their normal free-wheeling patterns, but there was an urgency and excitment about it all normally missing from the peacetime campus.

In February 1944, the Air Force informed Transylvania that they intended to terminate the contract with the College by June because of its distance from the pilot-training area. In May the cadets departed. A student reporter commented that

the campus looks deserted. We'll miss their marching and singing, the clatter in the "messhall," the "Hup, two, three, four" that we had so much fun with. Ewing Hall is dark and deserted.[23]

For the administration, the termination of the contract intensified the problem of keeping the college open. The "military faculty" had to be released, the College lost the small profit

[23]*The Crimson Rambler*, March 4, 1944.

from the government's use of its facilities, and the campus was dismally deserted. Yet the Board continued to support the aim of maintaining as normal an operation as possible by securing more women and attracting more religion majors by using Hume Logan's resources to build up the Department of Religion.

The 1944 spring quarter enrollment was 115 and Frank Rose, who was to assume the presidency of Transylvania seven years later, was sent out to recruit students. The recent choir trip had hopefully aroused student interest. An operating deficit of $13,400 by the end of June was reported, but the College had survived another year. The students credited acting-president Brown with providing the "characteristic energy, efficiency, and realism" necessary to survive.[24]

These grim times forced the administration and the Board to examine the strengths and weaknesses of the school. Alfred Powell, chairman of a special committee to survey the needs and suggest solutions, recommended that a financial executive be employed to be responsible for college publicity, church promotion, student promotion and raising funds. He also said that his committee thought the size of the Board ought to be reduced and composed only of persons vitally interested in Transylvania. Dr. Brown supplemented this recommendation with the comment that Transylvania had shown a sad lack of consistency and policy over the past twenty years in terms of leadership and financial promotion. There had been too many changes of personnel and too many campaigns which had resulted in a loss of support from churches, community and alumni. He proposed that the number of men engaged in promotion be raised from one to three: one for general promotion, the organization of alumni, and securing gifts; one for student recruitment, and one for church relations. The Executive Committee accepted Brown's proposals.

In April 1945, the Board employed Dr. Henry Noble Sherwood of the University of Kentucky as chancellor, a new position, to function as an administrative head to raise funds, recruit students, and improve church relations. Dr. Brown

[24]*The Crimson*, 1944.

assumed the post of administrative dean. This arrangement was temporary at best, for it was assumed that McLain would resume the presidency when he was released from the Navy. This occurred in late 1945, and in January 1946, McLain was back on campus. Sherwood remained for a few months in a promotional position, but resigned in September 1946, to take a position with the Board of Higher Education of the Disciples of Christ in Indianapolis.

Not since the Civil War had the survival of Transylvania been so critically challenged as it was by the crisis of World War II. Without closing its doors Transylvania had endured, but not without cost. The operating budget deficit had risen from $22,000 in 1939 to over $147,000 in 1945. This was in addition to an old indebtedness of $96,500 which had been refinanced by Carrick in the 1930's and was slowly being paid off. McLain, in looking over the figures, saw a dim ray of light in the situation by estimating that the assets of the College had also increased during the war years, thus reducing the annual deficit of this period to about $14,000. There were a few other assorted items that also burdened the College's financial resources, such as the $19,000 borrowed to pay off the old obligation of the Athletic Council on the new gymnasium. But all this could now be faced with a degree of optimism as normal peacetime conditions returned. Men students could now plan on entering college without worrying about being drafted. And tens of thousands of veterans would be streaming into colleges across the nation under the GI education benefits. Their presence would confront colleges with new challenges, for the veteran was a unique college student. He was older, matured by various military experiences, with a more serious attitude towards his work. He had less time to waste. He usually knew what he wanted to do and how his college education would help him.

For faculty and administration alike, the post-war years signalled a new era in which the traditional collegiate education was to be reevaluated.

21

Innovation and Expansion

Frank A. Rose

In January 1946, Raymond McLain returned to Transylvania after serving in the Navy for two and a half years. While away from the campus he had had time to view the College from a new perspective and to mull over his educational philosophy. Now full of new ideas and brimming with energy, he was ready to confront a bewildering array of problems. There was, first of all, the fundamental question of the future of the small, church-related, liberal arts college in the post-war period. There was the stubborn, ever present problem of providing adequate physical facilities, not only for the present student body but also for the expected influx of veterans. There was the financial deficit, greatly increased by the lean war years.

As McLain worked with the Board on these problems, he warned against the temptation to oversimplify the situation or to make decisions on the basis of expediency. "The modern college," he told the curators, "is a microcosm of modern life, and is, therefore, complicated and many-sided . . . subject to multiple pressures, coming from all directions. . . . It must be sensitive to its many relationships, and its judgments and actions must take them into account." He mentioned the changing character of elementary and secondary education, and its effect on the future college student. He noted the changing standards in higher education, transfer and entrance requirements, standardizing and examining agencies, and educational philosophy. Churches, alumni, students and even the climate of public opinion, all impinged on the college. In his report to the Board on November 1, 1949, he stated that it is not the sole task of the college to respond to these pressures. Without ignoring them, the college must move forward through them, and establish its own peculiar identity. . . . It has long been our conviction that our future rests upon our ability to build a sound, attractive program of Christian education that will increasingly reveal its own worth and justify itself. This is to be done through a devoted, qualified faculty and is to be supported and sustained by at least a minimum of essential facilities.

McLain believed that colleges such as Transylvania must play a unique role in American education — and must do so to survive. He was well aware of the pressures such colleges faced with the anticipated expansion of tax-supported universities. President Walter Groves of Centre College had sent McLain a copy of an address he had made on this subject. He pointed out that in the period from 1921 to 1946 enrollment in tax-supported institutions rose 292 percent and the percentage of all students going to them in Kentucky rose from 59.7 percent to 79.5 percent, while the percentage attending the independent church-related colleges in Kentucky had dropped in those 25 years from 50 percent to 20.5 percent. All indications pointed to a tremendous expansion in tax-supported institutions. What would justify the continuing operation of the independent, church-related college? Groves suggested four factors: (1) private independent education was essential to freedom in a democracy; (2) such colleges encouraged individual initiative and resourcefulness; (3) these colleges offered a faculty-student relationship infrequently obtained at large universities, thus cultivating individuality, and (4) the Christian college was the church's demonstration of its belief that the Christian faith embraced the whole man.[1]

McLain reaffirmed these sentiments. "For a long time," he said, "I have felt that the religious values, moral values, and spiritual values should not be marginal. . . . If they are necessary to individuals, they are necessary to education."[2] The complete resources of rationality must be brought to bear on the problems, he continued, and morality must encompass ra-

[1] Walter Groves, "The Christian College Today," Miscellaneous Correspondence Box, Transylvania University archives.

[2] Raymond McLain, Frankfort, Kentucky *State Journal*, December 9, 1948.

tionality, and religion encompass both. McLain also believed that educational experimentation could be more easily and quickly undertaken in the small college, freer as it was from the more elaborate, status-conscious departmental bureaucracy of the large university. The small college could act as the educational laboratory in the national higher education structure in which promising new ways of learning might be tested.

Concepts of what a Christian college was or should be varied widely between those who viewed any educational experience as an avenue to discovering truth and reality — making it, in an ultimate sense, a religious experience — and those who believed that a Christian college should be permeated with theological doctrinalism. McLain was frequently caught in the struggle between those opposing views and courageously stated his position in the face of some trying circumstances.

"Of course Transylvania is not atheistic," he wrote some disturbed parents, "and we have not taught in the curriculum the denial of the divinity of Christ."[3] The College was trying to do its best to fulfill its function as a small, liberal arts, church-related institution. From the days of the 1917 battle between the ultra-conservatives and the more liberal groups on campus, McLain concluded, the College has been viewed as somewhat progressive in attitude.

To a conservative minister who queried him as to whether dancing and smoking were permitted at Transylvania, and whether all the faculty believed in the virgin birth and bodily resurrection, McLain responded more tartly. These questions were out of order, he said. They were creedal in nature and not consistent with the fundamental principles of the church. "Therefore," he concluded, "not expecting people to ask me those questions, I do not ask them of those who teach at Transylvania. . . ."[4]

Questions concerning the nature and purpose of the church-related college continued to confront church leaders, the administration and faculty. Why, asked the members of the Christian Church, should they contribute financially or in any other

[3] McLain to Mr. and Mrs. Ralph H. Storm, July 3, 1947, Miscellaneous Correspondence Box, Transylvania University archives.

[4] McLain to the Reverend E. L. Hyatt, February 10, 1949, Miscellaneous Correspondence Box, Transylvania University archives.

way to this college? What church-related purpose did it serve? The administration viewed church support as crucial to its financial welfare but wished to remain free from church dictation of the college programs. The faculty, increasingly diverse in its academic, geographic and religious backgrounds, struggled with the question of what was distinctive about education in a Christian tradition and environment, or with the relation of Christianity to the classroom.

McLAIN BELIEVED educational innovation essential in light of the needs of a changing American society in the post-war world as well as imperative for the effective continuation of Transylvania. He had triggered some significant changes even before Pearl Harbor with Transylvania's departure from the traditional five-course semester system to the quarter system with its concentration on the large-course concept and deeper immersion in fewer subject areas. Now that the war was over, further changes were made. McLain and the faculty believed that pre-war education had placed too great an emphasis on vocational training, had been too scattered, fragmentary and superficial, had become too standardized and routine, too provincial in its emphasis on western civilization, and too easily diverted from the main task of learning by involvement in subsidized athletics and social activities. These deficiencies they hoped to correct.

The Procrustean, required-course system for graduation was replaced by more individually-designed patterns to be worked out between the student and his advisor. Such patterns would be a combination of the new general education courses, departmental courses and certain highly specialized non-credit courses. Requirements in foreign languages and mathematics were removed. The keystone of this new program was the structure of specially-created general education courses. One college official explained that

> this has become a closely integrated world; we wanted courses and procedures which by their breadth and nature would make the student better adjusted to it. Too frequently, earlier curricula leading to the A.B. degree had been superficial and fragmentary

with an overstress on departmental, pre-professional, or semi-vocational subjects.[5]

Various faculty members were released for a quarter or two to design such courses, assisted by a $12,000 grant from the General Education Board of New York City. Some of the first courses developed were the Science of Life, the Social World, and Western Civilization. Thus a student, instead of taking an introductory course in zoology or botany, would take an integrated course combining the insights, methods and information from a variety of scientific areas. The Social World did the same for the areas of economics, sociology and political science, in an attempt to create "a scientific approach to the study of society, examining the main structural and functional features and influences that exist in all societies, and the nature of these in our own society."

To these were later added general education courses in language, Philosophy and Religion in Life, Western Art, Introduction to Music, Oriental Civilization, and Types of Great Western Literature. These courses provided a broad base from which the student could derive perspectives on a wide panorama of natural and human phenomena, and which for many proved to be excellent guides to areas of their greatest interests. This basic curriculum remained largely unchanged until the institutional self-study of the early 1960's which resulted in a substantial revision of the general education program, though not of its rationale. For the most part it was a successful and exciting program that did a great deal to energize the College's academic life and to make Transylvania's curriculum distinctive and attractive.

In addition to the stimulus the faculty received from their development of, and involvement in, a novel curriculum, they were encouraged to become better teachers by funds allowing them periods away from the classroom for creative activity and research. This was made possible by a grant from the Carnegie Foundation of $4,000 annually for five years to which the College had to add $1,000 annually. Transylvania was the only Kentucky college participating in this nation-wide program

[5]*Transylvania College Catalogue*, 1947.

which the Carnegie Foundation hoped would substantially improve the vitality of college teaching.

FROM WRESTLING WITH the problem of defining the nature and purpose of Transylvania and developing a unique educational program to undergird it, McLain turned to the more mundane but equally demanding and essential task of providing adequate physical facilities for the students. Colleges across the land were preparing for the great influx of veterans to the campus as a result of the novel provisions of the GI Bill of Rights, the most massive federal financing of higher education since the Morrill Land Grant Act. As early as February 1945, the Board had appropriated $15,000 to convert a wing of Ewing Hall into apartments for married veterans. Hagerman Hall on Second Street was acquired to house freshmen. The Federal Public Housing Authority allocated twenty family-type housing units for married veterans attending the College. These wooden, ramshackle dwellings were hastily erected, with some student labor, on Thomas Field where once Transylvania had battled its football opponents. These dwellings were ready for occupancy early in 1947.

Students and veterans poured in as expected. By the time McLain returned, the enrollment had climbed to 219 and by the fall of 1946 had shot up to over 500, of which 265 were veterans. The curators hastened to set a maximum of 550. Despite this, the total enrollment for 1946–47 which included the summer session was 616, though this tapered off towards the prescribed maximum in the next two years.

Improved plant facilities were also needed. Plans for a new gymnasium and library had been drawn more than twenty years earlier but had been inevitably delayed in their construction by depression and war. Plans to involve the community in constructing a sizeable gymnasium and civic center as a war memorial were proposed, but they never materialized. Fund-raising for a new library was more successful, since an incentive gift was given by the Lilly Endowment of $100,000 for a new library if Transylvania could secure the matching funds.

The removal of the College of the Bible to its new campus across town gave more room for Transylvania to expand, but the problem of how to use or dispose of the massive and archaic old building puzzled the Board until a plan was worked out to rent it for a few years, assume title to it and then raze it.

Despite Transylvania's shaky financial condition, McLain decided that action on a new gymnasium and library should no longer be delayed. On July 1, 1947, ground was broken on the southwestern corner of the campus for the ground level unit of the new library, and in December, a contract was let to build the first unit of the gymnasium. Though it would be seven years before the new library was completed, and ten years before the new gymnasium-auditorium became a reality, the necessary first steps had been taken.

Transylvania's limited financial resources were also evident in the low faculty salaries. Though they had risen slightly from the stringent levels of the depression years, professors still earned an average of only $3,300 and others a few hundred dollars less. One college program that did not burden the financial resources of the institution was intercollegiate athletics. Though McLain was convinced of the need for a new gymnasium to house the physical education program of the College, he was not concerned with subsidizing talented athletes to produce winning teams for an intercollegiate schedule. The war had forced Transylvania to eliminate its intercollegiate football team, and although there was some talk of reviving it, the expense of this activity and McLain's conviction that no special grants should be provided for athletes precluded the possibility of successfully resurrecting football. For a college with limited resources and different priorities, it was a wise decision. Basketball and baseball remained the major intercollegiate activities.

"We're trying to take our sports seriously on an amateur basis," McLain pointed out. "It's a courageous step in the face of sports being a big business in big institutions, but it's the thing we've tried to do."[6] He hoped that Transylvania could schedule its games with schools which operated on a similar policy, but this was not always possible. Whatever the effect on the attitude of the students participating in intercollegiate competition, the consequence of this policy in terms of suc-

[6]*Lexington Leader*, May 31, 1951.

cessful performance was painfully obvious. Transylvania teams consistently lost, not every game but most of them. Students turned out in small numbers and rather half-heartedly for the games. Coach Harry Stephenson found it difficult to secure enough personnel, competent or otherwise, for the teams. But McLain was convinced that athletics should be treated the same as music, dramatics and journalism — one of a variety of activities in which the student might participate without financial subsidy.

The impact of the veterans on campus life was substantial and controversial. For many of the married veterans, some with small children, extracurricular activities and social programs were of marginal interest. They took their studies seriously and were concerned with getting a degree and moving on to a job. For some of the unmarried veterans who had come to college because they were in a transitional period of readjustment and needed the opportunity to think things over — or just to pass some time and postpone making any decisions — the campus was a pleasant way-station. Older than other students and toughened by service in the armed forces, they presented unique challenges to the administration and the faculty. President McLain concluded in his annual report of June 1947, that "the vast majority of the veterans proved to be conscientious, capable, and surprisingly cooperative."

IT WAS IN THE SUMMER of 1947 that the College and its president were once again called upon to defend its historic liberal tradition and academic freedom. McLain had recently employed Thornton Sinclair, a resident of Fort Thomas, Kentucky, as professor of political science. Sinclair had an impressive and impeccable array of degrees from Miami University, Harvard and Columbia. While studying in Germany in the 1930's he had married a German woman and had made the perilous decision to remain in Germany during the bitter war years. He returned to the United States with his wife after the war, having been cleared by the FBI and the State Department, and was looking for a teaching position. McLain had thoroughly investigated Sinclair before employing him and had received only the highest recommendations. Suddenly, on June 19, 1947, there appeared in the widely circulated syndicated column of Walter Winchell a vicious attack on Sinclair, accusing him of having high Nazi connections and behaving traitorously toward the United States during the late war. The local press could not resist exploiting this item, and McLain was soon besieged by phone calls and letters from alumni and others in the community demanding an explanation, if not Sinclair's immediate dismissal. Such notoriety would have been difficult to handle at a major university. For such a small college as Transylvania, the effects could have been disastrous. McLain boldly faced the wave of hostile inquiry and quietly but firmly responded that he had every reason to be more than satisfied with Sinclair's loyalty to the United States, his character and his competence. Neither Sinclair nor his wife were Nazi sympathizers. Within a few months the furor had died down and Sinclair proved to be an admirable and valuable member of the faculty.

Another unique appointment, free of controversy, made by President McLain was that of Victor Hammer as artist-in-residence. Born and educated in Vienna, this fine artist, type designer and printer came to the United States in 1939 to escape the horrors of living within the Nazi regime and the impending war. This remarkable man was the epitome of all that Viennese cultural tradition symbolized. Deeply steeped in the intellectual and cultural heritage of western Europe, he was another example of the benefits America reaped from the flow of brilliant refugees, forced to leave their homes and seek asylum elsewhere. Transylvania could not offer Hammer a handsome salary, but Lexington and this college campus provided the kind of compatible environment in which he could work. He was able to enlarge his income by offering painting classes to the community (McLain was one of his students), taking an occasional commission for a portrait such as those of McLain and Rose. He was also a master of designing and printing fine volumes which became collectors' items. Though his involvement in Transylvania's main educational process was tangential, yet his association with the school and the community was a treasured one, for his personality and talents enriched all.

An invaluable project was also being undertaken during these years. Dean Leland Brown spent endless hours, in addition to his teaching and administrative tasks, working on the old museum in the attic of the science building. From all over the campus he had painstakingly accumulated bits and pieces of the early scientific equipment used to teach courses in natural philosophy and medicine over a century earlier. This amazing array of materials has drawn admiration of specialists across the country and high praise from the Smithsonian Institution.[7]

Despite the vitality of these years, the large student body and the innovative educational program, the College fell deeper into debt. Income between 1938 and 1948 had doubled but so had operating expenses. By the end of the fiscal year in August 1948, Carrick reported a total indebtedness of $351,057 of which $192,557 was a total permanent fund liability and the remainder a constantly-growing operating deficit. The situation became increasingly critical as enrollment started to decline with the departure of veterans. By the spring of 1951 enrollment had dropped to about 250 and a deficit of $50,000 for the year was anticipated. Despite this situation, McLain believed that Transylvania was "at its strongest point in the last half century of its history."[8] Ample pre-professional programs were now being offered, and Transylvania was sending more graduates to medical schools than any other college in Kentucky except the University of Kentucky and the University of Louisville. The College had been one of the original participants in the Washington Semester program sponsored by the American University in Washington, D.C. McLain believed the College to be one of the best liberal arts colleges in the South. Despite this optimism, he predicted that "we are unquestionably in for some difficult years. I think the next two or three will be the worst. . . . I do believe, however, that we can get through the period without endangering the true nature of the college."[9]

Whether it was the prospect of continuing the desperate

[7]L. A. Brown, *Early Philosophical Apparatus at Transylvania: passim.*

[8]McLain to Malcolm Watt, February 12, 1951, Miscellaneous Correspondence Box, Transylvania archives.

[9]McLain to Clinton Harbison, March 6, 1951. Harbison File in Box II–I, Transylvania University archives.

struggle to solve Transylvania's financial troubles or not, McLain informed the Board in June 1951, that he was re-signing, effective August 31. He had accepted a position as executive director of the Commission on Higher Education of the National Council of Churches of Christ in the U.S.A. It was his belief that this new position would give him greater influence in higher education. He expressed his regret at leaving a position he said he enjoyed so much. Lexington was a wonderful place for gracious living. The Board of Curators, he said, was "broad-minded and long-visioned. . . . The faculty has exhibit-ed a remarkable oneness of spirit, which has resulted in distinct and permanent educational advances."[10]

The new president, he recommended, should be a church-man, a fund-raiser, and be well-informed as to the nature of an educational institution. Increased church support was essential to get Transylvania out of debt. The departure of McLain left a real vacuum at Transylvania, not only because of his leadership but also because of the active role of Mrs. McLain in promot-ing community interest in folk-singing, folk-dancing and folk traditions. Yet it was to be Transylvania's good fortune to fill this void with one of the most handsome, energetic and popular presidents the college ever had.

FRANK A. ROSE FIRST CAME to Transylvania as a student from Meridian, Mississippi. A pre-ministerial student during the war years, Rose participated actively in a variety of campus organizations such as Lampas, the Student Council Honor Council, Pi Kappa Delta forensic fraternity and *The Crimson*. He also served as student minister to the Wilmore Christian Church. Graduating from Transylvania in 1942 and completing his seminary training at the College of the Bible in 1946, he worked for awhile as admissions officer for Transylvania and taught some courses in the Department of Religion and Philoso-phy. In 1946 he accepted the pastorate at the First Christian Church in Danville, where he made an impressive record both in the church and community.

[10]McLain "Report to the Board of Curators, June 11, 1951," McLain Papers, Transylvania University archives.

In announcing Rose's appointment to succeed him as president, McLain told students that "Mr. Rose is a young man. He will be one of the youngest college presidents in the country. This is all in his favor in student relations and other aspects of the total program of the college. His ministry in the Danville church has been one of the most inspiring in the state."[11]

Confronted with a crisis of financial indebtedness and declining enrollment, the new president threw the remarkable resources of his determination, energy and idealism into pulling Transylvania out of its financial morass and securing the necessary physical resources to implement the educational goals and excellent academic program. Rose's efforts to increase church support were upheld by the executives of the Christian Church and the College of the Bible. This young Disciples' minister vigorously challenged his ministerial colleagues and their congregations with a frankness and urgency that galvanized them into action. He bluntly told them that if Transylvania was to survive they were going to have to save it with larger gifts than they had ever given and by recruiting more students. He preached in scores of churches across the state, and addressed women's and men's organizations of these churches. No church was too obscure, no congregation too small for him to visit and discuss the problems of the world in general and those of Transylvania in particular. He shared his educational ideals with them, telling them that the purpose of a Christian college was to offer a liberal arts education in the framework of religious and moral values. The crisis in the world, he said, was a lack of moral and spiritual leadership. Education at schools like Transylvania should help the graduates to provide such leadership. He criticized the student who sought only security instead of seeking knowledge. To one of the graduating classes he said:

> Transylvania has given you an education that should make you a sensitive, Christian citizen of the world. It is our hope that you have discovered the habitual vision of greatness which is to serve man and not destroy him. . . .[12]

Rose's crusade for church support was a success. To help

[11]McLain, "Memo to the Transylvania Students, July 27, 1951," McLain Papers, Transylvania University archives.

[12]*Lexington Leader*, June 8, 1953.

pay off the $417,000 debt, churches pledged $113,000 a year for the next few years which would be divided between debt retirement and current expenses. Though this total pledged amount was not always reached, a substantial percentage of it helped to fill the empty College treasury and provided that financial boost essential to Transylvania's survival. Not only did the churches provide immediate and direct financial aid, they also assisted in the vital area of increasing student enrollment by encouraging their young people to consider Transylvania for their college education. At a time when colleges across the nation were suffering a 10 to 15 percent drop in enrollment, Transylvania enjoyed a substantial increase, and Rose was optimistically looking ahead to the late 1950's when the growing national birthrate would bolster this increase even more.

Rose was not content to depend on sharply-increased church giving as a permanent financial answer to the college's money problems. Not only was such a source subject to other justified demands and the influence of a fluctuating national economy, it was not in itself sufficient to meet all the financial and physical needs of the College. To secure such additional funds, a large-scale campaign was necessary. Rose also believed that Kentucky's private industry should express its commitment to private enterprise by supporting the independent private colleges in Kentucky. To this end, he led a cooperative effort among the presidents of the eight private colleges to organize the Kentucky Independent College Foundation dedicated to annually soliciting funds from Kentucky industries and businesses to be divided equally among the colleges.

A large-scale campaign to raise money for Transylvania was developed in consultation with a professional fund-raising agency. The campaign was scheduled to coincide with the 175th anniversary of the founding of the college, and the development program was so designated. The goal was to raise $1,500,000 with which the College's indebtedness would be paid, a new gymnasium auditorium erected, endowment increased and a fine arts center created out of a renovated College of the Bible building. A sensational launching of this campaign was planned to include a visit by President Dwight Eisenhower. Charles Allen Thomas, noted scientist and outstanding alumnus of Transylvania, who was acquainted with Eisenhower because of Thomas' work on the atomic bomb project and as a consultant on nuclear matters, was greatly influential in persuading the President of the United States to make the trip to Lexington as part of an impressive schedule of events.

The program started on April 23, 1954, with an address on "Priorities in Education" delivered at a morning convocation in Morrison Chapel by Colgate W. Darden, President of the University of Virginia. Later that afternoon, an address on "Priorities in Science" was delivered by Charles Allen Thomas from a special platform built on the steps of Old Morrison. Here President Eisenhower, Senator John Sherman Cooper,

President Dwight D. Eisenhower

Governor A. B. Chandler and other dignitaries sat. President Eisenhower then made a few remarks and concluded by saying that

it seems to me that everybody who in the past has graduated from this institution, or who today is privileged to serve it, or to be here as a student, has a great heritage of tradition which cannot fail to enrich his life as long as he shall live.[13]

There then followed the dedication of the new Frances Carrick Thomas library, named for the mother of Thomas, with appropriate remarks being delivered by Raymond McLain. That evening there was a dinner at the Lafayette Hotel at which Henri Bonnet, the French ambassador was the speaker. Thus was General Lafayette's visit to Lexington and Transylvania of 1825 once again commemorated.

The presence of President Eisenhower at the ceremony launching the 175th anniversary development program gave a tremendous impetus to the drive. Under the leadership of former Governor and Senator A. B. "Happy" Chandler and R. M. Watt, president of Kentucky Utilities, the campaign was ably directed, first appealing to the Transylvania community of curators, administration, faculty, students and alumni, then to the Lexington community, the state and the nation.

By the summer of 1954 a victory dinner was held in Lexington celebrating the progress of the program in securing $500,000 from Lexington. Louisville contributed $162,000 specifically earmarked for the new gymnasium-auditorium. By December 1955, Rose was able to report that a total of $715,955 had been collected by the 175th anniversary program and that more was expected. A grant of $105,400 from the Ford Foundation for permanent funds, part of the gigantic nationwide distribution of funds to colleges by the foundation, helped to swell the total. In November 1956, Rose was proud to announce the receipt of $200,000 from the estate of Amelia McAlister Upshur to be used for the completion of the new gymnasium-auditorium to be named McAlister.

By April 1957, it was announced that $1,178,809 had been subscribed with $800,000 of that amount in cash. The College's indebtedness had been considerably reduced, the new library dedicated and the new gymnasium completed. In the fall of 1957, negotiations with the federal government for a $1,000,000 loan to construct a new girls' dormitory were successfully completed. Faculty salaries were raised, as were tuition and board fees. Rose's remarkable achievements in these few short years,

[13] Quoted in *The Crimson*, 1955.

marked especially by the 175th anniversary program and campaign, resulted in his being honored by the national Junior Chamber of Commerce as one of their choices for the ten outstanding young men of the year for 1954.

The impact of these events was substantial. There was a new spirit of confidence among the faculty and administration concerning future prospects of the College. The new buildings on campus, especially the library and gymnasium, stimulated increased enthusiasm in the academic and athletic fields. Rose differed with McLain's philosophy of volunteer amateurism in intercollegiate athletic competition, and reinstituted the system of athletic scholarships, particularly in basketball. He enlisted the talents of young C. M. Newton, recently graduated from the University of Kentucky and Adolph Rupp's elite corps, to coach the team. The editor of *The Rambler* expressed student sentiment in saying:

> Transylvania is an institution surrounded by tradition — part of that tradition is the losing of most basketball games played during a season. You'll probably agree with me in saying that the college ought to shed at least this part of the tradition.[14]

The tradition was indeed shed. Under the guiding hand of Newton, and his temporary replacement Hugh Jones while Newton was in the service, the team moved from seasons of two-or three-game wins to seasons in which it was winning seven, then nine, eleven, fifteen and nineteen games. Student enthusiasm at the games also rose, especially when they moved to McAlister. Baseball did not fare as well, but tennis and golf enjoyed some winning seasons.

The intellectual vitality of the campus was enhanced by the John Hay Whitney Foundation grant for the Embree lectureships which enabled the College to bring to the campus such men as Elmer Davis, Julian Huxley, and Aldous Huxley. J. B. Rhine intrigued the students with his talk on parapsychology. The International Relations Club initiated the Model United Nations at Transylvania (MUNAT) for Kentucky high schools in the fall of 1956, in the midst of the Hungarian revolt and the Suez crisis. This dramatic session was the first of a number of successful annual MUNATS. The Drama Department provided

[14]*The Rambler*, November 21, 1952.

the campus with exciting performances of such plays as T. S. Eliot's *The Cocktail Party* and Franz Kafka's *The Trial*. Young promising pianists such as Claude Frank enhanced the musical offerings. These were exciting years that pointed toward a bright future for Transylvania.

During his presidency, Rose had strengthened the academic program, completed the Frances Carrick Thomas Library and McAlister gymnasium-auditorium, paved the way for construction of a new girls' dormitory, established good working relations with the Disciples churches and brought the College to a new recognition in the eyes of the public. By a well-publicized and reasonably successful development program, he had substantially reduced the College's indebtedness and raised its credit rating. He had turned the tide of the College's fortunes and placed it on a path of growing strength and confidence.

In the fall of 1957, after six of the most strenuous years of his life, Frank Rose announced that he was resigning in order to accept the presidency of the University of Alabama, following the precedent set by Alva Woods over a century and a quarter earlier.

Irvin E. Lunger

22

Expansion and Consolidation

The years from 1954 to 1970 were ones of phenomenal growth for a college that for much of its history had remained relatively stagnant in size and physical plant. Frank Rose had provided the momentum the College needed for its expansion, and the curators were faced with the difficult task of replacing him. A committee, headed by Frank Dickey, alumnus, curator and then president of the University of Kentucky, completed its work with the selection of Irvin E. Lunger.

A native of Pennsylvania and a graduate of Bethany College, Lunger continued his studies at the University of Chicago, making a brilliant record there as he acquired his M.A., B.D., and Ph.D. degrees in record time. Prior to his coming to Transylvania, he provided an energetic pastorate at the University Church of the Disciples of Christ at the University of Chicago, participating in a wide variety of community activities and contributing his leadership to the Community Renewal Program of Hyde Park in Chicago, one of the major urban projects in the country from 1952 to 1955. Invited by Frank Rose to become Dean of Morrison Chapel and professor of religion at Transylvania, Lunger accepted and embarked on a new phase of his career. The change from the center of a large urban community to the relative quiet of a college campus and Lexington must have been dramatic, but it gave him the opportunity to serve in an area in which he had a profound interest. In the spring of 1956 Dean Leland Brown, who had suffered a heart attack the previous summer, indicated his wish to give up the position of academic dean, and Lunger was appointed to replace him. Rose and Lunger worked together to improve and streamline the administrative and academic structure of Transylvania. His work as dean, combined with his wide administrative experience, convinced the curators that Lunger had the necessary qualifications to assume the presidency when Rose moved to Alabama. Lunger assumed that responsibility in December 1957, and was formally inaugurated in April 1958. This tall, dark-haired, well-poised man had the incisive intellect and ability to strike at the heart of problems that faced him. He administered the affairs of the College with decisiveness and directness, along with a good measure of amiability, tact and common sense. As a college president, he brought to the task a desirable combination of scholarship and practical administrative ability.

As President Lunger assumed the leadership of Transylvania, he was determined to clarify first the existing status of the College and then delineate the needs and goals of the institution. The College had drawn upon permanent funds from time to time to finance current operations despite admonitions from its auditors. It had always been the intention of the curators to replace these funds when the financial condition of the College improved. As of August 1958, the accumulated operating deficit was $148,910 but this was a substantial reduction from the $417,000 deficit Rose had confronted several years earlier. Lunger believed that the time had come to abandon this practice of borrowing from the permanent funds if the confidence of the financial community and future donors was to be won. He told the Board that in the future current funds would be kept entirely apart from permanent funds which would now be divided into separate endowment, scholarship and plant funds. A new special fund was to be created to contain all assets that had no prior designation of the donor until the Executive Committee decided how to use them.

In previous years $435,594 of the endowment funds had been used to underwrite current operations and this amount was now restored to the endowment fund which amounted to $651,514 as of August 1958. The scholarship fund contained $223,176, and the plant fund $3,219,082 of which $1,000,000 was owed the

U.S. Government for the loan to build Forrer Hall girls' dormitory. The total permanent assets of the College in 1959 were estimated to be $4,252,421.

With the financial status clarified, Lunger then presented the curators with a number of goals for the next decade which he believed essential to the strengthening of Transylvania. These included an increase of student enrollment to 750 by 1970, a marked improvement of faculty salaries and an adequate retirement program, and a great increase in permanent funds. There was also the pressing demand for improved physical facilities such as restoring Old Morrison, erecting a humanities building, converting Graves Little Theater into a fine arts center, a new building for the social sciences and a new wing on Ewing Hall. He was glad to report that a gift of $250,000 had been received from Mrs. William M. Haupt in memory of her husband, a former curator. This was the largest gift the College had ever received up to that date, and it was to be used to erect a new humanities building.

In December 1960, he reaffirmed and expanded the above goals in a bold, challenging and vigorous report to the Board. There was a tone of urgency to it that seems, in part, to have been created by the significant increase in the number of applicants for admission and the realization of the inadequate resources of Transylvania to accommodate a larger student body satisfactorily. Emphasis was placed on recruiting an excellent faculty, raising admission standards, balancing the vocational and liberal arts aspects of the curriculum and questioning the traditional racially-exclusive practice of the past. He also pointed out the necessity of an accelerated building of physical facilities. The new dormitory for women had been completed in the fall of 1958 and named after the Reverend Samuel H. Forrer, a distinguished Presbyterian minister and Transylvania alumnus, who contributed generously to the building's completion and furnishings.[1]

[1] While a student at Transylvania, young Forrer had run out of money and was faced with the prospect of having to leave school but President Crossfield found the necessary funds to enable him to stay and graduate. Now, Forrer, in turn, had come to the aid of his alma mater. His gifts to Transylvania during the 1960's exceeded a half-million dollars.

Finally, Lunger said, there was the issue of creating a new image for Transylvania. "Many people," he asserted, "still think of Transylvania College as a little, struggling, debt-ridden, academically inferior, church controlled southern school — living in the memories of a glorious past."[2] There was a need to show Transylvania as a truly independent Christian liberal arts college that was academically excellent.

In the spring of 1960 the old College of the Bible building was razed to make room for the new Haupt Humanities building. The architect for this and most of the other buildings erected on the campus during the 1950 to 1970 period was John Gillig. He was committed to the concept of creating a campus with a basic architectural harmony, using Old Morrison as the central model to which the other structures should relate. Though some observers thought that Gillig's buildings lacked unique style and originality, he did succeed in avoiding the architectural eclecticism of many college campuses today.

The urgent need for a new dormitory resulted in making plans for a building for freshmen men, the idea being that rather than combine all men in one dormitory, more individualized attention could be given freshmen men and an *esprit de corps* developed among them. The structure was erected adjacent to Ewing Hall and named after Dyke Hazelrigg and his father — both curators through the years — who contributed substantially to its construction.

The Haupt Humanities building, completed in December 1960, and Hazelrigg Hall were built in record time, the former in seven months and the latter in eight months. Completion of these buildings greatly alleviated the desperate lack of adequate classroom and dormitory space. The new humanities building, with its neo-Georgian style and white clock tower, gracefully flanked Old Morrison in the center of campus.

Upon Lunger's recommendation the Executive Committee adopted a new policy regarding the construction of new buildings in 1958. It stated that no academic building would be constructed unless the funds were in hand or in sight, and that no dormitory would be built unless half the funds were in hand,

[2] Report of Lunger to the Board, December 10, 1960.

Haupt Humanities Building

since dormitories were income-producing. No change was made in this policy until a science center was constructed in 1969.

For some time Old Morrison had been in great need of repair and restoration. The campaign for funds to finance this task was sparked by the interest and support of the Junior League of Lexington. In 1961, $175,000 was expended to restore the exterior of Old Morrison to its original form and to remodel the third floor to provide offices for the social science faculty. The dingy exterior stucco was replaced, the hip roof flattened and strengthened, the brick eyebrows over the windows removed and small-paned windows restored. The result was a stunning success. The exterior of Old Morrison looked as close to its original as it had since Gideon Shryock finished it. When the City of Lexington designed a new seal, it came as no surprise that Old Morrison was placed in the center of the design. In 1966 the U.S. Government officially designated the building as a Registered National Historic Landmark.

As the growing enrollment placed increasing pressures on Transylvania's dormitory facilities, an addition was built onto Forrer Hall in 1962, and the following years two new dormitories for men were constructed behind Forrer Hall. The new dormitories were named Jefferson Davis and Henry Clay to commemorate the historic connection of these men with Transylvania.

The largest building project of the mid-1960's was the erection of a fine arts center. Despite the continuing vitality of the fine arts program inaugurated by President Braden, there had never been adequate facilities for it. Conversion of the old gymnasium into the Graves Little Theater had been a boon to drama, but art and music had to manage in various odd corners on the campus. Now with the munificent gifts of Board member Myrtle Mitchell totalling $673,500, of which $575,000 was designated for the fine arts center, plans for the new building could be drawn with the involvement and assistance of the fine arts faculty. The Board gave final approval in the spring of 1964 for constructing a building to be called the Mitchell Fine Arts Center. The Graves Little Theater and Ewing Hall were demolished to make room for the large structure. Financing of the $1,800,000 structure was substantially aided by gifts from Mrs. Anna Pearce Carrick, Dr. Halford J. Morlan, and Margaret V. Haggin, and the Haggin auditorium, the Carrick Theater and the Morlan Gallery memorialized these donors.[3]

The Mitchell Fine Arts Center was completed in the fall of 1966, and dedication ceremonies were highlighted by the premier performance of Rouben Mamoulian's version of *Hamlet*, with Mr. Mamoulian in attendance. A crisis developed when Philip Chapman, who was playing the lead role, broke his ankle shortly before the opening performance. By imaginative staging, Chapman was able to deliver some of the soliloquies from a wheelchair, while director William Thompson filled out the rest of the role, book in hand.

With the completion of the Mitchell Fine Arts Center, the art, music and drama students now had adequate facilities. An additional boost to the music program was the gift of a fine

[3]Report of Lunger to the Board, June, 1967.

$75,000 Casavant Freres organ given by the Codell Construc-
tion Company of Winchester, Kentucky, in memory of James
C. and John R. Codell. A number of organ recitals throughout
the year enriched the musical offerings.

The almost unceasing building program of the 1960's was
capped with the most expensive and ambitious project of all —
a modern, well-equipped science center. The old Carnegie
Science Building had long failed to provide satisfactory facilities for the growing number of students desiring science programs. Drawing up the plans was a mammoth task, and the
science faculty under the able leadership of chairman Dr.
Monroe Moosnick assisted the architects in this challenge. The
cost of the new science center was to total $2,800,000, the high-
est ever paid for a building by Transylvania. Completed in the
fall of 1970 and formally dedicated with an impressive ceremony, the center was appropriately named after Leland A. Brown,
whose contributions to Transylvania as a scientist, teacher, ad-

L. A. Brown Science Center

ministrator and restorer of the old medical and scientific teaching apparatus were invaluable.[4]

Work had no sooner begun on the science center when the College was stunned by the burning of Old Morrison. Fire was discovered in the basement of the historic structure in the early evening of January 27, 1969. The heat and smoke made it difficult to get at the source of the fire which roared up through the heart of the old building, gutting the center of it, including the back of the chapel. Fortunately the valuable Jouett paintings were hanging near the front of the chapel, and though blackened by smoke and damaged by heat, were able to be saved and remarkably restored. The wings of the building, in which the administrative offices and records were located, were not seriously damaged, although smoke and heat left their marks. Nothing can describe the sense of dismay in the hearts of all who watched the smoke pour out of that noble building that cold, wintry night. The outpouring of sentiment from college and community alike for Old Morrison and what it symbolized for all Transylvanians was remarkable.

It was with a sense of relief and gratitude that it was learned the basic structure of Old Morrison was still sound and could be restored. The price tag for rebuilding was $1,100,000 which insurance covered only partially. Coming as it did on top of the heavy financial strain of constructing the science center, it was not an easy decision to borrow funds for this new project. There was really no alternative, however. Old Morrison was Transylvania's most important historic symbol, and an administrative building was essential. In the plans for a restored Old Morrison, pressures of the new and old conflicted. If the building were restored to its original interior design, it would not meet the needs for adequate administrative space. The decision was made to restore Old Morrison to the original exterior as it had been before the fire, while constructing a new, modern, fireproof interior. Since it no longer served as a general assembly hall for the student body, the original large chapel was

[4]Martha Strickland left $213,959 to Transylvania and it was applied to the cost of the Brown Science Center and the main auditorium was named after her. Mr. and Mrs. Richard Prewitt provided a greenhouse for the Science Center and attractive landscaping.

The Old Morrison fire, January 1969

reduced in size and redesigned. An entirely new lower floor was created, housing the service department, air conditioning units and other mechanical equipment.

In the rededication of Old Morrison on May 9, 1971, former President McLain returned to deliver the main address in which he spoke of this new Old Morrison with its modern interior and traditional exterior as symbolic of the College itself. It represented the continuing historic identity of the institution, approaching its 200th anniversary, while reflecting the capacity of the College to adapt itself to the impact of the modern age.

Looking back from 1970, the previous two decades of building were nothing short of incredible in comparison to the long period before. Transylvania's total plant worth had been estimated as $3,219,082 in 1958, but fourteen years later this figure was $11,407,624. And in the same period the gross value of the College had risen from $4,252,421 to $13,746,024. Such remarkable expansion reflected, in part, the vast national expansion of both public and private institutions of higher learning during this period. There was a growing assumption that a college education was essential for success in the business and professional world. More young people — and there were more of them — planned to go to college, and the years of continuing prosperity created the affluent society that could afford to send them, especially to the large tax-supported institution.

FOLLOWING THE NATIONAL TREND, enrollment at Transylvania expanded rapidly in the 1960's. In the fall of 1958, 425 students were registered, of whom 67 percent came from Kentucky. By the fall of 1965, 798 had registered, and the peak was reached in the fall of 1968 when 884 students attended. The percentage of those coming from Kentucky dropped to about 50 percent as a greater emphasis on recruitment in the Northeast brought sizeable contingents from New York, New Jersey and Connecticut. Geographical distribution widened, indicated by the fact that in the late 1960's classes were composed of students from as many as 35 different states and a dozen foreign countries. This changed the character of the student body as diversity of attitudes and life-styles became more apparent. Despite Transylvania's continuing relation to, and support from the Disciples of Christ, the number of students from this church attending Transylvania diminished significantly.

An important development in the area of student admissions during this period was the recruitment of black students. In his 1960 report to the Board, President Lunger had bluntly raised the issue as to whether the traditionally racially-exclusive practice, if not policy, at Transylvania should be continued. The times were certainly against it as more and more of the segregationist barriers were being demolished by judicial decree and congressional action. Existing admission policy did not prohibit the admission of academically-qualified black students, but few applications had been received. More encouragement was now given for able black students to apply, and in the fall of 1963, Lula Bee Morton, an outstanding Lexington student, became the first black student to be enrolled in the regular A.B. degree program at Transylvania. Other able and gifted black students followed her example, and though the number remained small, their contributions to Transylvania life were significant. In 1969 students elected a black student, James Hurley, to be Mr. Pioneer.

The decade of the sixties was almost unprecedented in the radical change in student appearance, manners, ideas and actions in the nation. Though such a change was contemporaneous with major convulsions in American society centering around the revolution in civil liberties and the place of the black in that society, and the trauma of the Viet Nam War, it is hard to determine to what extent these were the causes of campus revolution. The long hair and beards, the prevalence of blue jeans and the increasing latitude of the spoken and written word, all reflected the change. This student generation challenged the traditional and established society more dramatically than any student generation had ever challenged it before. Students of the 1950's had frequently been labeled as security-minded, conformist and passive. The mark of many of the students of the 1960's was non-conformism, commitment and activism, although probably the majority of students, as they had in the past, tended to remain rather uninvolved.

As early as the spring of 1960, Transylvania students had participated in "sit-in" demonstrations in Lexington stores, restaurants and theaters to protest existing segregation practices. The issue of the Viet Nam War was hotly debated on campus, though, unlike other campuses, there was no violence at Transylvania. The Kent State University shootings in May 1970, shocked Transylvania students, and many of them participated in an all-night vigil on the steps of Mitchell Fine Arts Center and in the sunrise memorial service that followed. The appearance of about 600 University of Kentucky students who had marched from across town to seek sanctuary from police and national guard surveillance posed a temporary crisis which was wisely handled and no violence ensued.

There were other grim moments during the 1960's that students were not likely to forget: the shocking murder of a stu-

A T-Day Campus Sing at Old Morrison

dent, Betty Gail Brown, found strangled in her car in front of
Old Morrison in October 1961; the Cuban missile crisis which
cast the threat of nuclear war over the entire nation; the assas-
sination of President Kennedy and the memorial service held in
Old Morrison in which the college community expressed its
sorrow at this time.

With the growing diversity in dress, it was to be expected
that the campus dress code would be challenged and modified.
The days when students dressed for dinner and ate by candle-
light were over. Required convocations also fell by the way-
side. Other traditional modes of religious expression such as
the Student Christian Association and its retreats, and the ac-
cent on religion programs disappeared, though one could not

say for certain that students were any less interested in the basic religious concerns of man. The old modes no longer seemed adequate or appealing, and new forms had not yet been developed.

This was also the decade of experimentation with drugs, especially marijuana, and this campus could hardly expect to remain immune. The extent of its use was difficult to determine, but the administration was conscious of its responsibilities not only to discourage its use and distribution, but also to protect students against unwarranted search and seizure raids of the local authorities.

The growing demand that students be allowed a greater degree of control and freedom in matters of drinking and visitation between men's and women's dormitories was met by a flexible liberalization of college regulations in these matters despite the realization that agreement on such matters could never be expected from the older college constituency of alumni and church members.

The desire of some of the students for a greater voice and more effective role in the agencies that ran the College resulted in adding student representatives to the Administrative Council, Board committees and several of the key faculty committees. Yet the Student Council itself seemed to suffer from the traditional student apathy as far as being a significant influence on campus.

Some students volunteered for the Peace Corps, others worked in the Appalachian Volunteer Program in eastern Kentucky and still others acted as tutors and big brothers to the children of Transylvania's immediate community. Still the editorials of *The Rambler* attacked the general student apathy, and the president of the Student Council echoed the complaint. Doubtless there was a great deal of student apathy. There always had been and presumably it would continue in the future, for college life, in part, was marked by adolescent introspection and a rebellion against assuming duties, responsibilities or leadership. Compared to the 1950's a larger percentage of students became involved in issues which transcended the campus. Curiously, the intensity with which students interested themselves in off-campus issues did not result in their greater involvement in on-campus activities.

One source of student enthusiasm remained the basketball team which under C. M. Newton had begun to move out of the depression of perpetual defeat to impressive seasons, winning its first KIAC championship in 1958, and claiming a berth in the NAIA tournaments in the 1962–63 and 1964–65 seasons. When Newton left Transylvania to follow Frank Rose to Alabama as head basketball coach, it was a stroke of good fortune that Lee Rose, a former Transylvania basketball star, was persuaded to replace him. Under his inspiring leadership, Transylvania teams began to establish phenomenal records, culminating in the best season ever, 1970–71, when the team won 21 games and lost 3. For several years the teams were chosen to participate in the post-season NCAA college tournaments.

THE DECADE OF THE 1960's saw the size of the faculty substantially enlarged, its quality improved, and its salaries and fringe benefits dramatically increased. The academic marketplace of the 1950's in which college teachers felt superfluous had become a seller's market as the tremendous expansion of colleges and universities necessitated a corresponding growth of faculties. New Ph.D.'s were hired at a rapid rate and were soon in short supply. President Lunger impressed this fact on the curators and said that if Transylvania were to improve its faculty, it would have to compete vigorously in the open market.

Transylvania had an especially difficult task in raising salaries to a nationally respectable and competitive level because they were so low to begin with. At the time of McLain's administration, the highest faculty salaries were around $3500. By Lunger's first year as president, the minimum salary for a full professor with a Ph.D. was $6000, associate professor's $5,500, assistant professor's $5,000 and instructor's $4,000. By 1971 total faculty compensation, including fringe benefits, was $18,165, $14,822, $12,378 and $10,126 in the respective cate-

Frances Carrick Thomas Library

gories. The number of faculty ranged from 49 in 1960 to 72 in 1969 with the percentage of earned doctorates around 50 percent.

To encourage faculty members to continue their development as scholars and to enrich their resources as teachers, sabbatical leaves were initiated in 1967. When funds were available research grants were awarded interested faculty to assist them in various professional projects. More funds were available for travel to meetings of professional associations. The traditional informality of faculty organization and functioning was replaced by a more formal structure when a faculty constitution was promulgated in 1967. It clarified the composition and responsibilities of the various faculty committees and councils and specified the method of nomination and election of faculty to them. Frequently amended, the constitution in recent years has provided for greater student participation in certain key faculty committees.

Though a few of the Transylvania faculty had produced scholarly publications before the 1960's, there now was a significant increase in this area, reflecting the growing commitment and creativity of the faculty in this basic area of the academic community.[5] The faculty also sponsored and participated in such all-campus events as forums on Hegel, Bertrand Russell, Copernicus, and the Phi Alpha Theta panels on books of contemporary interest. Assisting the faculty in their desire to stimulate the intellectual atmosphere on campus was the impressive array of visiting lecturers. In one memorable year, W. T. Stace, P. A. Sorokin, F. S. C. Northrop and Paul Tillich spoke to the students and the community. In other years the campus was host to Harlow Shapley, Stanley Kunitz, William Arrowsmith, Willie Ley and Walter Kaufmann, to name a few.

Improvement of library resources was critical to the improvement of the academic quality of Transylvania. Adequate library acquisitions had been sadly lacking in the previous decades. Now, as funds became available, priority was given to building up the book collections, enlarging the qualified staff and improving the physical facilities. In 1949 when the College of the Bible moved to its new campus, it took with it all of its books which for years had been combined with Transylvania's. This seriously depleted an already modest inventory and left the College library in an almost poverty-stricken condition. The invaluable collection of the so-called Old Library, numbering nearly 12,000 volumes and consisting mainly of rare medical

---

[5] Among the more notable publications of the Transylvania faculty during this period was L. A. Brown, *Early Philosophical Apparatus at Transylvania*, Ash Gobar, *Philosophic Foundations of Genetic Psychology and Gestalt Psychology*, John Bryden jointly with David Hughes of Harvard, *An Index of Gregorian Chants*, Albert McLain's books on American vaudeville and William Cullen Bryant, Charles Holmes on Aldous Huxley, and Cara Richards and Ray Ware on texts in their fields of sociology and economics, and Benjamin Lewis' editing of *The Moral and Religious Predicament of Modern Man*, the essays delivered at Transylvania by Stace, Sorokin, Northrop, and Tillich.

volumes, could not really be considered part of the working collection available to or used by the average undergraduate.

As of 1960 the working collection of the library numbered only 17,500 volumes. Thanks to foundations, grants and sizeable increases in college appropriations for book purchases, the working collection in the decade of the sixties was increased by 47,000 volumes. The richness of the library's collections was significantly enhanced by the gift of Miss Clara Peck in 1958 of her rare books, valued at that time at $72,500. In 1969 J. Winston Coleman, outstanding historian of Kentucky and a long-time friend of the College, decided to will Transylvania his unique and invaluable collection of over 4,000 books and pamphlets on Kentucky. With a recent generous federal grant to the College for the purpose of cataloguing the Old Library, it could be anticipated that greater use of Transylvania's holdings would be made in the future by writers on the history of medicine and Kentucky.

A CONTINUING CONCERN of the faculty was the curriculum. One of the major advantages of a small college is that substantial changes in curriculum, calendar and faculty organization can be debated and effected with greater facility in a shorter time than in large universities where the procedures are more cumbersome. From 1949 to 1962 the basic features of the Transylvania curriculum had remained largely unchanged, but the self-study of the 1960–62 period provided an excellent opportunity for evaluation and change. The basic philosophy of the liberal arts college, general education courses and requirements for the A.B. degree were discussed at length. The attitude of the faculty at that time favored stiffening the requirements and adopting a more prescriptive general education program. Requirements in mathematics and modern foreign languages, which had been dropped in the 1940's, were reinstituted. Instead of the existing disparate general education courses in the area of the humanities, a new two-year series of integrated humanities courses was developed, necessitating a remarkable effort on the part of the English, philosophy, religion and fine arts departments to create a truly inter-disciplinary program with team teaching. Some of the older general education courses were dropped, reorganized or absorbed into new courses, and the student now had to take four courses a quarter in order to cover the new program and yet leave room for the major.

The new system went into effect in the fall of 1964, and that same year a new dean was appointed to head the program. He was John Bryden, a former Transylvanian of the 1930's who, along with Dr. Delcamp, had done so much to promote the music programs. After securing his Ph.D. at the University of Michigan, he had gone to the University of Illinois and then to Wayne State University. He was director of their extensive humanities program at the time President Lunger persuaded him to come back to his alma mater to pick up the reins from the hands of the retiring Dean Brown. It was an appropriate time for a man of his quickness and vitality as the University embarked on new programs. He was also deeply committed to increasing faculty salaries and fringe benefits.

By the time of the second self-study in 1970, the faculty had changed its attitude towards the heavily prescriptive program initiated only a few years before. Whether this change was due to a normal cyclical desire for variation or induced by the changing attitudes towards higher education evidenced by students and certain educational leaders is hard to determine. In any case the program was altered so students could now choose required courses from among a great variety of diverse courses in the basic general education areas, with the option of omitting one of them entirely. The mandatory requirements of mathematics and a modern foreign language were modified to the extent of placing these subjects among the options.

REMARKABLE ALSO DURING this period was the degree to which the curators became involved in various aspects of the College. While it was true in the early days of the University that the trustees had engaged in such matters as drawing up rules for student conduct, employing and dismissing the faculty as well as the president, specifying the contents of the curriculum and even participating in year-end examinations, those days had long passed. By the twentieth century, most of the curators regarded their role as largely advisory, mostly in financial matters. The few meetings a year were largely taken up with the curators hearing reports from the president and other administrative officers, and conveying their approval or occasional criticism. They were expected to contribute financially, but beyond that they rarely participated in campus matters.

President Lunger and a few of the curators believed this situation should change, that the curators should become better informed and more actively involved in the College's activities. Greater care was given to the choice of new curators to achieve a broader scope of geographical distribution and professional diversity, and especially to choose those individuals who had the potential of becoming actively and significantly involved in the life of the College. The able leadership of such chairmen of the Board as Dyke Hazelrigg and J. Douglas Gay, Jr., helped immeasurably to make the Board a more vital element in directing the affairs of the institution. The longtime devotion and service of such men as Alfred Powell and Caruthers Coleman, to name only two, greatly strengthened the Board's role.

In line with this aim of involving the curators more significantly in the life of the College, Lunger suggested to the Board that it assume the responsibility for defining the institution's goals for the future, now that the initial goals specified by the president at the opening of the 1960's had to a great extent been achieved. With the bicentennial approaching in 1980, the definition of the school's goals at this time assumed an even greater significance. The Board, challenged by this novel responsibility, appointed a Planning and Development Council under the chairmanship of Clair Vough, a major executive with IBM. The Council then established four committees to assist it in this work: the Committee on the Liberal Arts, the Committee on New Programs, the Committee on Physical Facilities and the Committee on Finances.

The Committee on the Liberal Arts was assigned the task of determining what the goals of a small liberal arts college such as Transylvania should be. Under the chairmanship of Earl Wallace outstanding educators from across the country were persuaded to come and consult with the committee or submit their ideas in writing. In part, the aim of this group as Mr. Wallace viewed it was to search out those qualities associated with colleges of the first rank and determine to what extent Transylvania might aspire in acquiring those qualities and prestige in the years ahead.

Leading educators and executives of major foundations were asked what they believed would be essential for the small liberal arts college to survive and function in the future. Some of their suggestions included association with prestigious universities for guidance and support, additional financial assistance, larger enrollments, and, if possible, novel programs unique to the school. In line with this latter idea a proposal was developed to establish an International School of Business Administration with special emphasis on Latin America, training corporate personnel in the language, history, and culture of the countries in which they would be operating as well as business expertise. A substantial grant from the United States Department of Health, Education, and Welfare was critical to its establishment, however, and when this was not forthcoming in 1971 all plans for the new school were dropped.

The beginning of the decade of the 1970's saw a significant change in the direction of higher education in the United States as a levelling off of economic expansion led to reduced financial support from state and federal agencies. With the end of a period of unprecedented growth and some overexpansion of the nation's colleges and universities, these institutions were forced to reassess their plans and priorities. Many college-age youth were becoming increasingly skeptical of the necessity for a college degree for personal fulfillment or a job, and enrollments across the nation began to taper off and decline.

Having now served as president longer than any of his predecessors, Irvin Lunger announced that he would retire as of July 1976, and the search for a new president began. Lunger could look back over his long administration with well-deserved pride and satisfaction. Building on the achievements of McLain and the educational creativity of the program he initiated, and of Rose who strengthened that educational system and saved the college from financial disaster, Lunger had insisted first on regaining for the institution a large measure of fiscal integrity. He had overseen an amazing construction program that created an almost entirely new campus. The size of the student body had more than doubled and improved in quality and diversity. The faculty had been enlarged and improved, about 56 percent holding the earned doctorate. Two self-studies had led to exhaustive examination of the curriculum and subsequent substantial changes in the academic program. The pre-professional programs were expanded as more students chose to enter the fields of law and medicine. The administrative staff was reorganized time and again to achieve the most efficient and productive use of personnel. Under Lunger's leadership, the Board of Curators organized themselves into working committees to keep the curators better informed, involved, and committed to improving Transylvania. President Lunger had brought additional prestige and respect for the University by his own untiring service in a multiplicity of community activities. Though Transylvania presidents had been noted for their involvement in community organizations and activities, no president had occupied so many positions of leadership in these organizations nor been more frequently honored by the community than Lunger.

No one would deny that this remarkable record was established during one of the most expansive and affluent periods in the history of higher education in America. The great increase in the number of students going to college in the 1960's was a nationwide phenomenon that benefited hundreds of other institutions as well as Transylvania. Yet the transformation of the school from a rather static, self-contained college to one of expanding resources and broadening horizons was phenomenal.

By January 1976 a new president had been chosen. He was William Kelly, serving at the time as president of Mary Baldwin College where his outstanding record impressed Transylvania's Board of Curators. A native of Virginia and a graduate of Virginia Military Institute, he combined his military training with a love of literature and went to Duke University to acquire a Ph.D. in

American literature. Teaching in this field at Michigan State and the newly established Air Force Academy in Colorado Springs, he became increasingly interested in college administration, and having gained some experience in that area he accepted the presidency of Mary Baldwin College. Though continuing the tradition of his predecessors who had served as presidents of Transylvania in being attractive, energetic, and competent, he did break a longstanding precedent in being the first to hold that office since 1865 who was not a member of the Christian Church (Disciples of Christ). However, his long and active association with the Episcopal Church had in no way hampered his administration of Methodist Mary Baldwin College, and it appeared that a similar effective relationship with the Christian Church and its historic connection with Transylvania could be achieved.

Throughout the spring of 1976 the new president frequently visited the campus to familiarize himself with the wide range of his responsibilities and after moving to Lexington in August he assumed the full burden of his office. His formal inauguration, set in the format of a symposium on higher education in America, was held in April 1977. The sense of a substantial change in administrative leadership was amplified by the fact that not only was a new president at the helm but a new academic dean, Walter Emge, and a new vice-president for the area of student affairs and plant operation and supervision, David Palmer, joined him at about the same time. Changes in admissions, publications, and alumni relations staffs followed shortly thereafter. The area of development was emphasized with the appointment of Thomas Ackerman.

New ideas, new programs, and new personnel all generated an atmosphere of excitement along with the inevitable strains accompanying the need for adaptation by the faculty, staff, and students. Within the next two years Transylvania changed its calendar from the quarter system, introduced at the time of World War II, to a two-semester system with a special May term, a change that provoked more grumbling among the students than the faculty which, on the whole, found the change an improvement. Plans were set in motion to revamp the traditional academic departmental structure by establishing major curriculum area divisions with subsidiary subject program subdivisions. Most innovative, and almost immediately a striking success, was the establishment of a Transylvania Community Education program. Similar programs existed nationwide, and the neighboring University of Kentucky and the Fayette County Public School system offered types of these programs, but Transylvania hoped that the character and accessibility of its campus and resources and the unique course offerings would attract various segments of the Lexington community. The new administration also introduced a more effective organization of student affairs and a higher degree of professionalism was applied to this area.

The usual stubborn problems of adequate plant maintenance, rising energy costs, security, and parking still continued to plague the administration and various solutions were tried to solve them. However, in the matter of student enrollment and recruitment at a time of declining trends across the country, Transylvania not only held its own but increased its numbers.

Throughout all these changes, however, the traditional high quality of academic standards was maintained as evidenced by the remarkable success of Transylvania graduates being accepted at leading law and medical schools across the country. The University was especially honored when Jeffrey Green, a 1978 graduate, was named a Rhodes Scholar.

Given the excitement and optimism generated by new administrative personnel and consequent changes introduced by them, given the increased leadership, drive, and dedication of the Board of Curators to forwarding Transylvania's progress, it was little wonder that plans for the celebration of the bicentennial of the founding of Transylvania were conceived in an atmosphere of high expectation. Former Transylvania president Frank Rose accepted the responsibility of chairing the bicentennial planning activities. Under his guidance a variety of significant and appropriate activities were planned in conjunction with the Board's commitment to a major capital funds campaign to provide a substantial endowment for Transylvania in the years ahead. Additional funds to finance the construction of a new student center, already in the blueprint stage, also had to be raised. Substantial pledges from the Board members themselves promised a success in this area unprecedented in Transylvania's history.

Thus the celebration of Transylvania's bicentennial was to be more than a nostalgic evocation of the past. It would be rather an occasion for not only pointing with pride to the University's remarkable history and achievement, but assessing its present resources as plans were conceived to make Transylvania's role in the future of American higher education as creative and significant as it had been for the past two centuries. Given the enthusiasm and commitment of the Transylvania community, and the University's historic tradition of overcoming adversity, there was every reason to expect that this goal would be attained.

Epilogue

In looking back over the two hundred years of Transylvania's history, certain major features, stages, and recurrent themes are discernible. In the 1780–1865 period Transylvania sought to establish itself as a non-denominational public institution in pioneer Kentucky to become, if the state were willing, Kentucky's university. After a period of modest growth under trustees with strong Presbyterian affiliations, the Holley years of 1818–1827 saw the amazing advance of Transylvania to become the most influential university in the West, matching in size and educational quality its sister institutions in the East, until the countervailing forces of sectarian hostility and state indifference succeeded in forcing Holley's departure and producing a subsequent decline of the University. Only the revival of the school under Methodist auspices temporarily halted this decline and pointedly showed the trustees what whole-hearted denominational support could do. When in 1865 the opportunity developed to ally the University with a dynamic Protestant sect, the Disciples of Christ, the trustees accepted the invitation to join with Kentucky University. Despite this denominational affiliation John Bowman tried to transcend the limitations of this sectarian identity and create a state university, but the experiment collapsed and Bowman left shortly thereafter. From the 1880's to the 1930's, Kentucky University (Transylvania) and the College of the Bible became almost a functional unit despite their separate legal identities, as for many years they were administered by a single president and operated jointly in many other ways. Despite protestations of non-sectarianism, Transylvania was viewed by the public with some justification as a Disciples' college, and it drew most of its students and support from that church. Despite this, the character of its faculty and its curriculum prevented it from becoming a typical "Bible school." The College treasured its historic tradition of freedom of thought and a commitment to the liberal arts. The 1930's saw the beginning of disentangling of the College of the Bible from Transylvania, culminating in the departure of the former from the latter's campus to a new one of its own.

One of the major recurrent themes that has run through the long history of the University has been the struggle between those men and policies which, for want of a better term, might be called liberal — emphasizing freedom of thought and inquiry — and those persons and beliefs which contended for a narrower, orthodox and conformist view. Toulmin was the first target of the orthodox because of his friends and questionable Protestant beliefs. The smoke had barely cleared away from that struggle when Holley's arrival signaled new combat. Transylvania would "pursue the liberty of philosophical, political, and religious investigation, unawed by civil and ecclesiastical power," Holley boldly proclaimed, but the opposition proved too formidable for him. John Bowman, dreaming of a great state university, was expelled by his own denomination, while the forces of McGarvey ferreted out any proponents of Darwinism. In 1917 the forces of orthodoxy, so successful in the past, instigated a trial for the exposure of such infidels as Crossfield, Fortune and Bower, but this time they suffered defeat. Again in 1947, a Transylvania president, Raymond McLain, was challenged to defend his institution and faculty from the vicious attacks of a famous columnist. Once again academic freedom was victorious over the pressures of fear, suspicion and rumor, and that tradition has been preserved by Lunger, despite occasional pressures that would erode it.

Today Transylvania proudly bears the rich heritage of achievement and failure, of victory and defeat, of good fortune and adversity. The long roster of distinguished alumni, nearly a hundred of whom have won a place in the *Dictionary of American Biography*, that splendid collection of American notables, is a priceless asset. The number of outstanding alumni seems disproportionate to the small campus and limited resources of the University. The hundreds of doctors, lawyers, congress-men, senators, governors, ministers, scientists and business leaders as well as the singular notables such as Jefferson Davis, Stephen Austin, John Breckinridge and John Harlan, who studied on this minute campus with its handful of buildings, provide persuasive testimony to the influence of this institution.

Transylvania University has passed through many stages, identities, and crises. In the past twenty-five years it has experienced unprecedented expansion, change, and physical building. Yet the fundamental question as to the future role in American higher education of this modest-sized, liberal arts college and its traditional church relatedness still remains.

Though sharing with other leading colleges and universities a profound commitment to the liberal arts as central to education, Transylvania's compact student body offers the special value of small classes, greater personal contact between the student and faculty, and greater visibility of the student as a unique individual in the collegiate community. These advantages do not guarantee a richer educational experience, but in combination with a lively intellectual quest stimulated by a concerned and able faculty, a greater opportunity is provided for rewarding self-examination and the development of meaningful values.

The history of higher education in America has been to a large extent rooted in the Christian tradition and learning, therefore, took place in the context of the moral and spiritual values of that tradition. The nineteenth century saw an unfortunate particularization of this tradition as each Protestant sect seemed determined to establish its own college. Many such collegiate ventures failed. Others succeeded so well that in the growing secularism of a scientific and technological American society they severed all ties with the founding sect. Some colleges established by churches have redefined that relationship in the light of the needs of both church and school today. Transylvania's church relations have passed through two stages, an early one closely uniting the College, the church and the College of the Bible, and a more recent one emphasizing a flexible but still meaningful connection with the Disciples.

In the multiplicity of institutions of higher education in America where scientific positivism and vocationalism have become increasingly predominant, the need for some colleges to place a study of the humanities and moral and spiritual values in a central position is crucial. It is here that colleges such as Transylvania, costly in comparison with the large tax-supported institutions, may continue to exert an essential and profound influence on the character and quality of higher education. As stated in its official purpose, Transylvania seeks to

> equip the student for a socially useful and personally rewarding life by bringing the resources of the past to bear upon the realities of the present and the uncertainties of the future . . . and . . . recognizing the proliferation of knowledge . . . stresses ways of knowing rather than mere accumulation, while simultaneously fostering a responsible attitude toward others, an awareness of self, a commitment to higher values, and a lasting capacity for personal growth.

The University's financial well-being will depend, in part, on the belief of parents and students that this kind of educational experience merits the cost, on the belief of alumni and other donors that colleges such as Transylvania form an invaluable part of America's educational tradition, and on the belief of state officials that the educational resources of their state should be seen as a totality of the private and public institutions, deserving such financial support as is feasible, and thus preserving a diversity of educational opportunities for their young citizens that would enhance and enrich the commonwealth.

Entering its third century, Transylvania University, endowed with a rich historic heritage few colleges of its size could match, has firmly resolved to create as significant a future in American higher education as it has done in the past.

Bibliography

Bailyn, Bernard, *Education in the Forming of American Society*, Chapel Hill, 1960.

Bishop, Robert H., *An Outline of the History of the Church in the State of Kentucky*, Lexington, 1824.

Bower, William Clayton, *Through the Years*, Lexington, 1957.

Broome, Edwin C., *A Historical and Critical Discussion of College Entrance Requirements*, New York, 1902.

Brown, Elmer E., *The Making of Our Middle Schools*, New York, 1903.

Brown, Leland A., *Early Philosophical Apparatus at Transylvania*, Lexington, 1959.

————, *Rafinesque Memorial Papers*, Lexington, 1942.

Browne, Warren, *Titan vs. Taboo: The Life of William Benjamin Smith*, Tucson, 1961.

Bucke, Emory S., ed., *The History of American Methodism*, 3 vols., New York, 1964.

Buley, R. Carlyle, *The Old Northwest Period, 1815–1840*, Indianapolis, 1950.

————, and Pickard, Madge, *The Midwest Pioneer*, Crawfordsville, Ind., n. d.

Caldwell, Charles, *A Discourse on the Genius and Character of the Rev. Horace Holley*, Boston, 1828.

————, *Autobiography*, Philadelphia, 1855.

————, *A Discourse on the Vice of Gambling*, Lexington, 1835.

Call, Richard Ellsworth, *The Life and Writings of Rafinesque*, Louisville, 1895.

Cappon, Lester J., ed., *The Adams-Jefferson Letters*, 2 vols., Chapel Hill, 1959.

Cash, W. J., *The Mind of the South*, New York, 1941.

Chroust, Anton-Herman, *The Rise of the Legal Profession in America*, Norman, Oklahoma, 1965.

Clark, Thomas D., *A History of Kentucky*, New York, 1937.

————, *The Kentucky*, New York, 1942.

————, *Kentucky, Land of Contrast*, New York, 1968.

Coit, Thomas W., *An Inaugural Address Delivered in the Chapel of Morrison College, November 6, 1835*, Lexington, 1835.

Coleman, J. Winston, Jr., *Lexington During the Civil War*, Lexington, 1938.

Cossaboom, Ewing O., *A Brief Sketch of Transylvania University's Law Department: The Pioneer Western Law School, 1799 to 1912*, Cincinnati, 1973.

Davenport, F. Garvin, *Ante-Bellum Kentucky*, Oxford, Ohio, 1943.

Davidson, Robert, *The History of the Presbyterian Church in the State of Kentucky*, New York, 1847.

————, *A Vindication of Colleges and College Endowments. An Inaugural Address Delivered in the Chapel of Morrison College, November 2, 1840*, Lexington, 1841.

Dupre, Huntley, *Rafinesque in Lexington, 1819–1826*, Lexington, 1945.

Eaton, Clement, *Freedom of Thought in the Old South*, Durham, N.C., 1940.

Eberson, Frederick, *Portraits: Kentucky Pioneers in Community Health and Medicine*, Lexington, 1968.

Godbold, Albea, *The Church College in the Old South*, Durham, N.C., 1944.

Halsey, LeRoy J., *Memoir of the Life and Character of Reverend Lewis Warner Green, D.D., With a Selection From His Sermons*, New York, 1871.

Hening, William W., *The Statutes at Large: Being a Collection of All the Laws of Virginia, From the First Session of the Legislature in the Year, 1619*, 13 vols., Richmond, 1809–1823.

Henkle, M. M., *The Life of Henry Bidleman Bascom*, Nashville, 1854.

Hofstadter, Richard, and Metzger, Walter, *The Development of Academic Freedom in the United States*, New York, 1955.

Hofstadter, Richard, and Smith, Wilson, eds., *American Higher Education: A Documentary History*, 2 vols., Chicago, 1961.

Hofstadter, Richard, and Hardy, C. DeWitt, *The Development and Scope of Higher Education in the United States*, New York, 1952.

Holley, Horace, *A Discourse on the Death of Colonel Morrison*, Lexington, 1823.

Hopkins, James F., ed., *The Papers of Henry Clay*, Vols. 2, 3, Lexington, 1961–63.

————, *The University of Kentucky: Origins and Early Years*, Lexington, 1951.

Jenkins, Burris, *Where My Caravan Has Rested*, New York, 1939.

Jennings, Walter Wilson, *Transylvania: Pioneer University of the West*, New York, 1955.

Jillson, Willard Rouse, *A Transylvania Trilogy*, Frankfort, Ky., 1932.

Judd, Romie, *The Educational Contributions of Horace Holley*, Nashville, 1936.

Knight, Edward W., *A Documentary History of Education in the South Before 1860*, Chapel Hill, 1949.

Knight, Grant C., *James Lane Allen and the Genteel Tradition*, Chapel Hill, 1935.

Lee, Rebecca Smith, *Mary Austin Holley*, Austin, Texas, 1962.

Levin, H., ed., *The Lawyers and Lawmakers of Kentucky*, Chicago, 1897.

Lewis, Alvin F., *History of Higher Education in Kentucky*, Washington, 1899.

Littell, William, *Political Transactions in and Concerning Kentucky*, Frankfort, Ky., 1806.

MacIver, Robert M., *Academic Freedom in Our Time*, New York, 1955.

Martin, Asa Earl, *The Anti-Slavery Movement in Kentucky Prior to 1850*, Louisville, 1918.

Montgomery, Ruth, *A World Beyond*, Greenwich, Conn., 1971.

Morro, W. C., *Brother McGarvey*, St. Louis, 1940.

Newcomb, Rexford, *Architecture in Old Kentucky*, Urbana, Ill., 1953.

Norwood, William F., *Medical Education in the United States Before the Civil War*, Philadelphia, 1944.

Osler, William, *An Alabama Student and other Biographical Essays*, London, 1908.

Parish, J. C., *George Wallace Jones*, Iowa City, 1913.

Perrin, William H., ed., *The History of Fayette County, Kentucky*, Chicago, 1882.

Peter, Robert, *The History of the Medical Department of Transylvania University*, Filson Club Publication No. 20, Louisville, 1905.

Peter, Robert, and Peter, Johanna, *Transylvania University: Its Origin, Rise, Decline, and Fall*, Louisville, 1896.

Philipson, Rabbi David, ed., *Letters of Rebecca Gratz*, Philadelphia, 1929.

Pierson, George, *Yale College: An Educational History*, New Haven, 1952.

Pollitt, Mabel Hardy, *A Biography of James Kennedy Patterson*, Louisville, 1925.

Posey, Walter P., *The Baptist Church in the Lower Mississippi Valley, 1776–1846*, Lexington, 1957.

Ranck, George W., *The History of Lexington, Kentucky*, Cincinnati, 1872.

Rankins, Walter H., *Augusta College*, Frankfort, Ky., 1957.

Reed, Alfred Z., *Training for the Public Profession of Law*, New York, 1921.

Robertson, George, *An Outline of the Life of George Robertson, Written by Himself*, Lexington, 1876.

Robertson, James R., *Petitions of the Early Inhabitants of Kentucky to the General Assembly of Virginia, 1769–1792*, Filson Club Publication No. 27, Louisville, 1914.

Rodabaugh, James H., *Robert Hamilton Bishop*, Columbus, Ohio, 1935.

Schmidt, George P., *The Old Time College President*, New York, 1930.

————, *The Liberal Arts College*, New Brunswick, N.J., 1957.

Sonne, Niels, *Liberal Kentucky, 1780–1828*, New York, 1939.

Stevenson, Dwight, *Lexington Theological Seminary*, St. Louis, 1964.

Sweet, William Warren, *Methodism in American History*, New York, 1954.

Swinford, Frances K., and Lee, Rebecca Smith, *The Great Elm Tree: Heritage of the Episcopal Diocese of Lexington,* Lexington, Ky., 1969.

Tewksbury, Donald, *The Founding of American Colleges and Universities Before the Civil War*, New York, 1932.

Thompson, Ernest T., *Presbyterians in the South: Vol. I: 1607–1861*, Richmond, 1963.

Townsend, William H., *Lincoln and His Wife's Home Town*, Indianapolis, 1929.

Wade, Richard C., *The Urban Frontier: The Rise of the Western Cities, 1790–1830*, Cambridge, 1959.

Wagers, Margaret Newnan, *The Education of a Gentleman: Jefferson Davis at Transylvania, 1821–1824*, Lexington, 1943.

Wayland, John W., *The Bowmans: A Pioneering Family in Virginia, Kentucky and the Northwest Territory*, Staunton, Virginia, 1943.

Whitsitt, William H., *Life and Times of Judge Caleb Wallace*, Louisville, 1888.

Wright, Louis B., *Culture on the Moving Frontier*, Bloomington, Indiana, 1955.

W.P.A., *Medicine and Its Development in Kentucky*, Louisville, 1940.

Manuscripts

Edward Everett Papers, Massachusetts Historical Society

L. Gay Papers, Massachusetts Historical Society

Horace Holley Papers, Transylvania University

Robert Peter Papers, Transylvania University

Willard Phillips Papers, Massachusetts Historical Society

Shane Collection, Presbyterian Historical Society, Philadelphia

Various files of clippings, correspondence, and documents, Transylvania University

Periodical and Pamphlet Literature

Catalogues of Transylvania University and Kentucky University

Coleman, J. Winston Jr., "Lincoln and 'Old Buster'," *The Lincoln Herald*, XLVI (February, 1944).

The Collegian

The Crimson

The Crimson Rambler

Delcamp, Ernest W., "Transylvania, The Pioneer College of the Western Wilderness," *Kentucky Progress Magazine*, Vol. II (April, 1930).

The Focus

Godbey, Edsel T., "The Governors of Kentucky and Education, 1780–1852," *Bulletin of the Bureau of School Service*, XXXVII (June 1960).

Leavy, William, "A Memoir of Lexington and Its Vicinity," *Register of the Kentucky Historical Society*, XL (January 1943).

Loewenberg, Bert James, "Darwinism Comes to America, 1859–1900," *Mississippi Valley Historical Review*, XXVIII (December, 1941).

Mayo, Bernard, "Lexington: Frontier Metropolis," *Historiography and Urbanization*, Baltimore, 1941.

Mitchell, Thomas D., "Valedictory Address," *Annual Announcement of the Medical Department of Transylvania University*, 1840.

Newcomb, Rexford, "Transylvania College and Her Hundred Year Old Greek Revival Building," *Art and Archeology*, XXIX (June 1930).

The Tablet

The Transylvanian

Unprinted sources

Minutes of the Board

Minutes of the Executive Committee

Minutes of the Faculty

Minutes Books of various literary societies at Transylvania

Field, Elizabeth S., "Gideon Shryock, His Life and Work," an unpublished manuscript in the Transylvania University archives.

Milligan, A. R., "Historical Review of Kentucky University, Read at the Fortieth Anniversary of Union with Transylvania," unpublished manuscript in the archives of Transylvania University.

Wright, John D., Jr., "Robert Peter and Early Science in Kentucky," an unpublished doctoral dissertation, Columbia University, 1955.

Documents

Kentucky Senate Journal
Kentucky Documents
Acts of the General Assembly
Kentucky House Journal

Newspapers

The Apostolic Times
Kentucky Gazette
Lexington Daily Press
Lexington Herald
Lexington Intelligencer
Lexington Morning Herald
Lexington Observer & Reporter
Lexington Reporter
Louisville Courier-Journal
Louisville Ledger

Index

Adams, President John, 29, 61, 69
Adelphi Society, 96
Agricultural & Mechanical College, 194–97, 199–200, 207, 211–17, 219–23, 226–33, 235–36, 274, 314–16
Allen, James Lane, 38, 243–46, 296
Alpha Delta Theta, 350
Alpha Gamma Chi (later Alpha Lambda Tau), 350
American Colonization Society, 105, 163, 166
Andrew, James O., 167–68
Anti-Gambling Society, 97
Apostolic Times, 220, 222–23, 225, 229, 231
Atchison, David Rice, 93
Audubon, John James, 73–74
Augusta College, 106, 160, 163

Bacon College, 190–93, 196
Barry, William T., 87, 91
Bartlett, Dr. Elisha, 156
Bascom, Rev. Henry Bidleman, 160–64, 166–71
Battenfield, Ben F., 336–38
Berea College, 165
Bethany College, 193, 202–03, 267
Bishop, Robert Hamilton, 48, 58, 70–71, 113
Bledsoe, Jesse, 87–91
Blythe, James, 29, 39, 42, 46–50, 54–56, 58, 70, 79–81
Boar's Head (Sigma Upsilon), 296, 349
Bonfils, St. Sauveur Francois, 164, 373
Books & Bones, 297, 349
Boone, Daniel, 2, 4
Bower, William Clayton, 320–23, 336–38, 340, 360, 369
Bowman, John Bryan, 190–201, 207, 209, 212–14, 216–23, 225, 227–33
Boyle, John, 139
Braden, Arthur, 365–73, 375, 377–78
Bradford, John, 19, 24, 26
Breckinridge, John, 89

Breckinridge, Robert, 179
Brown, James, 39, 44, 52, 87
Brown, Leland A., 77, 384–86, 388, 398–99, 407
Brown, Dr. Samuel, 33, 39, 44, 78, 83, 97
Bryden, John R., 367, 372, 424–25
Buchanan, Dr. Joseph, 20, 52, 79
Bush, Dr. James, 150, 154, 173

Caldwell, Dr. Charles, 65–66, 83–84, 87, 97, 109, 115, 120, 148–49, 155
Calhoun, Hall Laurie, 321, 336–38, 340–42
Campbell, Elmer, 365
Carnegie Public Library, 273
Carnegie Science Building, 275, 319, 345, 413
Carrick, Spence, 378, 389
Cave, Rev. Reuben Lin, 258–59, 261–63, 265
Cecropian Society, 293, 294, 349
centennial celebration, 189, 264–65
Centre College, 106, 165, 302–03
Chalkley, Lyman J., 274–75
Chandler, Albert B., 351, 403–04
Chi Omega, 300, 349
cholera epidemic, 86, 129–30, 170
Christian Church in Kentucky (Disciples of Christ), 193, 204, 206, 211, 217–29, 221–31, 233, 317, 359, 362, 385–86, 392–93, 401–02, 417
Christian Standard, 322, 337–41
Civil War, 185–88, 194, 209, 216
Clark, Champ, 284–88
Clark, George Rogers, 9, 24
Clay-Davis Hall, 412
Clay, Cassius, 125, 152, 166
Clay, Henry, 52–55, 59, 62–65, 87, 103, 105, 107, 110–11, 113, 118, 124, 127, 130, 152, 162, 166, 170
Clay, Laura, 250
coeducation, introduction of, 250–52
Coit, Rev. Thomas, 145, 146

Coleman, Caruthers, 462
College of the Bible, 200, 203–04, 206, 210, 219, 221, 223–24, 228, 230, 233, 238, 242, 244, 246, 249, 251–52, 255, 257, 321–22, 329, 336, 338–39, 341–46, 360–62, 366, 368, 375–76, 377
College of the Bible building, 255–56, 395, 410
Commercial College, 211, 249
Cooke, Dr. John Esten, 79, 149
Cooper, Thomas, 56–57
Cornelia Society, 294
Craig Hall, 283, 328
Crimson, 295, 298, 300, 309, 320, 335–36, 382
Crimson Rambler, 298, 339, 348, 352, 357–59, 377, 380–81, 405, 420
Crooks & Crones Society, 349
Cross, James C., 149–50
Crossfield, Richard, 317, 318–22, 325, 327, 329, 332–33, 336–41, 345, 380

Davidson, Rev. Robert, 26, 67, 124, 145–47, 159
Davis, Jefferson, 93, 264
Delcamp, Ernest W., 321, 351, 367, 371–72
Delta Delta Delta, 300, 350
Desha, Gov. Joseph, 109–13, 115
Dodd, James B., 176, 181
Drake, Dr. Daniel, 79, 81–82
Dudley, Dr. Benjamin, 79–85, 148–50, 152

East Hall, 330, 386
Eberle, Dr. John, 149
Eclectic Institute, 132–33, 151
Eisenhower, President Dwight, 402–04
Ella Jones Hall, 319, 330, 386
Everett, Edward, 36, 64, 126
Ewing Hall, 283, 327–28, 335, 386–87

Fairhurst, Alfred, 242, 249, 320, 340, 341
Fishback, James, 52, 54, 79, 113
football. *See* sports

Forrer Hall, 406, 409, 412
Fortune, Alonzo, 321–22, 336, 337, 340
Fox, John, Jr., 296
Frances Carrick Thomas Library, 395–96, 404, 423
fraternities, 299–301
Freeman, Clarence, 321, 371

Garrard, James, 9, 31
Gay, J. Douglas, Jr., 426
Georgetown College, 165, 190
Gillig, John, 410
Graham, Robert, 193, 201–03, 206, 214, 220, 228, 230, 249, 268, 276
Graham Cottage, 276
Gratz, Benjamin, 180, 208
Gratz, Henry, 208, 262
Gratz Park, 24, 28, 39–41, 49, 58, 208, 262, 273, 319
Graves Little Theater, 373–74, 412
Green, Rev. Lewis W., 181–82
Greenup, Christopher, 10
gymnasium, 253–55, 304, 351–52, 365, 396, 404–05

Hall, W. Scott, 387
Hamilton College, 275–76, 288, 344, 347, 360–61, 374
Hammer, Victor, 398
Harlan, John, 143–44
Harmon, Andrew D., 346–47, 358–63
Haupt Humanities Building, 377, 409–10
Hazelrigg, Dyke, 426
Hazelrigg Hall, 410
Henderson, Richard, 3
Henry, Roemol, 372
"heresy trial," 1917, 336–42
Holley, Horace, 56–77, 83, 87, 90–91, 98–118, 138
Holley, Mary Austin, 61–64, 75, 115–16
honor system, 289–90, 356, 374
Hunt, Francis K., 175

Innes, Harry, 13

Jefferson, Samuel Mitchell, 273, 320
Jefferson, Thomas, 1, 7, 14, 26, 31,

44, 61, 69, 87, 128, 133
Jenkins, Rev. Burris, 266–73, 275–
  80, 284, 306
Johnson, Madison C., 143–44, 152,
  180, 194
Johnston, Albert Sidney, 93
Jones, Ella, 330
Jordan, David Starr, 354–55
Jouett, Matthew, 19, 38, 67, 80, 124

Kappa Alpha, 300, 349
Kappa Lambda, 97, 299
Kelly, William, 427–28
Kentucky Academy, 28–32, 37, 50
Kentucky Gazette, 13, 14, 19, 21, 24,
  33, 58, 103
Kentucky School of Medicine, 173–
  74, 259–60
Kentucky University, 190–316
Kentucky University Academy, 206–
  08, 249, 252–53, 262, 270
Kentucky University Medical Depart-
  ment, 261
Kentucky University Prohibition Club,
  291
Kerr, Charles, 274
Kincaid, George B., 175

Lampas, 297
Lard, Moses, 220, 230
Leland A. Brown Science Center,
  413–14
literary societies, 95–96, 292–96,
  348–49
Logan, Benjamin, 10
Logan, Hume, 384–85, 388
Logan Hall, 282, 328
Long, Crawford W., 156–57
Loos, Charles Louis, 203, 238, 242,
  247–54, 256–57, 272
Louisville Medical School, 148–49
Lunger, Irvin E., 407–11, 421, 425,
  426–27
Lutz, John, 132, 139

Marshall, Thomas A., 142, 144
Matthews, John D., 179–80, 183
Matthews, Thomas J., 132, 298
Mayes, Judge Daniel, 139–40, 143
McCartney, Thomas B., Jr., 272, 314,

317–18, 321, 345–46, 364–65, 373
McDowell, Samuel, 9
McGarvey, John W., 203–06, 218–
  26, 228, 231, 242, 244–45, 249,
  251–52, 277–78
McLain, Raymond F., 371, 381, 383,
  385–86, 389, 390–93, 395–400,
  404, 416
McLean College, 330
McVey, Frank L., 343
Mermaid Club, 296, 349
Methodist Episcopal Church, 106,
  158–63, 167–71
Milligan, Alexander, 249, 265–66,
  320
Milligan, Robert, 193–94, 206, 221,
  224–25, 228
Mitchell Fine Arts Center, 412–13
Mitchell, James, 12
Mitchell, Thomas, 149–50
Moore, James, 21–25, 30, 37–39, 41,
  45, 46
Morrison College, Morrison Chapel.
  See Old Morrison
Morrison, James, 41, 104, 123–24,
  126–27
Moss, R. E., 295
Myers, Irene T., 271–73, 321

Newton, C. M., 405, 420
Nicholas, George, 18, 33, 39, 44, 87
Norton, Mrs. Charles, 354, 372

Old College Lot. *See* Gratz Park
Old Morrison, 127–32, 135, 139, 182,
  209, 224, 252–53, 264, 268, 329,
  411–12, 414–16
oratorical contests, 294–95
Overton, James, 79–81

Patterson, James Kennedy, 184–85,
  187, 201, 214–15, 222, 234, 236–
  38, 243
Patterson, Col. Robert, 16–17
Peers, Benjamin O., 132–39, 145, 151
Periclean Society, 293, 296, 349
Peter, Dr. Robert, 80, 150–54, 164,
  173, 176, 178, 186, 187, 201, 214–
  15, 220–21, 223, 243
Phi Kappa Tau, 350

Phileseubian Society, 294
Philothean Society, 293– 94
Pickett, Joseph Desha, 215, 218, 221, 225
Pi Kappa Alpha, 349
Pi Kappa Delta, 349
Pisgah Presbyterian Church, 28, 30, 47
Pope, John, 54, 87
Powell, Alfred G., 426
Presbyterians, 5– 6, 10, 12, 14, 24– 28, 30, 41– 43, 48, 56– 57, 59, 63, 99– 101, 104– 06
Priestley, Joseph, 25– 26
Pyatt, Charles Lynn, 371, 375

Rafinesque, Constantine Samuel, 70– 77, 113, 353– 56
Redden, Charles G., 276
Reeves, F. W., 360
Reign of Law, The, 243– 45
Rice, David, 9– 13, 18, 29, 105
Richardson, Dr. William, 79, 81– 83, 149
Ridgely, Frederick, 33, 39, 44, 78– 79
Robertson, George, 140– 42, 144, 175
Rose, Frank A., 400– 401, 404– 06
Rose, Lee, 420

St. Clair, Luella Wilcox, 276
Selin, William Edward, 306
Shelby, Isaac, 8– 10, 23– 24
Sherwood, Henry Noble, 388– 89
Short, Charles W., 132, 149– 50
Shryock, Gideon, 127– 31
Sigma Sigma Omicron, 350
Sinclair, Thornton, 397– 98
Smith, William Benjamin, 243– 44
Snoddy, Elmer E., 323– 25, 336, 338, 340– 41
Spanish-American War, 262– 63
sports, 301– 02; football, 276, 302– 07, 335, 350– 51, 367, 384, 396; baseball, 307– 08, 405; basketball, 308– 09, 351, 405, 420; track, 309; tennis, 310, 405
State University, 314– 16
Steele, Andrew, 28, 30
Stephenson, Harry, 397
Stewart, Willis T., 335, 351
Story, Joseph, 69– 70

Taylor, James, 192, 197
Thomas, B. A., 275, 345
Thomas, Charles Allen, 402– 03
Ticknor, George, 68– 69
Todd, Col. John, 6
Todd, Rev. John, 6, 10– 11, 20, 23, 45
Toulmin, Harry, 25– 28, 30– 31
Transylvania Academy, 206– 08, 249, 252, 262, 270
Transylvania Company, 3– 4
Transylvania Day, 352– 53
Transylvania Institute, 152
Transylvania Journal of Medicine, 81, 86
Transylvania Land Company, 24, 28
Transylvania Law Department, 33, 39, 43– 44, 87– 92, 108, 123, 139– 45, 147, 152, 158, 163, 172, 175– 76, 206, 216, 249, 256, 273– 75, 320
Transylvania Medical Department, 33, 44– 45, 58, 70, 77– 87, 108, 119– 20, 123, 130, 139, 147– 58, 163, 172– 74, 187, 216, 259– 61
Transylvania Philosophical Society, 52, 96
Transylvanian, 251, 254– 55, 262– 63, 280, 290– 93, 295, 297– 98, 304, 306– 07, 309, 315– 16, 331– 32, 382

Union Philosophical Society, 96, 125
University of Kentucky, 343, 362. *See also* Agricultural & Mechanical College, State College

Wallace, Caleb, 7– 8, 10, 12, 14
Wallace, Earl, 426
Warfield, Elisha, 79
Wayland, Francis, 134– 35
Welsh, James, 39, 41– 43
Western Military Institute, 176– 77
Whig Society, 96, 125
White, Henry, 191, 194, 202, 214, 232– 33, 246– 47, 249, 288
Wickliffe, Robert, Jr., 152– 53
Wilkes, L. B., 220
Wilkinson, Gen. James, 9
Williams, John Augustus, 214– 15
Wilson, Isaac, 20– 21
Withers, W. T., 221, 226
Woods, Alva, 118– 27, 132

Woolley, Judge Aaron, 143–44, 170
World War I, 331–33, 335–36
World War II, 381–83, 386–87, 389

Yancey, Hogan, 306–07
Yandell, Lunsford P., 148–49, 151